TAKING SOUTHEAST ASIA TO MARKET

Taking Southeast Asia to Market

Commodities, Nature, and People in the Neoliberal Age

Edited by

JOSEPH NEVINS
and
NANCY LEE PELUSO

Cornell University Press *Ithaca & London*

First published 2008 by Cornell University Press
First printing, Cornell Paperbacks, 2008
Printed in the United States of America

Library of Congress Cataloging-in-Publication Data
Taking Southeast Asia to market: commodities, nature, and people in the neoliberal age / edited by Joseph Nevins and Nancy Lee Peluso.
    p. cm.
    Includes bibliographical references and index.
    ISBN 978-0-8014-4662-7 (cloth : alk. paper) — ISBN 978-0-8014-7433-0 (pbk. : alk. paper)
    1. Commercial products—Social aspects—Southeast Asia—Congresses. 2. Natural resources—Southeast Asia—Management—Congresses. 3. Neoliberalism—Southeast Asia—Congresses. 4. Southeast Asia—Commerce—Social aspects—Congresses. 5. Southeast Asia—Commercial policy—Congresses. 6. Human ecology—Southeast Asia—Congresses. 7. Globalization—Environmental aspects—Southeast Asia—Congresses. I. Nevins, Joseph. II. Peluso, Nancy Lee. III. University of California, Berkeley. Center for Southeast Asia Studies. IV. Title.
    HF1040.9.A785T35 2008
    381.0959—dc22   2007049023

Cornell University Press strives to use environmentally responsible suppliers and materials to the fullest extent possible in the publishing of its books. Such materials include vegetable-based, low-VOC inks and acid-free papers that are recycled, totally chlorine-free, or partly composed of nonwood fibers. For further information, visit our website at www.cornellpress.cornell.edu.

Cloth printing   10 9 8 7 6 5 4 3 2 1

Paperback printing   10 9 8 7 6 5 4 3 2 1

Contents

Acknowledgments

This book grew out of a conference held in 2005 at the Center for Southeast Asian Studies at the University of California, Berkeley, and a postconference push to put together a volume. Along the way we have accrued the usual pile of debts for intellectual, bureaucratic, and other sorts of labor. Not all of the participants in the project are actually visible to the new reader, and we would like to acknowledge them here.

Several excellent discussants at the conference—Annette Clear, Frank Hirtz, and Aihwa Ong—provided insightful and constructive critiques of the papers. Their commentaries provided significant direction to the authors and editors as they reworked their papers into the chapters of the book. Greg Acciaioli, Mayumi Ishikawa, Noboru Ishikawa, Tomas Larsson, Piya Pangsapa, and Jerome Whitington also presented papers at the conference. Their presentations and comments on other papers greatly enriched the gathering while providing rich intellectual fodder for the book project.

At the Center for Southeast Asia Studies, we thank the Center's chair, Peter Zinoman, for his support throughout this process, and Thuy Pham, the program representative, for her administrative help. Most critical and central to the book's completion, however, was the work of the center's vice-chair, Sarah Maxim. From the time that the conference was a mere idea through the completion of the smallest details of the final manuscript's production, Sarah dedicated herself to seeing this project reach its goal. She has been a source of ideas, critique, and good humor throughout. We cannot thank her enough.

We would like also to express our deep appreciation to Dorian Fougères for his outstanding research and annotated bibliographic work on a wide body of literature that served as the raw material for the introduction. In addition, Dorian provided excellent feedback on an early version of the introduction, as did Ken MacLean, Keith Barney, and Daromir Rudjnyckyj.

We are also deeply indebted to Denise Leto, who worked painstakingly to create a single bibliography out of the many chapters—a Herculean task in itself—and typed multiple versions of the introduction and conclusion; to Jeannie Koops Elson, who helped correct and beautify the prose of some of our contributors; to Darin Jensen for sharing his bountiful cartographic skills and producing the book's map of Southeast Asia, and to our other mapmakers at York University and the Australian National University.

Peter Wissoker, at Cornell University Press, was supportive of the project from the first and had excellent ideas for organizing and conceptualizing the volume. The two anonymous readers of the full manuscript provided detailed and constructive feedback. John Raymond was a sensitive and consistent copyeditor, while Susan Specter and Karen Hwa helped smooth production-related matters. The University of California's Pacific Rim Research Program gave us a small grant that helped to pay for a number of the costs associated with the volume's production. The original conference was funded by the Center for Southeast Asia Studies and the Institute of International Studies at UC Berkeley.

JOSEPH NEVINS AND NANCY LEE PELUSO

Abbreviations

AAC	annual allowable cut
ACC	Aquaculture Certification Council
ADB	Asian Development Bank
ANT	actor-network theory
APKINDO	Asosiasi Panel Kayu Indonesia (Indonesian Wood Panel Association)
ASMINDO	Asosiasi Industri Mebel dan Kerajinan Indonesia (Indonesian Furniture and Handicraft Association)
BRIK	Badan Revitalisasi Industri Kehutanan (Wood Industry Revitalization Agency, Indonesia)
CAP	Consumers' Association of Penang
CBD	Convention on Biological Diversity
CBNRM	community-based natural resource management
CPB	Cartagena Protocol on Biosafety
ECAFE	United Nations Economic Commission on Asia and the Far East
EGAT	Electrical Generating Authority of Thailand
EPZ	export-processing zones (Vietnam)
ESQ	emotional and spiritual quotient
FDI	foreign direct investment
FGHY	fast growth, high yield
FTA	free trade agreement
GAP	good aquaculture practices
GMO	genetically modified organism
GPS	global positioning system
HCMC	Ho Chi Minh City

HKm	Hutan Kemasyarakatan (community forest)
ICA	International Coffee Agreement
ICRAF	World Agroforestry Center
ICT	information and communication technologies
IDP	internally displaced person
IMF	International Monetary Fund
IPHHK	Izin permanfaatan hasil hutan kayu (timber extraction permit)
IPR	intellectual property rights
IUPHHK	Izin usaha permanfatan hasil hutan kayu (timber utilization permit)
IZ	industrial zone (Vietnam)
KKN	*korupsi, kolusi, dan nepotisme* (corruption, collusion, and nepotism)
KNU	Karen National Union
LFA	Land and Forest Allocation
LFAP	Land and Forest Allocation Program
LMO	living modified organism
LPFL	Lao Plantation Forestry Limited
MAF	Ministry of Agriculture and Forestry (Laos)
MBC	Malaysian Biotechnology Corporation
MGE	Myanmar Gems Enterprise
MNC	multinational corporation
MOSTE	Ministry of Science, Technology and Environment (Malaysia)
MOSTI	Ministry of Science, Technology and Innovation (Malaysia)
MPI	Indonesian Forestry Society
MSC	Multimedia Super Corridor (Malaysia)
NGO	nongovernmental organization
NIC	newly industrialized country
NRE	Ministry of Natural Resources and Environment (Malaysia)
PAS	Parti Islam Se-Malaysia
PES	payment for environmental services
Rp.	Indonesian rupiah (unit of currency)
SAM	Sahabat Alam Malaysia (Friends of the Earth, Malaysia)
SESKOAD	Sekolah Staff dan Komando Angkatan Darat (Indonesian Army Staff and Command School)
SKSHH	Surat Keterangan Sahnya Hasil Hutan or Certificate of Legal Forest Products
SPDC	State Peace and Development Council (Myanmar)
TAO	tambon administrative organization (Thailand)
TNC	The Nature Conservancy
TRIPS	Agreement on Trade Related Aspects of Intellectual Property Rights

TVA	Tennessee Valley Authority
TWN	Third World Network
USOM	U.S. Operations Mission
VGCL	Vietnamese General Confederation of Labor
WTO	World Trade Organization
WWF	World Wide Fund for Nature

TAKING SOUTHEAST ASIA TO MARKET

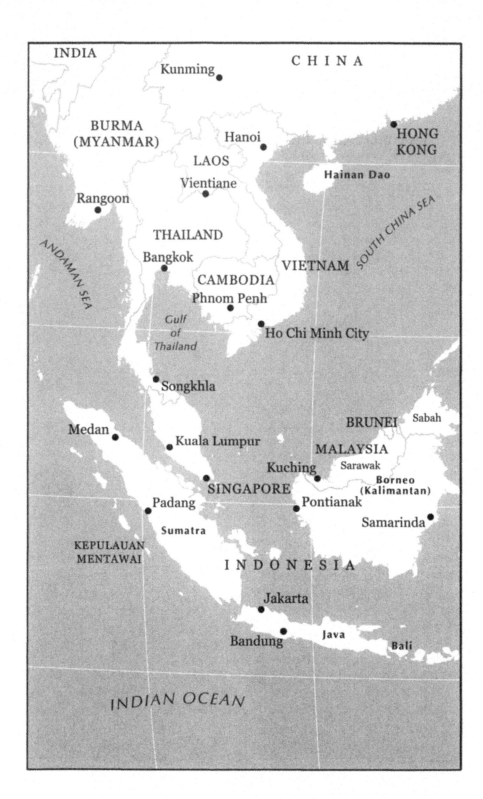

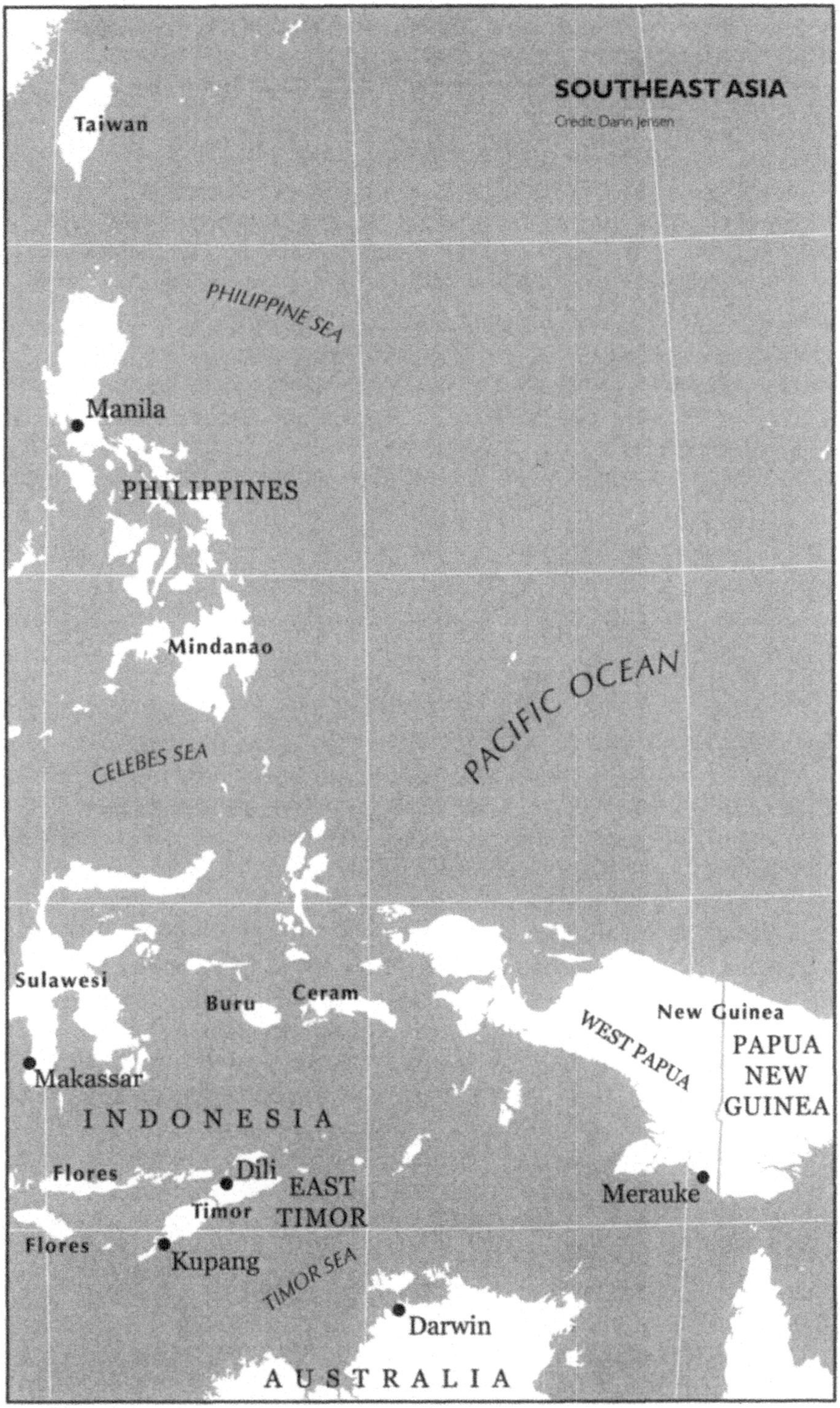

SOUTHEAST ASIA
Credit: Darin Jensen
Taiwan
PHILIPPINE SEA
Manila
PHILIPPINES
Mindanao
PACIFIC OCEAN
CELEBES SEA
Sulawesi
Buru
Ceram
New Guinea
WEST PAPUA
PAPUA
NEW
GUINEA
Makassar
INDONESIA
Flores
Dili
EAST
TIMOR
Timor
Merauke
Flores
Kupang
TIMOR SEA
Darwin
AUSTRALIA

Introduction

Commoditization in Southeast Asia

JOSEPH NEVINS and NANCY LEE PELUSO

> A commodity appears, at first sight, a very trivial thing, and
> easily understood. Its analysis shows that it is, in reality, a very
> queer thing, abounding in metaphysical subtleties and theological
> niceties.
>
> —KARL MARX (1867)

> The problem is that by nature capitalism is indiscriminate
> and inclined to reduce everything—including human beings,
> their labor, and their reproductive capacity—to the status of
> commodities.
>
> —NANCY SCHEPER-HUGHES (2002)

> Commodities surround us and we inhabit them as much as they
> inhabit us. They are everywhere, and in part define who and
> what we are. It is as if our entire cosmos, the way we experience
> and understand our realities and lived existence in the world, is
> mediated through the base realities of sale and purchase.
>
> —MICHAEL WATTS (1999)

Commodities are old and new. They are old in that things we use, value, trade,
buy, and sell have long been part of human society. New commodities constantly
appear as hitherto uncommodified realms of life are made into items for exchange. Recent examples include bottled water, wildlife, and outer space. Meanwhile, "old" commodities are repackaged, redefined, or enclosed in novel forms
and reworked through new regimes of production, distribution, and consumption, imparting newness to the old.

Our concerns in this book include how and why commodity-producing processes in Southeast Asia have changed; how these changes relate to neoliberalism and globalization; and to what extent they are unique or characteristic of

such changes wrought elsewhere. In pursuing these concerns, the contributing authors focus on the dynamic relationships between commoditization, nature, people, and places in Southeast Asia. They address questions of how particular sites, resources, and people in this dynamic and heterogeneous region have constituted and have been shaped by neoliberalizing and globalizing waves sweeping the world. They also demonstrate how regional, national, and local histories and geographies of Southeast Asia mediate these allegedly ubiquitous and homogenizing forces. Our point is not only that we need to understand histories and geographies to show changes in commodity production but that comparisons of past and present commodification processes show how the very definitions of nature, people, and places are changing with shifting social relations and political-economic contexts. In turn, what are defined as commodities are also changing.

Since the rise of capitalism, commodities have been integral to the making of global and regional economies and everyday life. As Marx pointed out long ago, however, the social relationships and therefore the politics of production processes are often obscured by a focus on, or fetishization of, the end product—the commodity as a thing—and its profit-making capacities and exchange value. The work of those who produced the commodities, the social relationships that shaped and were shaped by their lives and the production processes, are typically hidden by the glorification of these inventions and their sale as commodities. Moreover, the role of "nature" in the production process and the specific constraints and opportunities that different resources, environments, and places afford both the production and distribution of commodities are even more frequently taken for granted.[1] For decades now, Marxists, political ecologists, and other scholars have told the hidden stories of commodities, untangling the links between commoditization and other social relationships.[2] This book seeks to build on this work by exploring the political ecological dynamics of producing nature, subjects, and places as commodities in various parts of Southeast Asia.[3]

Why focus on Southeast Asia? This region, made up of the nation-states of Brunei, Cambodia, East Timor, Indonesia, Laos, Malaysia, Myanmar, the Philippines, Singapore, Thailand, and Vietnam, is renowned as the site of some of the world's fastest growing, most dynamic, and diverse economies. Its high-tech industries and advanced agricultural production processes operate in spaces adjacent to the homes of millions of smallholders and forest-dependent people.[4] It contains great ecological diversity and resource wealth while being the site of some of the most devastated landscapes.

These factors dovetail with the deep history of mass violence across the region, and the particular characteristics and roles of authoritarian states in Southeast Asia in postcolonial "development" processes.[5] First, the strength and length of time that authoritarian state rule and state-led development, or both, prevailed in nearly all Southeast Asian countries has been longer than in many regions. Second, most Southeast Asian countries have endured military-dominated regimes or extended periods of martial law (Malaysia being the exception) for some period of postcolonial rule. Third, authoritarian states in all these countries have played major roles in initiating, maintaining, and transforming enclosures of natural resources—whether they be land, mineral deposits, or fisheries—for private and state accumulation. Enclosure involves appropriating land, resources, and people both to turn them into commodities and to "free"—or create—a labor force to work and make capitalist accumulation possible. Though state landholdings have taken a variety of forms in different countries and areas therein, states and state agencies in many cases have become the primary landholders/landlords through the expropriation of rural and urban people's lands, often without compensation, and of land deemed by colonial and national authorities as "empty," "abandoned," or "available" for "development," "conservation," or "national security" purposes. Since enclosure is an inherent step in the making of commodities, shifts in these historic processes merit close consideration and unpacking. Finally, brute force and systematic social injustice have partnered with the "opening up" of areas and the disciplining of populations and property rights for commodification, and with the enclosure and the transformation of people and "nature" into marketable products (Blomley 2003; Glassman 2006). These processes are part of commoditization by definition (Marx's "blood and fire"), and whether we are talking about overt or structural violence, Southeast Asia's natural and human wealth and its strategic global location have contributed to the region's being the site of some of the most horrific political violence of the twentieth and twenty-first centuries.

This violence was preceded and initialized with the forceful "opening up" of the region by European colonial powers and the "disciplining" of particular populations for the sake of commodity production and sale (see, for example, Stoler 1985; Clarence-Smith 1992; Fasseur 1992; Morton 2000; Tarling 2001; Fernando 2003). It has continued in the postcolonial era as part of shifting global power struggles. Political violence over the loyalties of people and the control of nature continued through the devastation wrought by the Pacific War, the "hot" Southeast Asian wars of the globe's "cold war" period, and other forms of post- and neocolonial violence (see Chomsky 1993; Marshall 1995; Robinson 1995; Lens 2003; Nevins 2005; Roosa 2006). This violence lives on, structured into the very landscapes and social fabrics of many Southeast Asian places (Kamm 1995; Dreyfuss 2000; Griffiths 2003; Nevins 2003; Stellman et al. 2003). Such violence creates social distortions that underlie the unjust relationships between some localities and the global political economy (Nevins 2005), ones that help reproduce a "violence of everyday life" (Scheper-Hughes 1992). Millions of lives from Vietnam to Myanmar to West Papua have been sacrificed over the last few centuries in pursuit of commodities.

These periods of extreme state political violence and the resulting (and typically continuing) injustices help constitute what is "new" and "unique" about commodification and accumulation in the Southeast Asia of the late twentieth and early twenty-first centuries. State violence, or the threat of it, was foundational to the growth of capitalism in Southeast Asia—a point that has been largely and strangely unexplored in comparative studies of the rise of postcolonial economies in the region. Although many of the authors in this book do not write directly about the relations of violence and commodity production, we recognize that postcolonial clashes—often classified simplistically as part of the cold war—laid a basis for uniquely Southeast Asian expressions of neoliberalism, property rights, and enclosure.

In this introduction, we look to the region's wide variety of political regimes to make this argument. The region's nation-states represent political-economic configurations that range from state socialism to military oligarchy to state capitalism to nominal democracy (and combinations of these). All share histories of state authoritarianism, political violence between state forces and particular population segments, and, in most, continued threats of state, military, or privatized political violence. Even the extreme differences between the current regimes of Myanmar, Vietnam, Laos, or Indonesia, for example, are informed by certain commonalities in regional, national, or local histories. We show that, like primitive accumulation through enclosure, violence in Southeast Asia has not occurred only at some initial moment but recurs or remains a threat, albeit in different forms (De Angelis 1999; Perelman 2000; Hart 2004; Harvey 2005). These violent forms are produced and reproduced in different epochs and eras through new types of enclosure that enable primitive accumulation. These include racialized access to resources or job opportunities, the initiation of new kinds of property rights, the appropriation of land and resources by states and capital, changing legal and policy frameworks of resource management and governance, as well as brute force or the threat and fear of it.

Commodity production in Southeast Asia as elsewhere is dynamic in ways that reflect Polanyian "double movements" of state-market relations or state-market-society relations (Polanyi 2001). Resistance to dispossession, appropriation, disciplining, boundary making, and exploitation has long characterized commodification processes in different parts of the region. As opposition is also a product of social and cultural milieux, including the cultural practices generated through political economy, the performance or production of resistance and counterclaims are often what differentiates one case or site from another. Much such resistance is about resurrecting the "social"—the part of the social fabric needed for a dignified human existence but undermined by the commodification process—and making sure it constructively informs matters of commodity production, distribution, and consumption, as well as resource access and control (Hart 2006).

Combining the cultural with the political-economic, and embracing the multidirectional dynamisms of commodity regimes, the chapters in this book shed new light on specific examples of commodification, while illustrating how they relate to the production of people, nature, and places in Southeast Asia. But first, we turn to a brief history of the ways in which Southeast Asia's commodity production is a contribution to, a basis of, and a backdrop to contemporary forms of neoliberalism, the enclosures that continue to animate and undergird neoliberalism, and the production of people and nature as "new" and "old" commodities.

Commodities in Southeast Asia: From Colonial to Neoliberal Eras

Before the arrival of Europeans in the region, the area called Southeast Asia had long produced, consumed, and exported a variety of commodities. The region had been integrated into long-distance trading networks dominated by Arab, Indian, and Chinese merchants before the arrival of the European powers. The pursuit of commodities—spices such as pepper, nutmeg, and cloves—brought Europeans to the region. Once there, they greatly expanded their search for commodities. The extraction and eventual production of primary commodities such as timber, rubber, coffee, tin, petroleum, and tea linked the region to markets across the globe (see Wolters 1967; Hall 1981; Marshall 1995; Morton 2000; Reid 2000).

The Portuguese were the vanguard of the European presence. By the sixteenth century they had violently seized control of much of the region's lucrative spice trade (see Hall 1981 and Wolf 1982). From the beginning, European imperialism—which soon involved the Spanish, Dutch, English, and French—had to deal with resistance from local populations, which was countered with physical violence. The Europeans fought with one another as well as with Ottoman, Chinese, and Arab traders as they competed for control of access to people, places, and resources for trade. By the early nineteenth century Portugal was a marginal player, relegated to the eastern half of the sandalwood-rich island of Timor, while the Dutch, the British, and the French dominated the area (Hall 1981; Boxer 1969). The division of Southeast Asia into distinct colonial realms was directly related to the production of nature and people (laborers) as commodities and to the competition for control over them.

The consolidation of French rule in Indochina exemplified the intensification of commodity production in the late nineteenth century. Although the French were relative latecomers to the area, the catalyst for their expansion was the major economic downturn in the 1870s known then as the Great Depression. That depression resulted from myriad factors, including the overproduction of certain commodities and declining transportation costs that had facilitated the shipping and sale of goods across the globe. As a result of the downturn, many European countries and the United States intensified their searches for new investment opportunities and markets. This led to expansion and consolidation of markets at home and created fierce competition for control of other regions of the world that could provide cheap raw materials, labor, and became markets for European manufactured goods. Besides the "scramble for Africa," new colonies in Asia and the Pacific were established. The terms of rule in some of the existing ones were changed to enable greater levels of capital accumulation. As part of the process of consolidation and expansion, colonial powers and their agents forced or strongly encouraged people in many areas to become producers of particular commodities (Wolf 1982, 310–53).

Moreover, just as laissez-faire capitalism and liberal philosophies of governance were taking hold in Europe, the 1870s began the era in the Netherlands East Indies, British Malaya, and India known as "the liberal period." In the Netherlands East Indies, many of the feudal-style labor relations and production processes on which the Dutch colonials had built their strategies of governance and extraction were replaced by arrangements more in line with liberal principles of "free markets," including production of an "un-tied" (nonfeudal) labor force that worked for wages and paid taxes in cash and not in labor, kind, or other services. Through colonial constitutions, sovereignty declarations, and the signing of treaties with various local "rulers," Dutch officials began to create the legal-institutional environments through which commodity production and trade would proceed. In some of the British colonies—Burma, Malaya, Singapore—liberal principles were also the foundation of the earliest colonial policies (see, e.g., Furnivall 1956).

Through a variety of strategies, including the leasing of concessions for plantation agriculture and the control or taxation of trade in market centers or seaports, new forms of control of the production and flow of commodities were put in place. These economic practices depended on enclosures to enable primitive accumulation of various sorts. Land laws were written and imposed and notions of "free" and "unencumbered" lands or property were invented and embedded into the political-economic logics of these colonies. State or Crown lands were made available to agricultural enterprises—the major form of colonial accumulation at the time—to lease from state authorities. Forest laws were written and enforced throughout the region beginning around the same time (1865–1919). The notion of "political forests"—whether these were called reserves, Crown lands, state forests, nature monuments, or other terms—became a major mechanism by which colonial and later contemporary governments would enclose vast tracts of land and resources, in the process dispossessing forest farmers and other forest-dependent peoples. It was through these enclosed forests that primitive accumulation by state agencies, corporate interests, and powerful individuals in strategic positions became possible in both the colonial and later periods. The simultaneous rise of science and "scientific management" in the colonies both depended on enclosure and state territorial controls and helped produce a gloss on what was really transpiring (Peluso and Vandergeest 2001; Galudra and Sirait 2006).

Specialization within the colonies went hand in hand with capitalist development and the expansion of commodity production. Whole regions became specialized in the production of some sort of raw material, food crop, or drug. Sometimes this involved government/corporate appropriation of indigenous production and trade in certain products (cinnamon in Vietnam and Sumatra or teak in Siam, Burma, and Java, for example); at other times, the products were completely new to the area (coffee in Vietnam or Portuguese Timor; rubber [imported *Hevea* brasiliensis] in Malaya, Sumatra, and Borneo; cocoa in Sarawak and Sulawesi). As the economies of particular areas became increasingly concentrated on monocultures or tree crops, they required increased importation of foodstuffs and laborers—leading to specialization in other geographic zones. By the beginning of World War II, commodities such as timber, rattan, resins, rubber, copra, pepper, and other forest products and plantation crops were pouring in to local and world markets, as were tin, gold, silver, nickel, coal, and oil from this region (Wolf 1982, 310–53).

Despite commodity booms after World War II, the limitations of national economies dependent on primary commodities were not lost on the new political leaders of Southeast Asian nation-states. Industrialization became increasingly attractive as a development path. Some national governments fostered import-substitution forms of industrialization through domestic industries that aimed to produce relatively simple products for local consumption (e.g., bicycles and rubber-soled shoes). But a variety of factors—including the small size of some domestic markets, the economic inefficiencies of insulating domestic producers from foreign competition, and the compressed time and space that Southeast Asian countries had to "catch up" with industrial powers—limited the success of import-substitution approaches (Hart 2002). For such reasons, industrial policy increasingly invited and welcomed foreign investment. In this regard, Singapore's declaration of independence from Malaysia in 1965 and the resulting need for the new country to revamp its industrialization strategy was a key development. Given Singapore's size, it could not produce at levels that would make its products affordable to its citizenry. It had to engage in production for global markets (Owen 2004, 379–85). These forms of global production were not called "neoliberal" when first instituted—indeed, they were seen as part of state-led development. Although the Singaporean state is still highly involved in the city-state's development, in other places such practices have become symbolic of changes toward neoliberalism. The result has been the rapid transformation of various postauthoritarian regimes in the region to sites friendly to the production of a variety of new commodities—from garments to microchips to automobiles to shrimp. In addition, commodities long associated with the region, such as coffee, lumber, and precious metals, are being produced through new regimes and sold in new trade networks.

In Southeast Asia, as throughout most of the so-called Global South, neoliberal policies were implemented with the specific goal of facilitating economic growth through increased investment and growth in export production (Block 2001, xviii; Sawyer 2004, 7; Ong 2006, 11). The rise of Southeast Asian economies was thus predicated significantly on foreign investment, unlike in Taiwan and South Korea where domestic savings and investment fueled growth. In the late 1980s Japanese capital began to locate relatively labor-intensive aspects of manufacturing to Southeast Asia, thus initiating a decade of rapid economic growth. (This shift was an outgrowth of the 1985 Plaza Accord whereby the G-5, the world's then-five biggest economies—Britain, France, Japan, the United States, and West Germany—took measures to depreciate the value of the dollar vis-à-vis the yen so as to help the United States break out of a recession and reduce its trade deficit with Japan.) Japanese capital had already been active in fueling primary resource sectors in the region, particularly timber, as early as the 1960s (Dauvergne 1997). Further growth ensued after investment from Hong Kong, South Korea, and Taiwan soon followed suit, as did, later, more speculative forms of capital from international portfolio managers and banks. Thus, when international investors began pulling their investments out of the region in 1997, Southeast Asian economies were highly vulnerable (Bello 1998, 426–27).

Though coming late in global terms to Southeast Asia, and still not "arrived" in some places such as Myanmar, neoliberal policies and increasing amounts of foreign investment have led to significant shifts in the structures of national economies throughout the region. In Indonesia, for example, approximately 2 percent of the value of its merchandise exports was manufactured goods in 1980; by 1999, the figure was 54 percent. In the cases of Malaysia and Thailand, the corresponding figures were 9 percent and 80 percent, and 16 percent and 74 percent, respectively (Rigg 2003, 239). Recent changes in Vietnam and China indicate equally dramatic jumps.

Let's step back briefly to examine neoliberalism and put it into political context. Neoliberalism is also referred to as market liberalization, privatization, Thatcherism, Reaganism, market fundamentalism, or the Washington Consensus (Block 2001, xviii; Harvey 2005, 1–3). As the latest manifestation of capitalist forms in increasingly globalized commodification processes, neoliberal promoters claim that self-regulating markets work in the best interests of consumers, producers, nation-states, and the entire global economy. Like other mechanisms of accumulation, however, neoliberal policies and practices need to curtail alternative forms of accumulation. Although capitalism needs alternative forms of accumulation to thrive—think of the importance of public schools or unpaid domestic labor, for example—alternatives of the "wrong" sort undermine the ability of capital to expand. A nationalized telecommunications infrastructure or water as a public good, for instance, both serve to limit possibilities for private investment and profit. Thus, following on the heavy national and international investments in state-led capitalism or state socialism, neoliberal projects have entailed not only privatizing such public goods but also weakening the social welfare activities of the state. In certain forms, this has the effect of, or demands, the shift of the state's responsibility for the well-being of individuals and societies to the private sector—corporations, concessions, civil society groups, religious organizations, individuals, or, in the most abstract way, "the market" itself. Like other ways of producing things and people and processes as commodities, neoliberalism at the extreme pushes to extract "the social" from new commodity forms. Even in governmental contexts that do not broadly support neoliberal sensibilities, spatial and temporal exceptions have been made to accommodate some aspects of neoliberalism (Ong 2006).

Neoliberal discourse drives international aid and programs and constitutes the international push toward the selling or redistribution of public goods to private interests. It does so in part by promoting the deregulation of finance and trade and the liberalization of national economies by allowing allegedly "unfettered" foreign investment. Yet neither "markets" nor market actors act alone in these endeavors. Opening up an economy and a society (to unregulated investment) involves other technologies of control, such as the curbing or dismantling of labor unions and the deregulation of industry, agriculture, and resource extraction—thus enabling "market relations" to determine the direction of change—and the loosening of restrictions on financial transactions. The effects of these controls occur not only in the realm of increased trade and production but also in that which defines state protections of citizens, subjects, and environments.

Globally, neoliberalism emerged out of a series of political-economic changes and shifts in the 1970s and 1980s. These included the breakdown of Keynesianism, the adoption of monetarist polices by Washington, post-Maoist reforms in China, the fall of the Soviet Union and the Berlin Wall (Harvey 2005), and the increase in the debt burdens of many developing countries (Heertz 2004). Also central was the war against the countries of the "second" (the Soviet Union and its satellites) and "third" worlds that challenged U.S. or Western hegemony, or both.[6] In Southeast Asia, the overthrow of Indonesia's Sukarno government, which the United States and Britain helped to destabilize in 1965–66, and the U.S. war in Vietnam, one in which Australia also participated, were highly significant moments (Kolko 1988; also see Blum 2003; Chomsky 1993). Out of this confluence of multiple events, policy trends, and political violence, and through the work of powerful national and international institutions and actors, the market became triumphalist (Peet and Watts 1996) and neoliberal forms of "development," "aid," and "investment" were normalized.

The imaginings underlying neoliberalism are purported to be grounded in late eighteenth and early nineteenth century "liberal" thought, one that proponents trace back to philosophers such as Adam Smith, David Ricardo, and Thomas Malthus. As the power of European monarchies was receding, the "principles" of the market seemed to be a kind of wonderful "discovery," an alternative to the subsiding of feudal practices and the oppressive actions of emerging nation-states. Then and now, however, the actual practices involved in supporting liberal or neoliberal policies differed from the theories about them. Then and now, the production of so-called free markets involved coercion and the expropriation of land, resources, and labor through disguised forms of primitive accumulation.[7]

Southeast Asia stands out globally in these neoliberal processes due to the length of time it took for some of the countries to be directly affected. One reason mentioned earlier is the depth of authoritarian power that characterized most Southeast Asian national economies. Although the forms of authoritarianism varied from stark military power (Myanmar) to state socialism (Vietnam, Cambodia), to modified military power (Laos under the Pathet Lao, Indonesia through Suharto, the Philippines through Marcos), to hidden authoritarianism and heavy, top-down police power (Singapore, Malaysia, Brunei) and some briefer experiences with military rule (Thailand), heavily centralized, authoritarian rule has played significant roles in modifying or mediating the particular effects of neoliberalism. These authoritarian practices and forms have been bolstered by state claims of "Asian difference," most famously pronounced by former prime minister Mahathir of Malaysia and Lee Kuan Yew of Singapore as "Asian values." In the 1980s and 1990s, "Asia can say no" was a frequent refrain of various Asian leaders (Ong 2006, 1). Echoed in different ways through the paternalisms and patriarchies of power in Indonesia, Thailand, the Philippines, and Vietnam, the gloss of Asian values helped cement an image of both national unities and regional commonality. Thus, for example, even though the major capitalist countries such as the United States and Britain helped enshrine Suharto, Indonesia's heavy-handed ruler from 1965 to 1998, discourses of Indonesian nationalism, Asian difference, and, of course, Indonesia's great nationalized oil and timber wealth kept some of the neoliberal institutions at bay for a long time. Similar discourses and natural resource endowments enabled Malaysia to do the same. In the socialist/Communist countries, single state parties and military rule played key roles in determining the shape—and the presence or not—of foreign investments, whether through assistance, loans, or direct investment.

With the exception of Thailand and the Philippines, where neoliberal institutions and processes took local forms earlier than elsewhere in Southeast Asia, the breakdown of state authoritarianism began in the late 1980s and early 1990s, when revolutionary political-economic changes were brought on by localized crises with globally reverberating effects. The first of these changes was the transformation of Vietnam, Laos, and Cambodia's socialist economies, which was related, of course, to changes in China and the Soviet Union. The second was the Asian financial crisis, which had varied national and subnational effects, with regional and global implications. The crisis most directly affected the authoritarian government of Indonesia, leading to the fall of Suharto after thirty-two years of dictatorship, and contributed to the subsequent emergence of East Timor as an independent nation-state. Malaysia weathered the crisis rather well because of Mahathir's monetary policies before and during the crisis. Thailand and the Philippines suffered economic setbacks that particularly affected the middle classes and the poor, but did not experience revolutionary changes in their governance processes. The third set of changes took place in the late 1980s and 1990s in the postsocialist or current socialist states of Myanmar, Cambodia, Laos, and Vietnam. These involved the military or an authoritarian party taking or retaining power and facilitating increased commodification of land and natural resources. This was done directly by an increasingly violent military in Myanmar, while Cambodia and Laos each embraced new development programs and international aid under their military-socialist (Laos) and "old" monarchist (Cambodia) governments. In Vietnam, the Communist Party began to encourage substantial foreign investment and championed the expansion of the private sector.

How much of a norm is neoliberalism in Southeast Asia, given the realities and patchiness of its implementation suggested above? What we suggest in the next section takes us further toward explaining the "uniqueness" of Southeast Asia in the allegedly global neoliberal moment of the early twenty-first century. Commodification processes here are proceeding in many settings that retain the residues of authoritarian, centralized government; military or other forms of political violence enacted against citizens in these states; and enclosures by states, private interests, or international nongovernmental organizations (NGOs). These conditions have produced new forms of old commodification and accumulation processes in ways unique to Southeast Asia.

Commodification and Ongoing "Primitive Accumulation" Processes

The commodification of people (and land) was and still is a component of what Adam Smith called "previous accumulation" and what Marx renamed "primitive accumulation." Primitive accumulation was not part of Smith's theories on the creation of markets, states, and civil society but underpinned his assumptions about how this would take place (Perelman 2000). Ricardo and other liberal economists who built on Smith's theories continued this tradition of ignoring the histories of enclosures and expropriations that had to take place in order for Smith's theories to "work." Marx famously insisted that "conquest, enslavement, robbery, murder, in sum, force" are critical and often hidden components of both the primitive accumulation process and ongoing forms of accumulation and state power. Violence, whether structural or brute force, is what enables the creation of a subject population "free" to work as wage laborers for commodity producers (Farid 2005).

In Europe's colonies in Southeast Asia, the processes of previous accumulation often differed from those in Europe, although they also involved forms of enclosure, expropriation, and violence. Yet, to many observers in Europe the violence of commodification in the colonies either remained invisible or was represented as justified; the triumphant stories they heard were about production, improvement, profits, and conversion to Christianity (Wolf 1982; Multatuli 1987; Vlekke 1959). However, the production of tropical crops such as tea, coffee, indigo, sugar, opium, and tobacco, as well as the very production of "natural places" such as forests and parks in Southeast Asia, involved extensive seizures of land and resources and exploitation of people.

Forms of colonial violence and resource appropriation are well documented and the details are beyond the scope of this introduction. However, it is crucial to understand how the political violence of the late 1950s through the mid-1980s—at different times in different sites—created the preconditions for the commodity production economies of what became capitalist Southeast Asia. In addition to the wars and insurgencies going on in what was then called Indo-China, Thailand, peninsular Malaya, Sarawak, Brunei, and Indonesia faced insurgencies and "emergencies" of a sort that Peluso and Vandergeest (n.d.) have called "alternative civilizing projects." These alternative projects threatened the nature of state power and the orientation of civil society, with their visions for the future based on internationally influenced but locally framed forms of socialism, communism, and Islamism. In other words, the future fates of these Southeast Asian nation-states were not yet clear—nowhere was it written in stone that they were fated to become the planet's fastest-growing capitalist economies and approach the achievements of the newly industrialized countries, or NICs, to become "Tigers" and models for development planners the world over.

Hilmar Farid (2005) has argued this recently for Indonesia, focusing on the areas of the greatest state-orchestrated mass violence against the Indonesian Communist Party, Barisan Tani Indonesia (Indonesian Peasant Front), and other left-wing organizations: Java, Bali, and Sumatra. The primitive accumulation argument is relevant to other parts of Indonesia and Southeast Asia in a different way. The most extensive territories of forest enclosure in this forest-rich region were not the product of colonial forestry, but were constituted after World War II (Peluso and Vandergeest 2001; Vandergeest and Peluso 2006a, 2006b). The political violence of the cold war era gave many of these enclosures their final push, solidified the normalization of state-owned forests, and, in their wake, forest and marine parks, nature reserves, and other "protected" areas. Because the chapters in this book are about new resources, environments, and constructions of people, they contribute directly or indirectly to the notion that primitive accumulation has not disappeared but its forms have become normalized ("legalized") and thus enable further accumulation (De Angelis 1999; Perelman 2000; Farid 2005).

Besides winning an ostensibly political battle for the hearts and minds of the southern and insular parts of Southeast Asia, and establishing major capitalist economies therein, these cold war–era battles also provided the means and rhetoric for new and old sorts of enclosures—those critical components of Marx's primitive accumulation and Smith's previous accumulation. Not only were these enclosures accomplished through the allocation of resource-rich land to corporations and other sorts of private enterprise but they also were taken over by various state agencies for "national enterprises." These parastatal and government agency enclosures included oil and natural gas operations, mineral production areas, production forests, and plantations. Although national state enclosures in some cases continued enclosures initiated by colonial governments, in many cases they were new or took stronger institutional forms of exclusionary resource claims. They are varied in form and impacts, but need to be understood as having set the stage for further commodifications. The timber, gem, and oil industries, for example, across the region were dependent on national enclosures and reconfiguration of property rights (MacLean, chapter 8; Li, chapter 7; Gellert, chapter 2, in this book). In most cases, they were initially enabled by state violence in resource-rich areas, often against "insurgents." The populace's subsequent fear of state violence helped bolster state capacities to continue to monopolize and enclose forests, mines, seas, and plantations—and set the stage for commodification of both new and old genres.[8]

Violence and structural controls took different forms in Vietnam, Laos, Cambodia, and Myanmar. These histories of state accumulation through planning, however, began to change as these countries began to restructure their economies and transition to first limited and then broader forms of capitalist production and trade.

Against these formative backdrops of state violence and enclosures enabling accumulation, we see how a varied set of postindependence forms of primitive accumulation helped to facilitate the region's rise as both a development model and—in some parts—as a laboratory for at least embryonic forms of neoliberalism. Indeed, for global financial institutions such as the World Bank and International Monetary Fund, Southeast Asia—usually along with East Asia—was, through much of the 1990s, the paragon of supposedly free market development, yet one brought about through significant state intervention. It was there that the Asian "tigers" or "dragons" performed their miraculous economic growth. And it was there that the precariousness of the presumed miracle was painfully revealed beginning in mid-1997 when many of the region's fastest-growing economies underwent precipitous downturns (Rigg 2003, 3). One commentator suggested that this was the twentieth century's second biggest surprise—the first being the fall of the Soviet Union (Bello 1998, 425).

This crisis had cultural, social, and political effects of huge proportions. In Thailand, for example, an increasingly established middle class found itself unable to invest and accumulate even at the small scales that they had begun within the past decade (partly as a result of early adoption of neoliberal strategies). Around the region, massive construction projects slowed down or stopped. Urban construction workers and other laborers returned to rural areas where work was scarce. More workers, especially women, took opportunities to work in Saudi Arabia, Taiwan, Korea, and elsewhere (Breman and Wiradi 2002), creating new sorts of transnational connections, dependencies, and opportunities. While the downturn facilitated the adoption of stringent neoliberal strategies, it concurrently energized alternatives. In Indonesia, besides the downfall of Suharto, the financial collapse and return of laborers to rural areas can be connected to the massive land occupations in Java, as well as to the rise of non-party-affiliated peasant unions and other associations on an unprecedented scale (Fauzi 2005; Lucas and Warren 2003). At the same time, the steep economic decline fueled both decentralization processes and growing interethnic and sectarian violence in Indonesia, the Philippines, and elsewhere. Even where formal decentralization is not occurring, such as in Myanmar, local and district competition for access to resources and legal/illegal resource markets is increasing (Barney, chapter 5; MacLean, chapter 8, in this book). Sometimes competitors are international corporations.

Moreover, the growing strength of China was increased after the crisis, blocking the achievement of "tiger" status aspired to by Southeast Asian nation-states that had not yet achieved it (Barney, chapter 5). As Chinese entrepreneurs and multinational companies with linkages to the Chinese market increasingly gain control of territorial concessions and resources in Laos, Indonesia, Thailand, and Vietnam, observers consistently note the difficulties of competing with that regional giant.

Commodities, Capitalism, and a World Economy

Nothing is intrinsically a commodity; production for sale on the market is what made things commodities.[9] Something is made into a commodity in a particular context and under certain conditions. Things (or people, places, or "nature" itself) may be commodities at one time and not at another; they can move in and out of the commodity state (Kopytoff 1986; see also Appadurai 1986a). Commoditization involves the establishment or recognition of some kinds of property rights, so that regularized and state-controlled transactions can take place between people transferring rights over particular things to one another.

Although commodities have always been with us, commodities have only become *central* to our ways of seeing and living in the last two hundred years or so (Watts 1999, 305). At the same time, commoditization—the process through which "everything comes to acquire a price and a monetary form"—is an ongoing process, and an incomplete one, because the commodity process can never replace all the other ways in which things (inanimate and living) are socially valued (Appadurai 1986a; Kopytoff 1986). Yet, beyond markets, commodity orientations have penetrated contemporary capitalist societies so profoundly that we can speak of them as commodity-producing societies, ones in which almost everything is potentially for sale, as one of the epigraphs to this chapter states (Watts 1999, 305–6, 312–13).

Until the nineteenth century and the rise of capitalism, as Polanyi (2001, 45–48) famously argued, the economy was always "embedded" in society—in other words, it was "submerged in" social relations, politics, and religion.[10] Thus, precapitalist markets did not shape all the principles determining the production and distribution of goods and services. As capitalist social relations spread and intensified, the economy has become increasingly "disembedded," creating situations in which social relations and politics have become relatively subordinate to the economy. The logic of the market system, divorced from its origins in social and environmental contexts, increasingly determines the terms of our existence. But as Polanyi points out, this shift has never been—and, indeed, can never be—a total one. That said, the spread of capitalism has led to market forces mediating an increasing amount of social life everywhere.

Nonetheless, commodities continue to be shaped by nonmarket social relations. All commodities have "social lives" that inevitably are intertwined in noncapitalist social relations, meanings, and sorts of value. Because such relations and meanings differ across space, time, and society, the material and cultural effects and implications of commodification vary (Polanyi 2001; Appadurai 1986a; Jackson 1999). What and who become commodities, and when and where they are commodified, both emerge from and reflect social relations and histories at all points of production and consumption. For much of human history, for example, people's bodies were made into commodities, in the form of slaves. Even in the case of slavery, however, the meanings of being a slave, the ways slaves were produced, and the terms—the relations—of slavery, were neither universal nor unchanging (Reid 1983). Hence, even if commodities are "a universal cultural phenomenon" because the exchange in objects and services is "a universal feature of human social life," the ways commodities are produced and related to or embedded within the larger sets of social relations are destined to vary (Kopytoff 1986, 64–68).

The origins of a socially valued thing and its transformation into a commodity inform how social actors respond to its commodification. For Polanyi, land (or bounded nature), labor (work by human beings), and money ("a token of purchasing power" brought about by the state or banks) are all "fictitious" commodities in that they were not "objects produced [specifically] for sale on the market," unlike manufactured goods or food, for example (Polyani 2001, 75–76).[11]

While capital treats these things as commodities—and thus produces "fictions" that allow them to be bought and sold on the market—market relations simply cannot be "the sole director of the fate of human beings and their natural environment[s]." If this were to happen, it "would result in the.demolition of society" (Polanyi 2001, 76). Polanyi thus argues that there are limits to how much humans can be exploited and abused without severe social dislocation. We can extend that argument to "nature" by noting that we cannot limitlessly pollute waterways, extract natural resources, and destroy landscapes without eventually undermining society's ability to sustain itself (O'Connor 1996). Thus, while market forces under capitalism are driven by efforts to expand, there will always be countermovements "which blunt...the action of this self-destructive mechanism." Such countermovements might involve the development of state policies and regulations to protect people, the environment, and money from the free market, or practices of civil society, individuals, and institutions. Polanyi calls these linked forces the "double movement" (Polanyi 2001, 75–79). It is this double movement that produces and reflects the tensions of commodification that remake people, places, and nature.

Producing Nature

In thinking about the myriad ways commodification produces nature, we conceive of nature in terms that are materialist (e.g., ecology, natural resources, land) and idealist (e.g., perceptions and representations of "nature" and "the natural"), while acknowledging that there is no untouched, pristine "Nature" independent of people's perceptions and actions. In this regard, nature is always what many call "socio-nature" (Swyngedouw 1999). Many of the pieces in this book build on Neil Smith's (1984) pathbreaking work on the social production of nature and the ideas of society-nature dialectics introduced by Piers Blaikie (1985). The term "socionatures" pulls together old and new forms of enclosure, primitive accumulation, and privatization involving different forms of state-capital-society-nature connections, emphasizing that these processes are not discrete categories but heterogeneous, overlapping, contradictory, and mutually constitutive. These connections are achieved through institutional and discursive forms of legitimation, outright violence, and the disciplining of new forms of practice.

As the authors in this book demonstrate, these practices and transformations reshape our ideas about landscapes and nature for novel kinds of commodity production. Changes and privatizations of access or control over nature and resources deploy various legitimating techniques, including the terms of science, moral authority, and violence to justify and further their projects. This results in the development of unique forms of accumulation that articulate with the specific characteristics of particular resources and with the production of new forms of knowledge about these processes and their associations with different or new owners and users.

Although the debates about "what is Nature?" have both drawn on and challenged philosophical ideas ranging from those of Aristotle to those of Marx, Bacon, Darwin, Malthus, and Erlich (Soper 1995; Merchant 1980), discussions of Nature's production as a commodity is relatively new. Whether this is said to take place through processes labeled "privatization," "nationalization," or "enclosure," both states and private entities are developing new ways of gaining access to and control over whole segments of territory as well as over the individual resources that are constituted through enclosure and primitive accumulation (Midnight Notes Collective 1990; Coronil 1997; Katz 1998).

The privatization and enclosure literatures tend to speak to different audiences: the former to more policy-oriented, institutional analysis or technically oriented NGOs; the latter to a more left-leaning academic cohort trying to analyze the new forms that capitalism is taking in the twenty-first century under neoliberal market triumphalism (Blomley 2003). One irony of this capital and capitalist-led charge to privatize or "publicly" enclose everything—and to create new sorts of commodities and global demands for them—is that it often converges with activist agendas that seek to redress the inequalities produced in earlier, often highly centralized social formations (John McCarthy 2004). Global activists hoping to clean up or save the environment—for example, through the creation of "best practices" in food and fiber production (Vandergeest, chapter 12 in this book), the promotion of small-holder property rights, or the setting aside of tracts of land in attempts to protect wildlife and certain habitats or ecological formations—generally do not conceive of their efforts as modes of commodification (Li 2007, and Li, chapter 7 in this book). On the other hand, the notion of "saving Nature by selling it" (McAfee 1999) has taken hold in many nongovernmental organizations, transnational and local alike (Potter, chapter 10 in this book). This mantra has helped accelerate the enclosure, privatization, and commodification of nature, as well as the normalization of these processes. In other words, formerly contradictory forces are articulating in new ways that enclose so-called natural spaces and natural resources, often expropriating these from the very folks who created them in forms mistakenly labeled "pristine" (Katz 1998; Brush 1999; Hayden 2003; Agrawal 2005; Li 2007).

The drive to preserve "Nature," to create "ecological sustainability," or even more old-fashioned and explicit production strategies aimed at "improvement" or "development" result in restricted access to the enclosed resources and spaces. At times, these restrictions end up ignoring or further marginalizing already vulnerable populations, ones not imagined as "belonging" to a particular space despite their active presence within it (Walker 2004). Advocates of these enclosures also argue that they are for "the public good," thus tying the newly restricted "nature" to contemporary notions of the nation and citizenship (Coronil 1997; Comaroff and Comaroff 2000a; Zimmer 1998), and making them much more difficult for local users to challenge. Previous rationalizations for such enclosure also would have embraced "the greatest good" and drawn on state science discourses such as those employed to justify forest management under colonialism (Peluso 1992; Grove 1995; Bryant 1997; Sivaramakrishnan 1999; Hayden 2003, Galudra and Sirait 2006).

Contemporary claims about nature protection, as well as assertions defending landscape transformation for profit or "restoration," maintain important connections with these "old" discursive tools. At the same time, they embrace neoliberal policies and their underlying assumptions about the "best practices" for the land. In the process, the supposed legitimacy of certain practices and managers derives not only from science but also from the drive for state territorial power (Peluso and Vandergeest 2001). Ecological science, particularly conservation biology, has become a transnational discourse for claiming resources whether through de jure arrangements or de facto ones, indirectly, through other now-related discourses of neoliberal development (Li 2007; Hayden 2003; see also Haraway 1989). This discursive move shifts the terms of sovereignty and has major implications for the relative authority of nation-states and nonelected entities. The "greatest good" under these new terms implies a more inclusive national community (Smeltzer, chapter 11 in this book), as well as a more abstract humanity. In practice, however, it translates into select beneficiaries. This helps explain the rise of social movements against large-scale transformations and enclosures (on dams, see, e.g., Baviskar 1995; on parks, see Li 2007; Neumann 1998; Lucas and Warren 2003; Fauzi 2005). In too many cases people perceive or experience these nationalized or globalized "goods" as outright theft of their land, resources, and sovereignty (Perelman 2000; De Angelis 1999; Li, chapter 7).

In part, these local-global disjunctures come about because [stet capitalizations of nature and commodity] nature-as-commodity is a relatively new form of abstraction of value. Clearly, the commoditization of nature has taken place since the commoditization of land and agriculture—processes that can be traced back at least to the Romans (Williams 1973). But "Nature" became a new category in the second half of the twentieth century (Soper 1995), its definition changing in part because of the rising importance of "the environment" as an important category of science, institutions, law, and activism. Commodification, however, requires the establishment of property rights so that transfer, improvement, and the production of surplus are possible. Privatization and new enclosures such as parks have engulfed and reified both nature *and* environment (Neumann 1998; Hayden 2003; Coronil 1997; Smith 1984). At the same time that private property has become a dominant form of property, some people—in international conservation and environmental organizations, for example—are making claims about protecting the "global commons" through property rights. Nature protection and privatization—two forms of territorialization or enclosure—are not strange bedfellows at all, nor are their associations limited to this neoliberal age (Smith 1984; Arnold 1996; Grove 1995).

All sorts of new fictitious commodities have resulted through privatization and Nature enclosures. For example, the construction of an area as "primeval forest," "wilderness," or "untouched coral reef"—or more scientific-sounding names—is the first step toward making it into a park, and thus a first step in a trajectory toward commodity status. The making of national parks transforms nature by creating it institutionally—as a park, a protected and exclusionary site. The lands comprising these parks were bounded, reserved, controlled, managed, and rendered accessible in limited forms, just as other productions were histori-cally conceived and realized as commodities. Just like property rights, commod-ity relations are not about relations between things and people, but relations between people *about* things: in other words, they are social relations first and foremost (MacPherson 1978). Imagining a park as a commodity requires pre-liminary "work": the normalization of particular relationships and concepts as natural or desirable ways of the world. Even if hoped-for tourists do not arrive, other commodities arise in the form of nature protection services and "sustain-able" forms of resource extraction as defined by state or international environ-mental NGO managers. Sometimes parks serve as real or imagined collateral for multilateral loans or international conservation investment (Li 2007; Tsing 2004; Chapin 2005; Peluso 1993). The process also requires a certain type of power to enforce or inflict those imaginaries on the people who have alternate views, experiences, histories, and claims to those lands and resources. People in-side the bounds or in the vicinity of a park, who understand their surroundings as their gardens, farms, or backyards, have to be convinced—or forced—into understanding them as "parks." In this manner, "ways of seeing" are inherently mixed up with ways of being, claiming, managing, and using (Berger 1973). In the cases of large-scale landscape transformation included in this book, all involve some sort of enclosure—and various forms of conflict, control and violence that result (e.g., in this book, Biggs, chapter 6; Li, chapter 7; MacLean, chapter 8; Barney, chapter 5; Potter, chapter 10).

As these chapters show, landscape transformations and state enclosures cre-ate new commodities, but not always in the same way as classic enclosures by private individuals or states backed up by state legislation.[12] The conditions and relationships possible under neoliberalism constrain and reshape the old forms of enclosure and commodity production in new ways. State power remains a criti-cal part of the allocation of property rights for commodity production. Even in Myanmar, where neoliberalism seems far from a practice or a policy driver, the state (or pretenders to state power) is in the business of creating new territories—concessions—for the exploitation of gems. The violent practices of miners small and large within these concessions seem to be hybrids of old and new forms of enclosure (MacLean, chapter 8).

Sometimes new enclosures are intended to create commodities—for example, the damming of rivers in order to produce hydropower (Biggs, chapter 6). Moreover, "global demand" can be used as an excuse for creating corporate and state enclosures to produce high-value food or fiber crops (Barney, chapter 5; Vandergeest, chapter 12).[13] Although these might seem to be similar to the enclosures in eighteenth- and nineteenth-century Britain, the specifics of their production processes, their local forms of embeddedness, and the changed global contexts render them different. For example, it is through a complex array of international financial institutions, the rise of China as an economic powerhouse, foreign corporate interests, and international NGOs that the forest plantations in Laos discussed by Barney (chapter 5) have come about. Tsing (chapter 1) shows how the practices of entrepreneurs around the products of particular forests lead to new sorts of hidden enclosures and new forms of access and legitimation. Potter (chapter 10), while dealing with one of the commodities that made Java the jewel of Dutch colonialism—coffee—shows that the embracing of market-oriented activities (in this case, the cultivation of coffee trees in a protected forest area) does not always result in state-sanctioned enclosures or other kinds of support, particularly when the identities of claimants are represented as incapable of entrepreneurship or as destroyers of nature. A similar gloss is applied to the forest laborers in Tsing's story. As such, the political intentions and economic effects of key actors and interventions take different forms in different times.

In other cases, production of new commodities is both effect and cause of nature's transformation (Vandergeest, chapter 12; Fougères, chapter 9). Under these circumstances, state power or regulation is not necessarily "rolled back"—it simply takes different forms. The reframing of the Malaysian nation-state and its component peoples in advertising its new biotechnology initiative is perhaps the most obvious example of this (Smeltzer, chapter 11).

Such cases illustrate the complex dialectical relationship between local, national and internationally produced scales—sometimes in the form of new or old types of imperial power (Biggs, chapter 6; Li, chapter 7; Gellert, chapter 2; Vandergeest and Peluso 2006a, 2006b). At other times, corporate and state controls are hidden by terminology and practices that foreground "individual entrepreneurship" (Tsing, chapter 1; Fougères, chapter 9). Entrepreneurship, as a way of producing new subjects, achieves this in many diverse ways—Rudnyckyj (chapter 4) shows it appearing in the guise of Islamic practice in a West Java steel factory, Tsing sees it in the taming of "wild people" in "wild places," Gellert sees it in old and new institutional forms, and Fougères locates brand-new commodities in the new-old commodity chains of the southern seas. In a coupling that seems more benign, small-scale producers' desires may articulate with new market demands and concerns of first world activists as in the case of attempts to shape commodity production processes in the global South for the sake of social justice or sustainability (Potter, chapter 10; Vandergeest, chapter 12). New, local socionatures emerge thereby, along with all sorts of consequences, intended and unintended, seen and unseen (Walker 2004). As has been the case since European colonialism and before, international capital is a locus of profit making and legitimacy under neoliberalism and has often facilitated or led the move to abstract new forms of value from nature (Coronil 1997; Fougères, chapter 9; Barney, chapter 5; Tsing, chapter 1; Biggs, chapter 6). Particular forms of environmental regulation characteristic of neoliberalism and new forms of international governance facilitate this process (Hayden 2003; Bridge 2002; Bridge and Smith 2003; Vandergeest, chapter 12), and also help differentiate the forms and processes of nature commodification in the present from those that were most prevalent under colonial "improvement" regimes (Li 2007; Tsing, chapter 1) and under state-led development (Gellert, chapter 2).

Science also gets in on the act of regulation as both its subject and object: science is mobilized to create private property rights for corporate entities, as in the case of biotechnology (Smeltzer, chapter 11), often at the same time other sciences such as conservation biology are mobilized to demand defense of the public interest and the redefinition of what is "public"—through the consumption of organic coffee, or insistence on sustainable production and nature protection (Vandergeest, chapter 12; Potter, chapter 10; Li, chapter 7). Of course, many of these "publics" have privatizing characteristics, intents, or tendencies. In this regard, science, nature, politics, regulation, and profit are all connected (Demeritt 1998; Bestor 2001; Chalfin 2004; Vandergeest, chapter 12; Smeltzer, chapter 11; Barney, chapter 5).

Scientific technologies do not only make these products and processes possible but they establish or help establish the political and regulatory technologies associated with particular regimes of accumulation (Prudham 2005). How these political and regulatory technologies, social movements, and other responses to capital constitute new double movements or new alliances are empirical questions, unfolding in new sites and ways all the time.

Where Nature is the subject and object of commodification, it matters greatly what forms, scales, and qualities constitute it at various points in the commodification and exchange processes. In other words, the "nature" of "Nature" makes a difference, as does the political-economic context in which its commodification unfolds. Thus, one can find examples of "wild" commodity prospecting in the forests of a supposedly highly disciplined country—the United States—and highly controlled forms of production in Indonesia's "wild Borneo" (Tsing, chapter 1). In both cases, the commodity process reflects and reshapes nature and people as well.

People and Commodities

People make commodities, and commodities shape people's identities, circumstances, and social relations. Human bodies—as slavery, prostitution, human trafficking, and commercial pornography have illustrated—have long been for sale (see Kopytoff 1986; Blackburn 1997; Reid 1983). Despite the notion of human labor and bodies as fictitious commodities, body parts, in the form of trafficked organs from the living and the dead, have become commodities in the neoliberal era. Given that the flow of organs is typically from the destitute to the rich, they are symbolic of profound power imbalances within localities and across the globe (Scheper-Hughes 2002; Kopytoff 1986).

The commodification of people and bodies has typically entailed violently subjugating them or forcefully driving them from their land and thus compelling them to engage in wage labor (a form of self-commodification as the worker must sell his labor since he or she is devoid of all other possessions or means of producing a living) (see Marx 1992; Perelman 2000). It was the transformation of these hitherto noncommodities into saleable entities through enclosure, privatization, and primitive accumulation that enabled the rise of capitalism, and, arguably, its continuation (De Angelis 1999, 2004; Perelman 2000).

Processes creating appropriate subjects to enable accumulation are complicated and nuanced, as well as less visible oftentimes, particularly when they take place across global spaces. Through a variety of techniques—ranging from overt violence and laws to institutional practices and different forms of persuasion—people are meant to become disciplined in ways conducive to commodity-production regimes (see Potter, chapter 10; Rudnyckyj, chapter 4; Trần, chapter 3; Tsing, chapter 1). For example, Rudnyckyj shows here how spiritual disciplining through a new "brand" of Islamic practice is used to train workers and managers at a steel production factory in Java as the factory makes the transition from state owned and run to privately owned. In Vietnam, as shown by Trần (chapter 3), different historical modes of disciplining labor, guided by radically different ideologies, clash in the lives and actions of women workers who are empowered to demand their rights as the factory seeks to become more competitive in world markets. State agencies and international institutions, as well as ordinary schools, for example, can train individuals in such a manner to ensure that they have a proper outlook—in addition to the necessary skill set—to facilitate and normalize commodification and thus make the associated social relations seem natural and unchangeable. Trained technocratic "experts" then carry out their work in such a way that it effectively fetishizes the commodity in question by obscuring the inherently political and contested nature of its production (Biggs, chapter 6; Rudnyckyj, chapter 4).

Such "disciplining" can take contradictory forms. At particular times and places, docility and following orders are deemed appropriate; at others, "wild" workers are valued and cultivated. These differently disciplined subjects fit into different spatial and temporal contexts and are meant to produce according to the specific needs of the commodity (Tsing, chapter 1; MacLean, chapter 8). Hence, the production of neoliberal subjects also involves the creation of an autonomous individual who embraces and reproduces the logic of classical liberalism (Freeman 2000; Sawyer 2004).

Subject making is not limited to the realm of the purely economic; all sorts of subjectivities are involved in enabling accumulation. In selling shea butter to middle-class and wealthy or activist Europeans and Americans, for instance, the Body Shop cultivates people- and nature-friendly consumers by claiming to embrace "alternative" forms of production and consumption, while remaining a corporate capitalist enterprise underneath it all. At the same time, various companies market this commodity to African American women in the United States by stressing the plant's African roots, hoping to reinforce or create the sense of an African diasporic community (Chalfin 2004). Contemporary forms of capitalist accumulation have produced new subjects and actors, such as environmental activists (see Vandergeest, chapter 12), under many and varied capitalist regimes. The process has now become so normalized that people reproduce themselves as laboring, environmental, or otherwise disciplined subjects (Willis 1977; Agrawal 2005; Li 2007).

The chapters in this book also show how producers and other actors construct or reinforce identities and subjectivities and practices favorable to commoditization. Again, as Rudnyckyj shows for Java, state and private interests utilize a particular variant of Islam to produce "flexible" neoliberal subjects—from factory workers to managers. This then produces subjectivities with implications far beyond the realm of commodity production. In a neoliberalizing Malaysia, narrow "ethnic" nationalism is no longer in vogue and the nation's historical ethnic differences are officially valorized. Thus, "old" exclusive notions of nationalism based on race and ethnicity are being replaced by more inclusive forms that embrace difference (Smeltzer, chapter 11; cf., Moore, Kosek, and Pandian 2003). In this regard, capitalist accumulation and "multiculturalism" assist each other.

Commodification also brings people and places together in new ways, blending identities, creating new ones, and marginalizing others. This is clearly illustrated in Vandergeest's chapter about changing commodities and commodity production practices in Thailand. Li (chapter 7) also demonstrates that competing notions of what makes a commodity influence the positions people take in relation to new commoditizations. In war-torn Myanmar people move to take advantage of mining opportunities, marginalizing previously settled groups and reproducing violent state practices. This has sharpened ethnic and racial differences within the country (MacLean, chapter 8).

How individuals and groups respond to commodification, however, and what subjectivities result, depends on many axes of difference, such as socioeconomic class, race and ethnicity, nationality, gender, and ideology. In other words, these processes are contingent, as so many of the chapters in this book stress (e.g., Tsing, chapter 1; Li, chapter 7; Vandergeest, chapter 12; Trần, chapter 3; also see Fernandes 1997). For example, owners and managers of Vietnamese garment factories construct specific notions of womanhood such as docility and obedience to authority, while many women workers draw on socialist principles of equality and their place-based identities to challenge their reduction to commodities (Trần, chapter 3). The commodification of people is not only contingent but contested, against attempts to make them more "flexible"—a trait highly valued by capital (Ong 2000). In resisting, people struggle to "defestishize" or "singularize" themselves, to ensure that they are treated first and foremost as human beings (Kopytoff 1986). These struggles are shaped by historical and geographical circumstances and associated moral economies—realms of interaction between a society's ethical foundation and economic activity—in which commodification takes place (see Thompson 1971; Scott 1976). The variety of contestations also illustrates agency; ordinary people are not mere objects of totalizing forces such as capitalism, neoliberalism, and globalization (Thompson 1975; Chalfin 2004; Tsing, chapter 1; Trần, chapter 3). At the same time, specific commodity regimes can lead to unintended and unanticipated outcomes (see Hall 1996), which may unexpectedly empower marginalized groups and places (e.g., Chalfin 2004; see also Vandergeest, chapter 12; Potter, chapter 10; Rudnyckyj, chapter 4).

At the same time, as in any social process, commodification can have unintended consequences and thus produce subjectivities that are unfavorable from the perspective of capital. Capitalist accumulation requires a certain stability to unfold, while engendering disturbance and upheavals that reshape socionatural relations as much as economic ones. As a result, people often rebel against the fiction's constructs that would make them or their homes into commodities, thus providing frequent examples of old and new forms of Polanyi's "countermovements" (Sawyer 2004; Potter, chapter 10; Rudnyckyj, chapter 4; Smeltzer, chapter 11; Trần, chapter 3).

State and capitalist interests, however, do not stand still. In the case of Indonesian villagers who transgress the boundaries of newly declared national parks, for instance, the former residents are rendered criminals from the perspective of the state and some international nongovernmental environmental organizations (Peluso and Vandergeest 2001; Li, chapter 7). Criminalization and efforts by state and nonstate actors to prevent challenges to and trangressions against established power—for example, the implementation of state-protected forest regimes (enclosures by another name) and the outlawing of particular forms of organized labor activism—have gone hand in hand with the production of people and nature as commodities since the beginnings of capitalism (Thompson 1975; Peluso 1992; Sahlins 1994; Neumann 1998). It is such reactions by capital and its allies within the state apparatus and countermoves by those who resist commodification that make commodity production such a dynamic and contentious process, one with profound implications for the well-being of people, nature, and places across Southeast Asia and throughout the world.

PART I

New Commodities, Scales, and Sources of Capital

I

Contingent Commodities

Mobilizing Labor in and beyond Southeast Asian Forests

ANNA TSING

commodity
fetishization

How do people and nature become labor and resources? The process surrounds us every day, yet we rarely think about it. Indeed, we are blocked from thinking by messages that tell us to take commodities, including labor power and natural resources, for granted. We forget the violence and seduction that make it possible for profits to be made from human and nonhuman lives. We call this mechanism of forgetting *the market*. To speak of the market asserts the primacy of calculation over the uncertainties of history. Pushing culture and politics aside, it offers invariant natural law.

In the glare of the market, as ideology, policy, and coercive practice, critics must learn to illuminate scarcely visible shadows: the contingencies of commodification. To call the histories of labor discipline and natural resource extraction *contingent* affirms that they did not have to happen that way. The process of making labor and resources must be repeated over and over to keep commodities flowing.

I am grateful to Yoon Hwan Shin for getting me started on research on Kodeco. The hard work, perseverance, and stimulating insights of Yongjin Kim made this stage of the research possible; he also corrected serious mistakes in an earlier draft. I am indebted to Eric Jones and Kathryn Lynch of the Institute for Culture and Ecology as well as Katie Bagby of Forest Community Research for their generosity in guiding my Oregon matsutake research. Mushroom monitors Kouy Loch, Kao Saechao, and Vern Oden were most helpful and giving of their time. My matsutake research forms part of a network that includes Timothy Choy, Lieba Faier, Michael Hathaway, Miyako Inoue, and Shiho Satsuka. Nancy Peluso stimulated this analysis by inviting me to speak at the UC Berkeley Center for Southeast Asia Studies conference "Producing People and 'Nature' as Commodities in Southeast Asia" and by her encouragement to write up work I worried was too preliminary. Lisa Rofel kindly read an early draft. Don Brenneis discussed pidgins with me. Tania Murray Li and her colleagues at the University of Toronto helped me think through revisions.

The process is historical, meaning that it changes as new elements emerge and combine. To highlight the contingency of commodification is not to abandon analysis to chance but rather to reclaim what we practically know against the system of silences that stifles public discussion of such histories.

Corporate fascination with the global scale in the last twenty years has further obscured the history of commodities. In expanding across the globe, corporations declared the whole globe already commoditized. This is "commodity fetishism": we forget the history of the commodity to imagine it only as the object of our desires. We are drawn into a world in which the existence of particular commodities is taken for granted, and we can debate only how best to use them. To bring back an appreciation of contingency, we must make ourselves curious strangers, using our skills to push back the magic of the commodity, revealing its constituent fragility.[1]

Links in the commodity chain offer this potential. On the one hand, they are the necessary elements of commodity fetishism: they make the commodity possible. On the other hand, chains are made in shady deals, violent expropriations, creative finance, racist exclusion, and smart inventions. They reveal the contingent histories of making capital, labor, and resources. The links in a global commodity chain are forged through the charisma and coercions of people involved in world-crossing encounters. The cultural differences that must be bridged through these encounters offer practical traction to the commodity chain, facilitating the flow of the commodity, as they also create potential zones of disturbance. Elsewhere I have argued that the metaphor of "friction" brings both traction and disturbance into view (Tsing 2004).

Friction is "the resistance to relative motion between two bodies in contact."[2] The metaphor reminds us that global connections do not slide into place without a process of engagement. These are awkward engagements—grinding, grasping, sticky, tripping, slipping. Commodification can be revealed in action by considering friction in global commodity chains. To look for friction is to refuse to see value as something predetermined and fixed rather than shaped and contested, as it is in most commodity chain analysis. Friction is the everyday crisis of the value form.

In this chapter I examine two different sites to get a better sense of the role of friction in one link of the commodity chain. Doing so describes two sharply contrasting ideologies of Southeast Asian forest labor. The two settings are Korean-sponsored logging in Indonesia and immigrant mushroom collecting in the U.S. Pacific Northwest. In each case, labor is mobilized through self-consciously cultural strategies. Such labor becomes one link in a chain of heterogeneous business connections. Japanese capital pioneered such chains across the Pacific Rim. No single corporate standard here dominates the field; instead, multiple management forms compete and interconnect. In this creative global management space, people and nature are remade as commodities through a range of cultural and political histories and practices.

My first case considers the commodification of forest labor in Kalimantan, Indonesia, from the perspective of Korean industry. The Korean Development Company, or Kodeco, was one of the first and most successful logging companies in Indonesia.[3] Kodeco is one of the least documented industrial enterprises in Indonesia, at least in Indonesian and English.[4] Yet Kodeco is famous in Korea, and several books have been written about company founder Choi Gye Wol.[5] To find out more about Kodeco's business practices in Kalimantan, I have been working with a Korean colleague, Yongjin Kim, to translate Korean research on Kodeco. We began with a biography of the founder: *They Call Me the King of Kalimantan* (Kwon 1994). In keeping with the racy title, the book turns out to be colorful, exciting—and quite revealing about management ideas.

My second case follows forest product commodification and its relation to a Southeast Asian labor diaspora in the United States. Matsutake, a cluster of mushroom species most commonly found in pine forests, is a highly valued delicacy in Japan. Never successfully cultivated, matsutake are gathered in forests all around the Pacific Rim. As with tropical logging, a key challenge in this sector involves recruiting motivated forest labor. In the U.S. Pacific Northwest, Hmong, Mien, Lao, and Khmer refugees have found a surprising labor niche in matsutake collecting. My observations here draw from 2004–05 field research, still ongoing.

Before jumping into these histories, I step back to explain my approach to commodification.

Managing Leading Edges

How do management cultures remake people and nature as the labor and resources they need for their enterprises? Immanuel Wallerstein's notion of "leading products" is helpful here (2004, 25–27). Wallerstein explains that totally free markets would make capitalism impossible because open bargaining would take away anything but the smallest profits. Although capitalists claim to support free markets, they actually do their best to undermine them. Sellers work to create quasi monopolies, perhaps through restrictions such as patents or state contracts, or through price collusion among a few firms. Quasi monopolies increase the rate of profit. When monopolistic conditions deteriorate, firms shift their capital to more promising sectors. The products pushed in these relocations of capital are the leading products. The succession of leading products is an example of the *historical,* rather than the merely *structural,* determination of capitalism: contingency matters.

Wallerstein looks at global capitalism from an immense distance, interested in those trends that define the age at a global scale; thus each age has one leading product. Those of us enmeshed in the multiple histories of capitalism might look instead for "leading edges," that is, the profit-making advantage that any successful commodity needs in a free market. There are many ways to create a leading-edge advantage. If a corporation is offered public resources, it has privileged—and free—access to profits from them. The superexploitation of labor can raise profit margins. Political coercion and bribery can defeat free-market bargaining. Control of the media or the sites of consumption may play a role. Commodification is only lucrative if these contingent formations can forge quasi-monopoly rates of profit.

Forests present special possibilities and challenges for leading-edge commodification. Forests offer multiple options for commercial products: trees, resins, bush meat, fruit, live birds, fungi, and much more. Many forests have long histories of commercial collection of multiple products. When many sellers and buyers participate, profits are small, however. To claim the leading edge for one product often requires smashing the dreams of other commercial collectors—and sometimes killing off their favored species.

Just as nature exceeds commercial goals, labor may also be "wild"—that is, *liar,* out of corporate and government control, as Indonesians authorities say. (Loggers and miners without licenses are *liar.* Wild animals, savages, and shifting cultivation are also *liar.*) Forests are hard to police as spaces of private or public property; despite the laws of the land, people manage to get in and to take resources out for themselves. Whatever the ambitions of resource corporations or the regulations of states, forest dwellers have their own ideas about how to use the forest. Disciplined wage labor is thus a special challenge in the forest; laborers might run off and create their own "wild" enterprises. To create a leading edge, forest-resource corporations must somehow make people work for them.

Labor's specificities are particularly evident where downstream and upstream segments of the commodity chain are divided into separate business entities tied by trade dependence, credits, subcontracting, development loans, or other "soft cooperation networks." Japanese capitalism established such networks across the Pacific Rim (Hatch and Yamamura 1996). Even as such patched-together chains have become generalized beyond Japan's reach, it is useful to consider their capitalization in the vivid language of Koichi Iwabuchi, who introduced the concept of "culturally odorless commodities" to explain Japanese marketing strategies throughout Asia (2002, 24–28). Iwabuchi argues that, in contrast to U.S. marketing, which promotes and glorifies U.S. culture, Japan has disseminated products that do not make consumers imagine the "fragrance" of Japan. Instead, products such as electronics are marked with a generic modernity.

Similarly, Japanese capital makes business happen, but rarely are Japanese investments marked as "Japanese." Rather than promoting imagined economic universals, Japanese capital is discreetly deployed through other Asians, encouraging a heterogeneity of corporate cultures within Japan's shadow. Japanese development loans provide the start-up money for other Asian businesses. Japanese trading companies and wholesalers set up privileged marketing and conditions of trade.

Other Asians bear the brunt of making leading-edge commodities. In Kalimantan, for example, Malaysians, Filipinos, and Chinese Indonesians bring timber to Japanese markets, while Koreans use Japanese development loans to supply a national plywood industry deeply dependent on Japan.[6] If these Asian entrepreneurs are caught in unscrupulous business practices, labor slavery, violence against local residents, or collusion with corrupt officials—the necessary components of leading-edge commodification—their Japanese sponsors are hardly held responsible. Rather than standardizing economic practices, odorless capital supports multiple and overlapping cultural economies in Asia and across the Pacific Rim.

This kind of capitalist expansion deserves analysis on multiple levels. Here I examine the relationship between the independent management cultures that proliferate in sectors dominated by odorless capital and the subjectification of labor. At this link, odorless capital becomes full once more of cultural odor. Odor emerges in local situations to motivate the work process and make the product possible. But this is not the odor of Japan, nor some cultural essence of other Asian entrepreneurs. Instead, a mélange of Western and Asian development discourses toss and roll together, taking advantage of local opportunities to make work happen. The odors are often patriotic, but this patriotism covers rather than reveals the structure of capital.

My argument, in short, is as follows: After 1965, Japanese money ironically made a Korean nationalism possible among a few privileged entrepreneurs; by chance, Indonesian timber was one target. At just that time, timber was becoming a "leading product" in Indonesia as government officials offered strategic concessions. In the context of anticommunist labor suppression in Indonesia, Korean nationalist entrepreneurs could imagine "native labor" within a colonial discourse of difference. The company created a faux-colonial management scheme for instruction through a pidgin language adapted to the naïveté of imagined natives. Although this management strategy did not succeed in the way it proposed to do, it did create a corporate enclave culture able to resist popular protest.

In the Oregon forest a very different commodification of forest labor took hold between Japanese money and the trauma created by the U.S.-Indochina War: a "wild" forest labor became available in which discipline was anathema to management concerns. Despite their economic importance, nontimber forest products in Oregon have not been privileged against competition within state-corporate alliances. In this political vacuum, poor-people's entrepreneurship—guided by U.S. American nationalist slogans about freedom and competition—found a place to thrive in the forest. A strong form of U.S. nationalism was nurtured here, the nationalism of entrepreneurial loners. No developmental pidgin instruction was needed to manage labor; instead, management asserted a competitive autonomy and expected multiple natural languages in the forest.

Two nationalist "fragrances" are found in these forests—Korean and U.S. American—but, taken alone, neither explains much about the structure and

history of capital. It is the contingent histories of commodity chain formation—
the frictions of the commodity chain—that allow us to appreciate these offshoots
of Japan-centered globalization.

Capital in the Forest I: Managing Lazy Natives

In a 2003 interview, Kodeco founder Choi Gye Wol recalled the happenstance
conjunctures through which his business was formed. To help out a Japanese associate in the 1950s, Choi entertained a West Papuan delegation in Tokyo until
they agreed to endorse making their half-island a part of Indonesia.[7] Indonesian president Sukarno, who wanted West Papua, was grateful, as was Korean
president Park Chung Hee, who wanted ties with Indonesia. Over time, the
gratitude of these two men made Choi's fortune, offering him the unprecedented
opportunity of investment in Indonesia. "God has guided me to do unbelievable
things," Choi reminisced (Simbolon 2003).

Personal histories are enmeshed with structural developments, and Choi's is
no exception. The 1965 Normalization Treaty between South Korea and Japan
laid the foundation for Korean business development by making Japanese money
available—through Korean public officials (Lie 1998). President Park's patronage of Choi expressed the formula through which Korean business took off with
the help of Japanese capital. Choi received US$3 million in start-up funds from
the Normalization Treaty accounts. With Japan's support, too, the Korean wood
products' export industry began growing in the late 1960s. Because of the devastation of Korea's forests, most of the wood was imported for processing. Choi's
opening was timely. Yet it was up to him to create a leading edge—to translate his
good timing into profitable business practices.

The year 1965 was important in Indonesia as well. After an abortive coup,
General Suharto, soon to be president, led the army and the populace in a massive wave of bloodshed; between five hundred thousand and one million people
were killed because of associations or alleged associations with the Indonesian
Communist Party. By 1968, when Japanese money became available for Choi's
entrepreneurship, Indonesia had been opened to foreign investors. The natural
resource sector—and particularly logging—was offered as the inducement for foreign entrepreneurs. Foreign businesses were aided by the suppression of protest—
and of labor organizing, which were condemned as Communist. The intersection
of Japanese capital providing Korean business opportunity and Indonesian labor
suppression made Kodeco seem imaginable. Still, disciplined forest labor is a special challenge, especially where people are used to making their living in forests
without corporate assistance.

Kwon Tae Ha's biography of Choi elucidates Kodeco's attempts to shape labor
through management culture (Kwon 1994). Kwon is a sympathetic journalist who
worked for Kodeco in South Kalimantan for several years. He writes for a Korean

audience eager to hear about a successful and patriotic businessman. *They Call Me the King of Kalimantan* offers a vivid picture of what Choi thought he could produce in the Kalimantan jungle—and what he thought he was up against. The enormity and strangeness of the forest discouraged the Kodeco team. "This place is originally not for people," he has the pioneer Koreans say (1994, 100). The forest itself seemed determined to thwart Kodeco's efforts: "It was like a war between the living jungle and human beings. The jungle obstructed any human approach. The jungle was quite malicious in that it wanted more human sacrifices as it became more destroyed" (1994, 115). Snakes jumped out of trees; scorpions hid in crannies. Trucks slammed into giant serpents coiled on the road, killing their drivers. Branches fell and workers were lost in the forest. Kodeco saw its role as fighting against this wildness, disciplining the forest. The biography suggests that a key step in the disciplining process was the making of a labor force that would not shirk in fighting the forest.

Choi's Indonesian associates helped him select a place in Kalimantan. They warned him away from places where the Communist taint was still strong. In 1969, as Choi began his business, foreign money was attractive to Indonesian administrators, and recent political events had caused a new political docility among potential workers. Yet abstract money and fear could not make a labor force: they had to be applied on location. Rubbing against the material realities of South Kalimantan, Kodeco commodified the forest through creative friction. The biography describes this process through a linguistic metaphor: the company had to develop its own pidgin to socialize workers. Only through Bahasa Kodeco, "Kodeco language," could workers be disciplined.[8]

The text itself best shows how management ideology worked on the imagined body of local labor. What follows is most of the chapter called "Bahasa Kodeco," as translated by Yongjin Kim (Kwon 1994, 127–32). I point out the components of creative friction through which this company pidgin forged its leading edge. (The book's original text is indented below. My interpolations within the text are in brackets. Parentheses are in the original.)

> Without the help of the natives, it is impossible to manage a business in a foreign country.[9] Choi Gye Wol knew this very well. Before he brought Koreans, he went to the forest to do research with the natives. Choi was much indebted to Idam Halid, who was the chairperson of the Islamic Party. . . . Religious leaders have power not only in the religious realm but also in the political one.
>
> Chairman Idam Halid helped Choi by sending his younger brother Hasbula, who had once been secretary to President Sukarno. It was Idam Halid's advice that persuaded Choi to settle down in Batulichin, South Kalimantan.
>
> "Go to the south. There are many communists in the east. Available land in the south is huge. That is a promised land of future development."

The massacre of suspected communists in 1966 prepared the way for labor and resource commodification. According to Choi's advisers, compliant labor is not available from communists. Meanwhile, only the coercive pressures of the district officer succeed fully to bring in the workers.

> The natives began to flock in. From time to time, a scout team went out to Kota Baru or Pagatan, which is three hours away by klotok (a small boat used by the natives), and they recruited people using a broken local language. However, it was Mr. Hasbula's efforts to influence district officers and their administrative staff that helped Kodeco recruit people.

Without local language skills, the Korean management has a difficult time recruiting workers. In this gap of communication, it is easy for the Koreans to imagine themselves as entirely different from Indonesian laborers. A great gulf separates them in which the ability to speak is one element. How can this gulf be explained? The natives must be lazy; civilized managers must teach them how to work.

> Indonesians were braver and more willing to work than I had expected. The only bad thing about them is laziness. Laziness—that may be an evaluation made in comparison with Koreans. Even nowadays, all Indonesian offices are closed from noon to two o'clock in the afternoon. This is the so-called "waktu siang" (siesta hours). They eat lunch, rest and sleep. You will see very few cars in the street. . . . During those hours, nobody works, and it is against the law to force anyone to work. That would be very strange to our Korean eyes, since we are normally satisfied with a quick cigarette time under a willow tree after lunch.

How can lazy natives become productive? They must be taught; they must learn language itself. To reach out, the company needs to create its own language.

> "Bahasa Kodeco" is a peculiar language made by the Korean staff, who inserted Indonesian words in Korean sentences. Doo cepat cepat (speedy) makan (eat) and doo cepat cepat kerja (work). "Doo" is the word for "do" in Chungcheong dialect.[10] When translated properly, it would be, "Hurry up, finish your meal and go to work ASAP." . . . A person who learned proper Bahasa Indonesia might not be able to understand it. But the natives in Kodeco understood it very well.

Most early employees were migrants, disciplined by other labor experiences. To management, however, they were always already "natives."

> Since Choi Gye Wol treated the native employees quite well, many people came looking for jobs. Three months after the pioneering setup, Kodeco launched its first ship to export wood. At that time, about three hundred native employees were working there. In June 1969, the first ship with six thousand cubic meters of wood, gained by sweat and tears, left Batulichin and headed toward Inchon.

An "episode" disrupts work: a labor stoppage! This labor action is not in the language of communism; it is almost entirely unspoken. The company has only stereotypes of the primitive to explain the situation. Such false stereotypes are facilitated by the self-conscious submission of Indonesian politicians to foreign business initiatives.

It was during those days that a funny episode happened to Choi Gye Wol. It was the day after the company paid salaries to its employees. At that time, Borneo was such a primitive place that money was unnecessary. [Note that this is completely untrue.] Because uncivilized indigenous people did not recognize the value of money, the company paid in rice instead of money. Out of three hundred native employees, almost no one—except a very few—appeared for duty. Each working place could not manage its daily duties.

"What the hell is this? Are they making a strike or something?" Choi did not know why. He urged his Korean staff to ask what happened to the Indonesians. At the same time, he himself went out to find his employees. Most of the Indonesians were sleeping, wrapping their bodies in sarongs (the traditional costume for Indonesians).

Torpor is a familiar characteristic of "natives."

"Bangun (wake up)! Bangun guys!" Choi and his staff woke them up. The natives, just half waking up and half sleeping, did not say a word, looking at their supervisors with their big eyes.

"Kenapa tidak masuk kerja? (Why didn't you come to work?)," a Korean asked one of them.

"Tidak apa-apa (No reason)," he replied, with an annoyed look.

"Why do you say tidak apa-apa! Why?"

Where does this disaffection come from? the Koreans want to know. They turn to a theory of history: Primitives cannot sell their labor power because they do not realize that they have wants.

"Saya sudah cukup (I have enough / I'm satisfied)."

"Cukup? What is cukup?"

"Look. There is a lot of rice. I don't have to work for the next three months."

It was frustrating. He meant that he would work only after consuming all the rice he had. This made the Koreans crazy! Choi was so speechless that he just began to laugh loudly.

"How naïve are they! If they are naïve like that, we have to find another strategy. Don't blame them too much."

What is to be done? The benefactor proclaims the coming of new desires. Meanwhile, quietly, he takes away the elements that make life possible without them.

Choi Gye Wol shifted the pay system from a monthly basis to a daily one. He also opened a PX [company store] that displayed plenty of merchandise, which could be bought with tickets.[11] He wanted to bring up the purchase desire and uplift the working spirit. [In the PX] there were daily products, parasols, umbrellas, transistor radios, and so on.

It proved to be successful. The number of employees increased and the production of wood increased as well. After twenty-six years, the place became a city with a population of six thousand. Not only people from the neighboring area but also from Java, Sulawesi, Sumatra, Flores, and Irian Jaya came to work there. In 1994 [at the time of his writing], on every tenth day of the month, which is the payday at Kodeco, eight hundred million rupiahs were released. The city became active and everybody looks as happy as during a festival.

POLITICAL coercion and economic strangulation are covered up and explained by the need to develop a pidgin language of goal-oriented cooperation between employees and employer. Rather than facilitating a broad range of communication between employer and employee, it directs work in a local enclave, thus the better to foreclose, at least for the moment, the development of fuller codes and wider worker access to connections and resources, political, legal, and otherwise.[12] The need for this pidgin is explained by the wildness and ignorance of the natives, who also, the biographer says, must be taught to work for a wage. The native's difference, imagined as lack of knowledge, can be tamed, together with the forest, through the pidgin of "eat quickly, work fast."

Amazingly, although the pidgin may not have had the socializing function Kwon suggests, it does seem to have been important in imagining a corporate culture capable of staving off external threats. In the 1970s and 1980s, Kodeco recruited most of its labor from outside South Kalimantan, and often among those already socialized by other logging enterprises. Many loggers came from Malaysian Sarawak, for example, where timber companies exporting wood to Japan had already logged much of the forest. These loggers had learned disciplined forest labor without Kodeco's management. However, Kodeco's corporate practices established a Kodeco enclave. The labor force identified with the company rather than with local residents. Most of the time local residents had little contact with the company. The pidgin imaginatively confined—rather than opening—communication.

Only in the 1990s did local residents come to Kodeco for employment in significant numbers—and this was because so much of the forest had been removed that other forest-based livelihoods had become more difficult to pursue.[13] Some local farmers found jobs with Kodeco as mechanics or plywood factory workers. It was then that Kodeco's management ideologies gained their most effective moment. New employees were sucked into corporate enclaves that alienated them from their previous neighbors. When protests rocked the forests, Kodeco employees did not participate.

Kodeco's policy was to consider the forests uninhabited. Timber—and later plantation—operations moved through villages, orchards, and fields. Community protest was limited by the enforcement operations of Indonesia's militarized

New Order regime. Even when laws protected villagers' rights, such laws were not enforced. When the Suharto regime fell in 1998, community protests blossomed. Kodeco was a target of considerable community dissatisfaction.[14]

None of this protest, to my knowledge, followed class lines. Opposition was entirely communal, that is, either religious or ethnic. Muslims protested that Kodeco had destroyed cemeteries. Dayaks protested that Kodeco had destroyed orchards.[15] Yet, despite such protests, this was a period of expansion for Kodeco. Kodeco was discussed by regional elites as a model company. In 1999, Kodeco was offered a huge new logging concession in South Kalimantan. Because the concession included Dayak villages and environmentally sensitive mountain areas, regional advocacy NGOs mounted an anti-Kodeco campaign (Tsing 2004). The protests gained considerable regional and national momentum (Wulan et al. 2004). But activists were unable to mobilize company insiders. Kodeco succeeded in projecting a convincing picture of internal solidarity. Despite dedicated efforts, activists could find little material about Kodeco's history and organization. The enclave remained silent. My slowly developing research on this topic responds to this silence.

Kwon's account of Kodeco's management style addresses this situation indirectly. Kwon draws attention to the role of patriotic Korean fantasies of colonial paternalism, which came to occupy a niche between Japanese mercantile expansion and Indonesian labor repression. Disciplined enclave labor was one result, creating a "leading edge" in the forest. Disciplined labor is not, however, the only way to success. I turn to a very different commodification of labor, in which expectations of the wild excess of entrepreneurial loners create the possibility of forest product supply chains.

Capital in the Forest II: "Wilding" Forest Labor

The Oregon situation is just as historically quirky as Kalimantan's. Once a heartland for commercial timber, the timber industry destroyed much of its own resource. Other forest products, including wild mushrooms, have emerged in the gap. The U.S. Pacific Northwest was connected to the transnational mushroom market in the late 1980s as a result of the conjunction of several unpredictable historical developments. The Chernobyl disaster in Russia had destroyed much of Europe's commercial mushroom crop because of radioactive contamination.[16] U.S. involvement in Indochina brought in new waves of otherwise unemployable labor, including both shell-shocked Vietnam veterans, who refused ordinary jobs, and Southeast Asian refugees without English language skills or, in some cases, any urban employment experience. Quite a number of rural Southeast Asians, displaced to California cities, flocked to the mountains of the Pacific Northwest to forage. Foraging turned out to be profitable.

Commercial mushroom picking in the Pacific Northwest began with mushrooms for the European market: chanterelles, boletes, and morels. Excitement rose, however, with the turn to matsutake mushrooms for the Japanese market. The American matsutake is a white mushroom with the same characteristic odor as its Asian relative. The decline of the matsutake harvest in Japan expanded the search for matustake across the Pacific Rim. In 1993, a conjunction of historical factors—including the relative dearth of matsutake from other areas—turned attention to the Oregon matsutake harvest. Picker prices for the most valued buttons reached a high of US$600 per pound.[17] No one has forgotten these high prices, even as prices fall and fluctuate, dropping as low as $1 per pound in 2004. The rush to find matsutake attracts several thousand pickers each year. Most are Southeast Asians, but the pickers also include Latino migrant workers, Vietnam veterans, and ex-loggers.

Canadian export companies, linked with Japanese importers, handle most of the trade; a number introduced mushrooms as a sideline to other exports to Japan.[18] Relations with traders and bankers in Japan have made these businesses possible. Yet, unlike Kodeco, the Canadian companies do not make their presence known in the forest. Instead, they work through a chain of independent contractors, including bulkers, who sell large quantities of mushrooms to exporters, as well as buyers, who buy mushrooms every day from pickers in canvas tents set up on roadsides during mushroom season. Although many Canadian export companies are run by Asian Canadians (e.g., Chinese, Filipinos, Japanese), their representatives in Oregon are mainly white Americans; the buyers are white and Southeast Asian. Although importers and exporters set the price and provide the money, buyers stress that each buyer and each picker is an independent entrepreneur.

The job of bulkers and buyers is to obtain a large and consistent supply of mushrooms. Instead of directly disciplining labor, however, they focus on the allure of the product and the process. As far as bulkers and buyers are concerned, mushroom collectors collect for the thrill of the chase. In buyers' imaginations, the field is egalitarian, competitive, and driven only by personal desire. This is just as much a false representation as the Kodeco management dream. It also depends on racial stereotyping. For example, bulkers and buyers consistently stereotype Southeast Asians as violent, traditional, patriarchal, and with closed families, with money the common ground with whites: no lazy natives here. These qualities, according to mushroom buyers, make Southeast Asians *good* pickers. Buyers and bulkers want labor to be wild, not disciplined. In their imaginations, only wild labor—violent, competitive, self-motivated, and driven—is good at bringing in the product. Different frictions create a leading edge.

In contrast to Kodeco, Oregon mushroom buyers are invested in the pleasures—and the dangers—of a wild, multispecies forest and a wild, undisciplined labor force. They emphasize and encourage the wildness of people and nature. This is because they see wildness as key to the forest's allure as a space of entrepreneurship. If Kodeco can only attack forests through disciplined labor,

Oregon mushroom buyers can only draw independent pickers through forest wildness. Rather than trying to separate management and labor, bulkers and buyers imagine themselves as equal to pickers. They manage labor, at least in their talk, by identifying with it; their freedom, they say, is the same. One bulker explained how, fed up with company discipline, he left his job at the Georgia-Pacific logging company; he never looked back as he headed for the freedom of the forest—a freedom shared with pickers. In wilderness is the leading edge.

A few textual excerpts can make these contrasts more vivid. Jerry Guin is a former Navy man who came to Oregon's forests to both pick and buy mushrooms. *Matsutake Mushroom: "White" Goldrush of the 1990s* is a diary of his adventures in the 1993 mushroom season (Guin 1997). Most of the book is devoted to lists of the fluctuating prices of mushrooms, the places he went to find them, and the people he met. However, on the few occasions that he allows himself a flourish of excitement, metaphors of wild independence come through clearly. From the title on, he evokes the U.S. gold rush:

> Looking for "white gold" is a quest fueled by curiosity and greed, much like the quest of the 49ers of the last century, a true tale of high expectations, hard days and low yield, of great competition for cash literally growing in the ground. I lived the adventure among thousands of others racing against time to strike it rich before the season ends. (p. 4)

Independent work unites buyer and picker in a common logic of pursuit.

> October 9, Saturday. People are so frantic to find the elusive mushroom, it seems every rig you see is going faster than just a few days ago. (p. 47)

The independence of the pickers makes them throw aside trappings of politeness and civilization.

> October 11, Monday. Well, the greedy grubstakers are out in force with a real sense of urgency. Old clothes, unkempt appearances, knife stuffed to the side. All wear baseball caps to hide messy hair, and have red eyes from the dust and smoke. Filthy vehicles full of plastic buckets, baskets, and plastic bags are everywhere. The urgency only stops once the picker has been paid. Then a quietness seems to prevail. Slowness and tired movement with their only interest being food and rest till dawn; then out of the starting blocks again. (p. 49)

The challenge and danger of the escape from authority are the motivation for the chase. Guin describes buying—the real money-making venture—as an afterthought.

> October 19, Tuesday. During the trip I reflected on the successes and letdowns of the venture: the misery of living in and out of the back of my pickup, the dust, the cold, the washboard roads, the competition, the letdown of expecting to find huge

patches only to come across digs that someone else had made, the elation of finding the first mushroom each day with fingers crossed for many more, the anticipation and surprise at high prices, the joy of watching people be successful, at least for the moment. Further thought brought me to realize the good fortune I had had by working in the booth [buying]. . . . I probably would not have made it this long had it not been for the nighttime booth work. (p. 54)

Guin is circumspect in his comments about Southeast Asian pickers. Like all the white buyers and pickers I met, he imagines a race of all against all. For the white buyers I spoke with, the main difference between whites and Southeast Asians is that Southeast Asians work as enclosed, unitary "families," while whites work as individuals. One buyer revealed common habits of pan-Asian stereotyping, "When they come out of the van to sell their mushrooms, Mamasan follows Papasan, and the kids all follow Mamasan. Papasan decides where they will sell, and they all sell as a family."

His comment helps us imagine the labor force buyers aim to incite: it is segregated and modular, with Asian families holding the place of white individuals. It is ironic to find that, at least in my preliminary observation, ties within picking teams are eclectic and unpredictable. A young Mien man brings his elderly uncle and the teenager who lives next door. Two Cambodian men who met picking return each year to enjoy each other's company. A Lao man is caught on a surprise visit from his wife while picking with his girlfriend. Still, buyers' imaginaries are not irrelevant. Buyers work to create an individualized labor force by changing the prices every evening, and sometimes within the same night, thus increasing competition. They ignore registration requirements and celebrate illegality. The labor force of their desires competes wildly to bring in the product.

In this context, too, Southeast Asian pickers devise their own interpretations of the chase. One Cambodian man explained to me that he first came up from California because his mother had been diagnosed with cancer. He had heard that matsutake had medicinal value and he wanted to bring her some. After the season, he brought some to her oncologist at the UC Davis medical center. He told me that the doctor took them, did some tests, and declared them worthless except as an aphrodisiac.[19] (I would love to have been there, since I can't imagine that any tests were done.) Eventually his mother died. Yet he returned to the harvest year after year for himself. A landmine had disabled him, and his relatives had refused at first to show him their picking spots; he wouldn't keep up, they claimed. They had left him alone on a forested hillside—but he had found mushrooms! After that, he kept going back to prove, and improve, his own health.

Although this is obviously a singular personal story, it resonates with stories other Cambodian pickers told me. One woman explained that when she came to the United States, she was so thin and weak she could barely walk. Only the tonic value of matsutake as well as the physical exercise of picking has allowed her to regain her health. For many Cambodian pickers, matsutake harvesting is the pursuit of health, not the gold rush. Yet this cultural difference is not an impediment; it is encouraged in the managers' and buyers' rhetoric of open competition.

Without a singular management, everyone expects a multilingual situation. No communication is expected except when buying Forest Service permits, where instructions are carefully offered in many languages. Even there, a competitive ethos makes all translators suspect: What secrets might they be passing? What special interests do they slip into their supposedly neutral talk? Southeast Asian representatives of government or nonprofit organizations are suspected of conspiracy. Southeast Asian mushroom buyers who can speak to pickers from their language group are suspected of subverting the accepted prices. Without a structure of integration, betrayal haunts every act of translation.

Buyers and bulkers occupy a space by the side of the road that allows them to mediate between the wild forest—as they imagine it—and the warehouses and offices of their parent companies. In the forest, every white man and every "Asian family" works for themselves.

Contingent Commodities

To create a labor force in the forest requires experiments in love, greed, persuasion, and coercion. This is a good place to look for creative friction. The forests of the Pacific Rim, increasingly caught up in subcontracting and indirect capitalization, are lively sites of semiautonomous management cultures, each aiming for leading-edge profits. Here Japan's "odorless" capital allows the formation of nationalist entrepreneurial experiments, from Korean faux-colonial discipline to U.S. celebrations of freedom.

The resulting forms of labor subjectification are *both* contingent historical assemblages, made from national and ethnic encounters, *and* dependent on their ability to form links within global circuits. If I have focused here on contingency, it is not to discount the linking process, with its requirements for economic intelligibility. Too often we let the requirement for intelligibility take over our analysis instead of considering how every link is merely "intelligible enough," that is, formed with friction. We imagine the linking process as guided by a uniform economic logic that lines up places and people like products in an assembly line. For both supporters and detractors, capitalism appears as itself a Fordist product of increasing standardization, even if the standardization is in flexible production. Instead, I want to open discussion of how the heterogeneous niches that make up global capitalism are formed—not as differentiated products of a flexible punching machine, but rather as historical congeries that may exceed previous logics even as they find successful articulations. This kind of rethinking of the commodity chain is necessary if we want to combat commodity fetishism.

We continually naturalize commodities, taking them as preexisting in our attempts to find them, make them, distribute them, sell them, or buy them. Perhaps this ability to naturalize commodities is what makes the consumer class around the world so cruel. The "neutrality" of the commodity allows us to know our status in relation to what we buy and to ignore the dehumanization of people and the destruction of nature embodied in those products.[20] To move beyond this complacency we need to re-historicize the commodity chain, attending to the dynamics I have been calling contingency and friction. To explore the cultural and political work involved in making nature into resources and people into labor allows us to imagine more.

My contrasts between industrial wood production in Kalimantan and the collecting of minor products in Oregon are intended to make contingency in the making of forest products more evident. In each case, capital in the abstract cannot make commodities without turning people into labor. Management ideologies alert us to the importance of political and affective commitments as well as material practices in this process. Kodeco's attempts to tame the wildness of the forest through the discipline of labor drew on colonial symbolism to create inequalities and then bridge them. Mushroom buyers in Oregon also invoke racial stereotypes, but their goal is to make the forest seem even more free and alluring in order to let labor go wild. That the gold rush might help mushroom production in Oregon and the myth of the lazy native might stimulate logging in Kalimantan are each examples of the cultural histories of commodification. The indeterminacies of these histories are key to the process of global connection. It is what is missing from economic formulas of supply and demand. It is the reason why specifically anthropological research is worthwhile.

2

What's New with the Old?

Scalar Dialectics and the Reorganization of Indonesia's Timber Industry

PAUL K. GELLERT

Timber is one of the world's oldest commodities. Its history of trade and production for exchange value began with shipbuilding by the world's core political and military powers during the early years of what some date as the birth of the world-system (Albion 1926). In Southeast Asia, and Indonesia in particular, exports of timber have occurred since as early as the thirteenth century (Knapen 2001, 335) and flourished under the rule of the Dutch East India Company (Peluso 1992). The particular characteristics of timber, including its spatial distribution and density, as well as the geographies and topographies where supplies are found, have shaped the specific processes of extraction, transport, and processing of raw timber into the commodities demanded in local, regional, and global markets (Barham, Bunker, and O'Hearn 1994). In the face of these characteristics, the commodification of timber continues to be reproduced, reorganized, and contested in myriad ways.

One of the most important dynamics in this historical reproduction of timber's commodification is the production of scale. Building on the work of human geographers (Swyngedouw 1997, 2004; Smith 1984; Castree 2003; Harvey 1996, 2003), I examine these dynamics in terms of "scalar dialectics" (Heynan and Robbins 2005, 7). As Heynan and Perkins (2005, 102) state, "Scalar dialectics elucidate the processes and relations that shape...environments, which, in turn, contributes to the production of regional, national, and global environments." Specifically, commodification not only occurs *at* particular scales but through a production and politics *of* scale (Swyngedouw 2004; Smith 1996). What is

The author gratefully acknowledges support from an Abe Fellowship of the Japan Foundation Center for Global Partnership during 2004 and 2005 to conduct the research on which this chapter is based.

meant by the production of scale is that "scalar configurations [are] the outcome of sociospatial processes that regulate and organize social power relations" (Swyngedouw 2004, 132). That is, social processes do not occur in a geographical vacuum but in particular spaces and at particular scales.

Moreover, the production of scale is dialectical. One key process social scientists have identified in extractive timber economies is the progressive depletion of the commodified resource base and the attendant underdevelopment of the extractive region (Bunker 1985). Depletion and other putatively separate "natural" processes (e.g., fire and disease) and "social" processes (e.g., struggles over access and control) and surplus accumulation reverberate back onto processes of ongoing commodification and accumulation (Ribot and Peluso 2003). Out of this dialectical struggle, "nature" is produced but not a nature separate from human action (Smith 1984; Castree 1995). Thus, to employ a more precise, less dualistic term, "socionature(s)" are created and transformed in the process of capitalist commodification (Swyngedouw 1999; Gellert 2005b). Commodification of socionature in the form of natural resource commodities makes the dialectics of scale especially relevant because questions of nature and environmental transformation are drawn in as "integral parts of the social and material production of scale" (Swyngedouw 2004, 132).

In this chapter, as part of this book's focus on the particular contexts of commodification, I focus on the organization and reorganization of commercial timber (e.g., solid wood products) extraction, production, and export from Indonesia. What is new in the commodification of timber in Indonesia during the last decade of rapidly changing social relations is a highly volatile contestation of scale after several decades of crystallization of social relations within repressive national-scale "development." During the New Order (1966–98), central political and military authorities dominated Indonesia, ensuring—both through memories of the violence that brought the regime to power and periodic exemplary violence—that contestation of the production of a national scale of timber extraction was ineffective and isolated. However, the Asian financial crisis and domestic political crisis of 1997–98 created an opening for renewed contestation of the dominance of the national scale of political organization and economic accumulation.

Nowhere has this been more strongly felt than in the natural resource commodity sectors such as timber. One of the conditions attached to a US$43 billion International Monetary Fund (IMF) structural adjustment package in 1998 was the dismantling of the marketing powers of the Indonesian Wood Panel Association (Gellert 2005a). The resignation of President Suharto several months later formed a conjuncture of unforeseen political and economic change. More generally the structural adjustment formed part of the contemporary triumph of neoliberalism, whose discourse and practices came late and haltingly to Southeast Asia.

Importantly, rather than consider neoliberalism as a social "thing" to be studied, scholars are increasingly cognizant of neoliberalization as a process (Heynan and Robbins 2005; McCarthy and Prudham 2004). The politics of scale and continued commodification of timber have been profoundly affected by the neoliberalization process. On the one hand, political transition away from authoritarianism has created an opening for a domestic rescaling of governance away from the center in Jakarta, the capital. New decentralization policies have bolstered the legitimacy of regional and district levels of government. However, old political forces, both private and government, are contesting this rescaling, and the resolution of such contests remains somewhat unclear. On the other hand, although beyond the scope of this chapter, regional rescaling is occurring as Chinese markets increasingly dominate the region, and the role of Indonesia as an extractive periphery to global patterns of consumption is being reshaped. Thus, the local and supranational scales appear simultaneously to be gaining in importance in a process of "glocalization" (Swyngedouw 1997).

Yet, the theoretical and political priority in social and geographical research "never resides in a particular geographical scale, but rather in the [socionatural] processes through which particular scales become (re)constituted" (Swyngedouw 1997, 169, cited in Brown and Purcell 2005). That is, scale is not ontologically given but produced. Although some scholars have been so disturbed by the foundational weaknesses of hierarchical notions of scale that they suggest eliminating scale from our analyses in favor of a "flat ontology" (Marston, Jones, and Woodward 2005), this move seems too extreme. Scales remain useful heuristic abstractions to guide our investigations of the empowerment and disempowerment of different actors and the resulting (in)justices (Jonas 2006). Therefore, following Mansfield (2005, 468), I seek "to ask about the ways (i.e., through what processes and for what reasons) different scales are produced and given significance at any particular time and/or place." In other words, when I write of different scales competing, threatening, and emerging "victorious," I am using a narrative shorthand to convey these dialectical struggles.

In this analysis, the national scale, like all scales, should neither be ignored as superseded through glocalization nor taken for granted as an ontologically given category (Mansfield 2005). In general, the nation-state maintains an interest in territorial control, including the internal territorialization processes that allow the state to determine who has what kinds of rights to resources (Vandergeest and Peluso 1995). In Indonesia, where the vast majority of the land is claimed by the Department of Forestry, the control of land has long represented "the foundation of agency legitimacy" (Peluso 1992, 17). In the era of decentralization, forestry ministers and civil servants have been keen to avoid any potential loss of their historical control over land (Peluso and Vandergeest 2001). The state has relied perennially on Article 33 of the Indonesian Constitution, especially its Clause 3, which states, "Land and water and the natural resources found therein shall be controlled by the state and shall be exploited for the maximum benefit of the people." This declaration has served to foster the historical development of a "political forest" (Peluso and Vandergeest 2001) as well as other national political claims to parts of "nature" that might be commodified. Although the territorial interest of the state and the department's institutional legitimacy may have dynamics of their own, maintaining control of logging rights is closely related to the perception of present and especially future material accumulation opportunities from the extraction of raw materials commodities.[1] Given the present difficulties of the timber industry in obtaining sufficient raw material, the future reconstruction of the state's role around new commodities is likely to become increasingly crucial.

Nature's Commodification under the New Order: The "Victory" of the National Scale

The commodification of timber in Indonesia in retrospect seems a very ordinary thing. But whereas Java's teak forests have a long history of extraction for Dutch mercantile interests (Peluso 1992), the long existence of lush tropical rain forests in the rest of Indonesia did not immediately result in commercial exploitation focused on timber (Knapen 2001). Although a variety of products were extracted from so-called natural yet significantly human-modified forests, the high diversity of the ecosystems and the lack of easily accessible pathways to them, both in terms of physical transport and social labor to access and exploit them, allowed the forests to be largely left alone. The change from "impenetrable jungle" to source of commercial timber occurred after the rise to power of President Suharto in the mid-1960s. The rapid move toward market openness fulfilled foreign exchange needs by liquidating the forest's timber stands.

Market openness was coupled with a nationalist imperative to centralize development in a unitary state. In the process of producing a "political forest," Suharto's New Order allocated the forests of Indonesia to private, government, and military concessions for commercial exploitation (Gellert 2003; Barr 1998). These forests were then used for domestic accumulation purposes. Beginning with Law No. 1 (1967), which opened foreign investment, and the Basic Forestry Law (No. 5, 1967), Indonesia's forests were allocated in large twenty-year concessions. By the 1990s, 585 concessions had been allocated, covering about sixty million hectares of Sumatra, Kalimantan, and eastern Indonesia to Papua (Barr 2002). Exports of wood panels, mostly commodity-grade plywood, were organized and controlled by the Indonesian Wood Panel Association, APKINDO (Barr 1998; Dauvergne 1997; Gellert 2003). Under favorable market conditions, exports boomed in the 1990s, and a domestic alliance of state and private power at the national level was parlayed into an international alliance with importers in Japan and other markets (Gellert 2003). The construction of these commodity-chain linkages was a social, political, and ecological achievement that stabilized accumulation at the national scale. However, this scalar achievement unevenly benefited a small coterie of industrialists and the leaders of the Indonesian state.

Commodities are subject to the logic of "accumulation for accumulation's sake" within a market framework (Castree 2003). Like other processes of capitalist commodification of nature, logging in Indonesia has simplified nature in two senses. First, logging creates and supports a narrowed sense of what counts as "nature." It is not the whole Indonesian forest but the small number of "commercially viable species," as the industry refers to them, that "count" for commodification and capital accumulation.

The commodification of a small number of *dipeterocarp* species were grouped commercially into simply red *meranti*, white *meranti*, and yellow *meranti*. Gradually, as depletion has made large desirable red *meranti* trees scarce, the industry and its longtime key markets in Japan have accepted new species such as *kruing*. Concomitantly, it is these commodified fragments of the forest that count for states that "see" the forest through such lenses and rely on profit-making enterprises and peoples to fund their own state projects (Scott 1998b).

Second, as a corollary, insufficient attention to the renewable side of resource extraction is common to capitalist extraction and production. In James O'Connor's (1988) terms this means that the "conditions of production" for continued extraction are not produced anew. Forestry, however, is always controversial in this regard because of the *potentially* renewable quality of forests. Debates continue to erupt over the pace of destruction in Indonesia as well as whether it is better defined as "deforestation" or "degradation" (see Curran et al. 2004). The debates are also reshaped amid the current debates about scale.

Third, these two simplifying tendencies lead to an understanding of the "differences" imposed on capitalist accumulation strategies by nature-based industries (Boyd, Prudham, and Schurman 2001). The basic problem with nature from the point of view of capital accumulation is that it is difficult to control. Nature, in all its complexity, may offer "surprises" and "opportunities" (ibid.), but especially in particular locations nature-based accumulation is highly vulnerable to depletion. Furthermore, the technologies of extraction, processing, and transport impinge on the kinds of investments—and profits—that can be made, as well as by whom, since the most capital-intensive resources require the participation and backing of nation-states and their financial institutions to be viable in the first place (Barham, Bunker, and O'Hearn 1994a).

Depletion of accessible supplies in Indonesia has spurred loggers, in characteristic ways, to seek alternative sources, or what Harvey (1996) calls a "spatial fix." At the beginning of the New Order, Indonesia's forests replaced those of the Philippines and Malaysia as Japan's primary source of logs. Over the decades since, logging has spread across and within regions of the Indonesian archipelago.

Extraction of timber has also migrated eastward, to Maluku and recently Papua Province, as well as northwest in Sumatra to Aceh. Although central government data show that Papua's contribution to total logging is about 7 percent for the past five years (Departemen Kehutanan 2004), there have been reports of significant illegal harvest and trade (EIA/Telapak 2005). Within logging regions such as Sumatra and Kalimantan (Borneo), technologies of extraction and transport have improved and distances from forest to mill have increased, although eventually most logs still float down the rivers to production centers. Logging roads have also penetrated the political boundaries of protected areas and national parks (Curran et al. 2004).

Overall, the process of commodification in the last forty years can be seen in terms of a contrast between statist and neoliberal periods. In the statist period, when timber was the Indonesian government's second most important source of revenue after oil and gas, the process of commodification engendered debates over limits on the state's ability to raise revenue—in James O'Connor's terms, the "fiscal crisis of the state" (O'Connor 1973). Whereas in North American timber extraction, the state "mediat[ed] the relationship between capital and nature by way of a state-private timber monopoly constructed under the rationale that this would somehow benefit local communities" (Correia 2005, 28), in Indonesia the state allocated forest concessions largely to private companies that benefited from military security and the overall stability of the investment climate. Suharto's New Order, in turn, benefited from the informal subsidies and payments that timber industrialists made to shore it up when necessary (Schwarz 1994; Barr 1998).

The state also used a discourse of sustainable development centered on the Indonesian Selective Cutting and Replanting System as a "paradigm" of sustainable forest management despite its multiple contradictions (Barr 2002). In its ambitions, the system was similar to the system of scientific forest management imported to Java from Germany via Dutch colonialism (Peluso 1992, 44–78), but in its minimalist implementation it fell far short of scientific forest management. Nonetheless, the repeated discourse of logging as sustainable in Indonesia was (and continues to be) used as an ideological justification for capitalist development involving appropriation of land, exploitation of commodifiable chunks of "nature," and other practices of "accumulation by dispossession" (Harvey 2003).

The neoliberal period of recent years has brought with it a more open struggle between capital and labor. That is, such conflicts seem to be no longer, or only to a lesser degree, mediated by the (national) state. Even corporate relations with the military are increasingly open. The same is true of the relationship between capital and nature, but the Indonesian state has only recently and very reluctantly diminished its role in natural resource sectors. The state had claimed these sectors beginning with the 1945 Constitution and earlier under the Dutch colonial state (Peluso 1992; Peluso and Vandergeest 2001).

Although neoliberalism is not new, international financial institutions have changed tactics from crude antistatism in the 1980s to support for "good governance" since the 1990s. Paradoxically, as Leftwich (1994, 367) observes, "effective adjustment in practice has required a strong, determined and relatively autonomous state, whether democratic or not." Thus, to call these oscillations between state and market periods is an oversimplification. It underestimates the strength of continuing struggles and implies that the state has disappeared in the neoliberal period (see Mansfield 2005). Far from it. Rather, the scale at which the relationship between capital and nature is mediated is being altered. Thus, to understand contemporary commodification requires a consideration of the political conditions underlying it.

Decentralization Dialectics: Post–New Order Openings in the Regions

The rescaling of natural resource management away from the national state might be considered the unfinished business of the post–Asian crisis period. On the one hand, the IMF structural adjustment during the height of the Asian financial crisis in 1998 can be understood as an attempt to rescale the governance of Indonesia's development to a supranational level (Gellert 2005a). As elsewhere in the world, structural adjustment encompasses neoliberal policies of trade liberalization, fiscal austerity, and privatization in favor of the construction of global markets for the benefit of global social classes, that is, those who benefit from global accumulation processes. In Indonesia there were unusually specific conditionalities imposed on the forestry sector by the IMF, including the dismantling of APKINDO's marketing monopoly and the opening of raw log exports. These neoliberal economic policies of trade liberalization, as well as opening to foreign investment, which were supported by international financial institutions, disempowered the central regulatory ministry (Forestry)—which was deemed corrupt.

The construction of a local scale, on the other hand, is an equally important counterpart to these supranational threats to the national scale. Decentralization is usefully understood as part of this dialectics of scale. The notoriously vague concept of decentralization is reconceptualized as a disguise for struggles between those who wish to alter Indonesia's development trajectory in the direction of local benefits and sustainable development and those who wish to concentrate the benefits from localized capital accumulation and state control. In this politics of scale, decentralization is not merely concerned with the capacity of local governments to acquire technocratically reassigned responsibilities but part of ongoing struggles for power and material benefits. Multiple groups had demanded reform of the authoritarian state of Suharto's New Order during its waning years. During and after the crisis, domestic processes of democratization coupled with external pressure from international financial institutions delegitimized the nation-state as the primary arena of governance. While some point to the protests of student groups and Muslim organizations as precipitating the resignation of President Suharto, others have emphasized the withdrawal of elite support, notably from within his cabinet. In sum, decentralization, as John McCarthy (2004) observes, was an "overdetermined" political outcome after decades of criticism of the social injustices and environmental degradation of development.

The critics were self-defined against development (*pembangunan*) of and for the national scale. Public euphoria at Suharto's resignation and dissatisfaction with the corruption, collusion, and nepotism (*korupsi, kolusi, dan nepotisme*, or KKN) associated with national-scale politicians created conditions favorable to assertion of local rights. In essence, many assumed that local management of forests and other natural resources would be more sustainable than the centralized state model (Resosudarmo 2004). The new president, B. J. Habibie, oversaw the passage of Law 22 on Regional Governance and Law 25 on Fiscal Balancing, both issued in May 1999. A new Basic Forestry Law (No. 41) was also passed in 1999, superseding the 1967 law.[2] But control over resource extraction and its benefits did not simply move to the regions. Moreover, as Beard (2003) demonstrates, collective action by communities may require lengthy processes of covert learning and planning.

An analysis that focuses on the dialectics of scale is different from one that merely examines socionatural change at multiple scales, as much of political ecology aspires to do. The most important difference is that a dialectical approach aims to avoid the "local trap" (Brown and Purcell 2005) of much political ecology. The local trap is a romanticization of local-level management and the assumption that local control *should* lead to more socially just and environmentally sustainable outcomes, barring some obstacle (see, e.g., Stone and D'Andrea 2001). This assumption leads, as Brown and Purcell (2005) observe, to research into the failure of devolution (e.g., Ribot 2002). In a dialectics of scale, what some may think of as levels are "inextricably tied together as different aspects of the same set of social and ecological processes" (Brenner 2001, 605). Moreover, a given social process cannot be thought of as inherently attached to, or operating primarily at, a particular scale (Marston, Jones, and Woodward 2005). "Political economy is not inherently 'wider,' and culture and ecology are not inherently 'local,'" as Brown and Purcell (2005, 612) note.

The implicit thrust of advocates of decentralization was that local communities would gain rights to the forest. For Indonesia's citizenry, in other words, decentralization qua the localization of scale represents the hope and opportunity for a more equitable distribution of rights of access and control (Ribot and Peluso 2003). In reality, however, communities are not gaining tenure. Despite civil-society pressure and experimental changes in laws, by 2005 a mere 0.2 percent of the national forest estate was under community tenure (Colchester et al. 2006, 40).

The key power gained at the regional (*kabupaten*) and district (*kecamatan*) levels was control of logging licenses. And this power was gained over the unified power of the central Department of Forestry to create the "political forest." During the presidencies of B. J. Habibie and Abdurrahman Wahid, district-level governments were given authority over allocation of timber utilization permits (IUPHHK) for twenty years on areas up to fifty thousand hectares and timber extraction permits (IPHHK) for one year on small areas of one hundred hectares (Fox, Adhuri, and Resosudarmo 2005; Barr 2002). For a brief period, there was a boom in the issuing of district-level permits under the decentralization laws. For example, in the East Kalimantan district of Berau, small-scale logging and especially forest conversion permits were allocated in 1999 and 2000 (Obidzinski and Barr 2003). In Bulungan District, over six hundred concessions were operational in 2001 (Samsu, Komarudin, and Ngau 2005).

This power was countered by a recentralization effort couched in terms of the central ministry's concern about misuse of the forests and the "lack of control" resulting in an illegal logging "crisis" (Casson and Obidzinski 2002). In 2002, President Megawati Sukarnoputri's government issued a new regulation, PP34/2002, that cancelled district and provincial rights to grant licenses.[3] Legally the rights of the regions to allocate logging concessions were thereby brought to a halt. In the case of Bulungan, the number of permits rapidly declined as central government pressure began to increase and also because forest areas inside the official forest estate were not allowed to be accessed and controlled by noncentral authority. In February 2004, the leader of the Bulungan District stopped issuing permits (Samsu, Komarudin, and Ngau 2005).

But, as Patlis (2005) has pointed out, the issue of which law supersedes another law is clouded in Indonesia, especially with respect to natural resource management. The struggle over the scale of control of timber extraction continues. For example, in Papua, where the governor has nominally supported the rights of communities, the provincial government colludes with the military in extracting valuable timber.[4] In February 2005, EIA/Telapak (2005) exposed illegal exports of *merbau* (*Intsia* spp.) logs to China at a pace of 3.6 million cubic meters per year. Nonetheless, it has been extremely difficult to question, let alone supplant, the nation-state's political claim to resources in the national territory.

Recentralization Dialectics: State and Private Reassertions of National-Scale Controls

The politics of scale that briefly upset the national dominance of the New Order period with a euphoria for the local scale and its implied benefits for equity and sustainability dialectically caused a backlash as state and private actors attempted to recentralize authority. As a result, the rescaling of logging as a national accumulation strategy has been achieved to a significant degree. However, the sustainability of this strategy at any scale (within Indonesia) may be approaching its ecological limits (Curran et al. 2004).

The private sector has an interest in clear rules and steady access to the remaining timber in Indonesia, regardless of whether the control is achieved at the national or local scale. But, the industry has faced triple pressures: several years of risk from local direct actions against their logging operations in the regions; increasing international pressure against their participation in a transnational industry that relies on illegal harvesting (see Obidzinski 2005); and real declines in the available timber stock. In response, rather than face the prospect of restructuring, which was widely interpreted as downsizing an industry that had exceeded its raw materials and financial capacity (e.g., Barr 2002), the industry sought to reestablish the strong national scale as its way of revitalizing the industry.

In a move reminiscent of the blurring of the public-private boundaries of the New Order, the Department of Forestry and the Ministry of Trade and Industry signed a joint decree in December 2002 to create Badan Revitalisasi Industri Kehutanan (Wood Industry Revitalization Agency) or BRIK.[5] The stated purpose was to prevent Indonesian companies from purchasing illegal logs and thereby to help alleviate industry problems by assuring consumers in Europe and North America that they are not buying products obtained from illegal and unsustainable sources. Although APKINDO's marketing powers had been dismantled in 1998 as part of IMF conditionality, BRIK is positioning itself to have comparable power over Indonesian wood product exports. In the Suharto era, APKINDO had used its private status to protect both the organization and its leader, Mohamad "Bob" Hasan, from public scrutiny (Barr 1998; Gellert 2003). The organization and those of other wood products industries wielded considerable power over government regulations, including the level of taxation and thus the state's collection of rent. In the years after Suharto's fall, Hasan was the only figure tried on forestry-related infractions; he was "caught in [the] backlash," according to journalist Richard Borsuk (2003), against Suharto-era corruption.

BRIK's establishment blurred the public-private lines. Although created by the government, the organization was established with a board of directors composed of wood industry executives, without government representation. Even an APKINDO executive expressed "confusion" about whether the organization was a private or governmental organization. And the Indonesian Furniture and Handicraft Association (ASMINDO 2004), while supportive of any help in obtaining raw materials, openly opposed the "intimidation" and membership fees that BRIK charges to create its infrastructure, dubbing BRIK's emerging power blatant rent-seeking behavior.[6]

Amid these squabbles among fractions of the wood products industry, BRIK has managed to achieve considerable power over wood-product exporters. It was given the task of conducting an audit of domestic firms to ascertain the amount of logs used by each. It has also required all forestry-related producers to have a new license in order to export wood products.[7] Its role is to collect the mill reports on wood consumption and the transportation documents for the logs,[8] and then approve the export licenses. In practice, there is a severe problem of forgery and reuse of the transport documents in the extractive regions, leading critics to worry about BRIK's focus on legality over sustainability in creating a self-certification system.[9]

The inherent ambiguity and manipulability of the emerging system of national control appears to be strengthening BRIK's hand. In principle, BRIK can check whether companies, individually and collectively, are producing in excess of their legal supply and whether each company is receiving supply with legal transport documents. The internal process for reviewing requests for export approval is computerized and avowedly efficient but completely shielded from public scrutiny since BRIK officials are adamant that opening their books to such scrutiny is an infringement on their right to operate their "private" business. Although BRIK's authority comes from the government, including the export authority specifically from the Ministry of Industry and Trade, thus far reports are not being provided to the government on a regular basis. In brief, as an organization that is more than a private association of exporters, BRIK represents a usurpation of public authority at the national scale. Nonetheless, the assertion of the national scale faces ongoing difficulties; in the first half of 2005 approved exports decreased by almost 25 percent.[10]

If BRIK is the new organizational face of concentrated institutional power favoring the large-scale wood-based industries, "revitalization" has become the industry's favored ideological construction in the face of mounting pressures. In a clear response to the reform agenda of then minister of forestry, Muhammad Prakosa, the industry has carefully constructed a program of revitalization. Prakosa had attempted to implement a "soft landing" proposal for the industry that reduced the annual allowable cut (AAC) dramatically from prior levels over 20 million cubic meters annually to 6.9 million cubic meters in 2002 and 5.7 million cubic meters in 2004 while rescaling the control of logging to the national level. In taking revitalization as part of its name, BRIK relied on the trope of sustainable and selective harvesting of timber at the very time that firms in the field were beginning to have serious difficulty obtaining raw materials. That is, while the exact level of the AAC is debatable, BRIK asserted that a much higher level of cutting than proposed in the soft landing policy could easily be sustained but offered no plan other than continuing the existing practices and relying on natural forest regeneration rates to produce this volume of timber.

Although the industry might have welcomed the clarity of central control, it instead continued to strike out against the ministry. As the new government of Susilo Bambang Yudhoyono came to power in 2004, the umbrella industrial association group, the Indonesian Forestry Society (MPI), published a new book recounting the previous six years of their struggle, *Revitalizing Indonesian*

Forestry: Maintaining Its Existence and Strengthening Its Future Role (Suarga, Komalasari, and Hidayat 2004). In this polemical book the industry puts forward its self-described weak position and the threats to its very existence. It counters the soft-landing policy and describes efforts to *membiarkan hutan bernafas* ("let the forests breathe"), including the environmental group WALHI's[11] call for a total logging moratorium, as dangerous to the Indonesian (i.e., national-scale) economy. The costs of continued logging to particular regional socionatural configurations, including to local rights and forest-based livelihoods, are left unexamined.

The power of the revitalization move to bolster the national scale became clear when the new minister, Malam S. Kaban, was installed in 2004 while championing a program of revitalization and offering rhetorical praise for the days of Bob Hasan's leadership of the sector.[12] Perhaps cognizant of the peripheral position of Indonesian exporters in a global capitalist economy, national political and economic leaders are thus pining for the (re)creation of a nation-state scale strong enough to withstand the winds of neoliberal globalization. Although he did not raise the annual allowable cut in Indonesia back to precrisis levels (as originally rumored), Kaban did raise it by about 50 percent to 8.1 million cubic meters for 2006.[13]

One additional factor in the struggle to reestablish the national scale cannot be ignored. The Indonesian military, which continues to obtain significant portions of its operating income through off-budget funding, has an interest in maintaining its access to the commodified resources of the whole archipelago. In addition to nationalist and geopolitical concerns about Indonesia's unity and territorial integrity, both individual officers and the military itself benefit from the extraction and security services that they provide. Ironically, in Aceh and Papua, where national sovereignty is in question, the presence of logging both financially supports the military and justifies its presence (to control "illegal logging").[14]

Ongoing Scalar Struggles and Socionatural Futures

Struggles over scale, including scalar dreams and real(ized) scalar projects, continue to have dramatic impacts on the peoples, natures, and places of Southeast Asia. Such struggles intersect with both territorialization by the state and the commodification of nature and the ability of different social groups to accumulate capital from the commodification process.

From this perspective, the New Order was the "triumph" of the national scale in a peripheral location. What this means is that control over access (Ribot and Peluso 2003) to raw materials important to global capitalist production was achieved first and last in the hallways of national leaders. It does *not* mean that the national scale has a reified existence within an a priori and hierarchical ontology of scale (Marston, Jones, and Woodward 2005). To be sure, "the national" is socially produced as much as any other scale (Jonas 2006; Smith 1984; Swyngedouw 1999).

It also means that the ideological apparatus bolstering the material flow of benefits and allowing the establishment of regularized and regulated extraction favored the national (construction of) scale and national unity. The nationalist, authoritarian, yet postcolonial regime of Indonesia's New Order achieved power through violence. President Suharto enjoyed promoting himself as the "father of development," and his protégé, the timber king Mohammad "Bob" Hasan also shrouded himself in the clothing of national development. As self-described nationalists, they fought international capital to garner national control of development, notably the creation of a downstream plywood industry. Hasan even took on the Japanese trading houses to monopolize the export stream of plywood to Japan and other markets (Gellert 2003; Barr 1998). During this period, local-scale powers and interests in benefiting from the commodification of the forest were suppressed while those opposing the commodification process itself were repressed, sometimes violently.

Since 1998, a process of "glocalization" (Swyngedouw 1997), or the production of supra- and subnational scales simultaneously, has occurred. Glocalization appeared to fit well with the rhetoric of neoliberalism. It relied at first on decentralization of the state's control of timber as a commodity within Indonesia. The violence of the state appeared to be giving way to the violence of the market. However, decentralization has not succeeded in wresting political and economic control of the forests away from the nation-state and the capitalist firms that the state supports. National-scale actors, rather, have focused their energies on recentralizing control and reestablishing the supremacy of the national scale. To be sure, the national scale that is produced in reaction to the social struggles over control of logging in subnational locations is not exactly the same national scale that existed during the New Order, given the different political, economic, and ideological apparatuses that constitute it. The production of viable sites of resistance and the dialectical production of other scales continue to be contested processes with important implications for the power of differently situated actors. Nonetheless, it is difficult to imagine a scenario in which the extraction of timber will be slowed before the "natural"—but very socionatural—processes of depletion are completed.

3

Contesting "Flexibility"

Networks of Place, Gender, and Class in Vietnamese Workers' Resistance

ANGIE NGỌC TRẦN

As Vietnam reintegrated into the world capitalist system after domestic market reform in the late 1980s and the collapse of the Soviet bloc in the early 1990s,[1] it engaged the global capitalist economy and flexible subcontracting production while maintaining a nominally socialist government. This reflects the state's complex and contradictory relationship to capital and labor; rhetorically it shows a commitment to uphold socialist ideals (especially labor equity), but it also facilitates the accumulation of capital.

The point of entry for my contribution to the study of labor commodification—or the making of compliant and "flexible" workers by factory disciplining—and workers' resistance efforts in the contemporary Vietnamese context is an examination of labor processes and relations in Vietnamese textile and garment industries. As one of the major centers of garment production in Southeast Asia, Vietnam is a magnet for foreign-owned businesses, most of which are subcontracting for large multinational clothing companies and retailers. They dominate the growing private sector, with activities concentrating in export-processing zones (EPZs) and industrial zones (IZs) in the south. Due to the highly competitive nature of garment production worldwide, controlling and disciplining labor are keys to the success of multinationals and the subcontractors overseeing production in Vietnam. Thus, the labor commodification process is central to the larger production process. I also hope to contribute to resistance studies by exploring protests against the commodification of garment workers in the unique context of a socialist country actively engaging global capital.

I thank Thu Hương Nguyễn Võ and other reviewers for their helpful feedback on earlier drafts, and Joe Lubow for his faithful support throughout this project.

Migrant workers play a key role in the narrative of the commodification of labor in contemporary Vietnam. Most of the workers in the EPZs and IZs are women who migrate from provinces in the north (such as Nam Định, a historic major textile/garment town) and central Vietnam (such as Quảng Nam) to work in the south. These migrant workers start off as apprentice workers in factories, but under the conditions of flexible production in global subcontracting they become less than human; they are turned into a commodity, and, like a lemon, "squeezed to the last drop" (Trần 2005). To cope with and resist the labor commodification process, they use all the tools and resources available to them: place-based identities; gender, social and cultural networks; and local advocates such as district labor unions and, increasingly, labor newspapers. I will illustrate how workers have reached out directly to *The Laborer* (*Người Lao Động*), the official forum of the Hồ Chí Minh City (HCMC) Federation of Labor Unions, as the state and the Vietnamese General Confederation of Labor (VGCL)—the central labor union—struggle to represent workers' rights and interests in the growing private and shrinking state sectors.

Through interviews with women strikers and leaders, labor newspaper accounts, government reports, and other secondary sources, I present a study of the labor commodification process and public labor protests against this process in socialist Vietnam. This concrete evidence from fieldwork in Vietnam examines a new form of Karl Polanyi's countermovements (Polanyi 2005), and thus contributes a feminist perspective on this aspect of globalization and resistance to the literature (Marchand and Runyan 2000; Perry 1993). I show that the case of socialist Vietnam, despite all of its contradictions, demonstrates that migrant workers and local actors can create a challenge to capital that is consistent with alternative visions of globalization (Bonacich 2005; Appelbaum 2005).

Polanyi's argument back in 1957 still explains the labor commodification process in Vietnam and provides justification why that process would bring about a countermovement or resistance:

> Labor is only another name for a human activity which goes with life itself, which in its turn is not produced for sale but for entirely different reasons, nor can that activity be detached from the rest of life. . . . To allow the market mechanism to be sole director of the fate of human beings and their natural environment, indeed, even of the amount and use of purchasing power, would result in the demolition of society. (Polanyi 2005, 51)

In the context of contemporary Vietnamese factories, I explain how global subcontracting and just-in-time delivery and production systems discipline workers and make them into compliant and flexible workers for flexible production. First, I explain how low-skilled and low-paid assembly work reduces workers to a replaceable, compliant, and disposable commodity, or labor commodification.

Then, I discuss how workers, as a collectivity, resist such factory disciplining in overt economic protests in labor-intensive industries. They use their cultural, kinship, and gender networks as bases to organize and support each other, as well as to protest against being treated like disposable commodities. I call this process decommodification, in which workers fight publicly to regain their sense of dignity and human decency. Because of both historical and geographic differences in their circumstances, Vietnamese garment workers perform resistance differently than these forms described in classic work by Lee (1998) and Ong (1987, 1997) about Hong Kong and Malaysian workers.

Kinship and gender play important roles in the activities and consciousness of both Malaysian and Vietnamese migrant workers, thus the role of cultural embeddedness.[2] However, unlike the subtle forms of resistance deployed by Chinese and Malaysian workers, Vietnamese garment workers and their allies use a variety of social networks—place, class, and gender-based—to organize ways to reappropriate power in direct and public ways to alleviate their situations.

For example, Vietnamese workers use public economic contestations with clearly defined and openly declared strike agendas, announcing concrete demands and resuming work only after their requests are met. This also differs significantly from the tactics of Malaysian factory women who used local cultural and religious practices to stop production (Ong 1987).

cool; investigate?

Making "Flexible" Migrant Workers (*lao động nhập cư*)

Making the workforce temporary and vulnerable is a common strategy used by multinationals in Vietnam and elsewhere in the world to commodify labor. Subcontractors taking orders from multinational corporations (MNCs) hire neophyte, young female workers for low wages and avoid paying benefits such as unemployment, social security, and health care. Over 90 percent of the Vietnamese garment workforce is made up of young women in their early twenties, which is similar to the situation in Malaysia and China (Ong 1987; Lee 1998). Most of these young female workers migrate from poor provinces in Vietnam; they are called "*lao động nhập cư*" (migrant workers). Workers concentrate in low-skilled, low-paid industries such as textile, garment, shoe, and toy manufacturing in EPZs and IZs nationwide (Hà Linh Quân, September 14, 2004). They successfully staged massive minimum-wage strikes in December 2005. By February 2006, workers in foreign direct investment (FDI) factories had gained a 40 percent increase in the minimum wage after such wages were frozen for ten years (1996–2005) (see Trần 2007b). *nice*.

Most workers come from poor provinces in the north (such as Nam Định, Thái Bình) and central Vietnam (such as Quảng Nam, Quảng Ngãi, Đà Nẵng). These migrant workers in the twenty-first century are similar to the "Lowell mill girls" of Massachusetts in the nineteenth century (thousands of young New

England farm women between the ages of fifteen and thirty who came to work in textile factories, 1823–1860s) and the Guangdong "maiden workers" in the Shenzhen Special Economic Zone bordering Hong Kong at the end of the twentieth century (Lee 1998). Most migrant workers can only afford to live together in very small rental units into which four or six workers are crammed. The average monthly rent for these dilapidated and unsanitary units ranges from about US$4 to US$10 per person (Hà Linh Quân, September 14, 2004).

Multinationals sustain job uncertainty to produce compliant and vulnerable workers. Most companies do not offer workers permanent labor contracts even after they successfully pass the one-year probationary period. This is the case of a Nam Định migrant worker, who in 2004 was offered another annual contract even after having passed the one-year probationary period in 2001. This violation happens regularly in East Asian companies, as district labor union officials acknowledged in the strikes conference in HCMC in 2004. Some workers receive no contract at all. For instance, Weihua Limited Company (a Taiwanese company in District 12, HCMC) hired 550 workers but signed only seasonal short-term labor contracts with 192 workers; the rest had no labor contracts. Similarly, a Japanese company employed 400 workers but none were offered a contract, while Lee Shin International Limited Company (a Taiwanese company) hired 450 workers, none of whom were offered labor contracts (Lệ Thủy, December 30, 2004). In all these cases, not signing permanent contracts is just one of many labor violations that have occurred in many East Asian factories.

Factory control and discipline aim to transform workers into compliant commodities. Workers have to be flexible to accommodate production fluctuations. They bear the costs of flexibility, while management accumulates the benefits. Workers' flexibility is very important because it ensures on-time delivery, which is especially significant in the fashion garment industry. When small-batch orders or imported materials arrive late, workers are expected to stay late to finish products in time to meet the factory's delivery schedule. They often face overtime work during peak seasons and underemployment during slow seasons. For all this flexibility and compliance, workers are rarely compensated for their overtime work (interview with Ms. BV, Women's Department in the HCMC Labor Unions, July 21, 2004).

Factory discipline coerces workers into doing overtime work. They can't decline these requests for fear of losing their jobs. Most workers end up enduring it until they can no longer withstand the exploitation and publicly protest this coercion (interviews with Ms. VTN and Ms. VTT, workers from Nam Định; and Ms. NTY from Quảng Nam in August 2004; Thùy Anh, August 30, 2005). One worker at Shilla Bags (a Taiwanese-owned factory in Bình Chánh District) showed me the overtime condition in her annual labor contract: "Depending on the urgency of delivery schedules, I agree to work overtime" (interviews with Ms. VTN, July and August 2004). Like most workers, she had no recourse but to sign it. This common practice is confirmed by most labor union representatives, as well as by management groups such as the Taiwanese Economic and Cultural Office and the Vietnamese Chamber of Commerce in HCMC at their August 2005 conference on strikes. Moreover, workers are punished if they protest this forced overtime work. At the Keyhinge Toys factory in Đà Nẵng (a growth city in central Vietnam), management clearly stated the company directive: "Overtime work is dependent on the agreement of workers; if they don't want to work overtime, then so be it!" Nevertheless, workers were laid off for one week as punishment when they protested in writing against overtime work for which they did not receive proper compensation (Hoàng Dũng, May 12, 2005).

The position of the state and the VGCL on gender roles in the global capitalist economy to a large extent facilitates foreign capital accumulation. This is reflected in their efforts to produce a compliant female worker, described as "law abiding," who is expected to carry the double burden of fulfilling responsibilities at work and at home and to refrain from participating in wildcat strikes. Local labor unions also promote a type of "superwoman" female worker (interviews with Ms. BV, 2005). *relatable for ♀ in general!*

Although they ostensibly fight for the rights and benefits of female workers, their official documents exhort women to fulfill the patriarchal expectations of the work-home double burden. Labor union campaigns expected women to be "Good in national affairs and good in domestic affairs" (*giỏi việc nước, đảm việc nhà*) and that "Women study hard, work creatively, and build happy families." In this context, "national affairs" in peacetime Vietnam implies working hard in factories while also fulfilling domestic household roles. They also spell out that the "art of being wives, mothers, and daughters-in-law" means reproducing traditional female roles "to build happy families" (Hồ Chí Minh Labor Federation 2004).

This rhetoric is conveniently used by management, especially in East Asian–owned companies. Management in these companies produces compliant and docile workers by relying on patriarchal authoritarian relations in factories, which is tolerated to a large extent by the state.[3] Most Taiwanese and South Korean firms in Vietnam are small- to medium-sized companies and operate on the model of a patriarchal family (Korean Trade Association office in Vietnam, 2005). In these companies, workers have to bow when they see the East Asian line leaders, supervisors, or technical personnel. Studies and newspaper reports show that some East Asian managers verbally (and in some cases, physically) abuse workers, leading to all forms of protests in these companies (MOLISA et al. 2004; Trần Đức, December 28, 2004). Public humiliation is a common authoritarian practice in these companies. While walking through the assembly lines of a textile factory in the north in 2003 with a South Korean public relations representative, I heard the South Korean line leader yell in Vietnamese over the loudspeaker, admonishing a particular assembly worker by her number with the message: "Work faster, work faster" (*làm nhanh lên*). Workers frowned, shook their heads, and complained to each other about such public humiliation.

Strikes as a Form of "De-Commodification"

A countermovement, in a Polanyian sense, of workers aimed at protecting their rights and interests against market forces exists in labor-intensive factories in Vietnam (Mittelman and Chin 2005, 20–26; Polanyi 2005, 53). Evidence shows that Vietnamese worker protests have some characteristics of a Polanyian countermovement; their forms of resistance, or decommodification, are public ones with a clear agenda to protect themselves against the negative aspects of market forces and to expose specific labor violations, most often in foreign-invested factories supplying the MNCs.

Workers resist being commodified, often engaging explicitly in efforts to decommodify themselves, refusing to be treated as less than human beings and protesting to demand their basic rights. Migrant workers are most vulnerable; they need their salaries on time to feed themselves, save some for their families, and take buses home to visit far-flung villages. Late or partial salary payment exacerbates their poor living conditions, since most migrant workers do not have the local support systems needed to help them through hard times in the south. Their protests are short and for urgent economic goals: from several hours to several days, just sufficient to grab the attention of management, the media, the local governments, and the labor union offices. They cannot strike for a long time without access to strike funds.

Strike laws in Vietnam, while progressive for a socialist country, do not empower workers' contestation against labor commodification. There have been over fifteen hundred strikes since strikes were legalized in 1995 up through June 2007. Most strikes occurred in factories with East Asian investment and management, and were spontaneous and without labor union leadership. Most strikes were classified as "illegal": the unworkable strike protocol (the version before its November 2006 revision) and unequal power relations in the commodification process stifle the ability to strike legally. Unions, at the factory level, often failed to obtain the required over 50 percent of workers' votes in order to strike. Most factory-level union representatives were employees who often were harassed and penalized for their labor organizing efforts. Many lost their jobs when collecting strike votes: "If I were to go around to collect workers' signatures, no doubt the owner would accuse me of inciting workers to protest and I would lose my job in no time," lamented a labor union president at a South Korean company in an industrial zone in the south (Hong Van 2005). A revised strike law, ratified in November 2006 and effective in July 2007, is aimed at addressing these weaknesses (Trần 2007a).

The number of strikes in Vietnamese factories has risen consistently, especially after the normalization of Vietnam-U.S. relations in 2000 when different types of global capital entered socialist Vietnam. More strikes occurred in factories with foreign capital and management, and fewer public strikes occurred in state-owned enterprises (Trần 2007b).

In the FDI sector, the employees of only 40–45 percent of companies were represented by unions, compared to about a 15–20 percent unionization rate in the private domestic sector. There are 5.6 million union members out of about 12 million wage-earning workers in Vietnam's state and private sectors (Mr. Trần Văn Lý, member of the VGCL Executive Committee and director of Foreign Relations, August 2006; January 2007). About 1.6 percent of the total labor force work in the FDI sector. Again, this statistic may be underestimated due to an ongoing privatization process which has been laying off state workers who might resort to working in FDI factories.[4] Given the ongoing privatization process (or "equitization," as the Vietnamese state calls it) in which state firms sell stock shares to their state workers and the public, transforming state companies into private enterprises, the official percentages of workers in FDI and non-state sectors may be underestimated.

Most strikes have taken place in companies with East Asian capital and management, especially those from Taiwan, South Korea, and Hong Kong, which concentrated in the south in labor-intensive industries such as garment/textile and footwear manufacturing. The top five investors in Vietnam as of mid-2006 are from East Asia: Taiwan, Singapore, Japan, South Korea, and Hong Kong (Ministry of Planning and Investment 2006). Most strikes occur in southern industrialized provinces with a high concentration of East Asian investment such as HCMC, Bình Dương, and Đồng Nai. I have examined elsewhere the patterns of strikes by ownership types, and found that while most strikes occurred in the FDI sector, workers in the state sector producing for the MNCs also protested, but their protests took more subtle forms such as petitions and complaint letters sent to local labor newspapers, to local state bureaucracies (such as departments of labor, labor courts, people's committees) and to labor unions (Trần 2007b).

Worker Networks and Alliances: Place, Gender, and Class

Migrant workers bond to one another as they re-create the lifestyles, work ethics, and cultural practices of their northern and central Vietnam hometowns or villages in southern worker communities, far from the support of home. Female workers in particular create strong bonds with one another during both good times and strikes. Many Nam Định women workers demonstrate leadership qualities that may have come from the traditions of resistance in their native place. Moreover, cultural connections between experienced strike leaders and lower-skilled workers help to protect them from being turned into a commodity in flexible production processes.

Thousands of migrant workers live, work, and look after one another in local "factory towns" adjacent to the EPZs in HCMC and its surrounding areas, where workers walk or ride their bicycles to work (Hà Linh Quân, September 14, 2004; fieldwork 2006). I found a special bond between northern and central migrant women workers who live in makeshift worker dormitories or rental units near the factories. Coming from poor provinces with similarly dire conditions in north and central Vietnam not only creates strong bonds among them but also develops a shared identity. One Nam Định worker intimated, "It is harder to get along with workers from the south because this is their land. They talk, cook, and spend their money differently." Another agreed about this special bond: "Workers from poor regions in the north and central get along better because they are used to hardworking lifestyles. Workers from the south often get into shouting matches with each other; they do not work very hard, and often give us a hard time."[5]

I interviewed several Quảng Nam workers in their rental units who then introduced me to a group of Nam Định workers during my fieldwork in Gò Vấp District in 2004. I learned about the typical patterns of the migrant workforce, which begins with some family members migrating first and then other family members joining them once the first group finds jobs and places to stay in the

Figure 3.1. Migrant workers in Ho Chi Minh City watching another worker's wedding video, August 2006. Credit: Angie Ngọc Trần.

south. The Nam Định strike leader at the Taiwanese company in Bình Chánh District came to the south first with her husband; her three brothers joined them later in a small one-bedroom rental unit. In 2004, her young son was still in Nam Định, being cared for by her parents. During the Vietnamese Lunar New Year holiday, she and another Nam Định worker took the bus home to Nam Định and then back to Gò Vấp together.

Cultural and religious activities strengthen this place-based bond. Many Nam Định workers are Catholic, so they often go to church together on the weekends. Since they share similar cooking styles and tastes, these women cook and eat their meals together; after work, they congregate at night, have informal gatherings on the weekends when they do not have to work overtime, and take the bus together to their Nam Định homes during holidays. MNCs appear to be savvier now in meeting workers' cultural needs in order to prevent potential resistance. The management of Sam Yang—a company in Củ Chi District that had been plagued with strikes—sponsored a "Singing with Workers" concert, in cooperation with *The Laborer* newspaper in 2004. The event drew an audience of over ten thousand workers and their families who braved the rain to enthusiastically hear the performers. The following year, *The Laborer*, a state TV station, and two other privately owned companies sponsored and organized this cultural event for workers in a major export-processing zone in HCMC (Trần Hiệp, August 24, 2005).

How does the nexus of gender and place-based identity relate to resistance? To what extent do Nam Định women workers carry on the resistance tradition, which dates back to resistance against the colonial French, in textile/garment industries? How do strike leaders use cultural categories such as "sisters" to connect with other workers in familial gender networks and protect them from being turned into commodities?

Vietnamese workers' native-place identity brings them together in protests against labor commodification, consistent with the kinship bonds/networks used in Shanghai strikes (Perry 1993) and the clandestine protests in Hong Kong and Shengzen factories (Lee 1998). Many Vietnamese women workers take leading roles in labor organizing and strikes. Most are experienced older workers who understand workers' rights and are conscious of recurring labor violations perpetrated by management. These proactive and experienced women gain valuable knowledge of labor regimes from networking with co-workers for years on the assembly line. They inform recently hired workers, both male and female, about the protests and cajole workers to join them. Relying on cultural bonding, experienced female strike leaders were able to recruit lower-skilled workers to join the protests because these young workers respect and listen to "*đàn chị*" (elder sisters) who can offer advice on the basic entitlements for which they fight. One leader told me in 2004 that as soon as the recently hired workers saw the experienced older sisters refusing to eat contaminated food and water sold by management in the cafeteria, they all followed suit, which then led to management's allowing workers to buy food from outside vendors.

In addition to gender, place-based identity, and cultural bonding, a sense of dignity and human decency brings migrant workers together to protest against being treated as disposable commodities or draft animals that carry the heaviest workload. Strike narratives reveal evidence of class consciousness as some migrant workers identify themselves as belonging to the "we workers" class and publicly expose blatant labor violations. Appealing to the workers' sense of dignity, strike leaders use this language to urge their fellow workers to stand up for human decency and join the strike. A Nam Định migrant worker who worked in a Taiwanese factory with no factory-level labor union told me in anguish in 2004, "We workers are human beings, not dogs and cats, so we deserve to have clean and decent meals, not contaminated food like this!" She and her co-workers boycotted the lunch sold by the factory cafeteria after finding worms in the soup and other dishes. That protest grabbed the attention of management, which switched to another food provider in response.

Native-place bonding does not always work to empower workers because it sometimes conflicts with management hierarchy at the factory. The effort to produce compliant workers for flexible global production can weaken the native-place bonds between the Vietnamese line leaders/supervisors and workers. One worker got along well with her line leader, a woman from a northern central province, who hired mostly northern migrant workers in her factory. Although the native-place bond (both came from northern provinces) enabled this worker to convince her Vietnamese supervisor to demand improvements in meals and sanitary conditions from the Taiwanese boss, on other issues the supervisor's allegiance to the management was stronger: "My boss allied with the Taiwanese boss and gave us workers a hard time. She never approved any workers' requests to take a day or two off, even on family emergency" (interview with Ms. VTN, July and August 2004).

Networking skills have become more relevant in labor organizing and decommodification efforts, especially in low-skilled assembly work. Many strike leaders have mobile phones to network and organize fellow workers. In this sense, workers too are mobile. They communicate with local labor newspapers and TV stations to spread the news about their upcoming strikes and to pressure management to come to the negotiating table. During my 2004 fieldwork, I saw strike leaders and investigative journalists from *The Laborer* contact each other directly using cell phones. As soon as one of the major investigative journalists at *The Laborer* learned about a water contamination problem at a Taiwanese factory, she contacted the female strike leader by phone and published a cover story in the newspaper the following day. This stimulated the manager to fix the problem promptly.

Knowledge is power in resisting labor commodification. If management takes advantage of the "flexibility" of workers by forcing them to work overtime, workers can take advantage of the most important aspect of flexible production, just-in-time delivery, to stall the whole production process. Many stage their strikes at the most strategic time—on the delivery date—or stop the machines at a critical stage, which paralyzes the whole production process. Knowing that MNCs fear losing their worldwide reputations if they do not abide by labor (and environmental) standards, workers inform local advocates, such as *The Laborer*, the local labor unions at various levels (ward, district, city), and the local departments of labor. They use an array of tactics to grab the attention of advocates such as chanting collectively in unison a simple message, "paying wages, paying bonuses," in front of the management office to demand bonus pay (a small amount to complement their very low wages, which enables migrant workers to take a bus home for the holidays); by squatting in front of the factory gate to obstruct "competitive" workers, management, and delivery; and by boycotting lunches and making noise during nap times so no one can rest and work efficiently (Trần 2005).

Evolving Roles of the State and the Labor Unions

Given the state's complex and contradictory relationship to capital and labor as it engages the global capitalist economy and flexible subcontracting while nominally maintaining a socialist government, how do these contradictions affect workers?

Workers engage the state on their own behalf, making use of the rhetoric of a workers' state. They make use of the state's rhetorical commitment to uphold socialist ideals, including an equitable society, by appealing to all parts of the state apparatus, using strategies ranging from writing complaint letters to the local labor newspapers to submitting their complaints to the local labor and people's courts. The evidence from workers' narratives and their complaint letters indicates different forms of protests. In public protests they rely on native-place identity, cultural bonding, and local advocates as tools to organize and fight back; in private complaint letters, they invoke the state's rhetoric to hold them accountable to their pro-worker socialist ideals.

The state's dilemma of sustaining its commitment to social equity (at least rhetorically) and facilitating capital accumulation is reflected in the VGCL's loss of control over the production process to the MNCs.[6] The VGCL is no longer a monolithic power and faces challenges at the central and local levels. Structurally, it is still the only mass organization of Vietnamese workers, and key labor union officials are Vietnamese Communist Party members. It has a well-established regional structure: central (the VGCL office in Hanoi), city (with two major federations of labor in Hanoi and HCMC), district/province (many are active near the EPZs), hamlet/ward, in the export processing zones and industrial zones (such as HEPZA in HCMC), and at the factory level (mostly absent in foreign companies). The VGCL also oversees an industrial union structure consisting of thirteen unions with a combined membership of seven hundred thousand members from state-owned enterprises directly controlled by some state ministries; seven labor unions covering workers at state corporations directly under the VGCL cover the rest of the 5.6 million union members. Internal structural weaknesses and an inadequate capacity to organize the growing private sector have weakened the VGCL vis-à-vis the power of multinationals.

Most factory-level labor union representatives, while structurally under the VGCL, receive salaries from management. Their financial dependency gives rise to conflicts of interest. In some cases, they even had to report specific union activities to management to get their support and funding (interview with Mr. DC, manager of a Taiwanese company, August 2004). Many VGCL officials recognized these structural weaknesses and have proposed solutions that will be ratified at their congress in 2008 (e.g., Trần 2007a).

Southern labor unions at the city and district levels better understand the workers' plight and respond more promptly and effectively to labor organizing and protests. Since the VGCL pays the salaries of union officials at city/district levels nationwide who work full time for union activities, they are financially independent of the foreign companies. Also, most union leaders at the district level are in the factory areas and therefore understand the factory situations and can respond to their protests in a timely manner, especially in factories without enterprise-level labor unions (interviews with Mr. Phạm Ngọc Đoàn, head of Gò Vấp Labor Unions, July and August 2004, and Mr. Hùng, then director of the Labor Management Department in HCMC Export Processing Zones, August 2004; Vĩnh Tùng, June 30, 2003). However, one dynamic and committed labor union leader in volatile Gò Vấp District told me about the difficulties in obtaining an appointment with the managers/owners and in reaching out to workers in nonunionized factories, especially during peak seasons when most workers have to work overtime. A district union leader also had an intimate understanding of the tactics of East Asian capital: "Taiwanese owners/managers were the trickiest of all foreign capitalists because they are knowledgeable about Vietnamese cultural practices and thus can give lip service to 'always protect workers' to appease the labor unions and DOLISA offices [local departments of Ministry of Labor at the city/ province/ward levels]. But in reality they do not implement these policies."

Lack of district labor union personnel and resources and restrictive company policies create barriers to establishing labor unions at the factory level. Workers in foreign-owned factories had lukewarm attitudes about the effectiveness of local labor unions, as one worker leader told me:

> The Gò Vấp district labor unions promised to pressure management to form a labor union at the enterprise level. They came down to the factory once, but spent most of their time with management, and walked briefly around the factory. There was not even enough time for us to ask questions, never mind going through the process of electing a labor union representative on the factory floor. I would have volunteered to be a union representative if I had been given a chance.

In workers' own voices, time pressure and the manner in which factory visits were conducted (indicating unequal power relations between management and labor unions) also played a role in their frustration with local labor unions.

Local labor unions, while structurally part of and paid for by the VGCL, have some level of autonomy in responding to labor problems in a timely manner without having to wait for orders from the central authority. Some district labor unions in strike-prone areas have made efforts to stand up to the MNCs and are not complicit in making "flexible" workers. Of course this depends on the dedication and ability of individual labor union officials, but general proximity to the workers makes the local union representatives more responsive to the workers' plight and accountable to them.

Alliances between local agencies assist the struggle against labor commodification. Local labor unions work closely with local state offices (such as the Ministry of Labor in HCMC) and with management to resolve labor conflicts. For instance, the District 11 Labor Union in HCMC received sixty-four formal worker complaint letters exposing labor violations between 1999 and 2004. They worked with management and local officials to resolve fifty-seven cases (an 89 percent success rate), winning settlements of US$47,000 for workers and the rehiring of sixteen workers who were laid off due to their participation in strikes. They also provided legal consultations to eighty-nine groups of workers on labor laws (Phạm Hồ, November 17, 2004).

New Space and Strategy for Decommodification Efforts: The Dynamic Role of Local Labor Newspapers

Labor newspapers, still the media arm of the VGCL, face a challenging balancing act between reproducing a type of compliant worker (according to the pro-FDI state policy) and creating a public forum for workers to voice their complaints, which otherwise would not be heard by management, enterprise-level labor unions, and local state officials.[7] There are two major labor newspapers, Lao Động (Labor, the media arm of the central labor unions, which is based in Hanoi) and Người Lao Động (The Laborer, the official forum of the HCMC Labor Federation). While Labor has national coverage of labor union activities and strikes and is more policy oriented, The Laborer has timely, on-the-ground strike coverage focused on the south and surrounding vicinities (see Trần 2007a). In January 2008, The Laborer reported massive spontaneous strikes demanding FDI companies to implement inflation-adjusted minimum wages based on Decree 168CP effective January 1, 2008.

The Laborer is the most influential and popular daily labor newspaper in the south. It continues to reflect an ideologically proper image of the work of local labor unions. However, its daily and weekly reporting on labor issues clearly demonstrates that it has some level of autonomy to give voice to workers, especially when local labor unions and state officials fail to respond to workers' urgent needs. Thus, *The Laborer*'s autonomous actions compensate for the contradictory positions of the state and VGCL on labor commodification and workers' resistance (Trần 2007a).

The Laborer has been successful in bringing key stakeholders to the negotiating table. Through its reporting in its biweekly "Rights and Responsibility" page of the "Labor Unions" section, this newspaper provides a social-justice justification for workers to stand up and fight for basic human rights, while also reminding workers to respect the labor laws. It also provides some space for management's perspectives. Approximately 70 percent of labor violations reporting on the "Rights and Responsibility" page are prolabor and 30 percent are from other perspectives (interviews with Ms. T, *Laborer* newspaper journalist, July, August, September 2004, and Mr. Q, *Laborer* newspaper journalist, July and August 2004). At least ideologically, investigative journalists are somewhat safeguarded since, as Vietnamese Communist Party members (albeit not all), they are charged with fighting for workers' rights. On permissible topics, while still being censored by the newspaper's editorial board, most of the reporting remains intact. In different columns on the "Rights and Responsibilities" page, investigative journalists expose management's labor violations and the weaknesses of state officials in protecting workers. Although these journalists are vulnerable to complaints and harassment by management, they feel that ideologically they prevail (interviews with Ms. T, 2004). *The Laborer* covers wide-ranging and significant issues of concern to workers; it offers a new site for workers' resistance. This new public space offers effective and potent resources: transparency, immediacy, and timeliness (see Trần 2007a and 2007b). The "Rights and Responsibilities" page exposes concerns about labor laws not being implemented as intended in the Labor Code and features the viewpoints of all stakeholders on labor issues. The "Policy Roundtable" column brings together state officials, managers, legal experts and other stakeholders to express their positions on labor issues, to explain specific stipulations of the labor code and to recommend concrete policy changes at the higher levels of state institutions. This process is significant because labor policy adjustments and changes can both improve the livelihood of workers and stabilize production for firm owners. Covering the explosion of strikes, this column featured a range of perspectives on nationwide debates and conferences on problems with the 1995 strike law, which had contributed to over fifteen hundred wildcat strikes (1995–June 2007), leading to the November 2006 ratification of the revised strike law.

In terms of immediacy and timeliness, *The Laborer* offers a twenty-four-hour hotline phone number for workers to report labor violations and impending strikes; this enables investigative journalists to cover unfolding conflicts. The newspaper staff is also ready to meet one-on-one with workers who, out of frustration, have gone directly to the newspaper's head office in HCMC to expose labor violations and injustices. Thus, it has become the first responder to most strikes that erupt in HCMC and its vicinity. Knowing that management is fearful of being exposed in the public media, workers often call local labor newspapers and union officials to intervene on their behalf and give interviews to the labor newspaper when reporters arrive on the scene. Once the story is exposed in the newspapers, all stakeholders at the local level collaborate to resolve labor-management conflicts. For example, one strike leader mentioned earlier complained to a *Laborer* journalist about the contaminated drinking-water tanks (storing unboiled hot and cold water) that made them sick and led them to bring their own bottles of clean water from home; in turn, *The Laborer* exposed this problem and other labor violations in a 2004 article, forcing management to make changes.

The most dynamic column in *The Laborer* is the weekly "Labor Law Counsel Forum" that facilitates direct dialogues between workers and managers/owners on particular cases. After exposing labor violations to the general public, it effectively pressures the perpetrators to be accountable for their actions and to redress their wrongdoings appropriately. Workers often submit their complaints on pay, working conditions, and insurance (health, unemployment). Most of the time, workers receive their entitled benefits or clarifications on company actions and decisions, or both. As soon as these issues are publicly exposed, management, unions, and state officials are forced to rapidly respond to labor violations or queries.

An example from *The Laborer* demonstrates the effectiveness of the "Labor Law Counsel Forum." In May 2005 a worker at An Phú Châu Garment in District 9 HCMC posted her complaint: "I worked for this company many years, and contributed to the social security fund every month. In 2003, I gave birth to a baby, but as of now I still have not received any maternity benefits." Her posting resulted in management admitting to their mistake and advancing money for her maternity entitlements. Mr. Đào Công Biên, the personnel office manager of An Phú Châu Garment company, responded:

> We acknowledged what the worker said is true. It is because of our company's lateness in contributing to the national Social Security fund that the district Social Security office did not pay workers' benefits. But we recently paid our overdue Social Security contribution, so the Social Security office is now in the process of paying maternity leave for workers. In the meantime, we are willing to advance maternity leave benefits for Ms. Tuyền.

The public posting led the company to address not only this worker's case but also to pay their overdue contribution to a government fund; consequently, this type of management response benefits more workers ("Labor Law Counsel Forum," *The Laborer*, May 17, 2005). Without the newspaper's intervention, or the worker's belief that she could use it to effect some recourse, the outcome may not have been the same.

What Makes Vietnam Different?

Workers' nexuses of identity—native-place bonding; social, cultural, and gender networks; skills and knowledge; sense of belonging to a working class—play a vital role in their protesting openly against the commodification process. Migrant workers re-create their ways of life in the south of Việt Nam to cope with labor commodification, engage the state, and use all the mechanisms they have at their disposal to contest management's domination. Thus, dependence on place-based identity does not necessarily become fragmented vis-à-vis mobile capitalism and flexible accumulation as Harvey (1990) cautioned (which perhaps is more relevant in the context of the multicultural U.S.). These migrant workers demonstrate how they connect in a new place (southern Vietnam), strengthened by networks of native-place (north and central Vietnam), gender and class, and fight locally against mobile global capital. This chapter thus gives compelling evidence of countermovements of labor organizing to fight for their rights.

However, it is not merely workers organizing along particular dimensions of identity and protesting to the state that have effected changes in labor practices in Vietnam's market socialism. Institutions founded under the full socialist regime—for example, labor unions and their labor newspapers—have been transformed and are contributing to transformations when the labor-capital relations established since market reform in late 1980s produce conflict and tension. This demonstrates the significance of history and geography in Vietnam, a socialist state that has embraced foreign investment and facilitated foreign capital's access to domestic labor. Although the labor-capital relations anticipated from foreign capital investment in a "poor" country may be the same in capitalist and postsocialist settings, the responses to them are not. Besides calling on their own social networks, these workers turn to instruments of propaganda established by the state. To some extent, workers' expectations, instilled by the ideologies they grew up with, have turned labor union media into instruments of protest during those critical moments. In this important manner, Vietnamese garment workers have more options than women workers in other Asian sites of production such as Malaysia (Ong 1987, 1997), China (Lee 1998), Indonesia (Caraway 2007), the Philippines (McKay 2006), and Sri Lanka (Lynch 2007).

What makes the case even more interesting is that these worker strategies are not without their tensions as they play out in institutions and settings that are themselves fraught with contradictions specific to socialist market contexts. These contradictions are affecting the VGCL's evolving relationships *within* the state, as officials are forced to deal with workers' demands. Although this labor organization has been complicit with other state bureaucracies in producing a type of compliant/law-abiding worker, consistent with the interests of foreign capital and the state's "political stability," its local offices are allying with other local state bureaucracies and its labor newspapers to champion workers' concerns.

This also sheds new light on the ways Vietnamese workers in a socialist market system interpret and fight for their rights (see Trần 2007a).

Moreover, the ongoing presence of these active labor newspapers, transformed in a different political era, has made a tremendous difference in the resolution of labor grievances when the central state and the VGCL are compromised or weak. Although Ong's concept of "zones of graduated sovereignty," an example of "neoliberalism as exception" in Southeast Asia, provides a framework to analyze state strategies in the EPZs and industrial zones in Vietnam (Ong 2006), her generalization about these zones being freed from national laws, especially regarding labor rights, as governments adjust their policies to the dictates of global capital, does not explain the active roles of Vietnamese local labor unions and labor newspapers, which are still very much part of the state structure, on workers' behalf. Thus the specific legacies of Vietnam's history and the manners in which Vietnamese workers embody socialist ways of seeing and being differentiate this case from others in Southeast Asia.

4

Worshipping Work

Producing Commodity Producers
in Contemporary Indonesia

DAROMIR RUDNYCKYJ

Kiyai Haji Syafiq, the head of the Islamic boarding school Pondok Pesantren Bany Lathief, scornfully dismissed recent efforts at spiritual reform in Indonesia as we sipped small glasses of tea together in early 2004. A small, sprightly man, Syafiq had mastered the cultivated eccentricity that was a hallmark of several religious leaders (*kiyai*) that I had interviewed in the area around Cilegon in western Java. He would grin mischievously behind impressively bushy eyebrows and raise and lower his voice in alternating fashion to achieve maximum dramatic effect. At one point he brought a particularly scathing litany of derision to a crescendo:

> The problem with Indonesia is that culture, religion, morality have all been de-stroyed. They have been eroded away by development [*terkikis oleh pembangunan*]. No one knows about true Islam. They only build mosques for show. Sure they pray a lot, but only for themselves. They only go to *pengajian*[1] to be part of the group. Religion has become ritual only. The *kiyai* these days are nothing but soy sauce peddlers [*penjual kecap*]! Damn them all! Who is that one? Zainuddin MZ.[2] He is nothing but a big clown. Aa Gym is the same. The good ones won't be heard. These *kiyai sontoloyo*[3] talk big but do nothing. They all have a bunch of big mouths.... Religion is just a commodity now. Protestantism and Catholicism are still pure, but Islam has become just a tool to sell commodities [*alat jualan komoditas*].

Older religious authorities such as Syafiq are threatened by upstart proselytizers who adroitly use mass media and technology to convey Islamic teaching, but often are not graduates of conventional Islamic educational institutions. These new preachers skillfully use mass media such as television, Microsoft PowerPoint software, and DVDs to appeal to an educated, middle-class audience.

However, Syafiq's critique, with its echoes of Marxian critiques of the "culture industries" (Horkheimer and Adorno 1972), raises questions about the status of new forms of Islamic practice in contemporary Indonesia. In this chapter I argue that the projects of spiritual reform that have garnered such a strong following in such a relatively short period of time are not as much about circulating a new commodity as about creating the conditions for new relations of production. Indeed, while the media-friendly forms of Islam may be viewed as marketing devices, what is perhaps more significant is the fact that Islamic practices are being invoked to make the subjects who sell, buy, or produce commodities—that is to say, as a means to produce those people who in turn produce commodities. Those enmeshed in these projects are instructed in "worshipping work," a term I borrow from proponents of this interpretation of Islam, but also use to show how labor is conceived and enacted as a form of religious veneration in emergent practices of spiritual reform. Thus, labor is both a form *and* a means of religious practice. Work is interpreted as a form of worship.[4]

In this chapter I describe and analyze a project of "spiritual reform" that attempts to address Indonesia's economic crisis through a transformation of the ethics of work and worship held by employees of state-owned enterprises slated for privatization. The proponents of spiritual reform seek to eliminate corruption, enhance workplace efficiency and productivity, repair relations between unions and management, and prepare employees for privatization. They expect to achieve these myriad goals by inculcating Islamic ethics among employees at state enterprises producing commodities ranging from steel to oil to rubber.

The ethnographic research on which this chapter is based was conducted over a year and a half in Indonesia, thirteen months of which were spent at a state-owned steel conglomerate, Krakatau Steel. At Krakatau Steel, the main vehicle for spiritual reform was called ESQ, for Emotional and Spiritual Quotient training. This program is the brainchild of a charismatic Indonesian businessman, Ary Ginanjar, and draws on a tradition of Qur'anic recitation, Islamic history, and business management programs such as *The Seven Habits of Highly Effective People*. The remainder of the research period compared the project of spiritual reform at Krakatau Steel to other such initiatives in Jakarta. This project was fortuitously timed because, as it was nearing completion, in December 2004 the Indonesian minister of state-owned enterprises signed a memorandum of understanding requiring Muslim employees of over one hundred state-owned companies to undergo ESQ spiritual training. In addition to Krakatau Steel, these include such state-owned companies as Pertamina, the state oil company, and PTP Nusantara, a state-owned agricultural company. Other companies that have introduced ESQ training include Telkom, the largest telecommunications company in Indonesia; Garuda, the nation's flag air carrier; and Pupuk Kaltim, the country's largest fertilizer company. In addition, the training was embraced by a number of government agencies including the Directorate General of Taxation and the Indonesian Army's Officer Candidate Training School (SESKOAD) in Bandung. A number of high-ranking generals and other military officials were strong advocates of the program.

In this chapter I examine interventions designed to facilitate the production of steel, a natural-resource-based commodity long regarded as pivotal to the project of Indonesian modernization. Under import-substitution industrialization policies that formed part of Indonesian policies during both the Sukarno and early Suharto eras, steel was considered a critical commodity for national development. However, although the country contains abundant quantities of other metal resources such as bauxite, silver, tin, copper, and gold, Indonesia has no domestic sources of iron ore of sufficient quality to produce steel. Therefore, from its inception a global commodity trade has been a necessary condition for domestic steel production. Krakatau Steel has historically purchased iron ore on the global market from Brazil, Chile, and Sweden. Spiritual training is one means through which corporate managers and union leaders sought to enhance the productivity and efficiency of steel production.

In this chapter I document the ways in which practices of market-oriented Islam were viewed as preparing employees to participate in a commodity market increasingly characterized by global competition. Thus, I will focus on how spiritual reform is expected to elicit a self-governing, entrepreneurial subject, exercising what one manager described as "built-in control." This subject is deemed commensurable with changing commodity regimes associated with neoliberal development policies.

Spiritual Reform, Commodities, Neoliberalism

A commodity is at the center of the project of corporate spiritual reform that I observed in contemporary Indonesia. Krakatau Steel produces a commodity that was absolutely critical to the state's project of modernization under previous nonneoliberal policies of import-substitution industrialization. One possible interpretation of spiritual reform would view it as the commodification of religion. This interpretation is part of the story I relate here, but such an interpretation presumes a separation of religion from the market. Rather than seeing the project of spiritual reform as representing the commodification of religion, I have chosen to focus on the interpretations of the proponents of spiritual reform themselves, who take spiritual reform as a means of enhancing commodity *production*. I argue that efforts seeking to combine spiritual reform with global management knowledge at Krakatau Steel sought to facilitate the more efficient production, circulation, and profitability of a commodity considered essential to the national project of modernization.

Kiyai Syafiq's assertion that groups like ESQ and charismatic, television-friendly proselytizers like Ary Ginanjar signified the commodification of religion in Indonesia is a common claim. Other Indonesian scholars, students, and activists commonly criticized the training on precisely these grounds. They objected that participation in the training required payment of between US$100 and US$300 in fees, considerably more than the monthly income of most Indonesians. For employees of companies such as Krakatau Steel, the fee was covered by the ample training budgets commanded by state-owned enterprises. However, criticizing this training program for charging a fee is a complicated line of criticism. For one thing, this criticism presumes that the domain of religion should necessarily be outside the market. As Talal Asad has shown, the presumption of the separation of religion from the political and the economic domains is itself a product of liberal theory (Asad 1993). The construction of religion as an isolable social-scientific category is an artifact of a particular, historically situated system of representation (Foucault 1970; Said 1978).

Furthermore, Shafiq's claim that Islam in Indonesia had become just a commodity evokes a notion of religion as somehow outside the circulation of commodities. However, according to historical accounts religion has never been completely external to the market in Southeast Asia. The introduction of Islam to the Indonesian archipelago was enabled by a busy commodity trade that linked the island chain with the Arabian Peninsula and the Indian subcontinent (Nakahara 1984). Furthermore, religious leaders such as *kiyai* had long held prominent commercial and business interests in Islamic communities in the archipelago (Abdullah 1986). The proponents of ESQ were also fond of reminding participants that Muhammad himself was an extremely successful trader. One young acolyte of Ary Ginanjar, the creator of ESQ, enthusiastically proclaimed the prophet's business acumen, "Muhammad had forty camels. Today that would be equivalent to owning forty BMWs!"

Interpreting ESQ and other spiritual reform projects in contemporary Indonesia as representing the commodification of religion ignores the fact that Islam in Indonesia, like the other "world" religions—Buddhism, Hinduism, and Christianity—that have thrived in the archipelago at different historical moments have done so precisely because trade in commodities such as food, cloth, and spices facilitated the transit of religion across great distances (Reid 1993). What is at stake in contemporary Indonesian projects of spiritual reform is not the radical transformation of a noncommodified set of religious practices into commodified ones. Rather, these projects entail the insertion of religion into a pattern of commodity production that is reconfigured from one defined by the boundaries of the nation to one defined more by transnational connections and neoliberal norms. From the perspective of proponents of spiritual reform, it does not so much introduce Islam into the market, as accounts focusing on the commodification of religion might presume, as it emplaces the market within Islam. What is perhaps more significant is that the proponents of spiritual reform presume that enhanced Islamic piety by corporate employees will enable the more efficient production and circulation of commodities such as steel.

Spiritual reform is intended to address changes in the Indonesian economy that resonate with the kinds of neoliberal transformations that Nevins and Peluso refer to in the introduction. These include planned privatization, the elimination of tariffs on imported commodities, the eradication of state subsidies and investment in the means of industrial production, and the rationalization of management and employment procedures. However, managers at Krakatau Steel and proponents of spiritual reform realized that these policy proscriptions could not be translated wholesale at this state-owned company, which had historically enjoyed guaranteed state support regardless of its profitability.

Islamic spiritual training is a central means through which managers and trainers sought to effect this transformation. The subject sought through this training in some ways resembles the *homo economicus* of neoliberalism, but also diverges from this ideal type.

An emerging body of social-scientific research has taken neoliberalism as an object of analysis. The more sociological of these accounts, mainly focusing on Europe and North America, suggest the progressive unfolding of a single universal logic and subjectivity (Barry 2001; Barry, Osborne, and Rose 1996; Rose 1999). Many anthropological accounts have taken neoliberalism as a technique of metropolitan power that remakes the specific sites in which anthropologists conduct their research (Comaroff and Comaroff 2000b; Ferguson and Gupta 2002; Sawyer 2001). My approach to neoliberalism is somewhat different. Rather than seeing neoliberalism as a universal logic, unfolding in Hegelian fashion and remaking the postcolonial world in its image, I have been interested in configurations that emerge in the conjunction of neoliberal technologies and localized practices (Rudnyckyj 2004). In so doing, I take neoliberalism as a flexible technology that produces new or remade configurations in assemblage with other processes and objects (Ong 2006), a conceptualization concretely demonstrated by the project of spiritual reform at Krakatau Steel.

Spiritual Reform and Producing Producers in Contemporary Indonesia

Above the cavernous half-kilometer-long floor of Krakatau Steel's hot strip mill, where twenty-ton slabs are heated to over 1,000 degrees Fahrenheit and thunderously flattened into smooth sheets of coiled steel, a huge banner reads "hard work is part of our worship."[5] In 2002, managers and officials of the company's labor union decided to implement what they termed a "spiritual reform movement" in order to enhance the Islamic piety of the company's six thousand employees. At Krakatau Steel, this unprecedented initiative required employees to attend "spiritual" training sessions totaling forty hours over three days in which they were introduced to a novel form of moderate Islam. These sessions drew on a stirring, if somewhat unwieldy, mix of Qur'anic recitation, American business management theories, Islamic history, and popular psychology.

As a critical cog in the national project of modernization, Krakatau Steel has played a central role in Indonesia's multipronged development strategy. In particular, corresponding with the import-substitution industrialization policies that guided one prong of the country's development strategies (Rock 2003; Thee 2002), Krakatau Steel received billions of dollars of state investment during the thirty-two-year presidential administration of the former autocrat Suharto. However, the state expenditures that for years guaranteed the company's viability were greatly reduced in 1998 after Suharto's resignation and the near bankruptcy of the Indonesian government. My research occurred in the wake of the political and economic transformations, referred to by Indonesians as *reformasi* (reform), that presented a host of new challenges to Krakatau Steel managers and employees. Enhanced labor rights and protections offered novel possibilities for political mobilization by factory employees, including the formation of a new and, for the first time, independent labor union.

On the other hand, the collapse of the Suharto regime also prompted sweeping economic reforms. These included preparations for sale of the company to private investors, the implementation of rationalized systems of employee management, and increasing international competition due to the deregulation of the domestic steel market. For employees, these transformations threatened the middle-class salary-and-benefit packages to which they had become accustomed. One foreman in the slab steel plant summed this transformation up by remarking that during the Suharto years "the social was the most important and profit was secondary," but that now "profit is number one and the social mission is number two." The companywide project of Islamic spiritual reform was one technique to address the host of political and economic challenges presented by reformasi.

Spiritual reform in contemporary Indonesia posits a new worshipping worker as an antidote to the country's recent economic problems, including the drastic financial crisis of 1997–98. This crisis was a painful period in which much business was brought to a standstill, hundreds of thousands if not millions lost their jobs, and Suharto resigned in disgrace. Within a few months the country's currency fell to just 12 percent of its previous value against the dollar. Spiritual reform seeks to help resolve the nation's economic crisis by enhancing Islamic practice among the nation's citizens. The creator of ESQ, Ary Ginanjar, justified spiritual reform by telling me that "at the root of Indonesia's political and economic crisis is a moral crisis." A principal goal of the company is "transformation." The ESQ company states that its mission is "to become an 'AGENT OF CHANGING' [*sic*] that is independent and respected in the process of transforming spiritual values through the development of human resources based in spirituality."[6] Referring to a common distinction also articulated by Kiyai Syafiq in the opening of this chapter, Ary Ginanjar explained that this moral crisis is a result of the fact that although most Indonesians are Muslims, they do not adhere to the tenets of Islam: "Religion is only like a ritual...just a ritual without spirituality." In contrast to Kiyai Syafiq's dim appraisal, Ary Ginanjar sees spiritual training as a means of changing religion from "just a ritual" to a set of norms that govern everyday life. He has developed a sophisticated program intended to enhance Islamic practice as a means of facilitating economic transformation. Spiritual reform directs its activities toward employees at some of the state-owned enterprises, government bureaucracies, and some private companies.

At Krakatau Steel, official ESQ training sessions were offered monthly during the period of my research from 2003 to early 2005. These sessions were delivered in a charismatic style reminiscent of American televangelists, initially by Ary Ginanjar and then, starting in early 2004, by his brother Rinaldi. These two figures had achieved celebrity-like status at Krakatau Steel and their renown was growing around Indonesia as well. In October 2005 the number of Indonesians who had participated in ESQ surpassed one hundred thousand men and women. At Krakatau Steel Ary Ginanjar and Rinaldi incorporated the most pressing challenges that the company was facing into the narrative of the training.

Two simultaneous challenges to the company occurred during my fieldwork. One was a decision by the central government to abolish all tariffs on imported steel, eliminating guarantees that had long protected the company from international competition and had ensured its continued viability. The second challenge was a global shortage of iron ore, the critical raw material for producing steel. This was widely attributed to tremendous economic growth and widespread infrastructure development ongoing in China. During one training session held in May 2004, Rinaldi focused on these two pressing issues, suggesting that they were challenges presented by God to test Krakatau Steel employees: "These problems are actually blessings from Allah. Allah wishes to prove to every level [of the company hierarchy] that we have entered the era of globalization and are able to compete." Thus, an economic crisis and transformations brought on by the integration of production systems, financial activities, and commodity markets were interpreted as a challenge to the individual religious piety of employees. Under import-substitution industrialization strategies development was conceived of as a national problem to be addressed through state intervention. However, concordant with a shift to the conditions of global neoliberal markets, development was reconfigured as a matter of individual accountability and spiritual practice.

Spiritual reformers took the problem of producing more disciplined producers as a key step in the overall goal of achieving more efficient production of commodities. Rinaldi concluded his oration, which likened globalization to a divine challenge, by explaining to the participants that "Krakatau Steel does not produce only steel, but human beings" (*Krakatau Steel memproduksi bukan baja saja, tapi manusia*). Thus, spiritual reformers were conscious of the reflexive nature of industrial production. Insofar as work is a form of worship, the production of commodities entails the simultaneous production of human beings (Lugo 1990; . Ong 1987). Spiritual training was taken as a means to simultaneously produce better Muslims, better commodities, and better workers.

The connection between work, worship, and individual ethical transformation is common in other contemporary projects of spiritual reform in Indonesia and other parts of the Muslim world. In addition to the ESQ program, another manifestation of what is referred to by proponents and participants as "spiritual reform" is a hugely successful Islamic business, the Manajemen Qolbu Corporation. This Islamic media and direct marketing conglomerate uses first an English word and then an Arabic one to yield a name that translates into Indonesian as Management of the Heart Corporation. The corporation was founded by the charismatic engineer-turned-television-preacher Abdullah Gymnastiar.[7]

The project of spiritual reform is directed toward Indonesia's economic crisis, but it proposes a radically different diagnosis of that crisis from other accounts. Indonesian nongovernmental organizations have roundly criticized international institutions, particularly the International Monetary Fund and the World Bank, accusing them of looking the other way while development aid and loans were siphoned off to line the pockets of a small, politically connected elite. In neighboring Malaysia, Prime Minister Mahathir Mohamad criticized a cabal of financiers led by George Soros for precipitating Malaysia's financial crisis. These approaches responded to the financial crisis in Southeast Asia in terms that echo a common world-systems-inspired analysis (Wallerstein 1974; Wolf 1982) in which economic and financial power is concentrated in global centers and in which peripheral countries are at the mercy of their financial machinations.

In contrast, the approach taken by spiritual reformers proposes a different kind of global vision as a diagnosis of the problem presented by the crisis. The crisis is not the result of structural inequality, it is a moral crisis, which can then be addressed through enhancing individual spirituality. Thus, it is not a matter of getting macroeconomic conditions right or policing the behavior of national elites, but it is more a matter of producing a new "spiritual" subject who is both individually accountable and amenable to new economic norms.

One senior manager at Krakatau Steel, Djohan, who had attended several years of graduate school in the United States, explained what "work as worship" meant. He connected it to his own ethical transformation, which occurred after he had participated in spiritual reform exercises. In somewhat stiff English he poignantly confided:

> You can manage your heart through the methods of ESQ....When someone asks for bribe,[8] if they have already managed their heart well, their heart will urge them "please don't do that!" Not just because one is afraid of the regulations, or afraid of the police, but also because they are afraid of our God. That is...built-in control....If you can manage your heart well, we can develop our built-in control.

Control for what? Not to violate prohibitions....The employees don't do corruption, not because they are afraid of their superiors, not because they are afraid of their leaders, not because they are afraid of regulations that will have them sent to jail. But I am afraid, why, because I have already seen how someone who does corruption is tortured in hell and I am ashamed [*malu*] to be seen by God who can see me doing corruption, so I don't do it.

Djohan suggests how a form of self-governing can be achieved through Islamic spiritual reform. This is a form of religious practice that facilitates economic transformation. Specifically, introducing religious piety into economic practice entails a shift from a political economy in which corruption was taken almost as an entitlement of senior company officials to one in which corruption is viewed as an obstacle to economic growth and efficiency. What is marked here is the failure of external forms of control and compulsion and the desire to incorporate an ethic of individual accountability.

Djohan's concern with developing "built-in control" among company employees is better understood in the context of a conversation that I had with him some months before. At that time Djohan had told me that reformasi had brought about "big changes in Indonesian politics" and a "change to a more democratic country." During the New Order[9] Krakatau Steel only had to cultivate a "close relationship with government officials because everything was controlled by the central government. Now," he continued with a smile, "people have more power...they are hard to control." In the eyes of a senior manager at Krakatau Steel, reformasi had transformed the way in which power could be exercised. Responding to dissent was no longer simply dependent on deploying the coercive force of the state. Rather, it involved the production of an entirely new producing and self-disciplining subject.

However, Djohan's turn to spiritual reform was not merely a matter of "deceiving" employees at lower levels of the company hierarchy. He was one of the first employees of Krakatau Steel to participate in the training and he testified to others about his spiritual awakening. An administrator of the company hospital told me that Djohan's testimonial about his experience of ESQ was a critical factor in the decision by hospital administrators to require the training of their employees. Furthermore, managers at Krakatau Steel were the most enthusiastic adherents of ESQ. The program was targeted at first at senior-level managers where corruption was deemed to be most egregious and the need to link individual spirituality to economic development was most pressing. Only subsequently were mid- and low-level employees included.

The Logic of Spiritual Reform

I participated in or observed the three-day ESQ trainings several times during this research project, as they proved to be excellent opportunities to initiate discussions about religious practice with Krakatau Steel employees.[10] Initially, I was a participant, as there was no ready category of observer in which an ethnographer could fit. Later, after participating a few times I was allowed to observe the trainings. This provided an opportunity to have discussions with participants and "alumni" about the program while it occurred. I was also able to get a behind-the-scenes view of the training. For example, as an observer I was able to see what happened to those participants who lost consciousness and were removed from the room.

One assistant trainer, Zulfikir, suggested how new commodity producers might be produced by describing the expectations for each day of the training. He referred to the first day as "ice breaking and conditioning" in which techniques are deployed to get the participants to open up to the possibility of changing themselves through the methods of ESQ. They are also "introduced" to the basic concepts on which the training is founded like emotional quotient and spiritual quotient. The second day, after the participant has been "broken down," they are "reprogrammed" through asking and then providing answers to existential questions such as "Where are you from?" "Where are you now?" and "Where are you going?" Zulfikir explained that participants are instructed "not to worship material things, property, their job positions, or their education." On the third day, participants are "built back up anew." Techniques to practice self-control over desire and emotional outbursts are introduced. Participants are encouraged to conceive of their life's vision and mission and what their goals are. Finally, the concept of "total action" is introduced through a hajj simulation described below. Total action refers to taking responsibility for one's actions at work and being proactive in one's career. This is an important lesson for employees of institutions that under the Suharto era were hierarchically governed and in which responsibility was usually the provenance of only a few at the top. Workers had become accustomed to waiting for orders from superiors before taking any on-the-job action themselves. However, this submissive disposition, while a central part of the New Order governing strategy, was taken to be no longer commensurable with the new economic norms in which the company found itself enmeshed. Spiritual reform seeks to transform passive objects of the hierarchical system characteristic of the New Order into "proactive" entrepreneurial subjects who will make decisions based on their own judgments rather than waiting for orders to come down from above.

What follows is a brief description of one three-day ESQ training session at Krakatau Steel in June 2004. The others I witnessed and participated in were more or less the same although certain elements were changed and the lead trainer changed from Ary Ginanjar to his brother Rinaldi about midway through my fieldwork. The training is structured around what is becoming a ubiquitous global form for conveying information, a Microsoft PowerPoint presentation. This presentation consists of the usual slides with graphs, charts, tables, and a litany of bullet points, but also with spliced film clips, colorful photographs, and popular music. The sound is sometimes elevated to earsplitting volume and the lights in the room are manipulated to maximize the dramatic effects of the points made. Further, the air conditioning in the room was turned to its lowest setting, enabling people to feel more comfortable during portions of the training that emphasized bodily contact, such as embracing.

The key argument during the first morning session of the training is that there is link between religious ethics and successful business practices. There is a lengthy display of content downloaded from a website for a Harvard Business School seminar titled "Does Spirituality Drive Success in Business?" held in 2002 in Cambridge, Massachusetts. Several key events that set the stage for the rest of the training occurred in the afternoon of the first day. After lunch, participants were invited to remove their shoes and sit on the thinly carpeted floor of the training hall. Moving from chairs to the floor created a more relaxed atmosphere and facilitated certain training activities in which chairs would present obstacles. Perhaps most importantly the removal of shoes and the absence of chairs evoked important physical characteristics of a mosque. Several times during the training participants were admonished to kneel in prayer toward Mecca.

Two critical events took place in the afternoon. First, a past participant of ESQ training at Krakatau Steel gave a personal testament about his experience with the program, referred to as "sharing." This "graduate" was encouraged to tell about his or her spiritual transformation. Although these accounts were only about ten minutes long, they were very emotional and the speaker usually cried openly. The major themes were a past history of personal inattention to Islam, a recitation of one's experience of ESQ, and finally a plea that the employees collectively "return Krakatau Steel to greatness" (*bangkit kembali*). Second, immediately following the sharing a long collective prayer was recited in the darkened room in which participants were encouraged to "remember" their mothers and ask for forgiveness for past violations against them. This collective paean of remembrance deeply resonated with the assembled participants. This session evoked the material and symbolic centrality of the figure of the mother in Indonesian domestic life (Koning 2000). Indeed, motherly love was a recurrent theme of the training. For the first time there were mass outpourings of emotion as many broke into tears while remembering improprieties against their mothers.

In the afternoon of the second day participants were instructed in techniques to memorize the *asmaul husna,* the "beautiful names," which describe ninety-nine characteristics of Allah in Arabic. A lecture on the "leadership principle" drew on the pillar of faith that emphasizes a belief in prophets. The principle was illustrated by a lecture on the relation of motivation to business success that recapitulated an article, "Pygmalion in Management," by J. Sterling Livingston that had been published in the *Harvard Business Review* (Livingston 1988). The leadership principle was further illustrated by clips from *The Message,* a 1976 film about the life of Mohammed that stars Anthony Quinn as Hamza, the prophet's uncle, and Irene Papas as Hind, the leading antagonist of Mohammed in Mecca.

Immediately after a lecture on what constituted productive labor, the most fantastic event of the training took place. This involves a simulation of the traditional Islamic practice of *talqin*[11] and was described as the "climax" (*puncak*) of ESQ training. People with high blood pressure, heart conditions, and pregnant women did not have to participate. In the darkened hall 250 participants sat in pairs embracing each other. One, playing the role of the angels of death Mungkar and Nakir, yelled, "Who are you?" "Who is your God?" and "What do you want?" while the other, playing the role of his or her own corpse, wept tearful declarations of repentance. *Talqin* is a funerary practice that consists of instructions offered to a corpse on how to respond to the questions of the angels of death, who will visit the recently deceased after the last mourner departs from the grave. The event connects work to worship to the afterlife and brings together one's worldly practice with other worldly aspirations.

Following this climactic moment, the culmination of ESQ training involved a final eight hours working on five physical activities based on the five pillars of Islam. These five steps were a "mission statement" based on the *syahadat* or Muslim confession of the faith; "character building" founded on the requirement to pray five times a day; "developing self-control" derived from the requirement to fast from sunup to sundown during Ramadan; "strategic collaboration" developed out of the requirement of each Muslim to pay alms (*zakat*); and "total action" based on the requirement that each Muslim make the pilgrimage to Mecca at least once during his or her lifetime, if they are able to do so financially. Interactive exercises were devised to illustrate each of the principles. Thus, for "strategic collaboration" each participant paired up with another, shined his or her shoes, and then reciprocally paid the other for the service. The funds were usually then collected and donated to charity. A common criticism of employees of state-owned enterprises was their poor customer service. The exercise was intended to illustrate that it feels better to serve than to be served.

The concluding exercise of ESQ is a simulation of three of the most important aspects of the hajj pilgrimage: *tawaf*, the circumambulation of the Kaaba; the *sa'i*, a ritual that consists of running seven times back and forth between the hills of Safa and Marwah in Mecca; and the stoning of *jamrat al-aqabah*, in which pilgrims hurl rocks at three representations of the devil. The chairs at the edges of the room were stacked neatly to maximize the usable space in the hall and the women and men were divided into two groups on opposite sides of the room. Three successive representations of the devil drawn on big flip charts were displayed. The participants were given little balls of paper that were vehemently hurled at the pictures. The *sa'i* was enacted by running back and forth across the room, with each participant completing seven cycles, while a dramatic historical video glorifying Krakatau Steel was projected on the screens. Finally, a replica of the Kaaba was introduced into the center of the room. Participants walked around it singing "*la illaha illallah*" while two videos were juxtaposed behind them on the projection screens. The first showed pilgrims circling the actual Kaaba in the Al Haram mosque in Mecca, while the second was a live feed of the simulated circumambulation taking place in the room. After this was completed the trainers saluted the participants with chants of "Hey, hajji, hajji, hajji." The alumni went around cutting a lock of hair of those that had "just completed the hajj," which also was modeled on the conclusion of the hajj to Mecca. The individual reform that was sought through spiritual training was thus likened to the transformation that one is said to experience during the actual hajj.

In describing this three-day ESQ training session at Krakatau Steel I have sought to show how work was interpreted as a form of Muslim worship by proponents of spiritual reform in contemporary Indonesia. Krakatau Steel and a number of other state-owned companies in the country, such as Pertamina, PTP Nusantara, Telkom, Garuda, and Pupuk Kaltim, introduced ESQ training to produce commodity producers who would be commensurable with the neoliberal norms of an increasingly global commodity market in raw steel. At the precise moment in which state guarantees for the domestic production of key industrial commodities were being reduced, the company had introduced a program that sought to enhance Islamic piety and workplace efficiency among company employees. The training is a carefully calibrated series of exercises whose point is that being a good Muslim is equivalent to being a good worker.

Producing Commodities, Producing Producers

Corporate managers and other executives of state-owned companies have adopted spiritual reform as a means of better competing in an increasingly transnational market where prices for commodities are determined by a market that is both internal and external to the nation. Before the implementation of neoliberal policies in Indonesia, commodities such as steel that were critical to the project of industrialization circulated in a market that was effectively bound by the nation. This national market was heavily affected by state intervention. However, now this market is even less subject to the dictates of state intervention, in the form of tariffs or subsidies. Rather, it is increasingly subject to global flows of capital and commodities.

In the eyes of managers at Krakatau Steel what is at stake in this transformation is not simply compliance with new policies tuned to the dictates of a neoliberal market but also the production of new laboring bodies. The managers committed to ESQ concluded that if the company was going to compete in this globalizing steel market, the norms under which the company had long acted would have to be transformed as well. The means of this transformation was a project of "spiritual reform" in which participants were introduced to a form of moderate Islam. The expected effect of these programs was the production of a laboring subject who would integrate a certain interpretation of Islamic virtue into his or her work, family, and recreational lives. This spiritual reform project was conceived of as the antidote to thirty years of unsustainable excesses and the corruption of the New Order, as well as the solution to competing in a much more competitive global steel market.

Injunctions to "save the company" are directly connected to the project of eliciting a proactive, entrepreneurial laboring subject. The success or failure of the company is linked to the individual labor practices of each employee. Thus, employees are represented as being individually accountable for the success or failure of the company as a whole. Long lectures attesting to the importance of spiritual belief and practice as opposed to materialism could be interpreted in two ways. One possibility would be to interpret these critiques of materialism as injunctions such that workers, given new rights to mobilize in the wake of two landmark labor laws, would not agitate for better wages, benefits, and working conditions. Indeed, there is some evidence to show that some managers saw ESQ as achieving precisely this effect.

Why then did managers direct ESQ not just toward lower-level workers but toward themselves as well? The relatively expensive "spiritual training" was intended less for line employees working in plant operations and was instead intended for higher-level managerial workers. The initial cohorts were made of the most senior-level managers and the subsequent cohorts were filled with employees of decreasing status. In fact, although the company initially planned to train all the workers, the program was ended after the six managerial grades of employees had participated. Therefore, many operators at the company, the lowest level of employees, never participated. No rationale was offered for this change in plan; it suggests that managers decided that the program was not suitable for lower level employees. Rinaldi expressed frustration at how difficult it was to hold the attention of lower level employees. Spiritual reform involved managerial-level employees subjecting themselves to a deeply moral interpretation of Islamic piety; it was not a technique for manipulating the rank and file.

IN this chapter I have focused on efforts in post–New Order Indonesia to produce new kinds of commodity producers against a background of broader shifts in the country's relative position to external economic and political forces. In a general sense these may appear similar to transformations taking place elsewhere in the world, insofar as they involve the turn to private rather than state investment, the elimination of national tariffs on key commodities, and a focus on greater efficiency, productivity, and competitiveness. However, ethnographic research reveals that the implementation of these kinds of policies takes a particular form in contemporary Indonesia.

I offer this account in contrast to other accounts of globalization (Goldman 2005; Rose 1999), which, although they offer important insights into contemporary economic transformations, risk reproducing the very representations they seek to critique. That is to say, claims about the homogenizing effects of globalization risk seeing the world from the same perspective as those institutions and agencies that are producing new neoliberal norms. The danger in reproducing this perspective is that these representations will become social facts (Rabinow 1986).

The perspective I have sought is that of employees and spiritual reformers at a state-owned company in Indonesia. From this perspective, globalization looks somewhat different. Empirical inspection reveals that neoliberalism is an inherently flexible technology of governing that is deployed in a number of different ways (Ong 2006, 13–14). Spiritual reformers and managers at state-owned enterprises in Indonesia argue that an ethic of individual accountability that is endemic to Islam can be neatly mapped onto a similar ethic that is assumed in neoliberal projects. The result is the creation of a subject that shares affinities with both Islam and contemporary capitalism, but is reducible to neither. Thus, mangers invoke a form of "built-in control" in which corporate employees are led by an invisible hand that is simultaneously that of God, the market, and the self.

PART II

New Enclosures and Territorializations

5

China and the Production of Forestlands in Lao PDR

A Political Ecology of Transnational Enclosure

KEITH BARNEY

In Southeast Asia there is a major trend reshaping rural landscapes and the political economy of natural resource development—China's unprecedented pace and scale of economic expansion and demand for resource commodities. China is the world's largest primary-forest-product importer, importing over one hundred million cubic meters of timber products annually since 2003 (Sun, Katsigris, and White 2004). China's increasing demand has resulted in a renewed impetus for illegal logging and forest degradation, and an intensification of struggles over access to resources, both within China and in neighboring countries (Katsigris, Bull, and White 2004). In this chapter I develop a case study of how international timber commodity relations, in combination with ongoing neoliberal-inspired reforms, articulate with and produce new practices of enclosure and loss of access to the commons in Laos.

This chapter will focus on the development of "fast-growth high-yield" (FGHY) tree plantations,[1] which are expanding in central and southern Laos. For a number of years, FGYH plantations have been viewed as a potential means of transforming Laos into a more efficient, globally competitive forest products producer—a "Finland-on-the-Mekong." Asian Development Bank (ADB) reports speak of the sector's potential in near-breathless terms, stating that plantations hold "the brightest prospects for economic development and poverty reduction in the country" (ADB 2005a, ii, 2). A number of international plantation firms have made high-profile investments in Laos, attracted by the potential for access to inexpensive, large-scale land concessions. A rejuvenation of resource investment interest in Laos is strongly tied to the infrastructure linkages being developed and upgraded by the ADB through their Greater Mekong Subregion program. Although they provided new opportunities for promoting resource megaprojects and industrial development in the Lao countryside, plantation firms seeking access to concession land can also shift Laos further into the "resource shadow" (Dauvergne 1997) emanating from more powerful neighboring economies.

Given the economic incentives to develop plantations of eucalyptus, acacia, or rubber, a "scramble" for land by actors seeking concessions has been developing in the Lao countryside. In a situation that shows parallels to the experience with land concessions in neighboring Cambodia, serious rural governance problems are quickly emerging in Laos, as state actors compete, or are manipulated, to allocate lucrative concessions to external investors. In Laos such projects are often being initiated without effective coordination, regulatory oversight, adequate social and environmental assessment, or an effective participatory framework to promote legal clarification and dispute resolution. In some cases, the plantation concessions secured by unscrupulous investors through political patronage networks are only thinly disguised "cut and run" logging operations. Other cases involve genuine plantation companies, but involve projects that are even more transformative of rural landscapes and villages, via deepening processes of state territorialization and intensive agro-commodity production.

The geographical extensification and intensification of capitalist relations in the countryside is described by Polanyi (1944) as produced by a series of "violent breaks" and enclosures, often accompanied by "double movements"—or social oppositions to the totalizing production and capture of fictitious commodities (including rural landscapes and peasant labor). From a geographical tradition, Swyngedouw (1999, 460) has written of a "tumultuous re-ordering of sociophysical space" under global capitalism. The transformation of socionatures, achieved through complex processes of de- and reterritorialization, are for Swyngedouw tied inextricably to a politics of scale.

As Laos opens to foreign investments and integrates with regional economies, the country is being swept into a broader agrarian transition occurring throughout the region. Yet, these transformations cannot be reduced to a simple extension of historical patterns of East Asian uneven development, enacted over a template of postsocialist Laos. The agrarian transition under way in Laos is unique, and constitutive of a historically derived, but also very contemporary and complex, assemblage of state agencies, actors, global institutions, natures, and development practices. In Laos, market-based land-reform programs link to new imperatives for resource production and profit, which are becoming linked to emerging global environmental regulatory practices. In many ways, the Lao experience with resource development is representative of a new phase in the deep historical relationship between East and Southeast Asia. In response to the dislocations and enclosures that accompany the transition to a market-based, export-led economy, the beginnings of a social "double movement"—with Lao characteristics—is discernable, although the eventual political form of this, and its implications in terms of strategies to maintain and enhance the legitimacy of state rule in Laos, are unclear.

In this chapter I will view these processes through the lens of a particular forest commodity in Laos—the pulpwood chip—and through a Japanese transnational company seeking to develop a plantation base to support a major manufacturing expansion effort in China. While promoting a version of rural industrial development based on capitalist exploitation of nature and labor power, this plantation project is also part of a complex and overlapping set of socionatural transformations that are combining in unpredictable ways and contributing to new risks and vulnerabilities for rural people in Laos. Ongoing land-tenure reform initiatives in Laos are central to the current process of plantation zoning and development, particularly in the mapping and production of "degraded forestland" as a new and distinctive administrative category of land use (see also Peluso 1992; Vandergeest and Peluso 1995). I place the practices and outcomes of tenure reforms and forestry projects within a FGHY plantation pulpwood commodity network, describing how plantation investments in Laos are in turn linked to regional and global growth trends in forestry, in which China in particular has emerged as a core arena of demand, production, and export. Ethnographically informed political ecology research into agrarian transitions in Southeast Asia and elsewhere (e.g., Li 2002b) can be usefully combined with commodity chains and network approaches (Dauvergne 1997; Ribot 1998; Sikor and Pham 2005, 405–28), both in terms of understanding the spatial structure and organization of these networks (e.g., Murdoch 1998; Leslie and Reimer 1999) and how "commodity power" under capitalism contributes to the production of new natures, new communities, and new geographies of resource access in the countryside.

"We are Saying Goodbye to Our Forests"

During research visits to Hinboun District in Khammouane Province during the burning season of early 2006, a group of villagers in Ban Sivilay[2] were engaged in cutting and clearing upland forestland for Lao Plantation Forestry Limited (LPFL), a subsidiary of the Japanese multinational Oji Paper.[3] With Oji's purchase of a 154,000 hectare concession in Borikhamxai and Khammouane provinces from BGA Forestry Ltd., LPFL secured exclusive prospecting rights to locate up to 50,000 hectares of degraded forestland in the concession area, and to convert these sites to plantations. Thirteen Ban Sivilay households employed by LPFL were busy in early 2006 cutting, burning, and clearing all of the standing trees in an 18.5 hectare area of secondary forest. Afterward, there was to be wage labor available for digging holes, planting eucalyptus seedlings, and applying fertilizer. In return, villagers received US$80 per hectare for land clearing and $2 a day for tree planting. Perhaps even more important than the direct cash income, however, the participating households could then plant a crop of upland rice in the cleared forests, between the rows of eucalyptus seedlings. As the area cleared was quality secondary forest, soil fertility in these locations was generally high, as were the corresponding upland swidden yields.

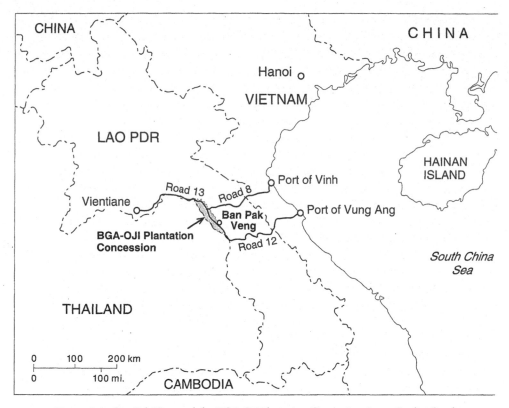

Figure 5.1. Ban Pak Veng and the BGA-Oji Plantation Concession, Laos. Credit: Carolyn King, Cartographer, Department of Geography, York University.

In 2006, fifteen other families from the village intercropped rice between the eucalyptus seedlings, in flatter lands that were cleared with the company tractor. For labor-poor households in the village, intercropping rice in these locations was an attractive option. Although the yields would be lower here, as the soil quality could be suboptimal or compacted from the tractors, and the trees were burned in a pile instead of through an ash-distributing swidden system, these families also avoided weeks of arduous labor to clear the land. In addition, twenty of Ban Sivilay's forty-eight households planted rice in their own upland swidden fields, separate from the Oji-LPFL eucalyptus plantation area. Five households also owned small areas of wet rice paddy located along feeder streams connecting to the Hinboun River.

Upland rice can be intercropped only for the first year of plantation operations, after which the eucalyptus canopy begins to close. But for villagers in Ban Sivilay, the LPFL plantation project has opened access to fertile forest-agricultural areas (though short term only, and at the price of relinquishing access for fifty years).

Figure 5.2. Village woman collecting *nor san* (a common local non-timber forest product and food source) in a degraded forest/swidden landscape, Ban Sivilay, Laos, February 2006. Credit: K. Barney.

Villagers had not made swiddens in some of these forests for at least fifteen to twenty years. Under normal circumstances, state land-use classifications under the Land and Forest Allocation Program would preclude villagers from clearing such forests; indeed, villagers claim they would be fined (based on the number of large and valuable trees cut) or arrested by authorities from the provincial and district agriculture and forestry offices for doing so. For the company's purposes, however, these forests were "degraded" and thus land that could be zoned for their eucalyptus plantation program.

The year before, in 2005, seventy-eight hectares of Sivilay village degraded forestland were also cleared with company bulldozers. Many Sivilay villagers were able to find employment with LPFL then as well, planting a crop of upland rice in between the rows of trees. For a village that chronically falls quite short of their annual rice requirements, 2005 and 2006 were relatively easier years for farmers.[4]

Villagers readily recognize that there are trade-offs attached to the plantation project. Although rice harvests have been above average for many, and a certain amount of cash earning opportunities have arisen from planting trees, substantial portions of former village swidden land have been transferred out of traditional village ownership and over to fifty years of company control. The loss of village forestland is also the backdrop for internal village political struggles, in which the present village headman and a respected former headman who held the position in the 1990s are allied in political opposition to a younger, dynamic and entrepreneurial villager, who, as village head from 2001 to 2003 signed the Land and Forest Allocation document zoning one-third of village forestland over to Oji-LPFL.

Poor and medium-income villagers alike are participating this year in cutting forest and planting trees for the company. The Sivilay village headman states, however, that villagers know they are clearing and burning the trees in these areas for the last time, and are doing so "without happiness. We are saying goodbye to our forests." Placed in a difficult position, negotiating among the company, district forestry officials, and other villagers (but receiving a US$50 per month salary from LPFL), the headman claims to be looking forward to retiring from village politics after his three-year term is completed.

In the context of authoritarian Laos, rural villagers have few options to voice direct opposition to state projects (Stuart-Fox 2004), particularly in relation to flagship, high-profile resource investments. Oji's village support program, which has included extending a plantation access road to reach the village, has been well received by villagers. Although there is significant dissatisfaction about the loss of village forestland to the plantation company, most villagers have adopted a pragmatic "wait and see" approach. However, others have been more outspoken, asking whether I could tell the Japanese company "not to take any more village land."

Under the Oji plantation project village agreement, based on the 2001 Land and Forest Allocation (LFA) process, 610 of the village's 1,833 hectares has been designated as "degraded forest" and zoned for potential development by LPFL. By the end of 2006, the company had developed one hundred hectares in this village location, while company interviews have suggested that further village land clearing is likely. The eventual effects of this plantation development on village food security are difficult to predict. Plantation employment opportunities can to some extent provide cash income for purchases of rice, but such work is sporadic. Village labor is required during land clearing, planting, and harvesting operations for the company, but very little for the years in between. Although in theory a plantations development program spread over the optimal seven years could simulate the conditions of rotational upland rice farming, a kind of eucalyptus *taungya* or agro-forest system, the basis for swidden agriculture is the fertilizing pulse from the burning of forest. There will be no such pulse after the first rotation, and, unlike with teak or other proven agroforest species, intensively managed eucalyptus plantations may degrade the soil to the point where subsequent intercropping of rice yields a much lower harvest, at least without significant additions of inputs. The available land base for conducting rotational swidden will decline significantly in Sivilay village over the coming years, a process tied directly to the allocation of "degraded" forestland—largely secondary forest (or fallow swidden)—to a commercial plantation company.

Lost Geographies of Swidden in Laos

The situation in Ban Sivilay can be taken as reflective of a wider policy-induced squeeze affecting the access of upland agriculturalists to swidden land across the country. In Laos, swidden agriculture is being zoned into increasingly restricted spaces, with cumulative problems emerging around soil and forest degradation and food security (State Planning Committee 2000). The Land and Forest Allocation Program (LFAP) of the Ministry of Agriculture and Forestry (MAF) is a central pillar of state land reform policy. As formulated, LFAP was considered a progressive tenure-reform policy, particularly in recognizing established village boundaries, the rights it granted villages to access and manage their forests, and the steps it provided for participatory, community-based land-use planning (Vandergeest 2003). But implementation of the LFAP at provincial and district levels has been plagued with inconsistencies, especially with the internal village land-use-zoning process. All village lands containing trees (in effect, anything other than paddy land) are classified through the LFA as "forest," and placed in five potential categories: protection, conservation, production, regeneration, and degraded forests. An early sign of a problem in the implementation of the LFA program was that village forestland was being zoned into unrealistic proportions—in 2000–2001 the ratio of land use zones in the LFAP was 91 percent in the protected forest categories and just 9 percent for village production forest (Ministry of Agriculture and Forestry 2005, 41).

Second, the LFAP in Laos has been often implemented in combination with parallel state policies aimed at stabilizing or eliminating shifting cultivation by 2010 (Baird and Shoemaker 2005). Yet hundreds of thousands of upland Lao farmers, both minority groups and ethnic Lao, remain dependent on upland swidden agriculture. In effect, shifting cultivation stabilization and the Land and Forest Allocation Program were set on a collision course with local livelihoods. The outcomes have been tied to accelerations of local inequality in access to productive swidden, and to increased soil and land degradation in the countryside (Ducourtieux, Laffort, and Sacklokham 2005). Participatory studies sponsored by the Lao government identify the LFAP as a primary source of new poverty creation and food insecurity in the countryside (e.g., State Planning Committee 2000). A significant body of research has concluded that the restrictive land-use provisions accompanying the LFAP around swidden agriculture have seriously limited the potential of villages to realize the intended benefits (Evrard and Goudineau 2004; Ministry of Agriculture and Forestry 2005).

Fewer, though, have highlighted the inherent conflicts of interest when a private sector–state consortium has a direct financial interest in zoning forestland as degraded in order to develop plantations. There are a number of donor-linked trial projects currently under way to move policy past the problematic LFAP system as administered under the Ministry of Agriculture and Forestry, for example, through a new national land management agency. Nevertheless, the continued understated goal of the MAF is stabilizing and eliminating what is termed unproductive slash-and-burn cultivation, and to replace swidden production methods with something better. A primary approach to ending swidden in Laos is through the promotion of modern, technology-intensive cash-cropping and tree-planting programs, where tenure rights are secure not only for villagers but also for companies and local entrepreneurs, and long-term investments can be planned. However, this approach also requires the expropriation of village, forest, and agricultural land.

The Land and Forest Allocation process does not provide an effective mechanism for communities to claim ownership rights over communal forestland. Under the 1991 Constitution and the 1997 Forest Law, all forestland officially remains classified as "state land." Hence, degraded swidden land, even as mapped within village territories as in Ban Sivilay, can be transferred out of village management and into state-company concession agreements. Although various donor initiatives are investigating the possibilities for communal land registration and titling, large-scale forestry, hydropower, mining, and infrastructure projects are proceeding—indeed, they are simultaneously being encouraged by the loans and policies of key donor agencies. Institutional safeguards for the recognition of common property rights in Laos are being implemented only during or after resource development projects get under way, while the land allocation system can be manipulated to suit specific development interests in gaining access to land. The political invention of one specific land use category in the Lao countryside highlights the implications of this process.

On the Natural and Legal History of Degraded Forests

Global commodity chains and their broader networks are inherently spatial. Considered as such, commodity networks can be viewed as interwoven into the spatial and territorializing practices of development, in ways that produce and regulate "local" socionatures and subjects in relation to new, broadly capitalist, imperatives. One of the key mechanisms through which plantation commodity networks take spatial form in Laos, and articulate with state tenure reform under the LFAP, is via the political invention of "degraded forests" (see Peluso and Vandergeest 2001).

In the approximately two-thirds of Lao communities where some form of Land and Forest Allocation procedure has been initiated, the LFA map is usually placed prominently near the center of the village or along the roadside. The map is intended to locate the village boundaries and to specify each distinct, participatorily defined land use zone. Different colors correspond to the agreed village land uses, with a corresponding land area in hectares. For example, in Ban Sivilay the land uses include *din kasikaam* (agricultural land), 85.34 hectares; and *paa sa nguan* (conservation forest), 171.00 hectares. Most villagers in Ban Sivilay claimed that they do not pay much attention to the map, and few could articulate specifically how it regulated their agricultural or livelihood practices. Villagers do know, however, which forests are likely to result in a visit from the district or provincial forestry office if cleared for swidden fields. In Ban Sivilay, official directives about acceptable land uses are more likely to be relayed personally during field visits by local or provincial officials rather than through the use of a map.

The LFA village maps nicely illustrate the contemporary role of the state as a key institution in the production of village spaces (e.g., Hirsch 1993; Agrawal 2001). What caught my attention with the map in Ban Sivilay was one particular land use category. In Lao it reads *din suan book mai bolisat bii jii ae* ("land for tree planting, BGA Company"). As mentioned above, 610 hectares out of a total village land area of 1,833 hectares have been allocated for the Oji-LPFL plantation project. With the exception of 13 hectares of streamside paddy, which was carefully mapped and labeled with GPS (global positioning system) instruments supplied by the company, any further village claims to land in this category were unacknowledged. A singular attention was paid to respecting paddy land—it was mapped down to the square meter—while all other aspects of village resource use were removed. The village land zoned for plantations is considered unstocked, "degraded forest"; without records of any land tax payments, villagers and households have no eligible claim to these spaces.

Under the terms of the concession agreement, Oji is allocating a one-time minimum compensation of US$50 per planted hectare to a village development fund.[5] For Ban Sivilay, this fund was used to extend a company access road 1.3 km to reach the village. Although the company claims that more compensation will be forthcoming, as of the time of writing there were no written guarantees as to the amount, form, or extent of compensation. That the BGA-LPFL provided material and financial support for the LFA process in the numerous villages located within their concession area highlights another key issue—the increasing internationalization of the Lao state (Goldman 2001), and particularly a process of market-driven land reform combined with private-sector territorialization. As the Lao state becomes increasingly internationalized, an exclusive focus on state actors in contemporary forestland territorialization processes can overlook the role of other key actors. The LFA maps in Ban Sivilay illustrate the close presence of BGA/Oji-LPFL in regulating local practices through tenure reform, and in determining which productive activities can occur in different spaces, and by whom. In Laos, many other private firms and development agencies are also providing financial and material support for mapping, zoning, and titling the terms of land use and the ownership claims over those lands. This draws our attention more directly to the role of, and the conflicts of interest involved in, international actors and global capital in reshaping de facto access rights for rural communities in developing countries through land reform programs.

There are various definitions for "degraded forest" in Laos, and there is also little clarity in actual implementation. The Ministry of Agriculture and Forestry uses an area of less than thirty cubic meters of standing timber to define "degraded forest." For the 1994–2003 ADB Industrial Tree Plantation Project, degraded forests were defined as forestland with less than 20 percent crown cover. The World Bank, following standard sampling measures, uses a timber volume of less than seventy to eighty cubic meters for determining degraded "production forest."

In the Lao legal framework (the 1996 Forest Law and the 1997 Land Law), forests (outside of National Biodiversity Conservation Areas) are to be classified into five forest categories. Degraded forests, the key category for plantation development, are defined in the Forestry Sector 2020 as "forests that have been heavily damaged, to the extent they are without forest or barren, that are classified for tree planting and/or allocation to individuals or organizations for tree planting, permanent agriculture and livestock production or other purposes in accordance with national economic development plans" (Ministry of Agriculture and Forestry 2005).

This legal definition does not incorporate specific criteria of crown cover or wood volume per hectare. It includes criteria about the quality of the forest found on that land ("damaged," "barren"), but also adds that degraded forests are simply those areas classified for tree planting or any other purpose that can be framed as a national development strategy.

To add to the ambiguity, elsewhere in the Forestry Sector 2020 descriptions of forest cover include the categories of "current forest," "potential forest," and "unstocked forest." Unstocked forest is defined as "forested areas in which the crown density has been reduced to less than 20 percent because of logging, shifting cultivation or other heavy disturbance. If the area is left to grow undisturbed it becomes forest again."

There are several further layers of obfuscation in these definitions. The first is that forests regenerate over time. To extrapolate a definition between current forest, potential forest, and unstocked forest, or between degraded and regeneration forest, is to make a more or less arbitrary distinction based on the present situation of land cover, projecting that situation into the future. A more fundamental source of ambiguity is between forestland classified on legal (cadastral) definitions and forestland classified on vegetation cover.[6] As with other countries in the region, the concept of degraded forests in Laos is associated with a significant obscurity: Is it based on a set of scientific criteria measuring characteristics of the vegetation, or on whether degraded forests are simply those forests declared and legally classified as such? (See also, e.g., Peluso 1992; Peluso and Vandergeest 2001.)

Identifying forestland territories as degraded forest is useful for the political project of evacuating these zones of substantive social, economic, or ecological significance. The ADB Forest Plantation Project proposal (ADB 2005a, i) refers repeatedly to "vast areas" of degraded forestland in Laos that is readily available for plantation entrepreneurs willing to make the investment. The suggested extent of degraded forest in Laos was included in a list of core regional comparative advantages that was to ensure the success of a proposed ADB $US15 million loan and grant facility to the plantations sector.

ADB reports reinforce the confusion around these definitions. An early Industrial Tree Plantation Program document estimated that in 1993 there was a total of 1.1 million hectares of degraded forestland in four southern provinces (ADB 1993, 6). In later documents, the extent of degraded forest in seven southern provinces is listed as being between 19,000 hectares (ADB 2003, 183) and 207,000 hectares (ADB 2003, 57). The 2005 ADB Report to the Board of Governors for the proposed Lao Plantation Forest Project (ADB 2005a, 28) leaves the question of degraded forest more open, stating that suitable areas would be identified according to scientific criteria—that is, a crown density of less than 20 percent or a slope of less than 20 degrees. Resolution and ground truthing of these parameters is to be accomplished using both economic considerations ("size and diameter distribution of trees by species and their quality") and a more social parameter ("threats that may affect regeneration") (ibid.).

Some project documents state that degraded forestlands are to be determined through Land and Forest Allocation exercises, which could represent a participatory approach to the issue. Another ADB consultant's report raises the question of whether, from the perspective of Lao villagers, they held any "degraded forest" at all. According to this study, the concept of "degraded forestland" is not well understood locally, even by village leaders (ADB 2003, 42, 48). For Lao villagers, degraded forestland would simply be recovering swiddens that will soon revert to a forest with larger trees.

Lastly, the *Operations Manual of the Lao Plantation Authority* (ADB 2005c, 30), a document where one might expect a more detailed consideration of informal land tenure and resource access issues, does not consider local common property resources in a substantive manner: "Degraded unstocked forests (forests with less than 20 percent canopy cover) will be used for establishing forest plantations. Some of these lands may be used for shifting cultivation. Government policy is to convert these lands to other land uses."

When I asked the provincial forestry department how they determine what is degraded forestland available for plantation zoning, there was a very simple answer. Junior staff busy preparing a map of zoned plantation land claimed that a more senior forestry staff member, who is charged by his superiors with implementing the village LFA programs in Khammouane in support of the Oji-LPFL project, was the arbitrator in deciding what forest was "degraded" and suitable for clearing. Although provincial foresters would be expected to be involved in local classification of degraded forests, in authoritarian, postsocialist Laos field foresters have limited scope to contradict the overall directives from senior party officials about the implementation of large-scale projects.

The ambiguity around degraded forest is functional to the actors who wish to allocate and zone such land according to their interests. For the ADB and the MAF or Finance Ministry, investors need to be assured that there are in fact significant areas of quality empty land available, to overcome the perception of the investment risks and the potential for delays entailed in project development in Laos. All levels of the forestry bureaucracy stand to gain from highly capitalized investment in plantations—from the stipends that supplement low public sector wages to the opportunities to implement various national forest policies, including the LFAP. The professional implementation of forest policy is much more possible with financing from a foreign investor. These agencies conceive of forestry as a modernizing project in which the loss of access to the commons will be compensated by wage-labor opportunities in a successful industrial plantation project. In the absence of Lao institutions that can translate laws down to local implementation standards, the differences between the de jure "political forest" and the de facto "forest of local resource use and management" are reinforced (Peluso and Vandergeest, 2001). A major part of the development problem in rural Laos is the general inattention to developing effective participatory mechanisms to clarify the implementation of laws by the major promoters of resource development initiatives in Laos; instead, the preference is to improve and clarify the implementation of policies as large-scale development proceeds (or even afterward).

Polanyi insisted on the distinction between true commodities and "fictitious" commodities—land (nature), labor (people), and money. Fictitious commodities are those which cannot be fully commodified for market production. In Laos, one particular socionatural system, composed of degraded forestland and swiddens, is being reinvented as a fictitious commodity that can be allocated and leased to international investors.

But for villagers in Ban Sivilay, the village's degraded forests are simply village forestlands, recovering swidden at various stages of regrowth. They are land for planting upland rice, for cattle grazing on the recovering swidden fields, for collecting edible plants, mushrooms, and useful forest products. The village's degraded forests are landscapes that they have produced, for which they have their own terms of description, and that they use nearly every day. Although these forests may be degraded by many scientific classifications, villagers certainly do not think of them in that way. They are the result of a complex amalgam of local practices—*village-forests*. To term these forests unstocked and degraded, as a "wasted asset" with "little or no alternative economic value" (ADB 2005a, 8), is to use a language that denies the substantial and well-documented role they play in sustaining villager livelihoods (Foppes and Ketphanh 2004).[7] The discourse of degradation also helps enclose culturally and economically valuable local common lands, with minimal obligation to compensate villagers (Nevins and Peluso, introduction to this book).

Zoning degraded forests in a rapid manner is central to the transformation of Laos into a viable regional and global plantation producer, however. In Laos, concessions are being allocated by various levels of government without standardized ground truthing or consideration of the quality of the forest cover. Nor is there an effective forum for local participation in forestland development programs that might recognize and build on the importance of village-managed swiddens and forests. Signs of a double-movement social response to the enclosures in rural Laos are emerging, however. While the political space for peasants to organize is quite limited, villagers have been arguing for established land and forest access with district and provincial authorities. In some cases, communities have refused to agree to alienate forestland to companies (for example, in the LPFL concession area). In the English-language media in Vientiane, news stories increasingly include accounts not only of more direct initiatives to address illegal logging but also of local understandings of the importance of even "degraded" forestland or livestock grazing land for rural livelihoods.[8]

A full understanding of the drivers of the production of new forestlands in Laos requires a regional and global perspective. Why are particular forest spaces in rural Laos being defined as degraded and enclosed and commodified for global production and consumption? What are the political-economic pressures involved? It is useful to situate the Lao plantation sector within a commodity network that connects sites across national and regional boundaries. The socionatural transformations and rural commodifications in Ban Sivilay must be interpreted not only in relation to state land tenure reforms or to the territorializing interests of transnational private sector actors but also, via timber commodity flows and demand trends, to industrial transformations in East Asian regional markets and the global economy.

From Hinboun to Shanghai: Global Supply Networks in the Plantations and Pulp Sector

The LPFL project in Laos is planned as one node in the offshore plantation supply sources for Oji Paper, Japan's largest pulp and paper producer. With 2006 revenues in the range of US$10.7 billion, Oji is the number-eight forest-products company in the world (PriceWaterhouseCoopers 2006, 8). The LPFL project fits into a commodity network that links sites in rural Laos to Oji's planned expansion into the Chinese pulp and paper market. In terms of global market pulp and paper production coastal China has been dominant in attracting global investment from the late 1990's. Barr (2002) has called the rise of China into global paper and paperboard commodity markets "the most significant trend, by far, in the global pulp and paper industry." Chinese pulp imports from 1997 to 2003 increased 26 percent per year, compared to 1.6 percent for the rest of the world (Cossalter 2004a). The projected inflows of global investment finance into the Chinese pulp sector between 2002 and 2010 are in the range of US$15–20 billion (ibid.), while the Chinese government has reportedly earmarked US$13 billion to finance domestic reforestation development between 2002 and 2020 (Brady 2004). These trends in forestry are closely linked to the overall trajectory of China's economic boom.

Such dramatic shifts in the Chinese paper sector are being matched by other Chinese wood industries, which have now become major importers of wood from Southeast Asia and the Russian Far East (Sun, Katsigris, and White 2004). Chinese wood imports doubled in the five years between 1997 to 2002, increasing from 40.2 million to 95.1 million cubic meters (ibid.). Recent data shows that China's total forest product imports have continued to increase rapidly, to 134 million cubic meters for 2005 (White, Sun, and Canby 2006, 6). As a result of these trends, the Chinese wood import complex now involves trade flows in the range of US$16 billion per year (ibid.). For some Pacific Rim countries logging activities are now at historical highs in terms of volume and value (Katsigris, Bull, and White 2004). Although China processes and then reexports approximately 70 percent of the timber volume it imports (White, Sun, and Canby 2006), this largely covers furniture and wood-based panels and is less relevant to the pulp and paper sector. Most foreign direct investments by the major players in pulp manufacturing are aimed at supplying the domestic Chinese market (Barr 2002).

The Chinese government has recently moved to close many of the country's small, heavily polluting pulp mills that utilize nonwood fiber, and to promote development of world-class wood-fiber mills that produce bleached hardwood and softwood kraft pulp (Barr 2002). This has been accompanied by an aggressive series of state subsidies, preferential loan and tax policies, "fast-track" approvals, and trade policies to support a revamped domestic paper industry (Brady 2004). Cossalter (2004b) reports on plans for eight greenfield pulp and paper projects in Hainan, Guangxi, and Guangdong provinces. These involve direct investments from some of the key transnational paper firms, including Stora-Enso, UPM Kymmene, Oji Paper, Asia Pulp and Paper, and Asia-Pacific Resources International.

The scale and speed of this development in China, and a series of constraints for siting sufficient plantation bases domestically, suggest strongly that a significant portion of the wood supply for these pulp projects will be imported for the foreseeable future (Cossalter 2004b). Detailed analysis of the associated fiber-supply status and plantation development options within coastal southern China is too complex a story to develop fully here, but Cossalter's preliminary conclusions are particularly relevant:

> The situation beyond 2009 will depend upon what the big players: APP, Stora-Enso, UPM Kymmene, Oji and APRIL will be able to plant in 2004 and in consecutive years.... Considering the various obstacles that several pulp companies are facing in their effort to secure an adequate plantation land base, it is likely that Southern China will remain largely reliant on imported wood chips beyond 2009. There might be a strong temptation, on the part of certain players, to fulfil their fibre gap from non-sustainable sources in countries with governance problems.

Laos is often included on lists of countries with forest governance problems.[9] A number of major plantation firms have shown interest in establishing plantations in Laos, including such major players in Asia as APRIL, APP, and Stora-Enso. The Aditya-Birla Group of India is presently mapping fifty thousand hectares of plantation concession agreements in Savannakhet and Khammouane provinces in southern Laos, aiming to develop an integrated plantation and pulp mill for rayon production. The ADB's efforts have been organized around reforming the Lao policy and land investment frameworks, developing large-scale and commercially viable smallholder plantation parcels, and attempting to promote Laos's suggested comparative advantage in plantations while simultaneously alleviating concerns over the extent of sovereign risk for foreign direct investments in the country.

Oji-LPFL represents the "flagship" plantation investment in Laos. Company annual reports explicitly link their plantation efforts in Laos and Oji's new greenfield pulp and paper manufacturing investment in Nantong, China, near Shanghai. The Nantong-Shanghai project is listed as a 1.2 million-ton–per-year integrated pulp and paper mill, with a total investment of US$1.7 billion. Securing the fiber supply for this mill will be an imperative for the company, given the new competitive pressures other investments in China are placing on the global fiber supply situation. The pressure on Oji-LPFL to gain sufficient access to plantation land to provide a source of stable wood fiber supplies for their capital investments in China will determine the priorities of LPFL in Laos. These are the significant economic imperatives and commodity relations that have become intimately involved in "defining degradation" and thus transforming the upland forest spaces of Ban Sivilay.

Toward a Geographical Political Ecology of Plantation Forestry in Laos

In this chapter I have focused on a set of territorial relations produced through the enactment of a particular global forestry commodity network in Southeast Asia. In many ways, and through direct donor investments such as the Greater

106 / KEITH BARNEY

Mekong Subregion program, Laos is being positioned as a new "resource frontier" for booming regional economies including China. It is through the requirements for intensively managed control of land that plantation projects should be viewed as particularly powerful modes of reconfiguring conceptions of forest and nature, of "de" and then "re"-territorializing countrysides, of rescaling access to the commons, and of institutionalizing new processes of inclusion and exclusion in rural political economies. Plantation forestry projects are prime examples of global resource commodity networks that produce spatially extensive rural development that in turn produces new meaning and controls over rural space. They are means of state territorialization (Vandergeest and Peluso 1995) by which new forms of global commodity control and accumulation are enacted.

In Laos, however, neoliberal ideology around development meets an authoritarian, postsocialist, but still largely agrarian society, and a state formation that is heavily dependent on foreign aid and foreign direct investment to maintain budget expenditures. Nature's commodification takes on particular characteristics in the Lao context. The political space for "double-movement" mobilizations of dissent against party directives supporting enclosures is constrained—but not absent. Under these circumstances, the power of global private and donor capital is in one sense increased (Goldman 2001), although just as often external disciplinary power merges with, and is effectively manipulated by, the interests of the political governing class in Laos.

In Laos, this territorialization is being enacted through the divergent processes of a transnationalized state, in which not only state agencies but also private sector actors, competing donor projects, new global regulatory frameworks, international NGOs, and the various imperatives of commodity networks, all influence the outcomes. Territorialization, enclosure, and commodification have taken on qualitatively different forms than their colonial and immediate postcolonial precedents (Peluso and Vandergeest 2001). At the same time, it would be simplistic to view Laos as a country governed according to neoliberal directives from the development banks. The interests at work in promoting plantation forestry in Laos extend beyond the promotion of commodity production for regional companies, although their factories are essential as the ultimate purchasers of the profitable wood chips to be produced in Laos. Resource commodification in Laos also becomes enmeshed with policies aimed at capturing not only the material benefits of development but also with enhancing territorial control and legitimating extensions of state power over upland forest spaces and peoples. This extends explanations of commodification based on an overarching understanding of "uneven development" to include the historical, political, and institutional ways in which new enclosures are produced and legitimated in different contexts—here, through the ambiguity of "degraded forests" in Laos.

In Laos, nature is produced, and plantation landscapes are "fixed" in part through the commodity production networks associated with large resource development projects, in a way that undermines the basis for community and common property systems. Resource commodity chain and network analysis needs to be more fully incorporated into the political ecology of forestry in Southeast Asia. A critical spatial-economic perspective in political ecology is important for moving beyond what Gellert has identified as a "changing geography of production" approach to commodity analyses (2003, 57). Rather than abandoning economic geography for an a-spatial commodity studies, however, it is through a historically—and geographically—informed political ecology that the full, often coercive, and at times violent relationship between global commodity networks, spatial-territorial power, forestland commodification, and agrarian transformation can be understood.

Relational understandings of globalization, commodity production, and rural change (Hart 2004), which incorporate the complexities of national to local politics, culture, territorialization, and livelihoods, may represent an approach that expands the possibilities for enacting different futures. A corresponding ethnographic challenge in political ecology is to demystify the political governance of commodities, socionatural space, and people, and ultimately to challenge new processes of environmental degradation and social exclusion.

6

Water Power

Machines, Modernizers, and Meta-Commoditization on the Mekong River

DAVID BIGGS

"There were no maps of the country, we had to make them," Lt. Gen. Raymond Wheeler said at a Bangkok press conference in 1958 after the former chief engineer of the U.S. Army Corps of Engineers had visited the Mekong River in December 1957. "Nobody had any data on river flow, or even any idea how to keep data. What I saw was a truly virgin river. Such sights disappeared in our country long before I was born" (Black 1969, 138). The trip was partly designed to rally congressional support for more spending in Southeast Asia. General Wheeler presented his visits as an exploration adventure, comparing several days of motorboat trips on the Mekong with the journey of the French explorers Jacques Marquette and Louis Joliet who surveyed the Mississippi in 1673. He and his fellow explorers—leading figures in international engineering—visited several ideal sites for hydropower dams on the river and they urged the United Nations to form a Mekong Coordinating Committee to oversee future efforts. Not surprisingly, this VIP adventure was a carefully scripted one—U.S. Bureau of Reclamation engineers and local military and civilian personnel had been studying these sites for several years (Schaaf and Fifield 1963, 84). More important than Wheeler's adventure story was his contention that an international basin development scheme in one of the most violently contested regions of the world would bring peace.

For Americans and other modernization advocates who visited the river in the 1960s, things eventually took a turn for the worse as militaries, guerrillas, and violent fighting ended this new venture. Peter White, writing for *National Geographic* in 1968, described the Mekong as a "river of terror and hope," one with rockets and tracers splitting the greenery while soldiers in F4 Phantoms, Swift Boats, and other craft searched out the Việt Cong and their allies (White and Garrett 1968). By 1968, the U.S. alone had invested US$115 million into what

David Lilienthal, architect of the Tennessee Valley Authority (TVA), criticized as an "international pork barrel approach" to development. The coordination implied in the Mekong Coordinating Committee's name had resulted in what Lilienthal called a "crazy managerial patchwork of scattered and unrelated studies" (Lilienthal 1976, 367). Lilienthal meanwhile traveled on to Vietnam where his consulting firm, Development and Resources Corporation, was drawing up plans for a proposed Mekong Delta Development Authority. Significant American commitment to Mekong development ended, however, in 1969 with Richard Nixon's presidency; many smaller initiatives followed until the Saigon and Phnom Penh regimes fell in 1975 (Ekbladh 2002, 369; Nguyen 1999, 167).

With regard to commodities and associated transformations of nature and society, what is interesting about the Mekong is that today the riparian nations, private firms, and international banks are actively reviving many of these old projects, most notably several dams on the Mekong mainstream. In 1997 the Electrical Generating Authority of Thailand (EGAT), once a major recipient of U.S. financial and technical assistance and the operator of several U.S.-funded dams, announced that it would cooperate with private companies to build and operate a dam on the upper Mekong in return for a share in the electrical power generated (International Water Power & Dam Construction 1997). More recently, a Thai consulting firm commenced new rounds of surveys on the lower Mekong, revisiting old sites such as the proposed Pa Mong Dam near Vientiane and Khone Falls near the Laos-Cambodia border (International Water Power & Dam Construction 2005). During travels in the Mekong Delta in 2000, I also witnessed several major reclamation and irrigation projects under way, all of them funded by international banks and based on designs first produced in the early 1970s. The once-scattered vestiges of colonial and cold war–era modernization appear to be reviving themselves, albeit under the guidance of newly emergent Chinese, Thai, and Vietnamese interests.

In this chapter I consider how such seemingly dead projects from the past can come back to life so easily despite significant political, economic, and environmental changes in the region. What factors have preserved a sufficient continuity in large-scale modification to water resources despite often violent regime changes and continuing tensions over heavily patrolled state borders? There is in the Mekong a remarkable persistence of the old ways of doing things—with power residing in the hands of state technocrats and wealthy businessmen, trends toward the colossal rather than the small (Nam Theun II Dam and the Upper Mekong Cascade), and the continued influence of foreign-educated technocrats and foreign consultants.

This persistent influence of reports, agencies, technicians, projects, and companies on the Mekong stems from a process I call *meta-commoditization,* a building of intellectual and physical infrastructures that permits both contemporary and future creations of commodities often regardless of reigning political ideologies.

In outlining a brief history of water-control schemes on the Mekong beginning with French colonial reclamation efforts in the late nineteenth century and continuing through American-backed projects in the 1950s, I intend to explain meta-commoditization historically, arguing that networks connecting people, machines, and designs from past efforts continue to shape present-day interests in building new dams and other projects. There are three component activities involved in meta-commoditization: *reconnaissance,* the collection and publication of data; *mechanization,* importing machines that turn existing water features into hydroelectric dams, flood control and irrigation works; and *legalization,* the production of decrees, treaties, and other documents that continue to carry weight in inter- and intrastate disputes.

The things produced by these actions—for example, data, maps, dams, and legal documents—continue to influence present-day designs and social relationships on the river, contributing to state actions that Vandergeest and Peluso (1995, 390) describe as *territorialization* where rulers and powerful agencies employ maps, machines, and other objects to extend their control over natural resources, especially in hinterlands. However, while territoriality presumes that military juntas, the politburo, or leaders of volatile democracies may be acting for their own political and economic ends, I consider an additional problem: whether the relationships between artifacts or things (and the humans who manage them) also constrain the future designs of states and related political debates. This calls into question the primacy of elite human agency and state politics in struggles over resources and responses to environmental degradation. In his work on Egypt, Timothy Mitchell raises similar questions about human agency in matters of economic development: "Is human agency a disembodied form of reason, observing, calculating, and reorganizing the world before it? Or is it rather more of a technical body, manufactured out of processes that *precede* the difference between ideas and things, between human and nonhuman?" (Mitchell 2002, 10; emphasis added) Like Mitchell, I maintain that the answer lies somewhere in the middle, in the transformative interplay between people, nature, and machines.

In this chapter I offer a historical sketch of the production of work sites, data, maps, and transnational professional communities from colonial to postcolonial eras in the Mekong River valley. These geographically and technically specific things have played formative roles in shaping debates over water power—both in terms of political control over water and in terms of the powerful commodities that water produces. I examine these processes by looking at colonial-era reclamation efforts in the delta and postcolonial studies of dams and other structures upstream. In colonial Cochinchina, French engineers and a private contractor dredged thousands of kilometers of canals to facilitate the expansion of an industrial and plantation economy. French and Siamese negotiations also were instrumental in placing the river within the territorial confines of modern states through navigation treaties; the river upstream became an important boundary separating what might be called the "geo-bodies" of Indochina and Siam (Thong-chai 1994). Colonial products of meta-commoditization—maps, mathematical models, technicians, machines, and infrastructure—played immediately into postcolonial, cold war nation-building efforts.

Hydro-Agricultural Machines

In the Mekong River valley, the first wave of economic and environmental change began a century before the French conquest as Chinese merchants and exile communities in the 1750s developed markets for rice, beeswax, and forest products, creating what Cooke and Li (2004) have called a Chinese water frontier. From the first years of the colonial conquest, the French presence in Indochina relied on this existing network of Chinese merchants and shipping companies to operate wharves and carry goods from the interior to market. The colony's early revenues did not come from commodity production but from taxing the Chinese firms that managed trade in rice, alcohol, salt, and especially opium.

The French colonization of Indochina relied extensively on existing Chinese commercial networks and nineteenth-century Vietnamese roads, canals, and fortifications, building modern works out of these existing frameworks. Since the first French attacks on Saigon in 1859, controlling activity on the waterfront and on waterways was essential. By stringing telegraph lines along the waterways and expanding the French navy's fleet of gunboats, French military commanders built Cochinchina from the water's edge and gradually expanded into the interior.[1] The delta's maze of rivers and creeks enabled *cannonières* to quickly respond to uprisings, and it was out of strategic as well as economic concerns that the government of Cochinchina invested heavily in constructing deeper waterways, connecting the delta's fertile hinterlands more directly with Saigon.

This reference to precolonial Chinese commercial networks and early colonial activities shows that processes of meta-commoditization were certainly already under way even before the colonial conquest; the admiral-governors of Cochinchina made the first moves to expand local infrastructure in the 1870s as Saigon's waterfront expanded and they initiated new hydrographic surveys of the area's rivers. In 1871, the Commission des Arroyos began studies on new water routes, sending military hydrographic engineers such as J. Rénaud out on gunboats to survey possible routes (Brossard de Corbigny 1878, 515). The first canal projects commenced construction in 1875 and were key inland transport links between the Saigon River and rivers in the Mekong Delta. They required several thousand conscripted laborers and dozens of military overseers. Despite spending relatively large sums, colonial engineers were soon disappointed to find that within six or seven months of completion all but one canal had failed due to intense sedimentation caused by the tides (Gouvernement Général de l'Indochine 1911, 84).

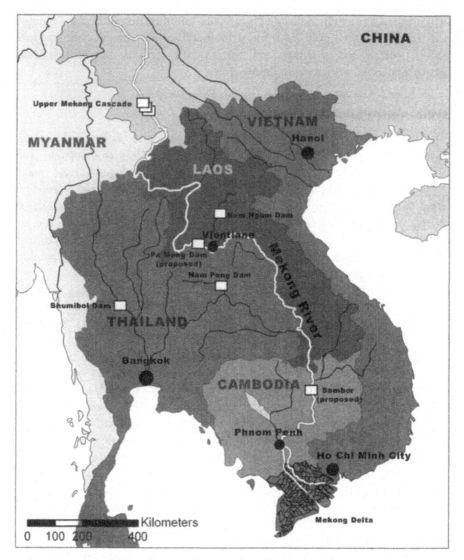

Figure 6.1. Mekong Valley dams and canals. The map shows the dams mentioned in this chapter and the dense network of canals dredged in the colonial era. Almost two dozen other tributary dams have been completed on Mekong tributaries and neighboring rivers. Credit: D. Biggs.

In the wake of mounting French opposition at home and continuing unrest in Vietnam and Cambodia, all of this nation building might have ended had a more liberal French government not been organized in 1879, putting the colony under civilian rule and resituating public works and other activities under the new guidelines of a *mission civilisatrice*. The civilian governor called for a more comprehensive study of delta waterways that would benefit both French and native interests while he expanded public institutions and ordered his public works engineers to expand construction of urban waterworks and market buildings. In this new reconnaissance effort, French engineers not only mapped the delta's rivers but also paid special attention to works produced by earlier regimes. Even in technical reports, engineers expressed their concerns that failing to build new waterways would not only undermine colonial economic interests but also threaten to erase "the work of civilization" initiated by Vietnamese governors and Chinese merchants in the past (Rénaud 1879, 66). Such statements by technicians echoed a common interest in documenting Vietnamese customs, traditional land rules, and historical landmarks such as roads, canals, and fortresses.

Reconnaissance should be viewed not only as producing data necessary to support future projects but also as connecting new projects to what engineers such as Rénaud perceived to be the existing social and physical landscape. Defining and categorizing old projects, commemorative steles, and property codes coincided with measuring channel beds and producing mathematical models; all of these actions were important to structuring a colonial image of the region's environmental and social past in a quasi-imagined, quasi-material community. Somewhat different from Anderson's (1991) notion of an "imagined community," this picture of the delta landscape, however badly interpreted, was nonetheless connected to real things—roads, forts, old canals, historic makers—with definitive physical properties.

The pivotal factor in the colony's decision to build waterways was the introduction of steam-powered dredging in the 1890s. Such machines consumed a wide path through the forests and swamps, traveling approximately one hundred fifty meters daily, and they replaced the trouble of controlling thousands of forced laborers with the convenience of a paid crew of less than a hundred. These new machines converted the work of digging canals into numbers and equations in the same manner that railroads did; progress and efficiency could be measured in terms of cost per cubic meter, accounting for capital and labor expenses and considering projected profits from transportation and irrigated agriculture per hectare. Dredges were the ultimate colonial "anti-politics machine" in Cochinchina, to use James Ferguson's (1990) term. The apparatus of men—French, native, skilled, and unskilled—and machines involved here so radically altered the social and ecological terms in which people managed water resources that it was difficult to oppose them. The dredgers, built in Paris yards along with other equipment such as several thousand meters of steel bridges erected by Gustave Eiffel's company, also increased French support for colonization because it benefited industrialists and skilled labor alike. The introduction of a public-works monopoly contractor likewise changed the economic and political terms of dredging, redirecting the bulk of capital invested in public works into companies headquartered in France (Vietnam National Archives Center No. 2 [VNA2]

1893). Montvenoux, a firm in the Loire Valley, was the only one to respond with a bid and a year later assembled the first three steam-powered dredges in Saigon (Gouvernement Général de l'Indochine 1911, 70).

Dredges and associated colonial machines—water pumps, rapid transit ships, and milling equipment—produced a new, short-lived frontier society in the wake of the dredges. Sitting high atop the dredge (see fig. 6.2) the usual crew of three Europeans—the engineer, captain, and chief mechanic—floated high above while Vietnamese, Khmer, and Chinese workers below cleared away stumps and finished banks in the wake of the clanking, smoking contraption. With such a distancing (anti-political) machine, the French pushed colonial roads and waterways into the most distant reaches of the delta with little significant resistance.

Turning this new web of waterways into a manageable system, however, perpetually eluded the French engineers. Each new canal brought complications to the existing network. The unprecedented and rapid scale of construction radically altered existing irrigation works, especially those built on the natural network of tidal creeks. As one observer noted early on in 1880, canals were "works of Penelope," costly projects that had no apparent end (Social Sciences Library—Hanoi 1881).[2] Dredging also frequently disrupted or destroyed existing villages, burying them under tons of mud, and waves of new settlers cut or burned forests that before 1880 had covered roughly a quarter of the delta's area (VNA2 1904).

Figure 6.2. Standing atop Dredge II at a height of some twenty meters are the three Europeans in charge of the project: the Public Works observer, the dredge captain, and the chief mechanic. Credit: Gouvernement Général de l'Indochine 1930, 29.

As dredging, settlement, and deforestation continued in the first decades of the twentieth century, engineers and their allies in government became involved in an increasingly complicated effort to shore up the water infrastructure.

The third aspect of river colonization, legalization, coincided with dredging as both natives and *colons* (a French term for colonizer, typically a plantation owner) brought complaints for damages to colonial courtrooms. These challenges over time resulted in decrees and rulings that more clearly delimited public, French, and indigenous property. One of the first large projects, Xà No Canal, cut through two of the most densely settled villages—Nhơn Ái and Nhơn Nghĩa—in the delta. The combined population in these two densely settled villages was more than four times that of the nearby colonial town, Cần Thơ (VNA2 1900). Local residents (including some who were naturalized French citizens) challenged the government to clearly define the terms of compensation for the destruction of crops. The leader of Nhơn Nghĩa village complained about damages and petitioned the government to allow him to cut a new opening to bring water back to the village. The chief engineer refused and the matter passed eventually to the governor-general in Hanoi. In deciding between several hundred farmers and a major French investment, the governor-general maintained rather creatively that the new canal-front property produced new commercial opportunities for the landowners that far outweighed the temporary losses caused to them by damage to their crops (VNA2 1902). Hundreds of such decisions over time more clearly delineated the boundaries between private and public domains. Water, flowing through the rivers and canals, was unquestionably the domain of the state, and this situation arguably continues today. Decrees and court decisions complemented the work of machines in forcing villagers to join the new economy or risk being left behind.

These processes of reconnaissance, mechanization, and legalization continued repeatedly into the 1940s, albeit with mounting political, environmental, and economic criticism coming from both colonial and indigenous groups concerned with widening economic and ecological crises. In the 1930s, colonial officials were especially concerned with alarming trends in land abandonment and increases in Communist-led organizing among the poorest tenants. The rapid expansion of waterways in the French model—what was largely a network of stagnant or polluted water—had turned many wetlands and forests into treeless wastes. Over two million migrants had come to the delta since 1880 with hopes of owning land and improving their economic standing; by 1934, most were in inescapable debt and often living in slavery-like conditions under powerful, mostly indigenous colonial landlords (VNA2 1944).

During World War II and especially the First Indochina War that followed, economic conditions worsened as the government sent fewer dredges to repair waterways and fighting destroyed many key points in the water infrastructure. The colonial landscape and the products of colonial-era meta-commoditization—dredgers, highways, railroads, dams, plantations, and ports—were especially targeted by insurgents who recognized that these things not only enabled troop movements and commerce but also reinforced liberal economic ideologies. Insurgents, however, were not antimachine; in fact, they often depended on them for their own movement, and visions of a nationalist future typically included increased industrialization. One elderly Việt Minh veteran, for example, reiterated his respect for Western technology when I asked him about a former French plantation located near where he lived. The veteran, Diều, was quick to condemn the owner for his allegiance to the French administration, but then he praised this colon's irrigation operations with the greatest compliment: "very scientific" rất khoa học.[3]

In 1904, Rémy Gressier installed steam-powered water pumps and sluice gates on a one kilometer by one kilometer grid of canals dug across his fifty-six-square-kilometer estate. He founded company towns at each one kilometer intersection of the main canal with a company store selling goods for company scrip in each center. Like rubber plantations in the hills north of Saigon, village names corresponded to their distance from the property's boundary—One Thousand Hamlet [Ấp Một Ngàn], Two Thousand Hamlet [Ấp Hai Ngàn], and so forth. Over the decades he added a six-story mill, an airstrip, a maternity clinic, and briefly operated a vocational center to train local youth (Société Géographiquede l'Indochine 1925; VNA2 1936). Although the land has been redistributed into small parcels since 1975, the villages still retain their original names.

Americans on the Mekong

Although the story of American technical advisers working on the Mekong is generally associated with dam projects and located upstream, the first commitments of American machinery and personnel occurred in Vietnam, especially the delta region where covert field agents and on-loan technical advisers such as Wolf Ladejinsky began to study the strategic and economic challenges of rehabilitating the delta's hydro-agricultural infrastructure to support nation-building efforts in Vietnam (Ladejinsky 1955).[4] The major agency responsible for these projects was the U.S. Operations Mission (USOM). Located generally within the confines of the U.S. embassy, USOM offices in Southeast Asia emerged in the 1950s as sprawling centers for managing both covert operations and aid projects. From 1950 to 1975, they fostered thousands of exchanges among local officials, engineers, contractors, scientists, and academics involved in related projects across the entire region.

The problems that American modernizers and their South Vietnamese colleagues encountered in their attempts to rebuild the delta's infrastructure after 1954 illustrate the complex ways that older, colonial-era networks of machines, documents, and people persisted despite unprecedented increases in U.S. aid to South Vietnam. For example, USOM-Saigon delivered two brand-new dredges in 1955, but it relied extensively on the old French monopoly contractor to

operate them and to train new Vietnamese technical staff. Given the comparatively higher wages offered by contractors, Vietnamese trainees tended to stay
on with the French contractor rather than move to public service. Although the
South Vietnamese Public Works Ministry eventually took control of all these
dredges after 1960, American construction firms soon entered the scene with
their own dredges and continued the private competition for skilled labor during
the American military occupation (VNA2 1966, 7).

Although American civil and military involvement greatly altered the scale of
construction (and destruction) after 1954, it did not significantly reverse earlier processes of meta-commoditization. In particular, failures to address legal
problems of land redistribution seriously weakened later efforts to win local support. The rapid escalation in American military involvement complicated rather
than corrected colonial-era processes. Waves of new machines—bulldozers, road-
building equipment, airplanes, and small engines—dramatically expanded a bureaucratic apparatus in South Vietnam that was still not prepared to handle the
volume of work.

Where Americans played a more formative role in altering the river was upstream in areas that before 1945 had been largely ignored by the French and Thai
governments. The American interest in building dams on the Mekong, however,
was somewhat accidental. The U.S. Bureau of Reclamation had already trained
several dozen Chinese engineers before 1945 in anticipation of building dams on
the Yangtze (not far from the present-day Three Gorges Dam). Completion of
Hoover Dam in 1936 drew scores of foreign visitors, especially from India and
China.[5] In 1939, the Bureau's state-of-the-art Hydraulics Laboratory in Denver
trained more than a dozen Chinese engineers in preparation for constructing
large concrete dams in the world's biggest potential market. As wartime conditions permitted in 1944, more engineers and officials from China came to Denver. Even Soviet engineers visited before 1945, traveling on what at the time was
a sort of hydraulic pilgrimage: Hoover Dam, Grand Coulee Dam, the Tennessee
Valley Authority, and the Hydraulics Lab in Denver. John L. Savage, chief design
engineer of Hoover Dam, even traveled to China in 1944 to initiate surveys there
(National Archives and Records Administration—Denver [NARA-D] 1950b).

With the collapse of the Nationalist Chinese government on the mainland in
1949, the interest of the United States in promoting hydroelectric and irrigation
projects rapidly shifted to China's periphery: to Northeast and Southeast Asia.
Responding to President Truman's Point IV Program to quickly aid modernization efforts in the third world, the Bureau of Reclamation initiated the World Reconnaissance Survey to identify potential hydro projects in the developing world,
especially in Thailand, the Philippines, and Indonesia (NARA-D 1950a). With
this new interest in containing Soviet and Chinese influence in the region, a new
wave of reconnaissance and training efforts commenced in the Mekong River
Basin to identify future sites for dams there.

Like the French in Indochina, this surge in American reconnaissance led to new legal and mechanical interventions, most notably the creation of multilateral committees and the involvement of multinational corporations as contractors to agencies and national governments. Truman repeatedly directed funding and technical assistance through international agencies so that this reconnaissance effort at least appeared on the surface to be international. On the Mekong, the responsible international agency for development was the United Nations Economic Commission on Asia and the Far East (ECAFE) headquartered in Bangkok. This public multilateral office, however, was overshadowed by the increasingly heavy presence of American military units throughout the region. USOM—Bangkok effectively became the center for all U.S. modernization efforts in the region while Vietnam increasingly turned into a battlefield. What advisers frequently called "the Mission" in Bangkok became a key player with ECAFE and the Mekong Committee in sponsoring surveys (Biggs 2006).

The Mekong Coordinating Committee, established by ECAFE and the riparian nations in 1957, resulted in a transfer of U.S.-initiated efforts to a less controversial multilateral institution. With the exception of a few dams constructed in Thailand and Laos, most of the Mekong Coordinating Committee's efforts until 1975 were reconnaissance missions. Construction was limited to several tributary projects such as Nam Pong in Thailand and Nam Ngum in Laos, and these construction projects were typically dependent on unilateral American aid with contracts for design and construction going for the most part to American firms. Given high levels of violence along the Mekong, there were few opportunities to commit funds, equipment, and people to build megadams such as the Pa Mong Dam on the main stream between Thailand and Laos.

Nevertheless, a very profound kind of meta-commoditization occurred in this enormous survey effort, preparing for a posthostility scenario that never materialized. Several thousand foreign experts and technicians, especially Americans, worked as contractors for U.S. and UN agencies on these projects. Their efforts centered on the proposed cascade of dams, but work across the river valley extended to related problems such as land reform, resettlement, and agricultural mechanization. As with French colonial public works in the delta, the most lucrative aspect of these projects was not realizing increased production in rice, electricity, or other commodities so much as the highly lucrative work of building infrastructure and consulting—meta-commoditization—that would allow the production of such commodities in the future. Equipment manufacturers, construction and engineering companies, and American citizens, especially liberals, supported modernization—just as French republicans had in 1879—under the premise that economic development might end ongoing military struggles peacefully.

This does not mean, however, that because they did not succeed in building the megadams they did not transform nature or society during this time. The extensive reconnaissance efforts of Americans and others produced many influential things that changed lives and environments in the region. Experts not only produced maps and data but they trained local residents and brought waves of imported machines to the region, especially small-scale water pumps, motorcycles, and generators. Also, while there may be some similarities between American policies on modernization and the French *mission civilisatrice,* the social and environmental transformations that occurred during the American era were often not the intended outcomes of American designs. Where Michael Adas has shown the endurance of an American civilizing credo based on repeated stories of technological dominance overseas (Adas 2006, 31), the reality then was that actual social and environmental changes often differed greatly from projected outcomes of specific projects. Peculiar, unexpected things often happened at project sites where maps, reports, and machines as well as the experts who learned to use them often moved in directions counter to American strategic interests. Many American members of the large community of experts charged with carrying out modernization programs even opposed U.S. government interests after working in the field for some time.

Perhaps the single best instance of this more complicated approach to reconnaissance concerns the work coordinated by American and UN agencies on Pa Mong Dam. Pa Mong was to be the centerpiece of the Mekong Cascade project, several times larger than Hoover Dam. It was to be President Lyndon B. Johnson's demonstration of peaceful U.S. intervention. In explaining to college students in 1965 why he was committing troops to Vietnam, he highlighted his administration's commitment to dams such as Pa Mong that would become America's "footprint" in the region, providing "food and water and power on a scale to dwarf even our own TVA" (U.S. Government Printing Office 1966). The scores of reports, sociological studies, pamphlets, and press releases that resulted from over twelve years of study on this project offer an interesting glimpse into the particulars of one modernization scheme.

The reconnaissance effort included Bureau of Reclamation preliminary studies, geological surveys, anthropological studies commissioned by USOM-Bangkok, and studies by the Ford Foundation. Taken as a whole, this collection of documents presents an incredibly fragmented picture of American modernization efforts, suggesting what Latham (2000) has described as competing "modernization ideologies" at work. One of the most important reports to run counter to U.S. government activities on the site was a Ford Foundation report by geographer Gilbert White published in 1962. This report expressed concern that the dam should not only be profitable in terms of generating electricity and storing water but that it also should bring immediate, substantial benefits to several hundred thousand people who would have to move from flooded valleys (White et al. 1962; Pa Mong Resettlement Research Project 1982).

American social scientists such as White introduced new social and psychological factors that in turn forced planners to recognize the political and social costs of resettlement associated with the dams. Like engineers, social scientists also brought their own ideological baggage with them, notably a tendency to rely on colonial-era ethnographic depictions of local people and their perceived ability to adopt new technologies associated with the hydroelectric dams. Such studies, often funded by USOM-Bangkok and later by the U.S. Agency for International Development, echoed popular colonial assertions about the inevitable path of development (civilization) from subsistence to traditional resource management. One study in 1969 even suggested that these different stages of development might apply generally to local states, contrasting Thai farming methods as "traditional water management" and Lao methods as "subsistence" (McDole 1969, 56). Another new voice in the reconnaissance effort was that of systems theorists. Like social scientists, they often criticized traditional engineering analyses for factoring out social costs, but their solutions typically called for more calculations based on computer-run algorithms (Ingersoll 1969). Although construction on Pa Mong had not yet commenced, several tributary dams were completed in this era, presenting opportunities to consider how instances of mechanization and legalization affected people on the smaller rivers. Nam Pong, a smaller tributary dam near Khon Kaen, Thailand, triggered widespread and unregulated clearing of upland slopes above the reservoir as thousands of farmers who were resettled from the valleys abandoned their resettlement zones and cut down the woods to survive (Huddle 1972, 93). The sale of irrigated land below the Nam Ngum Dam in Laos led to increased tenancy rates as military officers in Vientiane purchased title to the land from resettled farmers in exchange for allowing them to stay on the land and cultivate it (Southeast Asia Technology Company Ltd. 1978). Such dams, like canals in Cochinchina, delineated new boundaries between modern and traditional spaces, state and private property, and they ultimately concentrated ownership and wealth in the hands of wealthy urbanites while dislocating or impoverishing farmers.

Problems with the smaller dams and increasing violence after the 1968 Tet Offensive prompted the United States to reduce its financial and technical commitments to the Mekong Committee. The committee had already been in serious jeopardy with Cambodia's threat of withdrawal in 1968–69, and U.S. decisions to withdraw military forces from Vietnam in 1972 further weakened prospects for the construction of projects such as Pa Mong. The mood in Washington in 1972 had also changed, becoming strongly opposed to the war and to large infrastructure projects such as Pa Mong (Huddle 1972, 25).

Before leaving the topic of Americans on the Mekong, however, it is important to leave megadams for a moment and briefly consider how everyday life on the river changed in this period. Several million small internal combustion engines dramatically reshaped the water environment and local societies in this period. The four-horsepower and six-horsepower Kohler engines introduced by the American manufacturer in response to USAID programs stimulated a kind of hydrological and environmental revolution across the region that has to date received little if any attention. From their introduction in the early 1960s, such small machines became essential for families living in the war zones of Vietnam. One veteran in the Mekong Delta told stories of guerrillas escaping American jets strafing a free-fire zone by lifting the motorized propeller up and down to cut through thick mats of water hyacinth to reach cover.[6] These motors traveled readily across ideological lines and became important fixtures in rebel bases. Today, one often finds them in provincial history museums along with AK-47s, models of improvised explosive devices, and photographs commemorating the guerrilla wars of resistance. Such machines contributed to a radical shift in patterns of individual transportation and by 1974 even contributed to noticeable variations in water conditions where an estimated one million small engines were being used as improvised pumps for small-scale flood control in the delta (Netherlands Delta Development Team 1974). While American planners' attentions were generally focused on large dams and colossal structures such as Pa Mong, several million smaller machines played a significant role in the region's political struggles and ecological changes.

Meta-Commoditization and the Agency of Things

With the fall of the Saigon and Phnom Penh governments in 1975, construction of dams and other waterworks ceased to be a subject of much international concern until the late 1990's when nations and companies in the lower Mekong returned to prospects for building large structures on the river. The simple conclusion in light of this is that these new projects are simply being re-packaged from earlier American and even colonial-era "footprints." Arguing for this kind of historical and political continuity, however, greatly overemphasizes the role of the colonial state or American advisors in these matters and assumes an implausible continuity of state agendas from one era to another. John Perkins's best-seller *Confessions of an Economic Hit Man* (2004) makes a compelling case for such a history of covert policies propelled by international banks, U.S. agencies, and corporations colluding to engineer dependency through pushing expensive loans for projects such as dams. Although I find it plausible that many Americans, Thais, Vietnamese, Chinese, and others have schemed (and continue to scheme) to secure big-ticket projects for personal or political reasons, the "hit man" argument leaves several million people and their agro-environments as little more than victims to these appropriations. As Anna Tsing and others in this book show, closer investigation on the ground shows that farmers, loggers, factory workers, and others have been anything but passive in these recent processes of commoditization. Furthermore, political and economic alliances among elites in the region are so turbulent it is hard to believe that associations of powerful business and political leaders dating back to the 1950s are still responsible for realizing old colonial and cold war-era designs in the region today.

Perhaps the historical persistence of old projects has less to do with decisions at the top of society than with the complex webs of human and technological interactions at the middle and bottom. Certain technologies, such as internal combustion engines, have become so fundamental to daily patterns of life since 1960 that they have fundamentally altered political and economic choices at the bottom and middle of society. This more distributed approach to understanding the role of technology and materials in human societies has been a central topic for actor-network theory (ANT), a material-semiotic approach in science and technology studies that argues that complex and repeated interactions between different human groups, technologies, and natures produce environmental, po-litical, and social change (Latour 2005; Law 1992). Responding to ANT's more contentious argument for the agency of things, I do not propose that things in themselves—soil cores drilled in 1968, a still-working Caterpillar bulldozer from 1958, or even key plant and animal species—have agency. However, ANT's focus on the power of relationships between human communities and such things sug-gests a novel way to approach the kinds of problems covered in this book. Meta-commoditization and its products—maps, dam designs, 4 hp engines, reservoirs, property claims—produce both material and semiotic networks that may survive over decades despite frequent political upheavals at the top. The power of these networks or relations is perhaps most visible at the middle and lower economic rungs of society. A man or woman who has acquired a boat engine, for example, has a greater range of movement, can more easily escape in times of trouble, and may even prevent flood damage to crops by strapping that motor to a crude water pump. However, greater agency also comes with a price as the owner of such a motor depends on spare parts, imported fuels, and low fuel prices.

The idea of meta-commoditization proposed here is intended to redirect at-tention from powerful elite players such as the World Bank or autocratic govern-ments to consider instead the region's broader physical- and knowledge-based infrastructures and their deep roots in the colonial and postcolonial past. The three processes that I have described—reconnaissance, mechanization and legalization—have produced and re-produced important connections between human communities and technologies at specific sites. These relationships devel-oped both within and outside the world of economic hit men and engineering leaders such as General Wheeler. To understand how commodities are changing the lives of people in Southeast Asia, it is important to follow these relation-ships beyond the lives of autocratic rulers or internationally known figures from sites of initial formation to eventual locations in government archives, around abandoned project sites and in individual households. By following middle-level adventurers such as technical adviser Lyle Mabbott, who traveled the world su-pervising dam studies including that of Pa Mong, one finds a more widespread yet intimate history of exchange with local colleagues who in turn supervised local technicians operating fleets of imported equipment (White and Garrett 1968).

These professional associations and travels helped to transmit what Theodore Porter (1995) calls a "culture of objectivity" to the region that is still alive today. While prime ministers, presidents, and even governments come and go, these more intimate technological and social relationships formed between equipment vendors, boat drivers, engineers, and others have persisted and deserve greater attention before the watery threads in Penelope's robe unravel faster than they can be repaired.

7

Contested Commodifications

Struggles over Nature in a National Park

TANIA MURRAY LI

A national park is supposed to be pristine nature, a place where flora and fauna are left to thrive without disturbance. For many advocates of conservation, the wildness of this kind of nature imbues it with a particular kind of value—an intrinsic value, the value of a global heritage, a priceless treasure. For them, a park is the ultimate noncommodity. If they discuss the commodity value of the services nature provides, it is not to assert the commodity status of nature itself, but as a tactic to promote the survival of parks in a world dominated by commodity thinking.[1] Further, despite the structural similarity between the enclosure of a park and the enclosure of a plantation—a similarity especially visible for the victims of such an enclosure—conservationists do not see their projects in these terms. As Peluso and Nevins point out in their introduction, conservationists see their effort as part of what Karl Polanyi (2001, 141) called a countermovement—the endeavor to protect the noncommodity status of the elements essential to the maintenance of life. Yet the projects of establishing both the wildness and the noncommodity status of a park are best understood as just that—as projects, not as established facts. They are seriously unconvincing to the people most affected by these renderings of nature, namely, people living in the vicinity of parks who pay a tangible price for conservation when they are excluded from the use of park resources. In this chapter I explore contestations around the wildness and the noncommodity status of protected nature, drawing on a case study of Sulawesi's Lore Lindu National Park.

The term *project* twists together two threads of meaning: (1) the verb to project—to imagine or fantasize a particular scenario, as a slide show projects images on a blank screen; (2) the noun, a project, a purposive activity intended to bring about definite results. As Cronon (1996) and others have pointed out, nature-as-wilderness is projected in these ways. It invokes the fantastical notion of the untouched, yet it needs to be produced by practices of enclosing land, excluding farmers, and erasing signs of human labor and habitation. In the same manner people, if they are to be included in a park, must be projected as nature-loving, and produced to conform. Park border villagers, as I will show, have a counterproject, namely, to reclaim the right to use and sell park resources. They also have a counterprojection, as they imagine that people professing an interest in conservation are driven by the search for economic gain.

Counterprojections

Villagers who live around the Lore Lindu National Park and draw part of their livelihoods from it do not see the park as a noncommodity. They see it rather as a site of struggle in which different commodifications contend. They them- *such a* selves are fully involved in a market economy. Working under the protection *blatant* of and with financing from well-placed officials and entrepreneurs, they extract *statement* timber and rattan from the park for sale. They also clear patches of forest to *on people's* grow commodities: coffee, since the colonial period, and cacao since the 1990s, *behalf* when Sulawesi became one of the world's largest producers. In the past they also grew food there. Market values circa 2000 were such that the main objective of park-border villagers was growing cacao, a brown gold offering the prospect of money to pay for food, school fees, better houses and clothes, and other desirable goods. When conservation organizations attempted to stop them from carrying out their market-oriented activities, villagers attributed their motives not to the protection of the park as a noncommodity but to an alternate commodification that competed with their own. In the villagers' projection they were "small people" oppressed by greedy and powerful outsiders who wanted to profit from the park's resources at their expense.

I caught a glimpse of the villagers' counterprojection in 2003 when I heard park-border villagers offer a literal translation for the conservationists' claim that the park was "the property of the world," or a "global biodiversity resource." Villagers informed me that government officials had sold the park or divided it up between "nine nations" as payment or guarantee for Indonesia's foreign debts. Their tale of "nine nations" probably referred to an Asian Development Bank loan of US$32 million to the government of Indonesia, represented by the Forest Department, for an "integrated conservation and development" project that was supposed to protect the park. As the villagers imagined it, officials had mortgaged the park to the foreigners in return for project funds. If the conditions of the loan were not met—if the park was not protected—the foreigners would retrieve their money by laying claim to the park itself. The villagers were convinced that the foreigners had profit motives. If they did not want to profit from the park, why would they want to control it? Behind the talk of conservation, villagers suspected the foreigners wanted to sell off the park's genetic resources or mine there for gold.

The villagers also projected profit motives onto the officials who stood to gain from the existence of the ADB project and its associated income streams. As they saw it, officials had used a techno-scientific rationale as a ploy to withdraw sources of livelihood from villagers in order to create sources of livelihood for themselves. They knew for sure that some corrupt officials already were profiting from the park by organizing the "illegal" timber and rattan extraction. In relation to this particular commodification—one in which some villagers also participated—their objection was framed in terms of fairness and matters of scale.

"We are true to the constitution," a villager named Pak Ratu informed me. "The constitution says the land and water belong to the people, for their well-being. . . . It is the officials who are breaking the law. If we are wrong, they are more wrong. The logging companies steal timber on a big scale. Why are only the small people faulted? It should be fair." Pak Ratu had been sent to attend Indonesia's preparatory meeting for the 2002 Johannesburg environment confer-ence (a decade after Rio), an experience that had broadened his critical vocabu-lary. "Political ecology," he said, "means 'who is it for.'" At issue for Pak Ratu was not whether the park should be commodified, but whose commodifying practices would prevail—a question intimately related to who would reap the profits, and who would pay the price.

Contested commodifications also entered into the sad story told to me by Mama Yonas, a woman living inside the park on land that she had occupied in concert with a thousand households claiming to be landless and calling them-selves the Free Farmers Forum.

> We didn't have land [in the valley]. We were share-cropping sawah [wet rice fields]. To get somewhere, you need to have land. So in 2000 we decided to try in the park. We came in with twenty people, to clear two hectares. The usual pay was 5,000 rupiah but I offered my workers 10,000 rupiah because the work was hard—they had to cut big trees.
>
> Then a party of forest guards came by, fifteen of them. They came to my hut. I was getting the food ready for the workers. The workers ran to hide. They thought I had been arrested. So I gave the guards coffee and food. They stayed for one hour to eat. Then they said, "It's time for us to go. Do you know this is inside the park?" I said I know, but I need to eat. They asked me what I planned to plant. I told them candlenuts, cacao, durian, to replace the trees. I said I have nothing in [the valley]. They said, "Excuse us now" [i.e., they politely took their leave]. Then they started hacking at my hut and everything I had planted, cut it all to pieces, burned it down. I cried. I said, "God will see you. You have no pity." They just smiled. My cacao, coffee, chili peppers, they pulled it all up.
>
> I asked them, "Don't you eat chilies too? We are just going to grow crops, not take the land." They said, "You can't do that here, this place belongs to lots of na-tions" [banyak Negara yang pegang ini]. So I thought, does this belong to Indonesia or to some other country? If it belongs to Indonesia, it belongs to me too. Then

they left. My workers came back, and went right back to work, because I had already paid them. They went back to work, clearing the forest, brave—until it was all done. It was cleared, but we hadn't planted yet.[2] *And then what happened!?*

What Mama Yonas asserted was not a right to customary land, or to use nature in "customary" ways. It was an entitlement to land as a basis for livelihood in the context of a market economy. This kind of claim has been especially problematic for the park authorities and conservation organizations because it is difficult to contain. The livelihood needs of Sulawesi villagers are infinite, as is the population that might want a share of the park land to farm. Villagers all around the park circa 2000 were indeed making bold claims, cutting down trees to plant the new boom crop, cacao. They justified their actions in terms of customary rights to land used by their ancestors, wrongfully stolen from them when the park boundaries were demarcated or, as in the case of Mama Yonas, on the grounds of the right of citizens to access the resources needed for a decent life. The involvement of foreigners and the language of global values only strengthened their sense of local entitlement.

— dude this is indigeneity. Doromir is wrong.

I will now contextualize villagers' counterprojections in the history of agrarian relations in this part of Sulawesi, and then examine the conservationists' project of producing the right kind of natives to fit the niche in nature potentially available to villagers living in and around the Lore Lindu National Park—natives who would opt for conservation over profit.

Sulawesi Highlanders and Other Awkward Subjects

In his magisterial book *Nature's Government: Science, Imperial Britain, and the Improvement of the World*, Richard Drayton stresses the centrality of the idea of the profligate native in the justification of colonialism—the idea that "whoever was on the spot was wasting its resources, and...might legitimately be expelled, or submitted to European tutelage" (2000, 232). This myth is alive and well in national bureaucracies and transnational agencies that promote agricultural development and conservation. As Peluso and Nevins observe, it continues to be used to justify dispossession. Ruling regimes backed by science use a particular population's failure to improve (to turn nature's bounty to a profit) or to conserve (to protect nature for the common good) as justification to reassign resources to parties capable of making proper use of them.[3]

In Sulawesi, the first part of the myth of the profligate native—the failure of natives to turn resources to a profit—is rather easily refuted by reference to the villagers' evident proficiency in and commitment to market-oriented production. Yet this refutation runs up against well-intentioned efforts to defend villagers from the second part of the myth—that which accuses them of being poor stewards of nature. Although a few villagers have benefited from presenting themselves as nature-loving natives capable of contributing to conservation goals, most find this niche highly constrained. For conservationists prepared to include villagers in park management, Sulawesi highlanders are awkward subjects. Some background will help to explain why this is so.

For more than a century, villagers in Central Sulawesi have been enthusiastic commodity producers. They needed no coercion to take them to market—so long as the price and the conditions were just. In the highlands, which was subdued by conquest around 1910, Christian missions and the edifice of colonial administration depended on the capacity of the natives to pay taxes, school tuition, and church dues. Thus highlanders were coerced into coffee production in the early years, but they became keen producers of the crop as soon as flexible market channels were established and the price increased. In the Palu Valley colonial officials required every household to plant fifty coconut trees and an extra ten per additional family member (Weber, Faust, and Kreisel 2003, 414). Yet their coercion was superfluous: farmers in the Palu Valley had been planting coconuts since the seventeenth century, and they relied on the copra and oil as a source of income and a means to pay tribute. From the 1880s onward they planted millions more trees in response to good prices. Enthusiasm for commercial crops continued after conquest. Indeed, colonial officials observed this enthusiasm, since they issued further instructions that food production should not be neglected.[4] Concern that villagers would neglect food production in favor of commodities was a frequent refrain in the colonial archive across Southeast Asia, especially in the uplands. The problem, as officials saw it, was not how to make villagers into market subjects, but how to prevent them from responding to booming prices in ways that threatened colonial interests by stimulating large-scale migrations, increasing the need for imported food, outcompeting plantation-based production, or causing villagers to withhold their labor from the plantation economy.[5] The struggle—then as now—was not over forcing produce onto the market, but over the distribution of costs and benefits.

Specifically in relation to the Lore Lindu National Park, struggles over the costs and benefits of market-oriented production intensified in the late 1990s as smallholder enthusiasm for cacao threatened the project of nature conservation. The reason for this particular threat was local and specific, situated as it was at the conjuncture of several forces: (1) a massive rise in the price of cacao related to the crash of the rupiah in 1997–1998; (2) the low capital, low-tech character of cacao in its early stages, making it ideal as a smallholder crop: in 2001, 80 percent of Indonesia's cacao production was smallholder based; (3) an increase in population in the vicinity of the park, caused by poorly planned resettlement schemes and the spontaneous migration of smallholders seeking land for cacao; (4) processes of agrarian differentiation among smallholders, as some accumulated land and others were effectively dispossessed; (5) large-scale enclosures of land for plantations and the state-claimed forest, closing off the avenue of retreat—and of

[handwritten: ⌐ landless move into the park]

hope—for the landless; (6) increased enforcement of park boundaries as transnational conservation agencies supplied financing to step up park protection.[6]

This was the context in which landless farmers such as Mama Yonas took desperate measures to reclaim land from the park for smallholder production of cacao, at the risk of violent eviction—her own bitter experience. But enforcement could not keep pace with the pressure presented by thousands of land-hungry would-be cacao producers in the villages surrounding the park. It was in this context that the park-based conservation lobby, headed by The Nature Conservancy, set to work on another front: projecting park-border villagers as nature-loving allies in conservation and seeking to make their behavior conform by misrecognizing—and curbing—their market-oriented activities.

Making Categories Real

[handwritten: why the quotes, they are natives]

In the context of the villagers' interest in cacao, the project of producing nature-loving "natives" of a kind suited for inclusion in the park's management regime seems especially heroic. From the perspective of conservation experts concerned about the park, its natural landscapes should either be uninhabited or populated by people whose livelihoods and identities could be assimilated to nature. This assimilation is a projection, what Larry Lohman (1993) calls a "green orientalism" that involves making up an exotic story about a certain group of people and then imposing this fantasy on them.[7] Natives are nature loving; otherwise, they are not real natives. Yet producing natives to fit the slot conservationists have devised is no easy task.

Classificatory schemes, as Timothy Mitchell (2002) points out, are not models of the world, they are models for it. Arguably, producing suitably nature-loving natives is more difficult than producing disciplined labor, a project that can be accomplished by coercive means, including absolute dispossession. In the case of Lore Lindu, people living in and around the park had some choices. It was not easy to make them conform. Here I analyze the efforts of one conservation organization, The Nature Conservancy (TNC), and the elaborate scheme for natural-native production outlined in its 2001 draft management plan for the park.[8]

Faced with villagers' challenge to the legitimacy of the park and its boundaries and their desire to commodify park resources their way, TNC devised a containment strategy that focused on the system of park zonation. Since it was impossible to exclude people from the park entirely, TNC's goal was to confine human activities to the Traditional Use Zone, which made up 13 percent of the park's land area. Yet this was not simply a matter of acknowledging the villagers' existing practices and claims. The purpose of the Traditional Use Zone, according to the 1990 Conservation Law, was to allow "limited resource extraction of locally occurring species" (TNC 2002b, 2:100). The use zone had as its imagined subject traditional villagers gathering indigenous resources for use in

[handwritten right margin: see now this is your first problem!]

traditional, noncommercial ways. This concept fits uneasily with the reality of resource use inside the park. Nevertheless, for TNC fit had to be attempted in order to contain the villagers' challenge. The use-zone concept provided some room for maneuver and compromise. TNC expected that park-border villagers who were granted access to the Traditional Use Zone would be willing to sign conservation agreements binding them to stop agricultural "encroachment," timber extraction, and other "illegal" activities in a quid pro quo. For this to work, actors and activities suitable for the use zone had to be identified. This was much easier said than done.

One obvious problem was that many of the resources present in the park and valued by villagers are not actually indigenous—they are exotic. Ecologists advising TNC produced a long list of exotics that should ideally be eliminated both from the park and, even more contentiously, from surrounding villages. The list included coffee, cacao, dogs, cats, chilies, carp, deer, tilapia, and water buffalo (TNC 2002b, 2:65, 178). A second major problem was that the use-zone provision prohibits commercial extraction of resources (TNC 2002b, 2:69). It assumes that traditional systems of resource extraction prioritize subsistence use. This is incorrect. From around 1870, commerce has driven the ebbs and flows of resource extraction from the forests of Indonesia (Boomgaard 1997). Damar resin from the trees enclosed by the park was collected and exported for at least a century (1870–1970), and rattan was a major export in the 1980s and 1990s when many villagers derived a major part of their incomes from that source. A third problem was identifying an appropriate subject to fill the niche of the "traditional" villager, embedded in an appropriately traditional community. In this matter one particular village, Katu, emerged in a prominent but troubled role.

Troubles with Tradition

Katu village is located inside the park boundaries. It was slated for resettlement under the ADB project. With the help of some NGOs, Katu villagers mounted a strong campaign that resulted in the formal recognition of their right to remain in their village. The park director accepted their argument that they were indigenous people who held customary rights to land and resources enclosed by the park, and who had traditional wisdom concerning resource management and conservation. In this way, the Katu people and their allies successfully countered one of the myths identified by Drayton: the myth that profligate natives cannot be trusted with nature protection. Although TNC had opposed the park director's decision to let Katu village remain inside the park, it later turned the presence of Katu to its advantage, as Katu offered TNC an opportunity to make the category "traditional resource use" real. It served as a placeholder for the concept of traditional management anticipated in the use zone. It also served to mark a boundary, to explain why the rights and privileges of Katu *did not apply* to other, more ordinary park border villages. Katu was used, that is, to contain a much broader political challenge. But the containment was precarious. Park-border villagers disputed Katu's status as an especially traditional place, and they emphasized the need of all the park-border villagers for access to agricultural land. TNC's experts were also concerned that Katu might turn out to be rather ordinary, that is to say, market oriented, and worked hard to define and maintain the grounds of distinction.

The draft plan noted the disjuncture between concepts of tradition and existing practice. To qualify for the use zone, villagers—including Katu villagers—would have to demonstrate that they were indeed traditional. Put differently, concepts of tradition would serve to limit what villagers could do in the park. Thus, according to the draft plan, "Application of *adat* or customary practice would, presumably, restrict hunting to indigenous communities who have traditional hunting grounds. Techniques would, presumably, have to be traditional, thus ruling out the use of guns and wire snares" (TNC 2002b, 2:67). Set against these presumptions, Katu's practices were found to be deficient. Although the park director applauded the interest that the people of Katu showed in restoring their old rice terraces and planting them with biodiverse strains of local rice, he was disappointed when his exemplary traditional subjects joined the rush to plant cacao (TNC 2002b, 2:167). Less inclined to trust the wisdom of tradition, the TNC experts writing the draft plan argued that managers, not villagers, must decide which practices would be forbidden or permitted in Katu, guiding the villagers on an appropriate path (TNC 2002b, 2:84–86).

Making distinctions between social groups and allocating rights according to those distinctions was a central feature of the draft plan. In addition to the axis of indigenous/nonindigenous and traditional/nontraditional, the plan emphasized the distinction subsistence/commercial, sometimes amalgamated with a concept of scale (small/large). In relation to agriculture, for example, enforcement efforts were to distinguish between a subsistence farmer and a "commercial coffee planter" (TNC 2002b, 2:90). This might seem quite an appropriate distinction, appealingly populist, but it was disrupted by the actual pattern of livelihoods around the park. Almost all the coffee grown in the park in 2001 was sold, and no farmers in the vicinity of the park had coffee groves bigger than about four hectares. There was no distinct practice of subsistence coffee growing, nor was there a distinct class of "commercial coffee planters." Yet on the basis of this and related distinctions, the draft plan developed a scheme for classifying land users and determining the kinds of "action" that should be taken to control, reduce, or eliminate their activities. These sets of distinctions were set out in the following figure.

The classificatory grid formalized in the figure proposed a set of distinctions through which park authorities could apprehend, redirect, and manage extractive

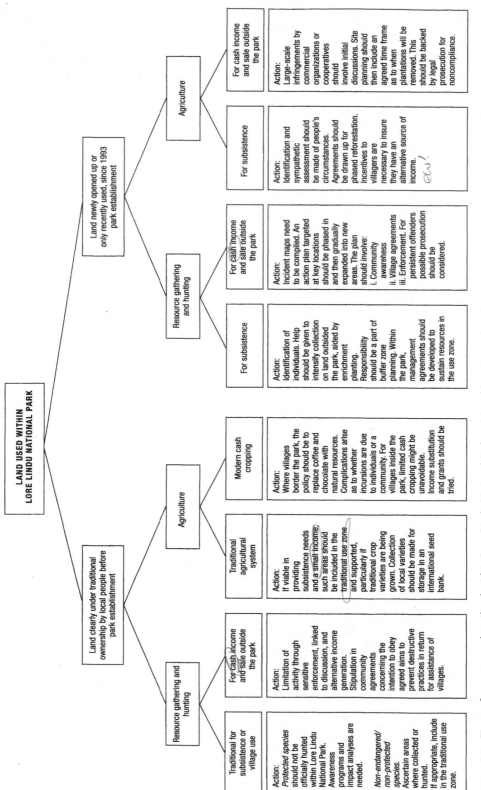

Figure 7.1. Types of areas currently utilized within Lore Lindu National Park and possible action to be taken.

and agricultural activities within the park. Yet, as I have explained, there was a gap between the reality of the grid and reality in and around the park. This gap could not be left unfilled. The draft management plan called for "precise mapping," the listing of "those people certified to exploit resources within the zone," and the preparation of protocols "specifying the type of community activities" that were permitted (TNC 2002b, 2:105). The boxes on the grid had to be filled with actual people and places that met the criteria. These maps, lists, and protocols had to stand up to scientific, legal, and bureaucratic scrutiny, since they had to be approved in Jakarta and then circulated to numerous officials (TNC 2002b, 2:107). How could this be done? In the effort to fill the grid, scientists proved to be just as awkward as villagers, as I will demonstrate with the case of rattan "management."

Rattan Regimes

Rattan extraction was one activity potentially permitted in the Traditional Use Zone. To qualify, it had to be sustainable and "traditional." The draft plan proposed that rattan collection, which was "claimed as a traditional activity but in the last twenty years has become a major local business," should be subject to "tight control measures, including codes of practice"—if, indeed, it was to be allowed at all (TNC 2002b, 2:66). To help fill the grid, TNC sponsored a scientific study of rattan ecology, collection, and use. But the findings of the study, conducted by Stephen Siebert in the late 1990s, did not support the preferred management strategy. Siebert's report supported critiques of the concept of sustainable harvesting as an "ecological fallacy" based in "utopian thinking." He was skeptical that technical criteria and practices for "sustainable harvesting" from forests could be devised. Despite widespread interest there were, he wrote, "few, if any, documented examples." Even if guidelines for sustainable rattan extraction could be devised, he pointed out that there was no scientific basis for predicting the sustainability of the park ecosystem as a whole. He also argued that the concept of sustainable extraction assumed that ecosystems, property regimes, and markets were stable and that extraction could in fact be controlled (TNC 2002b, 2:155). His study demonstrated that none of these conditions were present in relation to rattan in the park.

The idea that subsistence could be separated from commerce was a nonstarter in Siebert's two study villages west of the park in the 1990s. In one of these, Moa, 85 percent of households were highly dependent on rattan incomes to meet subsistence needs, and in Au the number was 58 percent. The search for rattan income, further, had attracted landless households to move into these rather remote villages—mainly indigenous highlanders who had sold off their land to incoming migrants busy buying up land for cacao. But by around 2000 Siebert found that interest in rattan collection was declining because there were no more suitable canes within ten kilometers of the villages, and alternative and more lucrative opportunities had become available (TNC 2002b, 2:149). Given the "phenomenal increase in the value of cacao," he argued, "it is unclear whether rattan will continue to be as economically important to area households at it has been in the recent past, and thus whether [villagers] will invest capital and labor in its management" (TNC 2002b, 2:157).[9]

Siebert also questioned the concept of *customary* rattan management. Minimally, management requires territorial exclusion. He found that the village head of Moa had attempted to declare an exclusive harvesting zone reserved for villagers. Outsiders could access the rattan only with permission. His study showed, however, that the headman's rules were not familiar to Moa's long-time "traditional" residents or to outside rattan collectors, still less were they enforced. Without tenurial security vis-à-vis the park and other collectors, the incentive for "sustainable management" was effectively zero. Thus, Siebert argued, in the case of the park a rattan tenure and management system would have to be devised and implemented from scratch. It could not simply build on "tradition" or "custom" as proponents of sustainable management assumed. The connection between village and territory was also precarious. A catastrophic flood in Au had cut the village in half, destroyed rice fields, and caused residents to relocate two kilometers downstream, far from the zone that would have been carefully mapped, classified, and monitored for their "traditional use" under TNC's draft plan. After the flood he found the people of Au "so busy rebuilding homes and rice fields, and planting cacao, that no one appears to be gathering rattan" (TNC 2002b, 2:156).

Based on his research Seibert concluded that programs for the community management of wild rattan should *not* be developed. Instead he recommended interventions to increase the productivity and sustainability of cacao and coffee on privately owned and managed lands outside the park, and the addition of cultivated rattan to the repertoire of farm-based perennials where farmers showed an interest (TNC 2002b, 2:157–59). Rattan, in short, was not a resource that villagers had an interest in "managing" in the park's use zone. Nor, argued Siebert, were there any other forest products of sufficient value to compete with cacao.

Although Siebert's report was included in the draft plan, complete with its dissident conclusions, TNC opted to ignore the scientist's advice. The TNC plan for the design of the Traditional Use Zone was premised on the concept of sustainable gathering of forest products according to traditional norms and new monitoring protocols that would bring expert knowledge, conservation requirements, and village interests into alignment. Thus the draft plan stated that Siebert's recommendations were "not in keeping with the general approach to resource issues within the Park. The way forward is generally perceived to be through Community Agreements" (TNC 2002b, 2:69).

Collaborative Management

Collaborative management was intended to fill the space on the grid reserved for conservation-oriented villagers who would assist the authorities in monitoring activities taking place within the park. According to the draft management plan, monitoring was to be conducted jointly by forest guards and villagers. A report on a monitoring exercise sponsored by TNC in a village east of the park revealed the difficulty of making this category real. The exercise was designed to measure the extent of damage to the forest on the village edge by means of transects. The results would be compiled in a database entered into a GIS system for long-term comparison and decision making by people—villagers as well as experts—with a shared concern to protect the park.[10] But who were these imagined villagers? Why would villagers want to help supply the park authorities with details of the "damage" their farming and extractive activities caused to the park? What interest, if any, did they have in biodiversity monitoring? Another conservation project at Lore Lindu also built a significant part of its program around "biodiversity monitoring systems." It envisaged the practice of monitoring as an educational tool to "precondition" the border population to move toward regulated resource use (CARE 2003, 6). It was a technique designed not so much to produce data as to produce new, environmental subjects.[11] But as the midterm evaluation of this project observed, a similar initiative elsewhere in Sulawesi had already been abandoned because of the "lack of clear legal basis ... and misgivings among locals about [the] utility of [the] system" (CARE 2002, 21).

The park director, who recognized the villagers of Katu as "an integral part of the Park Management system," was an enthusiastic promoter of village monitoring to detect and expel illegal loggers and rattan collectors. In his plans, monitoring by villagers would be backed by customary councils that would arrest the culprits and impose heavy fines. It would also be backed by a strengthened forest police supplied with more guns (ADB 2002, annex 14). This plan took no account of the way that some villagers profit from logging. The director assumed that logging was a net minus for villagers—the source of damage to their water supply, or the accusation that *they* were the ones engaged in illegal activity. He also overlooked the complicity of village officials and park guards in the logging, in organizing village labor and providing local "security" for logging syndicates. He overlooked the ways village leaders compete over the spoils, factionalizing their own villages, and compete with outsiders who try to log village lands (inside or outside the park) without making the proper financial arrangements. Under these conditions, the director's plan to "empower" villagers to monitor forests did not amount to support for their self-regulating, conservation-oriented, "customary" ways. It did not engage a unified community of people who cared about the park, and who together with park staff would challenge greedy and irresponsible outsiders. It amounted to a requirement that villagers should confront their co-villagers, village elites, and powerful outsiders, including officials—a recipe for vigilantism and violence.

The attempt to make self-governing, environmentally conscious communities real through managed encounters between villagers and planners produced some strange non sequiturs. A TNC report on a consultation exercise in a park-border village duly recorded that villagers raised the problem of their acute shortage of agricultural land and voiced their frustration at being cut off from their coffee and cacao crops when the park border was drawn in 1992. The report then stated "in this matter, the park managers and the villagers have the same interest in the Park, so it is hoped there would be an agreement with the purpose of preventing the occurrence of something neither party would want" (*menghindari hal-hal yang tidak diinginkan bersama*) (TNC 2001, 17). Interpreted liberally, this passage demanded village compliance with a state-decreed order, while conveniently ascribing that order to villagers' own desires. Yet at the time the report was written, park-border villagers did not believe that their interests and the interests of the park authorities were the same. They thought their interests were opposed. After so many outsiders had come asking the villagers to describe their problems but had failed to supply any answers, some villagers not only grew weary of "collaborative" planning, some concluded that they should simply help themselves—Pak Ratu and Mama Yonas among them.

Contentious Practices

From the moment park officials began delimiting boundaries in the unilateral manner typical of Indonesia's Forest Department, park-border villagers have contested their exclusion from agricultural use of park land. For villagers engaged in swidden cultivation, cutting down trees is an integral component of agriculture. As one villager stated during a dialogue session with park officials:

> We move our farms in order to retain soil fertility; we return to the land later; we don't exhaust the soil; we do clear the forest (*membongkar*) but we don't destroy it (*tidak merusak*). Our question is, will the Park authorities ever agree to that? . . . We doubt it. We want our customary land back and we will use it our way. We can't be accused of invading the Park when we are just taking back what belongs to us. (Yayasan Tanah Merdeka 2003)

For villagers intent on tree crop production, the goal is to replace less useful trees, "ordinary trees" (*pohon biasa*) as they put it, by more useful, more lucrative trees. Cutting trees in this part of Sulawesi is also the principal practice through which villagers assert customary rights over land. The pioneer who first clears a patch of primary forest acquires exclusive rights that are inherited by his descendents. These rights include the right of the pioneer to treat the land itself as a commodity, that is, to sell it to another person. Hence the villagers' fury at park officials who had sold or mortgaged "their" land to the foreigners. The scale of this problem was significant. Not only did TNC scientists find that hundreds of hectares of park land, in some places extending ten kilometers inside the borders, were planted with coffee and cacao (TNC 2002b, 2:20), they also confirmed the long history of agrarian land use. Up to 26 percent of the park area was under light or heavy anthropogenic forest, mainly former swidden land— hence potentially subject to ancestral claims.[12]

From the perspective of conservationists, the principal problem is that village practices fail to conform to their expectations about harmonious communities deeply in tune with nature. Thus a researcher involved in a German government–funded project, Stability of Rainforest Margins, bemoaned the villagers' lack of systems for "customary" forest management. "Traditional rules on forest resource use are almost absent," wrote Gunter Burkard. "Little restrictions on forest use were developed and no well defined traditional mechanisms to regulate resource use among community members have been created" (Burkard 2002b, 6). Villagers in the park border area, he found, also lacked a concept of collective benefit or responsibility. They had no local cohesion and little sense of community or mutual assistance in livelihood matters. Each family took care of itself, and theft of produce was common (Burkard 2002a, 33).

it's the "nature" idea that's wrong, not the "harmony" idea.

Yet, if we can avoid projecting the value of biodiversity protection onto villagers, it is far from evident why villagers should want to protect "ordinary" trees.[13] From my observations around the park in 2001 and 2003 I can report that villagers valued useful species and protected them when they were scarce. They avoided cutting trees on steep slopes and stream banks for the pragmatic reason that they did not want to see the fruits of their labor disappear in a flood. If, like Mama Yonas, they planned to restore tree cover on the land they claimed, it was mainly because this practice was consistent with their economic interest, currently focused on cultivating cacao.

read: their livelihood

From a longer term perspective, the customary system of forest classification and use critiqued by Burkard as not "real" management did in fact manage the element of nature of most concern to villagers. It managed rights to use and sell forest land and products. The system ensured that everyone knew what was theirs so that each could pursue their own livelihood goals without conflict with kin and neighbors. It did not manage what was abundant—ordinary trees—only what was valuable and scarce. The key scarcity of pressing concern to park villagers by 2001 was not the scarcity of trees but the scarcity of agricultural land caused by the Forest Department's unilateral imposition of a forest boundary that excluded them from their "customary" land frontier.[14]

economics aren't separate from life

Commoditization for All?

The Nature Conservancy was not ignorant of the commodity values forgone by villagers when they were excluded from the park, but it seriously underestimated the degree to which the villagers calculate their economic interest. The "income generating projects" (honey marketing, butterfly collecting, white-water rafting, ecotourism) TNC introduced to offset the villagers' losses and introduce them to the value of conservation foundered on the villagers' economic calculus. The income these projects produced (if any) was far lower than the value of their labor at local daily wage rates, and substantially less than the profits to be made from cacao. As Siebert demonstrated, villagers readily phased out rattan collection when it was no longer cost effective. They roundly rejected the logic Michael Dove dubs "rainforest crunch"—the logic that assigns poor people to the least lucrative economic niche (Dove 1996). They assessed their participation in TNC-sponsored conservation-awareness-building activities by the same market calculus. As one villager trained by TNC to help run village activities observed, "We got a certificate from those trainings, but what can you do with a TNC certificate? It is not accepted at the bank."

Recognizing these problems, conservation agencies are keen to experiment with a new generation of conservation projects that take the market orientation of villagers more seriously. The goal is to "accelerate development of markets for forest ecosystem services (such as watershed protection, biodiversity conservation and carbon storage), to expand markets of sustainably produced forest products and to advance markets that serve the interests of forest communities."[15] The assumption of these projects is that communities can be induced to manage forests sustainably not because it is their custom to do so, or because they have direct use for forest products, but rather because the economic incentives can be put in place to entice them. Yet there are two problems with this approach, as its proponents acknowledge.

First is the problem of the incomplete commoditization of nature. Thus far, markets for forest ecosystem services do not exist—they are still to be developed. The difficulties are formidable, not least because the costs and benefits of these "services" are separated by vast differences of scale. It was to make sense of jumping scales that park-border villagers devised their creative narrative about "nine nations" and their hidden agenda. Second, costs and benefits are separated by differences of power. Forest villagers seldom have secure tenure over forests, and so they are not in a position to sell forest-protection services. They are not in a position to commoditize nature. Much as they would like to do this, they have no effective means to follow the example of the officials who figured out a way to sell the park to "nine nations." The most they can do is to find ways to realize commodity values from the material they have at hand—forest products, and the agricultural products that replace the trees. Their effective, on-the-ground power to realize these values should not be underestimated. Indeed, TNC's program to produce nature-loving natives can be read as a recognition of the villagers' de facto powers to turn nature to a profit, even as it attempted to contain them. Yet on the scale of the park as a whole, should its nature-protection "services" ever be commoditized, without doubt the benefits would continue to flow to members of the elite—officials and entrepreneurs, often in collusion—who are in a position to grab and monopolize them by legal and illegal means. If conservation organizations proved incapable of shifting the market orientation of villagers, they have even less capacity to control the rapacity of entrenched elites, and no amount of planning, consultation, or micromanagement will change that fact.

Real Conservation

In this chapter I have examined contested commodifications and the project of producing nature and nature-loving natives in Indonesia's forest zone. Although conservation advocates envisage pristine forest as a priceless treasure that defies commodification, villagers contending with conservation agendas see the forest as a source of commodities—forest products, agricultural products, and land, each of which can be used directly or sold as sources of livelihood. Villagers project their own profit-seeking agendas onto the various parties who speak in the name of conservation—a reading that makes sense of many of the practices they observe, and fills the gap between their knowledge of who actually profits from park protection and the claim of conservationists to protect nature for the broader public good.

Unlike the villagers, and observing the situation from a vastly different position, I am prepared to take the agenda of the conservation organizations operating around the Lore Lindu National Park at their word. Although it is true that some individuals and corporations profit from conservation programs, in Sulawesi and in many other places park-based conservation as it is currently implemented is heavily subsidized by governments and individuals concerned with the public good. It is subsidized because it is unprofitable. It is unprofitable because nature's "services" are incompletely commoditized. Should they be completely commoditized, they would be even more vulnerable to destruction, for the reasons Karl Polanyi pointed out. This is the impossible context in which conservationists project an image of villagers as natives in tune with nature, and attempt to engage them as partners in a countermovement for the future of the planet. They run up against the hard reality that Southeast Asians, including highlanders on the forest edge, have been market subjects for at least a century, with consequences that cannot be wished away or readily reversed.

WHY IS THIS A HARD REALITY?
there's nothing wrong with selling stuff!
Li is thinking in the same nature/culture
divide that she condemns.

8

Sovereignty in Burma after the Entrepreneurial Turn

Mosaics of Control, Commodified Spaces, and Regulated Violence in Contemporary Burma

KEN MACLEAN

The number of extractive enclaves in Burma has grown dramatically over the past two decades, particularly in regions that were until quite recently sites of intense fighting between armed groups.[1] In this chapter I examine the competing modes of governance that have since emerged in these enclaves and the role that regulated—that is, nonlethal—violence plays in reshaping social identities for members of different ethnic populations living and working within them. Although conflicting forms of sovereignty exist in many postcolonial states similarly dependent on primary commodity exports (Hansen and Stepputat 2006), the spatial effects these practices produce in Burma differ in at least one respect. The sub- and transnational flows of capital, technology, expertise, and labor that make intensive forms of commodity extraction possible in the Burmese context do not—at present—disconnect the enclaves from the national spaces in which they are geographically embedded, as is increasingly the case in resource concessions elsewhere (Ferguson 2005; Tsing 2000; Hardin 2002). Instead, the flows, as they separately move through and between different extractive enclaves in Burma, result in a decidedly more paradoxical outcome: the simultaneous extension and erosion of centralized control over the commodities and populations found

The author thanks Mahn Nay Myo and those Burmese who shared their views with the research team at great personal risk (all names have been changed). Without their assistance and vast knowledge, this research project would not have been possible. I would also like to acknowledge the important contributions made by my colleagues at the Karen Environmental and Social Action Network and EarthRights International as well as the constructive feedback I received from the conference participants, the editors, and the anonymous reviewers.

therein. These contradictions are made possible by competing networks of regulatory authority and wealth accumulation (Roitman 2001) that have emerged in the enclaves, but now extend far beyond their boundaries. As a consequence, sovereignty has fragmented into competing "mosaics of territorial control" (Hardin 2002, ii) that make it difficult to determine where the Burmese regime begins and ends, institutionally as well as geographically, in many parts of the country.[2]

To support my contentions, I provide background on the political and economic circumstances that enabled intensive forms of resource extraction to resume in Burma's former conflict zones. A case study, which compares the processes at work in two different mining enclaves, follows, the details of which are based on interviews conducted inside the country between 2002 and 2005 with Burmese of different ethnic backgrounds who lived and worked in the enclaves either as horticulturalists, miners, loggers, rattan and bamboo harvesters, or charcoal producers. (Additional interviews were carried out with internally displaced persons [IDPs] in or near the enclaves and with individuals that recently fled these areas for refugee camps along the Thai-Burmese border.) After the case study, I return to the broader question of how resource concessions differentiate sovereignty and the populations within, but in ways that diverge from those found in other areas of Southeast Asia where neoliberalism is ascendant.

The Entrepreneurial Turn

Since 1989, the Burmese regime—currently known as the State Peace and Development Council (SPDC)—has brokered more than twenty cease-fire agreements with armed opposition groups across the country. While the cease-fire agreements did little to resolve the underlying political conflicts that gave rise to the insurgent movements, they nonetheless served a tactical purpose. Armed groups that "returned to the legal fold" (i.e., publicly acknowledged the legitimacy of the regime) were able to retain some administrative control over large and frequently discontinuous pieces of territory as well as the populations and resources within. In exchange, the cease-fire agreements made it possible for the regime's armed forces (Tatmadaw) to concentrate counterinsurgency operations in a steadily decreasing number of areas around the country. Together, these related processes have dramatically enlarged the amount of territory over which the regime can claim to assert its permanent authority.

By the mid-1990s, the regime's efforts to further consolidate its control over these former conflict zones shifted from a wholly militarized approach to one that placed greater emphasis on economic development. Although state-sponsored initiatives in the country's remote border regions formed a crucial component of this new security strategy (Lambrecht 2004), the regime increasingly relied on joint-venture agreements to help revitalize the country's economy, which had badly stagnated during three decades of centralized state control known as the "Burmese Way to Socialism" (1962–88). However, the move toward a more market-oriented economy did not signal an official endorsement of the values and practices associated with neoliberalism, which were then being (re-)adopted across much of Southeast Asia (Nevins and Peluso, introduction; Ong 2000, 2006, 1–27). The flirtation with the marketplace was instead prompted by a series of trade and investment sanctions that some Western governments and international financial institutions used to punish the regime for not complying with basic human rights norms. Unfortunately, attempts to isolate Burma economically as well as diplomatically since the late 1980s and thus create conditions for "regime change" have failed to produce their intended effect. Instead, the sanctions have ironically strengthened the regime's civil and military branches by forcing them to diversify their business interests and to develop new ones more quickly than might have occurred otherwise (Steinberg 2005).

One consequence of the entrepreneurial turn, which affected all levels of the regime, was the rapid conversion of previously contested spaces into commodified ones where large-scale resource extraction could openly take place. Although the precise details of the agreements the regime separately negotiated with twenty-two armed groups between 1989 and 1997 have never been made public, it is clear the number of joint ventures extracting gems, precious metals, minerals, tropical hardwoods, and other valuable resources dramatically increased in each of the former conflict zones immediately after a cease-fire was declared. Significantly, most of these joint ventures were not formally registered companies; rather, they were ad hoc entities that opportunistically linked military and commercial interests together in a particular place, though rarely on equal terms. Typically, these entities partnered members of different Tatmadaw field battalions, cease-fire groups, state-owned enterprises, and local entrepreneurs, especially those with access to foreign capital via transnational personal networks. Such strategic alliances, while not unique to Burma (Roitman 2005), nonetheless assumed a specific form in this context due to the pressures the regime faced at the time. Moreover, the very conditions that contributed to the proliferation of joint ventures in the cease-fire areas made it impossible for any one entity to monopolize the resources in a given enclave.

Three trends, which reinforce one another, account for this state of affairs. First, due to budgetary and ideological reasons, the regime requires all of its field battalions to be economically self-sufficient. This policy, introduced in the early 1990s, has encouraged the battalions to engage in a diverse array of activities to fund their operating expenses, which minimally include food, ammunition, and pay packets for the soldiers under their command. Of these activities, joint ventures are among the most lucrative since they allow the battalions to collect various rents (such as extralegal taxes and protection fees) in addition to a percentage of the commodities extracted. Second, decades of counterinsurgency operations have resulted in the extensive militarization of Burma's border regions. There are, for example, more than two hundred infantry battalions presently deployed on or near the country's eastern border (Thai Burma Border Consortium [TBBC] 2006, 17). Due to the density of these deployments, battalions frequently find themselves seeking to exploit the same limited number of economic opportunities. Lastly, most of the extractive enclaves in the cease-fire areas contain several kinds of resources, so concessions devoted to one commodity often overlap spatially with others, which results in shifting forms of competition and collusion between the joint ventures (MacLean 2007).

Over time, these practices have produced a curious paradox that complicates conventional understandings of sovereignty, which still privilege a state's monopoly over the legitimate use of force within a territory (Vandergeest and Peluso 1995, 385). On the one hand, the resource concessions have helped the regime to expand its military, administrative, and economic reach into areas of the country where it previously had little or none. On the other hand, the resource concessions have simultaneously undermined the regime's ability to exercise centralized control over these same areas since the joint ventures are able to divert a considerable portion of the resources they extract (rents as well as primary commodities) to members of their respective patron-client network, group, or locality (Verdery 1994, 16). Both processes have not only intensified efforts by the joint ventures to claim what remains of Burma's natural "capital" before someone else does, but they have accelerated the devolution of sovereignty into competing networks of authority and accumulation, which crosscut the regime's civil and military bureaucracy at some moments and bypass them entirely at others.

Cease-fire groups that lease gem concessions, for instance, are typically required to sell at least 10 percent of the stones they extract at twice-annual auctions organized by the regime in Rangoon or face the loss of their mining permits. The terms of this agreement, while unequal, are mutually beneficial; it allows cease-fire groups, such as the United Wa State Army, to convert profits from drug trafficking into weapons and legal currency—two important means by which they maintain their regional autonomy—by selling some gems through official channels and for the regime to extract rents from stones it would otherwise lose to buyers in Thailand, China, and India who purchase smuggled ones (ALTSEAN 2005, 6). By contrast, much of the gold mined in Burma remains in private hands as a hedge against severe inflation and official exchange rates that vastly overvalue the Burmese kyat by a factor of two hundred. To some extent, the contrasting spatial trajectories of gems and gold reflect precolonial patterns of consumption. They also highlight the regime's inability to regulate capital flows and the movement of other assets inside and across the country's territorial borders.

The case study that follows illustrates these processes, while exploring why mining enclaves in two separate regions of Burma produce similar patterns of enclosure and displacement despite significant differences in the commodities extracted; the history of armed conflict in both locales; and the ethnic populations within them. Although many of the similarities can be attributed to the under-lying logic of "primitive accumulation" (Marx 1972, 713–74), which organizes extraction in the mining concessions in common ways, the field data also reveals the ways in which the forms of regulated violence that joint ventures utilize in both enclaves generate different outcomes for the populations subjected to them. In some cases, these practices reinforce existing ethno-racial hierarchies, while in others they blur them. But in no case do these practices reflect regime-led efforts to reorganize national spaces or to "graduate" the rights afforded to those who work within different zones, as Ong has shown is the case in other parts of Southeast Asia where states selectively link some of their territory and popula-tions to global circuits of capital (2000; 2006, 75–80). Although a number of such extraterritorial zones exist in Burma, they are few in number and, with the notable exception of the Yadana Natural Gas Pipeline, they are not essential to the regime's economic survival. Instead, the practices at work in the vast major-ity of the country's extractive enclaves produce complicit subjects who engage in predatory behavior that destroys their well-being and the very ecosystems they depend on for their survival.

Lastly, since a detailed presentation of the field data can be found elsewhere (EarthRights International [ERI] and Karen Environmental and Social Net-work [KESAN] 2003; ERI 2007; MacLean 2007), the case study emphasizes the trends found in both mining enclaves as well as the flows (of events, people, and things) that unexpectedly connect them across space. In sum, the reorganization of the gemstone mining around Mogok in north-central Burma following a series of ceasefire agreements between 1994 and 1996 pushed hundreds of small-scale independent miners, many of which had worked the area for generations, to the margins. Beginning in 1997, a growing number of these miners, who are largely of Shan or Chinese descent, relocated to an area approximately one thousand kilometers to the southeast where they have since gained control of the informal gold-mining operations there. In the process the in-migrants have reproduced the very conditions that forced their initial departure, but this time on the Karen, who form the ethnic majority in this latter region. Although the dynamics of displacement in both locales exhibit significant similarities, the emphasis will be largely on events in Mogok for this is where the miners marginalized by the gem industry's consolidation first gained the knowledge and experience they later used to displace others. The emphasis shifts to the Karen at the end of the case study to explain why the sociocultural impacts of displacement have been more severe for them.

Settings

The town of Mogok is nestled in an upland valley approximately two miles wide and twenty miles long. Located in the extreme eastern corner of Mandalay

Division, along the western border of Shan State, Mogok has been a center for mining gems, especially rubies and sapphires, for eight hundred years. Due to the richness of its mineral deposits different political entities during the precolonial, colonial, and postcolonial periods sought to directly control the area or, as was more common, to secure access to the gems via regional trading and tributary routes (Turrell 1988). Despite these periodic struggles, most mining outfits in Mogok remained small-scale enterprises largely dependent on labor-intensive techniques. As a result, the environmental impacts of these mines on the valley's landscape were not irreparable, at least until comparatively recently.

Between 1962 and 1988, various armed groups fought against the Tatmadaw and one another largely though not exclusively to gain control of Shan State's valuable mineral resources, forests, opium fields, and, more recently, methamphetamine factories. In 1989, four regional and ethnically distinct armies controlling parts of Shan State entered into cease-fire agreements with the regime. However, much of Shan State remained engulfed in war until the mid-1990s as the competing armies and "anti-insurgency" militias fought for dominance. By early 1994 the security situation in the extreme western part of the state, which borders Mogok, had finally normalized. Later that same year the regime approved the Myanmar Mines Law, which abruptly reversed three decades of socialist policies as part of a broader effort to attract foreign investment, which was largely used to modernize the Tatmadaw (Selth 1996). Shortly after the law was announced, the military regime invited Burmese businessmen, primarily of Chinese descent, to invest in new mining operations in the gem fields north and west of Mogok. To further help revive this stagnant sector of the economy, which generated less than 1 percent of the country's official gross domestic product at the time (ADB 2005b, 307), the regime authorized production-sharing contracts for new deposits and profit-sharing contracts for existing ones (Moody 2000, 17–18). Tatmadaw battalions also deployed permanently to the region to provide security in conjunction with other cease-fire groups and ethnic militias. With these inducements in place, informal capital investment increased rapidly. By 2003, there were more than one hundred joint ventures employing hydraulic mining equipment imported from China, though much of the operating capital is rumored to be Singaporean in origin.

By contrast, alluvial gold deposits were not discovered around Shwegyin until the late nineteenth century. Since then individuals and small-scale business operations have continually mined the area, primarily to augment income from other economic activities such as subsistence farming, fruit production, and petty trading. Large-scale mining never developed in part because the gem deposits around Mogok were far more lucrative. But the violent conflict also played a significant role. For many years much of eastern Pegu Division, where Shwegyin is located, was at the epicenter of brutal anti-insurgency campaigns conducted by the Tatmadaw against the Karen National Union (KNU), an ethnically based organization that has fought since 1949 to create an independent nation-state for all Karen. The security situation improved during the early 1990s as most of the front-line conflict gradually shifted eastward into neighboring Karen State. Still, no major changes in the gold mining sector occurred until 1997 when the first wave of miners displaced from Mogok began arriving in Shwegyin.

Because some of these migrants were involved in negotiating mining concessions in Shwegyin, we know how these agreements were reached. According to informants, several migrants collectively approached Maung Ni, who heads Light Infantry Battalion No. 4 in Pegu Division, and Po Baing, a locally influential businessman of Indian descent, for permission to develop mining operations around Shwegyin through joint-venture agreements with the state-owned Mining Enterprise No. 2. Gen. Tin Aye, the commander for SPDC Division No. 66, eventually granted permission. In exchange, all three men allegedly receive substantial rents on mining equipment, the number of hired laborers, and the sale of property acquired under questionable circumstances. As was the case in Mogok, local Tatmadaw units and members of other armed groups routinely extort food, consumer goods, and protection fees from the concessionaires as well. Despite these onerous conditions, the newly established concerns sought and obtained seventeen concessions from Mining Enterprise No. 2. Collectively, the concessions produce an estimated five hundred kilograms of gold annually (Maung 1999, 124). This relatively modest amount was sufficient to create a "gold rush." Miners originally from Mogok and laborers from elsewhere soon flooded the area. By late 2003, more than one hundred Chinese-manufactured hydraulic mining units were in operation along the township's rivers.

Patterns of Attrition

In 1963, when Burma's military regime nationalized all of the country's mines, it suddenly became illegal to remove anything, including rocks, from the ground without a permit from the Ministry of Mines. This effort to assert state control over these resources conflicted with long-standing practice as mining claims had previously been secured through possession and typically passed from one generation to the next. Despite the policy change, the Ministry of Mines remained relatively powerless to enforce this regulation as people continued to mine clandestinely even in areas where the Tatmadaw exercised military control. The situation began to change in 1989 as limited international sanctions put in place the year before forced the regime to seek alternate ways of accumulating hard currency. In addition to legalizing joint ventures with foreign companies and negotiating cease-fire agreements with armed opposition groups, the regime also sought to formalize the mining industry as a whole by creating clear policies and laws to guide the commercial exploration and extraction of gems, minerals, and so on. Together, these factors dramatically improved the ability of the Ministry of Mines to monitor the industry, which grew rapidly during the 1990s (ADB 2005b, 307). Informants claim that ministry officials, Tatmadaw commanders, and the heads of several nonstate armed groups regularly collude with one another to manipulate the process the regime ostensibly created to promote greater transparency.

In Mogok, there are three loose categories of permit conflicts. The first involves disputes between the Myanmar Gems Enterprise (MGE) and the local SPDC Strategic Command Office, which oversees the Tatmadaw battalions operating in the area. As one miner described the relationship between them, "[They] are like husband and wife. If there is a disagreement, the strategic command will just take out the person from the MGE that disagrees." By this he meant the interests of the MGE are routinely subordinated to the Tatmadaw, who seeks out a new "wife" whenever it encounters any significant opposition.

The second entails frequent land seizures by military units and militias. These offer a more direct means to bypass the permitting process nominally controlled by the MGE. All mining sites, regardless of type, are subject to periodic surprise inspections by military intelligence officers, who determine whether tax rates should be increased based on the perceived quality and quantity of the gem deposits. If the site appears to be potentially rich, the inspecting officer can claim it for the Tatmadaw battalion in which he serves. The battalion is then free to auction the mining permit to a private company, who will then take over the site and make its own operating agreement with the Tatmadaw unit's commander. One local Shan miner claims that he witnessed twenty sites taken over in this manner. Independent Chinese businessmen and various companies subsequently "purchased" all of them.

The third type involves military units' developing sites to generate private income for their own battalions. They simply plant a flag in the area, which indicates that no one else is permitted to mine there, and soldiers are later posted to the site and fences erected to prevent anyone from approaching. Existing trench mines and small open areas, often seasonally cultivated as gardens, are frequent targets of military-owned backhoes and bulldozers. More enterprising units have forcibly evicted entire villages. In two affected villages, the inhabitants were not only denied compensation but were also forced to pay for their transportation to a new location. The military units additionally refused to allow the villagers to disassemble their wooden homes or to harvest food from their gardens and fruit trees before moving. They were, however, allowed to work for the state-owned company that gained the mining rights to the area as day laborers (keeping 25 percent of the value of the gems they mined), or as salaried workers paid by the month.

All of these conflicts are common in Shwegyin as well, but with one additional complication. Karen horticulturalists whose customary land-tenure practices are not recognized by the state still inhabit most of the land around Shwegyin. But

Tatmadaw battalions, rather than seizing the land outright, instead force its owners to "buy" their existing property or risk forfeiting it without compensation. As one displaced Karen villager explains, "In March 2003, the military came and took all the land around [the village]. They posted signposts and told the villagers that they had to buy the land if they wanted to grow anything on it or look for groundnuts. If you didn't buy your own land, you lost it. Other outside people bought the deeds and took over the villagers' land."

Those independent miners that remain pursue different strategies to preserve their livelihoods. In Mogok, independent miners often form small mining co-operatives, ones typically organized along ethnic lines. These groups practice what might be termed "guerrilla mining." That is, they use their tactical advantage—size, mobility, and flexibility—to locate sites in remote areas on the fringes of, or outside, concessions to avoid regular patrols looking for illicit mining operations. Should a site prove to be productive, these miners seek to rapidly extract as many gems as possible and then quickly sell their permit to another group before military intelligence, Tatmadaw units, or a cease-fire group seizes it along with their equipment and supplies. Additional bribes are often needed to avoid jail time. People caught mining in restricted areas claimed by military units face a mandatory three-year prison sentence. Some of these people later opt to become "prisoner-porters," who carry supplies for Tatmadaw units into front-line combat areas in exchange for a reduction in their sentence—a decision that underscores the severe conditions inside Burmese prisons.

For miners with little or no capital, there are two other options. The first is to become a laborer for outside mining interests. Given the high cost of living, high rents, and the low return on one's labor, this option is not attractive. Additionally, working conditions have significantly declined with the introduction of hydraulic mining and the area's militarization. Miners regularly risk drowning from flash floods and landslides during the rainy season, while workers who sort gems after they are removed from the pits do so under the tropical sun since much of the surrounding area is deforested. Workers also report that work breaks are rare and that they regularly face verbal harassment and physical abuse from the soldiers who provide on-site security for the companies. Theft, nonetheless, remains widespread and companies have resorted to body searches at different stages of the mining process to reduce losses. The second option is to leave Mogok and seek employment elsewhere, which is what a significant number of people have chosen to do since 1997. When asked why he left, a Shan miner, mixing traditional proverbs, explained: "We stay under the mango tree, but aren't allowed to eat mangoes. The people may own the land in Mogok, but we don't get any benefits. It's like the deer that has many fawns, but the tiger will always get them. Here, the tiger is the military. Mogok people don't want to stay anymore.... Now, the only rich people in Mogok are not from Mogok."

Around Shwegyin, "guerrilla mining" is paradoxically both easier and more difficult. The equipment needed to pan for gold is inexpensive and can be constructed easily out of local materials, as can sluices and small diesel-powered sifters with variable-sized screens—though they are considerably harder to hide and to move on short notice. Alluvial gold, unlike rough gems, also requires processing; the flakes typically need to be chemically treated with mercury to further isolate the precious metal—a highly toxic process known as amalgamation. Finally, the steepness of the terrain and heavy fighting outside the concessions sharply limit the number of areas where individuals and households can safely search for gold without facing violent retribution from armed groups. Such areas are about to become even smaller as the completion of the nearby Kyaut Nagar hydroelectric dam in 2008 will completely inundate other areas. As in Mogok, laborers working for outside gold mining interests are also subject to physical searches, but in "cleaning ponds." At the end of each day, gold miners are required to bathe nude to wash free all the accumulated dust and flakes stuck to their hair, skin, and clothes, which can amount to as much as one kyat *thar* (15.3 grams) of gold.

The problems associated with gem and gold mining are not limited to the consolidation of the industry by outside interests and the negative effects this has had on relations between labor and capital. The technology also has had devastating impacts on ecosystems. The first open-pit hydraulic mines appeared in Mogok in 1990. Previously, gem miners relied heavily on labor-intensive techniques that varied depending on the seasonal availability of water. But new hydraulic equipment offered a technological solution to the declining return on gems located deep in the valley's alluvial soils. Diesel-powered generators, pumps, and water hoses as well as other heavy equipment, such as backhoes and bulldozers, made it possible to extract gems far more efficiently—though at the expense of the region's watersheds. The tremendous pressure generated by the pumps has enabled miners to wash away entire hillsides, sending the topsoil and overburden down sluices where the materials can be easily sorted. Within a decade, gem miners had washed away nearly all of the valley's topsoil and tree cover, forcing people living in the area to import nearly all of their food. Equally visible are the socioeconomic costs. Gambling is widespread in Mogok. But more alarmingly, intravenous drug use and unprotected intercourse between miners and sex workers have increased, raising fears of a generalized epidemic of HIV-1 in reproductive-age adults.

These same problems have accompanied the miners who left Mogok for Shwegyin, but with an added complication. Tatmadaw patrols treat most of the areas to the east of Shwegyin as "free-fire zones" where they can shoot anyone on sight. Landmines are also used throughout the area. This state of affairs has made it impossible for Karen to practice shifting cultivation properly and, as a result, the limited number of upland areas still available to them are rapidly becoming exhausted due to overuse. Additionally, Tatmadaw patrols regularly seize or destroy crops to prevent food from reaching the KNU. The resulting shortage caused the price of paddy in Shwegyin Township to rise 25 percent in 2003 (Burma Border Consortium 2003, 51). At the same time, hydraulic mining is washing away lowland plots. Thus the in-migration of miners, simply by dint of numbers, has placed considerable pressure on the region's already tenuous food security. Many Karen now subsist on little more than rice gruel mixed with yams, roots, and bamboo shoots.

Complicity

Most attempts to understand forced displacement in Burma have for justifiable reasons focused on state-sponsored violence. The figures are staggering, with an estimated 540,000 IDPs in eastern Burma alone (TBBC 2005, 24). But the scale and severity of this ongoing violence has directed attention away from other forms of enclosure and forced displacement, such as those found in extractive enclaves that do not neatly fall into those caused either by armed conflict or large-scale infrastructure projects. This is not to suggest that violence is absent in and around the concessions. Physical and sexual assault, torture, murder, and illegal forms of military conscription occur in both locations. However, according to local informants the number and severity of such incidents has decreased. Similar reductions in lethal violence have been reported in other cease-fire areas of intensive commodity extraction (TBBC 2005, 26, 43).

What accounts for this trend is the economic competition between the joint ventures in the enclaves. They produce semiformal, if largely arbitrary and extralegal, rules, which help govern access to particular resources and the rents that different actors may levy. Although these rules take various forms, joint ventures prefer to use their personal connections with local representatives of the regime (e.g., civil servants, policemen, judges, and cadastral officers)—relations that are maintained through bribes—to pressure individuals who hold mining permits or own land to "sell" them at below market prices. A refusal to do so can result in bankruptcy, wrongful imprisonment, or other forms of retribution. But both lethal and nonlethal strategies eventually result in a similar outcome—displacement—as the competition between the joint ventures consumes everything in the enclaves, including entire landscapes. Hence there is immense pressure to strip anything of commercial value before someone else does (ERI and KESAN 2003; ERI 2007).

Given this outcome, what accounts for the influx of labor into the concessions and their compliant behavior once there? During the past decade, living conditions throughout much of Burma have deteriorated so much that many people have to participate in practices that are morally corrosive to themselves simply to survive. Repeated acts of aiding and abetting the regime—out of fear, indifference, or alienation—have arguably transformed many Burmese into "complicit subjects" (Kligman 1998) whose capacity for political resistance, much less the kinds of economic self-fashioning that have emerged in concert with neoliberal policies elsewhere, remain sharply circumscribed. Although a small number of "enterprising selves" exist in Burma, their flexible strategies for increased efficiency and profitability have little to do with personal desires for greater self-fulfillment or, for that matter, the welfare of others via the invisible hand of the free market (cf. Miller and Rose 1990). These individuals, who by definition maintain close and mutually beneficial ties with high-ranking SPDC officials and Tatmadaw field commanders, remain a tiny minority. Instead, Burma's extractive enclaves are populated almost exclusively by landless laborers. In some cases, these laborers are local inhabitants who have lost their land or livelihoods and now work for the extractive industries. But in most instances the laborers are economic migrants from elsewhere in Burma seeking work even though pay scales are rarely sufficient to meet daily expenses.

Importantly, this emergent proletarian class remains internally subdivided as the extractive industries exhibit a strong preference for hiring workers from the ethnic group of the owners, while paying men considerably more than women, even when they perform the same task. Mining companies, for instance, desire ethnic Chinese and Shan laborers, while logging companies typically hire Burmans. In a related fashion, the Tatmadaw battalions, cease-fire groups, militias, and armed opposition groups provide varying rates of "protection" depending on where the concession is located, what is being extracted, by whom, and when.

As Ong (2000) has pointed out, these practices afford graduated sets of de facto rights to different populations. However, the forms of identity and the different possibilities they afford in contemporary Burma are not connected to regime-sponsored efforts to segment citizenship in the enclaves to better link them with global gem or gold markets. Rather, the strategies for managing the populations in concessions reproduce long-standing patterns of interethnic discrimination, some of which predate the colonial formation of Burma, but in new geographic locations. Put differently, five decades of violent conflict, state-sponsored discrimination, and limited economic opportunities mean that the presumed relationship between space, place, and ethnic identity, which was reified in the 1974 Constitution, no longer holds, if it ever did. Shans are not consigned to "Shan State" any more than Karens can only reside in "Karen State" or Burmans in the seven administrative "Divisions" located in the country's center. Members of different ethnic groups have *always* been in motion, frequently forced motion, for a variety of reasons (Scott 1998a). What differs now are the outcomes.

Displacements Past

So far I have highlighted the similarities that exist in the mining enclaves surrounding Mogok and Shwegyin, specifically the forms of governance and regulated violence that joint ventures use to extract resources and to discipline the populations. Despite these similarities, the outcomes for the Karen are more severe due to past episodes of forced migration. In fact, the emergence of a politically coherent Karen identity out of numerous subgroups was a long process arising from a series of displacements that can be traced back to nineteenth-century policies, which established two competing sets of administrative rule within colonial Burma, the first based on equal rights within a centrally unified state and the second on a vastly more pluralized model that granted significant political autonomy to non-Burman ethnic groups that primarily lived in the country's border regions (Taylor 2002, 152). These contrasting forms of administration, and the natural resource concessions that frequently accompanied them—teak plantations in the case of the Karen (Bryant 1994)—helped reify ethnic and linguistic divisions into fixed racial categories, which continue today to justify a wide array of discriminatory practices (Houtman 1999, 59–78).

During the 1960s and 1970s, counterinsurgency campaigns forced lowland and hill Karen from fertile river valleys into more mountainous and isolated border areas to the east. This displacement reconfigured the basis of Karen identity once again. Intermarriage between plains and hill Karen, for instance, produced a culturally, linguistically, and religiously diverse population at the same time the KNU leadership was attempting to articulate its postcolonial vision of a homogenous and politically unified ethnic nation. Another paradox was the gradual creation of a two-tiered socioeconomic structure within the KNU itself. Much of its leadership had been educated in Baptist missionary schools in lowland towns and urban areas, while most of the troops were recruited from upland populations, who were either Buddhist or animist. Lastly, the relative geographic isolation of the KNU created by this eastward migration meant that extracting rents on cross-border trade, which included tropical hardwoods felled by Thai and Malaysian companies, became crucial for generating income, without which the KNU could not have provided social services or purchased weapons and ammunition (Bryant 1996).

For much of the next three decades, the Tatmadaw carried out seasonal campaigns to limit the flow of food, money, intelligence information, and recruits to armed opposition groups such as the KNU. During the 1990s, a more concerted effort to permanently hold territory by forcibly relocating dispersed rural populations into concentrated sites gradually replaced this strategy. By the end of the decade, the Tatmadaw's efforts "to drain the sea in order to kill the fish" had resulted in the destruction of more than twenty-eight hundred villages along Burma's eastern border (TBBC 2006, 20). While this massive wave of forced relocations prompted more than ninety thousand Karen to flee to refugee camps in Thailand, most opted to stay in Burma despite the ongoing violence. Of the estimated 540,000 IDPs in eastern Burma, more than half are Karen (TBBC 2006, 22). For these Karen, most of whom move several times a year either to avoid regime-sponsored violence or in response to it, displacement increasingly defines a particular way of being in the world. It is one that differs markedly from legal definitions that stress a person's forced separation from "home," as there is no identifiable home to which these IDPs can return.

Since the 1990s, when cease-fire agreements in nearby areas went into effect, the geographic territory in which it is possible to be a "Karen" living in Burma today without direct military pressure to assimilate or to otherwise adopt state-approved forms of identity has also decreased dramatically. Contemporary forms of Karen identity are, as a consequence, tied more than ever to what remains of the "the forest" as the last source of refuge, economic livelihood, and cultural integrity (Heppner 2005). This makes it all the more tragic that many Karen now participate in the destruction of "the forest" to earn a living. One KNU forestry official bitterly complained about the situation:

> Because of the SPDC [regime], we could not control our forest....They drove the civilians from the town into the jungle where they disobey the rule of [the KNU]. If you kill them, it will turn the civilians against you. But if you don't, they will continue to come and to cut the forest. No matter what you do to solve the problem, it will come back and bite you. (KESAN 2003, 25)

One could make a similar statement about the dilemmas posed by hydraulic mining with one additional caveat. Hydraulic mining, unlike clear-cutting, completely destroys the landscape, including its underlying soil structure, and thus precludes the possibility of regeneration.

Rethinking Concessions

The entrepreneurial turn in Burma, which began in 1989, has contributed to the (re-)emergence of extractive enclaves in spatially discontinuous zones across the country. This shift, although it coincided with the adoption of neoliberal practices and values across much of Southeast Asia, cannot be explained as a regime-led effort to more effectively govern its ethnically diverse population by graduating sovereignty or citizenship in accordance with market criteria. Rather, the entrepreneurial turn was prompted by a combination of international and domestic pressures that threatened the regime's ability to maintain sovereign control over the central core of Burma, much less to secure the remote border regions where more than two dozen insurgent movements were active. Although the cease-fire agreements and the resource concessions that followed from them helped reduce the severity both threats posed to the regime, they also created new and unforeseen ones—namely, the uncontrolled proliferation of ad hoc joint ventures operating in enclaves.

Fierce competition among these joint ventures has produced a number of "state effects," the term Michel-Rolph Trouillot coined to conceptualize how

Figure 8.1. Impact on the landscape after hydraulic mining, Shwegyin township, Burma. Credit: EarthRights International.

global flows are reworking the practices and processes national governments have long claimed a monopoly over (2001, 130). The most important of these involves the use of regulated violence to extract primary commodities and to discipline the population. Over time, these practices have fostered the growth of multiple networks of regulatory authority and wealth accumulation based on the continued redistribution of primary commodities, rents, and other assets across political, economic, and cultural boundaries. As a consequence, the regime's ability to exert centralized control over the enclaves and the translocal networks they sustain has paradoxically grown both stronger and weaker.

This case study also illustrates how different populations experience, understand, and react to their forced relocation in contingent rather than uniform ways—even where the economic, technological, and regulatory pressures contributing to their displacement and the production of complicit subjects are quite similar. Many of the miners originally displaced from Mogok, for instance, were able to move elsewhere and begin their livelihoods anew. Indeed, some of them have profited handsomely after switching from gem to gold mining. But for the

Karen living around Shwegyin the options are far more limited due to past and ongoing patterns of displacement.

These particulars aside, what purchase do resource concessions offer toward ethnographic studies of the "state" during an era discursively, but not always materially, dominated by neoliberal processes? One possible response entails returning to precolonial and colonial patterns of resource use and the transnational networks of relationships that made them possible to better understand the present-day reconfiguration of the "state." For example, Rebecca Hardin has illustrated how these interrelationships affect the *co-management* of valuable forested areas by nonlocal logging and conservation interests in the Central African Republic (2002). Concessions, she points out, refer not only to spatial units designated for economic exploitation but to a much broader process where various rights and obligations between state and nonstate actors are actually negotiated (2002, 3).

For my purposes, I wish to focus on the three features that Hardin identifies as increasingly characteristic of natural resource concessions under contemporary globalization, all of which apply to Burma. First, the negotiation of formal concession agreements occurs at the local or regional level rather than at the national level. Second, patron-client relationships, often involving nonstate entities, now mediate and sometimes even replace direct nation-state governance. Finally, the transnational rivalries engendered by these spatial practices reconfigure identity politics among local populations differently affected by these agreements in addition to altering the geopolitics of resource use (2002, ii). Taken together, these features suggest concessions are not simply legal agreements that, by virtue of their abstract and formal qualities, exist distinct from social practice (Mitchell 1991, 94). Rather, concessions are complex and historically constituted social forms that tend to obscure the very relations of power that animate them, much as Marx demonstrated with capital and the commodity form more generally (1972, 71–83). Put differently, it is our preoccupation with a concession's material properties—specifically the potential exchange value of the "commodities to be" located within them—that diverts critical attention away from how concessions are negotiated and the emergent modes of governance active within them. Examining these practices opens analytical terrain for reexamining our assumptions regarding the relationship of sovereignty to territorial space and identity formation, highly relevant concerns given the increasingly contradictory picture of the autonomy of the contemporary nation-state (Verdery 1994; Ong 2006, 1–27).

Such tensions appear quite clearly in Burma where, as I noted earlier, the regime has negotiated a series of cease-fire agreements with armed opposition groups. These agreements have ended fighting in some areas, fomented intra-ethnic armed conflicts in others, and weakened the resolve of many armed opposition groups to maintain a unified front. Although observers have focused on the strategic military ramifications of these agreements (Smith 1999), they have placed relatively less attention on their interlocking socioeconomic, cultural, and environmental ramifications that I briefly touched on previously. Among other things, these arrangements have dramatically expanded the area where different business interests can operate via "extra-state" networks, while blurring "theoretical ideas concerning the nexus of legality/illegality, state/non-state, and formal/non-formal power relations" in the process (Nordstrom 2000, 38). Of course, these binaries rest on the premise that we actually know both ethically and analytically where one domain ends and another begins.

But more to the point, the Tatmadaw (the state's armed forces) and the SPDC (the state's bureaucracy) are not the same thing. Although both institutions overlap considerably—active military officers hold all high-ranking government positions in Burma, for instance—they are not unified entities that think and act like persons, though ordinary Burmese and scholars alike often speak of them as if they were. Rather, both institutions consist of competing interests and actors that often work at cross-purposes to one another (and to those outside their direct purview) despite the regime's persistent claims to be the sole force capable of preserving Burma's "national unity" and "territorial integrity" (Houtman 1999, 59–120). In this regard, one must remember that power in Burma, specifically the ability to exert one's influence and to demand loyalty, remains firmly personalized rather than institutionalized (Maung 1983), hence the enduring significance of patron-client relationships and the complex forms of exchange they depend on that are not based on laws.

Given the complex nature of these competing networks of authority and accumulation, politico-administrative maps of Burma have become little more than "cartographic illusions" (Ohmae 1995, 7). Such illusions fail to accurately depict how these previously contested areas and the concessions located within them are actually governed and by whom. A more accurate representation would require a dynamic map with multiple layers to convey how momentary economic alliances anchored to particular resources bases have created different "mosaics of territorial control" (Hardin 2002, ii). Importantly, a growing body of field research indicates that these mosaics are not new per se; rather, they represent the intensification and geographical expansion of resource struggles that date back to the 1960s, if not earlier (e.g., ERI and KESAN 2003; ERI 2007).

Two final observations, both of which deserve further inquiry, follow. First, our understanding of postcolonial Burma remains one sided as most studies reduce the violent conflicts there to past and present ethno-nationalist struggles. Closer attention to the changing political economy of access to and control over the country's diverse natural resources should yield a more nuanced account of the role primary commodities have played in shaping when and where violent conflict occurs in Burma (Peluso and Watts 2001b). Second, the resource concessions also raise questions about the empirical "nature" of the regime, its own sovereign assertions notwithstanding. In other words, the processes at work in the extractive enclaves may simply be the most visible manifestation of broader rivalries between different networks of authority and accumulation that have always been in play, but are normally hidden by the façade of unity the regime's leaders publicly maintain through a combination of censorship, terror, and complicity. If indeed the regime has no institutional or geographic fixity, as many scholars of the state have argued (e.g., Trouillot 2001; Roitman 2001; Mitchell 1991), then greater ethnographic attention to how sovereignty is multiply asserted across Burma should shed light on how such translocal networks (rather than an authoritarian state) differently mediate the effects of neoliberalism at particular times and in particular places.

PART III

*New Markets,
New Socionatures,
New Actors*

9

Old Markets, New Commodities

Aquarian Capitalism in Indonesia

DORIAN FOUGÈRES

If you have ever ventured immediately southwest of Hong Kong to Lamma Island, you have seen them: bright red, green, and gold fish from coral reefs, swimming in long, narrow glass tanks that double as storefronts. These are "live reef food fish," soon to be steamed and eaten by wealthy seafood connoisseurs. Along China's southern coast, the practice of keeping coral reef fish alive until moments before cooking likely dates back centuries, although they only began appearing on the menus of Hong Kong's upscale restaurants in the late 1960s (Johannes 1995, 11). A regional trade linking East and Southeast Asia took several more years to develop. Divers from Hong Kong first depleted proximate fish stocks, moved into the Philippines in the 1970s, and into Palau and Indonesia in the 1980s (ibid., 12)

In this chapter I use the East Asian–Southeast Asian trade in live reef food fish (hereafter "live fish") to illustrate how the region's historical double movement of people, money, and equipment in one direction, and tropical marine commodities in the other, now occurs faster (taking hours instead of weeks or months) and in greater volumes (involving hundreds rather than dozens of tons) than ever before. Furthermore, although this trade has historical precursors and these seafoods move through long-established markets, I will argue that live fish constitute a new and unique type of tropical marine commodity. This distinction hinges on their biophysical forms—large coral reef fish—and their corresponding need to be constantly immersed in clean, cool, oxygen-rich seawater to survive. As a result, circulating these fish involves greater technological complexity and economic risk than other commodities extracted for export on Indonesia's reefs. The production of coral reef fish as live seafoods demonstrates capital's considerable ability to control and profit from tropical marine nature at the turn of the second millennium.

Live seafood production and trade concurrently illustrate the contested commoditization of labor under neoliberalism. In the two islands I studied in South Sulawesi, "Pulau Rantau" and "Pulau Tetap," fishers and divers, their patrons, and fish exporters have continually renegotiated social and labor relations. Over the past fifteen years the ties that bind them have changed in nonlinear fashion, involving various mixes of wage, contractual, and self-employed labor.[1] Most recently, the largest fishing and diving patrons have gained control over the production and domestic marketing of live fish from their islands, and they have improved their positions in the regional seafood networks that link their fish with distant consumers.

The live fish case is notable because its trade generally has been developed under neoliberal principles, yet it diverges from two of this book's themes. First, though authoritarian state institutions are key in Indonesia, they have not fostered the enclosure of the fisheries I examined. As scholars have long emphasized, fishing territories cannot be easily bounded and divided, hence restricting access and assigning individual private property rights is particularly problematic (Gordon 1954). Therefore, as I argue elsewhere, primitive accumulation in the live fish fishery has hinged on expanded credit and debt relations, rather than enclosure (Fougères 2005). Second, capitalist development in the fishery has depended on unrestricted flows of foreign capital. However, state institutions and joint ventures have not played significant roles in regulating the "live fish" fishery or channeling resources into it, as has occurred in Indonesia's other high-value fisheries (Zachman 1973; Bailey 1988) and resource sectors (Gellert, chapter 2; Tsing, chapter 1; in this book). Instead, private entrepreneurs have organized and underwritten the trade.

Aquarian Questions

Agrarian questions have reemerged at the turn of the millennium (McMichael 1997; Watts and Goodman 1997), and scholarly work focusing on questions of agrarian capitalism provides my point of departure in studying marine resources. A subset of this literature problematizes how the nature of an agricultural territory or a commodity inflects processes of capitalist production and circulation (Mann 1990; Talbot 2002b). Associated work in political ecology explores such phenomena in nature-based industries such as forestry and mining (Barham, Bunker, and O'Hearn 1994; Prudham 2005). My central claim—that live fish constitute a new and unique type of tropical marine commodity because of its biological characteristics—builds on this literature. My claim fits within a larger argument I make elsewhere that processes of capitalist development in both fishing and aquaculture are analogous but not reducible to those in agriculture, because these two industries are biogeochemically and biophysically based in water rather than in land (Fougères 2005). This basis in water affects uncertainty and risk—the central focus of this chapter—as well as enclosure and state intervention in specific ways, and these nature-based differences, I argue, merit the theoretical recognition of distinctly *aquarian* questions of capitalism and transition (ibid.).

My investigation of the amplified linkages between Hong Kong and South Sulawesi also draws from the literature on agrarian change and differentiation in Indonesia (Gerard and Ruf 2001; Li 1999; Hart et al. 1989). This literature is centrally concerned with historical changes in people's control over and access to productive resources in rural society, particularly land, labor, and capital, and with corresponding changes in the appropriation and distribution of surplus value. Here I broach the topic of aquarian change and differentiation, and refute a standardized portrayal of divers and fishers as the passive and powerless victims of foreign fishing enterprises from Hong Kong (e.g., Barber and Pratt 1997; Lowe 2000). This intervention builds on studies that have shown that while contemporary agrarian changes are linked to globalizing processes of commoditization, primitive accumulation, and the subsumption of labor and nature under capital, these processes only take shape through the countless interpersonal relations and agentful transactions that constitute everyday life in historically, geographically specific rural places (Li 2002b; Moore 2005).

Working from the premise that a commodity embodies overdetermined relations of political economy, culture, and nature (Coronil 1997; Watts 1999), I use a commodity chain analysis to structure my two arguments (see fig. 9.1). A commodity chain refers to (a) a sequence of processes extending from commodity

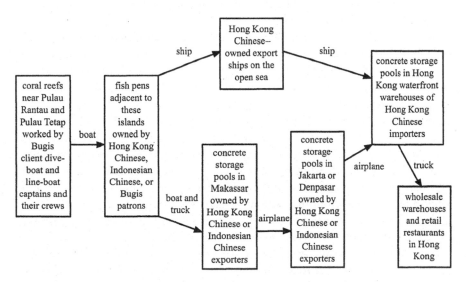

Figure 9.1. South Sulawesi–Hong Kong live-reef-food-fish commodity chain.

production through processing and sales, (b) the series of exchanges through which this commodity passes, and (c) the linkages that bind these processes and exchanges (Ribot 1998; Talbot 2002b). Although elsewhere I use a commodity chain analysis to highlight the creation, appropriation, and distribution of value (Fougères 2005), here I focus my analysis primarily on the nature-based complexities and risks bound up in the capitalist effort to bring a living commodity to market, and how actors have engaged these qualities through the use of new technologies.

Old and New Tropical Marine Commodities

Regional trade in high-value tropical marine commodities has linked diverse people, remote islands, and emporia in Southeast and East Asia for centuries. The earliest representatives of such trade consist of marine jewelry, namely corals, pearls, and tortoise shells: the circulation of these inert commodities through and around the South China Sea dates back to at least the third century CE (Gungwu 1958). In the sixteenth century, dried shark fins became the first tropical seafood to enter regional trade circuits (Blussé 1991). A trade in sea cucumber used for medicinal purposes emerged, and a century later edible sea cucumber entered the commodity stream, stretching as far as northern China and Japan (Macknight 1976). During the eighteenth and nineteenth centuries, sea cucumber funneled through Makassar (the provincial capital and export hub of South Sulawesi) became the major commodity that linked South Sulawesi's diverse traders with Xiamen and Canton in China (Sutherland 2000). In the late nineteenth century, a fermented marine food—shrimp paste—entered the regional market (Butcher 2004).

Beginning in the 1850s, trade in tropical marine commodities expanded to include living products. At this time a boom in the sale of tropical aquarium fish, "discovered" during German and other scientific expeditions, began linking markets in England and Scotland with coral reefs in Southeast Asia and other tropical regions of the world (Atz 1971). A century later, in the 1960s, a rejuvenated American and European demand for aquarium fish encouraged the rapid expansion of supply networks throughout the Philippines, Indonesia, and elsewhere (Johannes and Riepen 1995). These small fish could survive in transit with minimal care and technology. In the 1980s advanced aquarium technologies allowed collectors to sustain transplanted hard and soft corals. It remains unclear when a regional market for live seafood, specifically lobster, emerged in East Asia and Southeast Asia, but this likely predated or occurred simultaneously with the expansion of regional live-fish networks in the 1970s.

The production of high-value tropical marine commodities in Pulau Rantau and Pulau Tetap thus has relatively recent origins, and even though widespread production of tropical marine commodities in the islands extends back only a few decades, a skilled and enterprising labor force already existed when the live fish industry arrived in the islands. Until the late 1960s shipping services that involved seafaring throughout Indonesia, Malaysia, and Singapore had constituted the primary basis of island livelihoods. Around this time national freight lines running on diesel engines began replacing wind-powered Bugis trading ventures like those based in the two islands (Ridder 1988). Many islanders from Pulau Tetap turned their attention to lift-net boats, a new technology in the region that made it possible to catch large volumes of bottom-feeding fish—anchovies, sardines, little tunas, snappers—to supply local markets on the mainland. Capturing these fish involved uncertainty insofar as nothing guaranteed that fishers would find any while at sea. Furthermore, marketing these fish involved the nature-based economic risk of perishability: fishers had difficulty selling fish that had begun to decay.

Rather than turn to lift-nets like their neighbors, in the late 1960s many residents of Pulau Rantau began diving on the locally abundant coral reefs in search of high-value marine commodities. They chose this alternative based on the practices of a few families at the southern tip of the island who had Bajo ancestors and already based their livelihoods on diving. Since the island's settlement around the turn of the century, these free divers had collected *japing-japing*, a conical shell used in jewelry and for buttons. Diving became a commonplace occupation, particularly after 1967. That year a company based in Makassar sent a boat to the islands to recruit free divers for voyages throughout Indonesia in search of pearl oyster shells (also used in jewelry and making buttons). In the ensuing years most of the island's residents reorganized their trading ventures around pearl-shell diving expeditions. During the 1970s, this became the island's predominant economic activity.

Producing and circulating pearl shells involved relatively straightforward processes. On the reefs a diver would pry the sessile oyster from its coralline substrate either by hand or with a crowbar, place it in his dive bag, and continue gathering oysters until he had to surface for air. This gathering of a wild marine organism involved uncertainty, yet circulating the resulting shells involved no nature-based economic risk—on returning to shore the diver would split the oyster open and discard the muscular flesh, after which he or his patron could store the half shells indefinitely without any loss of value.

In the early 1980s divers adjusted their activities as the availability of oysters diminished. Many dove more frequently, sometimes for several days and nights in a row. Those with enough money invested in scuba gear, which allowed them to reach depths greater than forty meters, where pearl shells remained abundant. Likewise, almost all diversified their efforts by collecting sea cucumber alongside pearl shells, and the former commodity slowly replaced the latter as the island's economic mainstay. The imbrication of sea cucumber biology and a new, inexpensive diving technology introduced to Pulau Rantau in 1987 secured sea cucumber's primacy. This relied on using an air compressor to force air from the deck of a boat down to a diver through a thin plastic hose. Compressor diving equipment costs about two-thirds less than scuba diving equipment and requires crews of just four for operation. This made it possible for entrepreneurs with limited capital to invest in their own equipment and become captains of their own boats, and in some cases to eventually become patrons. Critically, while the equipment functioned poorly in deep waters, it worked well in the shallower depths (five to thirty meters) where sea cucumber thrived.

Compared with pearl shells, producing and circulating sea cucumber involved slightly greater complexity. Sea cucumbers are mobile rather than sessile organisms, although they move slowly and cannot defend themselves. After being captured, divers bisected and eviscerated the sea cucumber, and salted its empty body, which maintained its quality for a week. When back on shore divers boiled hollow bodies twice in saltwater, smoked them for two to six hours depending on the species, and dried them in the sun for three days. Afterward a diver or his patron could store the cucumber for months without spoilage or loss of value.

Around the same time that sea cucumber became popular, a local market for live rock lobster began to develop, creating additional niches for divers from Pulau Rantau to exploit. A few divers had once sent fresh lobster to Makassar for export in the mid-1980s, chilling them to stave off spoilage. In 1988 one particularly gregarious and enterprising boat captain met a businessman in Makassar who had recently begun exporting live lobster to Hong Kong, and the two agreed to work together. This would mark the commoditization of nature in a new form—live seafood—in the small archipelago. Producing this new commodity, however, presented significant operational challenges for the few divers who tried it. Lobsters make their homes in coral crevices and, like sea cucumber, have limited mobility. Yet they defend themselves when pursued, and if divers broke a lobster's limbs in the ensuing struggle, the lobster lost half or all of its market value. The adoption of cyanide diving technologies in 1992 encouraged rapid growth in the sector because it allowed divers to catch the defensive creatures without a struggle. Divers dissolved tablets of sodium or potassium cyanide in plastic squirt bottles filled with seawater; they then would dive down to the reefs and, using the long nozzles on the bottles, squirt the target lobster (and later fish) with the poisonous solution, temporarily stunning it. The newfound ease in capturing live lobster convinced dive-boat patrons from Pulau Rantau to begin supplementing their trade in sea cucumber with this new commodity.

Circulating live lobster posed new risks and complexities. The risk centered on mortality: if a lobster died, it garnered about one-third the price of a live lobster. Patrons subsequently learned to hold lobster in special pens floating at sea, and to feed them chopped fish every few days to maintain their size. Exporting live lobster also involved greater complexity than earlier commodities, because they required periodic immersion in fresh seawater to survive. When done by ship, exporters accomplished this by keeping the lobster in water compartments (a closed portion of a boat or ship's hull with holes in the bottom to allow water to flow in and out) during the ten-day voyage to Hong Kong.

Export by airplane involved a specialized packing process. First divers in Pulau Rantau submerged the lobster in icy seawater to make them lethargic. Divers subsequently took handfuls of wet sand and used this to cover each lobster's eyes, in order to minimize fighting when the lobster were next packed in Styrofoam boxes. Layers were separated by newspaper and stocked with small plastic bags of ice. Patrons then sent the lobster to shore by boat, and from shore to an exporter's warehouse in Makassar by truck. Exporters in turn sent them to Hong Kong by plane. If divers had caught them without cyanide, the lobster survived out of water between twenty and thirty hours, but those caught with cyanide survived for only about twelve hours. In the latter case, exporters had to first unpack the lobster, place them in concrete pools filled with saltwater for an hour, and then repack them. Lobsters caught without cyanide rarely died in transit to Hong Kong, while about 5 percent of those caught with cyanide did. Importers in Hong Kong paid exporters in Makassar nothing for those which arrived dead.

The Distinctiveness of Live Reef Food Fish

A market for live fish emerged in Pulau Rantau and Pulau Tetap alongside that for live lobster. A Hong Kong Chinese company based in Makassar first caught live fish with cyanide in the area's waters in 1989, followed by a second company in 1990 and a third in 1991. Foreign Chinese—not Indonesian Chinese—captains and crews piloted and operated these companies' large wooden catch boats, each outfitted with six or seven additional speedboats used to catch fish and bring them back to the main boat. Around twenty-five Indonesian divers from Lai-Lai, an ethnically Bajo island just off the coast of Makassar, worked as wage laborers on the monthlong trips these catch boats made throughout the Indonesian archipelago.

Capturing live fish posed greater challenges than previous commodities produced by Pulau Rantau's divers because fish can rapidly swim away when pursued or hide in coral crevices like lobster. In the early years of the trade, a handful of the island's independent divers (i.e., those not tied to a patron) joined the Hong Kong boats and were trained in the use of cyanide to catch live fish. As with lobster this involved divers diving down to the reef and attempting to get close enough to fish to squirt them with cyanide solution. If fish retreated into corals, divers had to break apart the corals to remove them, and then place them carefully in mesh dive bags. Divers also learned how to relieve the air bladders of the fish so they could survive in shallow depths. This involved properly locating the air bladder of a particular fish species and carefully inserting a hypodermic needle into the bladder, through which air then escaped. Once back at the central catch boat, crew members divided the fish according to species and size class, weighed them, and submerged them for several minutes in large plastic bins filled with an antibiotic solution.

Circulating live fish also involved novel technical difficulties: unlike lobster, they could not survive out of water for more than a few minutes. As stated earlier, taking these fish to Hong Kong's market thus required keeping them constantly submerged in cool, clean, oxygen-rich seawater throughout the entire commodity chain. When shipped by boat, crew members accomplished this by using water compartments. When shipped by airplane, entirely new techniques had to be developed, as explained later.

In the mid-1990s local production of live fish with catch boats stabilized. In 1993 companies based in Makassar built floating fish pens (like those used for lobster) in the waters surrounding Pulau Rantau, which allowed catch boats to store large amounts of locally caught fish for weeks at a time, instead of transporting them around the country. When fish arrived at the pens, a technician treated wounded fish with small injections of antibiotics or swabbed their wounds with antibiotic salves. Once deposited in the pens, the pen managers fed the fish regularly to maintain their weight (and hence value, with larger fish generally garnering higher prices). Technicians also monitored water quality around the pens, and moved the pens if terrestrial runoff during the rainy season threatened to infect the fish with disease and cause catastrophic die-offs, or if strong winds and swells associated with the east or west monsoon threatened to rattle the pens and cause additional fish injuries. The use of fish pens, furthermore, entailed the complementary use of dedicated export ships—large steel or aluminum alloy ships that came straight from Hong Kong via Makassar to Pulau Rantau's fish pens for the express purpose of exporting, but never catching, fish. One such ship could export fifteen or more tons of fish, compared with no more than four tons for a catch boat. From 1993 through 1996 one or more such export ships visited the island each month of the fishing season, typically loading fish at one or two other regional sites before returning home; no longer a fishing backwater, Pulau Rantau and Pulau Tetap had become a key node in the regional live-fish network.

The establishment of fish pens in Pulau Rantau's waters broke the monopoly of the Hong Kong Chinese boats over fish extraction, and made possible a shift in the control of production in the islands to patron-captain partnerships. This is because Hong Kong companies would not buy fish from anyone in the years before they built fish pens. But once they did so, and stationed representatives atop the pens to guard their fish, their representatives purchased any live fish caught by anyone regardless of their involvement with the Chinese boats. So patrons and their captains interested in extracting these valuable fish now had a buyer. Many patrons from Pulau Rantau and Pulau Tetap now turned their attention to live fish. Notably, patrons from Pulau Rantau did not work with their long-standing dive-boat captains to catch live fish at this time. Instead they recruited line-boat captains (i.e., those who used hook-and-line technologies to catch live fish) from Pulau Tetap. Since the 1980s captains from that island had watched their incomes decline as lift-net boats with electric lamps from the mainland out-competed their own gas-illuminated lift-net boats. The invitation to work with patrons from Pulau Rantau and catch live fish thus appealed to many captains in 1994, and over the next few years between eighty and one hundred boat captains, each with an additional one to three crew members, began to do this.

Increasing competition among live-fish export companies further stimulated local involvement in fish extraction by driving exporters to pay, via their fish-pen representatives, higher fish prices to obtain the fish caught by local patrons and their captains. Crucially, increasing competition involved not only new companies based on catch boats and export ships but new companies based on a revolutionary mode of transportation: airplane shipping. An Indonesian Chinese entrepreneur in Makassar had begun using airplanes to export live lobster in 1992, and in 1994 he began experimenting with exporting live fish in the same way. Although several of his early attempts failed, the former chemistry professor eventually perfected the complex technique.

Airplane shipping involved several innovative processes and technologies. First, getting the fish from the islands to the Sulawesi mainland involved transferring the fish from the pens to a transport boat with a water compartment that held three hundred kilograms of fish. Once the boat arrived at the mainland, a patron or exporter's assistants transferred the fish from the boat to a truck that was specially outfitted with one or two large plastic drums, each filled with chilled, fresh seawater containing dissolved antibiotics that was aerated constantly by an oxygen tank. Several hours later the fish arrived at a waterfront warehouse in Makassar, where an exporter's technicians unloaded the fish into large concrete pools through which they continuously pumped cool, fresh seawater.

Once the fish reached the warehouse, the most complex stage of the circulation process—packing—began. This involved using ice to slowly lower the temperature of the water from twenty-seven or twenty-eight to twenty-one or twenty-two degrees Celsius over two and a half hours, and then anaesthetizing the fish en masse by dissolving chlorophenicol in the water—a technique the chemistry professor had refined through trial and error. Next the exporter transferred the fish one by one from the water to a Styrofoam box lined with a thick plastic bag, simultaneously adding antibiotic-laden water at a water-to-fish ratio of 3:1. Additional assistants next inserted a plastic hose attached to an oxygen tank into the bag, hyperoxygenated the water, and quickly tied the inflated bag shut. Lastly, other assistants placed the lid on the box and taped it shut. When the exporter had packed all of the fish, assistants loaded the boxes into the waiting truck of a cargo agency, which then took them to the airport in Makassar. If a scheduled flight connection existed, the fish might arrive in Jakarta (or Denpasar) and then be immediately transferred to a plane to Hong Kong, where they arrived about twelve hours after leaving the warehouse in Makassar. If one did not exist, the exporter in Makassar collaborated with an exporter in Jakarta or Denpasar who picked the fish up at the airport, unpacked and placed them overnight in another warehouse's concrete pools, and then repacked them early the next morning for the flight to Hong Kong; in this case it would take about thirty hours to get the fish from Makassar to the final destination.

The need for intensive management at all nodes in the commodity chain points to the complexity and associated high economic risk that circulating live fish poses. Their need for constant immersion in clean, cool, oxygen-rich seawater to survive storage and transit represents a crucial biophysical requirement not seen in any other tropical marine seafood. If producers cannot meet this requirement and a fish dies, it typically loses all of its value. On the rare occasion that a captain can quickly sell the dead fish in fresh form to his patron, he may get one-third to two-fifths the live fish price, but if the fish has begun to decay and a captain can only sell it dried and salted, he will generally get only one-twelfth to one-eighth the live fish price. In turn, if a fish dies in a patron's pens and that patron can ice the fish and sell it fresh to an exporter, the patron generally receives around one-fourth the live fish price, while fish that have begun to decay garner no value.

The key variable in live fish survival is the duration a fish spends in captivity, and this explains the advantage of airplane shipping. Catch boats and export ships succeeded in keeping live fish immersed in fresh seawater through the use of water compartments, but these vessels visited Pulau Rantau and Pulau Tetap only periodically, and it then took ten days to make it back to Hong Kong. In this system of punctuated circulation, if fish waited in the islands' fish pens for one month before export, 15–30 percent of the fish died, depending on the species. On the way to Hong Kong mortality rates regularly ranged between another 25–40 percent of the fish. By contrast, with its low minimum shipment requirements (300–400 kilograms instead of at minimum eight tons for an export ship) and hence near daily exports, and its short transit times, airplane shipping markedly reduced the risk of fish dying before making it from the islands' reefs to Hong Kong. In this system of continuous circulation, only 1 to 2 percent of fish died while being held for two or three days in the islands' fish pens, with fewer than 5 percent dying in transit to Hong Kong. So although the cost of shipping per kilogram was higher for airplanes than export ships, the higher survival rates generated higher overall profits.

The advent of airplane shipping stimulated the rapid expansion of South Sulawesi's live fish industry. Intrigued by the success of Makassar's pioneering airplane-based exporter, more than a half dozen additional seafood-related Indonesian (and Indonesian Chinese) businessmen in the city entered the live fish trade and attempted to replicate his strategy. By 1996, however, only the two largest of these continued to ship fish by airplane; the rest had dropped out due to the financial losses they incurred from fish dying due to poor packaging before reaching Hong Kong.

The key point for the production of live fish in Pulau Rantau and Pulau Tetap's waters, and the marketing of these fish, is that Makassar's three remaining airplane-based exporters ran their large operations differently than the Hong Kong-based companies. Rather than hiring independent divers on a salary, or buying whatever patron-captain partnerships would sell them on Pulau Rantau's spot market, airplane-based exporters relied on credit-based contracting with patrons. Patrons who accepted credit to help increase their production in turn were required to sell their catches to the exporters who provided this credit. In the early years of the trade, credit was essential for patrons, who had limited financial resources. This was because the high price of live fish coupled with their high risk of mortality meant that circulating them required large amounts of money to cover purchases as well as deaths in storage or transit. By providing patrons with credit in the form of cash (or equipment) that the patrons then passed on to their captains, Makassar's airplane-based fish exporters (a) simultaneously underwrote expanded technologically cutting-edge production in Pulau Rantau, without directly supervising the extraction process, and (b) secured fish supplies through a forward market contract. This started shifting the control of fish marketing from Hong Kong companies based on export ships and wage labor, or on opportunistic open market purchases, to exporters in Makassar based on airplanes and credit-based contracting.

In 1996 another subtle event occurred that planted the seed for a further shift in the control of fish marketing that blossomed after the year 2000. In a move to gain a modicum of control over the sale of their fish to airplane-based exporters, three of Pulau Rantau's patrons built their own fish pens. These patrons were already able to produce some fish (and profit) with their own assets, even though they still depended on their contracting relationship with an airplane-based exporter to run their overall operations. In succeeding years this credit would slowly become a complementary source of financial capital used to expand production, rather than an essential input.

The amplification of capitalist relations between Makassar and the two islands between 1994 and 1996 also primed local production for what came next. The 1997 financial crisis in Asia—an event that fractured the "Washington Consensus," but did not necessarily stop the spread of neoliberal policies[2]—and its political fallout at the highest level of the Indonesian government in 1998 dramatically devalued the Indonesian rupiah, which in May 1998 fell to one-seventh of its 1996 value. Live fish exporters in Makassar began making windfall profits because Hong Kong importers had always denominated fish prices in dollars, yet the exporters had always paid island patrons in rupiah. So even though retail fish prices in Hong Kong fell by 1999 to half their 1996 value (McGilvray and Chan 2001), the rupiah's much greater depreciation meant that an exporter now received three to four times more rupiah per kilogram of fish than he had in pre-crisis years, even while he continued to pay patrons in rupiah at precrisis prices.

This potential for large profits helped to expand live fish production in South Sulawesi because it attracted a new round of opportunistic businesspeople in Makassar to the live fish trade. Fewer than ten live fish exporters (including export ship and airplane based) operated in Makassar in early 1997, but by the end of 1998 around twenty vied to purchase fish from patrons all around South Sulawesi. These fish exporters poured financial capital in the form of credit into places such as Pulau Rantau and Pulau Tetap in an effort to secure fish supplies through contracting with patrons.

Local production also expanded because almost all of Pulau Rantau's diving patrons reassessed their economic activities in the mid-1990s. One by one diving patrons and their captains began diverting their patron-derived credit, boats, and equipment to catch the live fish and lobster available on local reefs, instead of the increasingly scarce sea cucumber. The number of dive-boat captains that switched to catching live fish during this period numbered between sixty and eighty, each with three to five crew members. The entry of these divers into the live fish fishery beginning in 1997 coincided with a large increase in the use of cyanide in local waters. Almost all diving captains and crews used this technique because divers could catch two to four times as many fish as fishers using hook-and-line fishing over the same period. The burgeoning of cyanide diving marked the beginning of a shift in the control of production from one group of patron-captain partners—Pulau Tetap's hook-and-line fishers, who had dominated since 1993—to another—Pulau Rantau's divers (though some patrons worked with captains from both groups).

The widespread adoption of cyanide diving technologies in the late 1990s, while increasing the number of fish caught, also markedly increased the risk of fish mortality in circulation. Rather than 1 or 2 percent mortality, about 5 percent of live fish captured with cyanide died during the first day or two of being held in fish pens; and rather than 5 percent of the live fish dying during airplane shipment from Makassar to Hong Kong, 8 to 10 percent died. Patrons who relied on dive-boat captains, all of whom used cyanide, thus preferred to sell to airplane-based exporters. If they tried to hold fish caught with cyanide for a month to sell them to an export ship, most or even all of their fish might die.

Back in Makassar the bloated number of live fish exporters soon deflated. In the three years after 1997, live fish exporters in Makassar competed to contract fish by offering more credit and progressively higher prices to patrons, even though this made their own profit margins increasingly slim. About half of the exporters failed to cover their costs and could no longer continue operating by the year 2000; all but a few export ships stopped visiting the islands. By 2003 only eleven of the twenty-some exporters that operated during the Asian financial crisis remained. The shake-up in Makassar, however, did not negatively affect the patrons in Pulau Rantau and Pulau Tetap. Competition for the islands' fish remained intense, as the large exporters still battled one another in the market. In the islands, this meant that fish prices remained high even after the economic crisis peaked: even though their profits might have been slim, fish exporters had to pay high prices to secure enough fish to keep their businesses financially afloat, otherwise patrons would have avoided contracting with them entirely. In this way, patrons finally started seeing an increase in their profits. Additionally, in 2001 one exporter began denominating his fish prices in U.S. dollars, as was done in Hong Kong. This meant he would no longer capture the benefit of currency fluctuations—if the *rupiah* suddenly declined against the dollar but prices in Hong Kong remained constant, he would now pass the financial gain on to patrons—but it helped him attract clients. Other exporters soon followed suit.

Rising profits encouraged several prosperous patrons to begin changing their business practices around this time. Led by those who had built their fish pens back in 1996, patrons who had assets to independently finance their own operations began to pay off their credit-based contracts with airplane-based fish exporters, and to sell their fish primarily through the open market in Makassar. This move marked the onset of another gradual shift in the control of the marketing of Pulau Rantau and Pulau Tetap's live fish, now from airplane-based exporters to the archipelago's own patrons. By 2003, fourteen of the two islands' twenty-two patrons, including the three largest, had ended their credit-based contracting relationships with airplane-based exporters. They now could shop around and sell to the exporter that offered the highest price on a given day.

In 2002 several patrons in Pulau Rantau and Pulau Tetap began collaborating in their fish sales, further increasing the predominance of unfettered market transactions. Rather than relying exclusively on their own stocks to meet minimum shipment sizes of 150–200 kilograms worth of fish, which could take two or three days, patrons who had a significant yet inadequate amount of fish would solicit from a combination of other patrons the remainder needed to meet a quota imposed by an exporter. Just ten or twenty kilograms of fish from a few other patrons, all of whom received the same prices, allowed the organizing patron to meet shipment quotas faster. During the peak fishing season, this pattern of collaboration allowed patrons to send fish to Makassar once or twice or even three times in one day. Such collective sales also reduced the risks for patrons that were associated with circulating fish caught with cyanide, as they generally had only to hold fish overnight, subsequently losing only 1 or 2 percent of their fish before sale.

Aquarian Capitalism under Neoliberalism

Markets for high-value tropical marine commodities have linked South Sulawesi and southern China for centuries. The recent application of industrial technologies to production and circulation, however, has allowed capitalists in the region to extract and distribute new commodities, live lobster and live fish, based on entirely new commodity forms—the living rather than the fresh, dried, fermented, canned, or frozen. The development of this regional trade in live fish is particularly notable given the "nature" of "Nature" in this case—that is, the nature-based economic risk and technological complexity associated with trying to keep a large fish alive during (at minimum) a one-day voyage covering more than four thousand kilometers.

The context within which entrepreneurs in Hong Kong have extended live fish markets to encompass the coral reefs in Sulawesi, however, has involved more than antibiotics and airplanes. Indonesia implemented initial neoliberal reforms of its banking, trade, financial, and foreign investment sectors in 1983, 1986, 1988, and 1994, respectively (Jomo et al. 1997), and the amplification of the live fish trade in national waters began during this period. Although the trade would likely have developed regardless of these reforms, it is questionable whether it would have developed as quickly and in the same form as it did without these restructurings. Although the earliest traffic in live fish involved relatively slow catch boats and export ships, the advent of airplane shipping allowed for much more rapid physical transaction times. Taking advantage of potentially daily fish exports, however, in turn required equally expeditious payments and credits. Fortuitously, following three decades of strictly regulated foreign investment after 1967, international money transfers became commonplace in the 1990s and allowed for just such rapid financial turnover. Likewise, the liberalization of banking, trade, and capital restrictions meant that state-owned enterprises and joint ventures, by no means abandoned in other resource industries, now regularly operated alongside independently owned transnational corporations. In the live fish case, as private seafood importers from Hong Kong extended the trade throughout Indonesia's seas, state institutions never monopolized extraction and international sales, but instead limited their activities to immigration control, permitting, taxation, and food export inspection.

At the same time as aquarian capitalists in Sulawesi engaged the nature of fish and coral reefs, they also altered the regional economic geography. With the local price of reef fish quadrupling in a decade, divers and their patrons in Pulau Rantau and Pulau Tetap found themselves occupying what was fast becoming a significant node in the East Asian-Southeast Asian live fish network. Particularly in the aftermath of the Asian financial crisis, as live fish exporters in Makassar fought for increasingly small profits and market share derived from the islands' fish, diving patrons moved from contractually subordinated clients to economically and socially unconstrained sellers in Makassar's spot market. Nonetheless, despite a few attempts to sell fish directly to Hong Kong importers, these patrons never gained access to the live fish markets in Hong Kong, which hinged upon Chinese nationality or at least ethnically Chinese cultural identity. This limitation underscores that while efforts to restructure capitalist exchange along neoliberal lines can have significant effects and remain open ended, contests over the appropriation of surplus value from new Southeast Asian commodities remain grounded in the past histories and uneven geographies that constitute old markets.

10

Production of People and Nature, Rice, and Coffee

The Semendo People in South Sumatra and Lampung

LESLEY POTTER

Coffee, "a palpable and long-standing manifestation of globalization" (Topik and Clarence-Smith 2003, 2), is the focus for this examination of the production of people and nature in southern Sumatra.[1] Commodities such as coffee, which have been traded for centuries between peripheral tropical uplands and core metropoles, are no longer seen by scholars as simply economic or agricultural products, but as possessing social and cultural attributes (Appadurai 1986b; Bridge and Smith 2003) and as "producing" both their growers and their own version of "nature."

In this chapter I will examine the position of smallholder coffee growers in southern Sumatra, specifically the indigenous Semendo people, though other ethnic groups are involved, both indigenous and migrant. The Semendo are highly migratory, and will be studied in their home subdistricts in South Sumatra Province and in one of their migration destinations, Sumberjaya subdistrict in Lampung Province (see fig. 10.1).[2]

Coffee has been characterized as "everywhere a frontier crop eating the forest" (Topik and Clarence-Smith 2003, 391) and many of its Sumatran producers have been stereotyped as forest destroyers, both during the Dutch colonial period and in recent times. A careful examination of historical and modern evidence reveals a more complex and contested reality, especially in relation to the Semendo. In Sumberjaya, violent evictions of coffee growers from protected forest during the Suharto regime, have given way to a more moderate government stance since the demise of the regime in 1998. Reformation and decentralisation, plus the increasing roles of international research institutes and local NGOs, have had important effects.

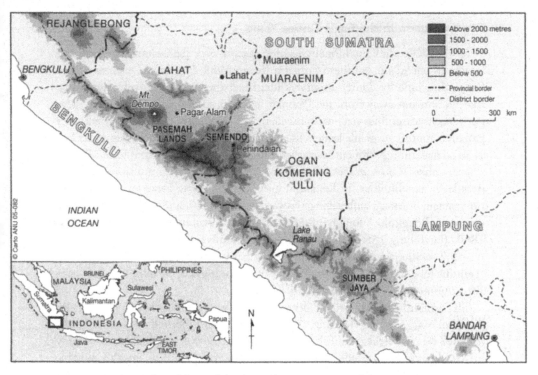

Figure 10.1. Semendo and Pasemah lands, southern Sumatra. Credit: Carto ANU 05-082.

Recent studies also demonstrate the impacts of globalization and neoliberalism on Sumatran coffee growers, who generally produce the lower grade robusta variety (*Coffea canefora*). They have suffered from low prices and international competition (especially from Vietnam), plus the antigrower organization of the marketing chain (Ponte 2002; Talbot 2002a). However, as producers of coffee agroforests and growers of trees, the Semendo group in Sumberjaya—together with its Javanese and Sundanese neighbors—has created a different kind of "nature," though one that is still excluded from the global market for organic or rustic coffees.

In their "homeland" in South Sumatra, other Semendo villagers have remained more isolated, reliant on return migrants from Lampung and incoming Javanese to expand their economic possibilities. Unlike their counterparts in Sumberjaya, they have suffered some neglect from government and a lack of interest from outside organizations.

To better understand the present, it is useful to explore the history of the Semendo in southern Sumatra and their relationships with rice fields, forests, and coffee gardens, long central to their culture.

The Semendo in the Early Coffee Years

By the 1860s the Dutch finally secured control over the isolated Pasemah and Semendo uplands in southern Sumatra (Sevin 1989, 89). Initial reports on the Semendo people by Dutch observers identified them as a relatively new group that had broken away from the Pasemah in order to embrace Islam. They were perceived as careful farmers, with excellent wet rice fields. Well disciplined, they gathered around a capable leader. Their high plateau environment was described as attractive, though difficult to access (Gramberg 1866; Pauw ten Kate 1869).

Java coffee (*Coffea arabica*) had been produced under compulsion for some decades by smallholders in Bengkulu and West Sumatra; however, the Cultivation System of forced coffee deliveries was ending in Java and in 1872 it ceased to operate in Bengkulu. Though unknown among the Semendo and Pasemah in the 1860s (Gramberg 1866),[3] free smallholder coffee began a rapid increase during the 1870s under the impetus of high prices, being described by van Gorkom as a "genuine folk culture" (Gorkom 1884, 266). Compulsory smallholder deliveries also continued in West Sumatra until 1908.

The Semendo already had a culture of out-migration, largely due to their tradition of *tunggu tubang,* whereby the eldest daughter inherited the family home, irrigated wet rice fields, and fish pond. As the *sawah* (wet rice) fields were highly prized, other siblings would often move from the village to find another suitable location for their *sawah,* usually along a riverbank. Although swiddens were also made on the forested hillsides, establishing *sawah* was always the goal. The first moves south into Lampung took place around 1876 (Prins 1935, 239), with settlers reaching Sumberjaya about ten years later. Four *marga* were established along the route, facilitating the movement south.[4] According to local tradition, it was some years before coffee was introduced to the new area, at the suggestion of Dutch officials (Kusworo 2004, 75).

The passage of the Agrarian Law of 1870 in Java (Domeinverklaring) marked the beginning of the long-lease system, whereby European planters were encouraged to produce export commodities on "wastelands." Although there was debate over the economics of such enterprises in such a remote region, in the 1880s Dutch planters began arriving in the southern Sumatran uplands, setting up coffee estates on the good volcanic soils around Mount Dempo in the Pasemah lands, in Rejang-Lebong (Bengkulu), and near Lake Ranau.[5] These activities encouraged smallholders to establish themselves near the estates. The high Semendo plateau, cut by deep ravines, was less accessible and not attractive to foreign interests (see the map).

Although large parts of the uplands were forested, on his ascent of Mt. Dempo in 1885 botanist H.O. Forbes saw to his surprise that the Pasemah lands were almost completely grass covered, except for trees growing in the ravines and gorges and on hills rising above the plateau surface. The volcano itself was forested, with rice fields and coffee gardens on its lower slopes. Forbes learned from villagers that no trees had been found on the plateau for the past three hundred years, an earlier forest having been destroyed in a great fire, perhaps an eruption (Forbes 1885,192). Parts of the Semendo plateau also carried *Imperata* grasslands, though the descriptions included large areas of forest (Gramberg 1866; Pauw ten Kate 1869). As those areas were more distant from the volcano, the grasslands may have originated from swidden farming on the plateau's poorer soils.

One detailed study of free smallholder coffee in southern Sumatra (in Rejang Lebong, Bengkulu) was critical of smallholder techniques as compared with those of nearby European plantations. The observer recommended pruning the bushes "down to the stump" and wider spacing for longer production: "With the European a garden is laid out for 30–40 or more years, with the native for 10–15 years" (Kraft van Ermel 1892, 22).[6] Some smallholder gardens had trees up to 3.5 meters high with thick trunks, but they were planted in swiddens without shade. Against such irregular planting was opposed the plantation model, with orderly, widely spaced trees and predictable harvests. The transitory nature of smallholder production, its uncertain and irregular need for labor, were criticized by Kraft van Ermel, a former *controleur* of the district. However, his criticisms were administrative, rather than environmental. He saw the coffee swidden system as productive, but lacking in organization.

Forester Z. Kamerling, reviewing this discussion thirteen years later, disagreed with the recommendation for wide tree spacing, arguing that such a pattern would only encourage weeds and invasive grasses. Believing that the coffee garden should be treated more like a forest than a plantation, he strongly recommended canopy closure, leaving a few forest trees to take care of soil protection (Kamerling 1906, 101). Unusual for a forester, he supported smallholder coffee techniques, including the practice of swiddening: "One thus, in fact, gets a transition to permanent cultivation in which the cultivation of perennials is the main thing and in which, in the first and second year, one grows annuals as a sideline" (Kamerling 1905, 626). The subtle environmental message saw *alang-alang* grassland (*Imperata cylindrica*) as the enemy of forests, with the close-planted coffee swidden combating that enemy.

Kamerling's survey found coffee to be widespread, but growers had suffered low prices due to overproduction in Brazil, and interest was declining (Kamerling 1906).[7] The first trials of the robusta variety (*Coffea canefora*), introduced to Java in 1900, were conducted in Sumatra in 1907: a sturdier and higher yielding type, this was seen as eminently suitable for smallholders. By 1911 a hajji from Semendo was demonstrating his small but productive robusta garden (planted following the advice of the local *controleur*), which impressed all with its enormous harvests, good prices, and low soil demands (De Bruyn Kops 1919, 77; Huitema 1935, 71). This was despite the fact that the Semendo district was considered backward, its people partly still heathen (Letterkerker 1916). By 1920 there was also strong interest in robusta coffee in the Pasemah lands of Lahat and Pagar Alam (Huitema 1935, 71, 94).

Under the shifting system, farmers would open a new field every year or two (preferably in the forest) and harvest coffee for up to ten years after two crops of hill rice. Trees continued to grow during the fallow period, being finally replaced after twenty years. This system caused rights to the fallow land to remain with the previous owner, rather than to become generally available, as would happen with an annual crop: "With the cultures for the market, which only came up in the last half century, the *adat* law could not adjust itself quickly enough to the changed circumstances" (Royen 1927, 183). Although the tall abandoned coffee allowed forest to regenerate in some areas, in others rough scrub or grass characterized the fallows.[8] The entry of a borer beetle in 1923 emphasized the usefulness of robusta: methods of control focused on removal of breeding sites through rapid harvesting (not possible with arabica) and keeping the ground clean under the trees. The physical extent of the gardens in southern Sumatra proved an obstacle, however, with so much additional fallow land through which the borer could spread. Hoedt compared them unfavorably with European estates in East Java, where control was much simpler (Hoedt 1929, 3).

Coffee Smallholders versus the Colonial Forest Department, 1921–24

In 1921 the new forest service in Palembang was becoming active and advocating numbers of reserves, including all hydrological and production forests in the Pasemah lands (Dienst van het Boschwezen 1921–22). The coffee swidden system was criticized by the forester A. Thorenaar, who made a clear connection between swiddens, *alang-alang* fields (especially on the Pasemah plateau), and soil poverty through frequent burning (Thorenaar 1922, 764). This seems to have been the first attack on a system that had previously received either encouragement or only moderate criticism from Dutch officials, and it was linked to the spread of institutional forestry into southern Sumatra. Unaware of the age and persistence of the Pasemah grasslands, Thorenaar attributed them to recent human activity. He was challenged by an agricultural officer named van Setten, who had encouraged the introduction of robusta coffee into the region (De Bruyn Kops 1919) and had worked for some time at Muara Enim, near Semendo territory. Van Setten noted that Semendo were "born farmers, who were unhappy without a wet rice field." He added: "One could hardly accuse these people, with their intensive *sawah* farming, of having impoverished the land through making *ladangs*" (Setten 1922, 107).[9] He also pointed out the existence of local closed forests, *rimboe larangan,* and strict marga rules over mountainsides where making a *ladang* was forbidden.[10] He quoted the *pesirah* (marga head) of Semendo concerning the need to keep steep slopes under forest: "Everyone...would like to pay one hundred guilders or more for such splendid, exceptionally suitable coffee growing land. But everyone knows that this would result in a water shortage in a few years and we could not plant our sawahs any longer" (Setten 1922, 113). Thorenaar replied: "The case of the Semendo is unique: everywhere else the Malays do not hesitate to burn the forest on the steepest mountain slopes for their agriculture. It is ridiculous to expect anything from the forestry insights of the Native" (Thorenaar 1922, 775). The correspondence continued intermittently for another two years, with Thorenaar castigating the "reckless" *ladang* farming, with forest cover restoration being left entirely to "nature" (Thorenaar 1924, 766). He obviously did not trust nature to do the job, as efforts were made to reforest the Pasemah lands with leguminous trees (*Albizzia falcataria*) and pines. The Forest Department was also said to have excluded local swiddeners from one large reserve on the pretext of "protecting" the forests, then it made the land available to European capitalists for plantation development (Setten 1922, 112). Thorenaar responded (1922, 774; 1924, 767–68) that the land had been found to be unsuitable for plantations and would remain forest. The clash of values between a supporter and a detractor of local agriculture is very clear in these exchanges, in which the combatants remained barely civil. The forester's attitude has modern echoes, with his preference for capitalist plantations over local swidden farmers and his efforts to restore the forests, even through the planting of exotics.

The inclusion of the marga head and his pronouncements about the need to keep uplands under trees, together with the information about the existence of closed forests, provides a unique insight into the Semendo group and their understanding of "nature," as opposed to the "scientific" knowledge of the forestry officer.

Transition to the Modern Period

The success of smallholder coffee in the 1920s was accompanied by moves toward a greater stability of production in the Pasemah areas around the Dempo volcano. The agricultural extension service introduced new seed and encouraged the use of shade trees and pruning. As coffee was always combined with rice growing, preferably wet rice, more labor was required to make these changes and Javanese young men seeking work moved from the coastal areas to the Pasemah lands (Tergast 1930, 18–20).[11] Shading and pruning evened out the harvests, so that the trees were not stressed by the bumper crops of the fourth or fifth season, which were usually followed by sharp productivity declines. Under shading, the need was reduced for frequent replanting of new fields and fallowing of older gardens, the result being a more permanent cultivation. Leguminous trees used as shade (such as *Erythrina subumbrans*) also provided mulch and nutrients. More distant plateau areas, such as the Semendo lands to the east, remained untouched by those innovations (Huitema 1935, 95). The uneven spread of shade prompted a further exhortation by agricultural consultant H. Vonk (1937, 368) who condemned the *ladang* coffee system as "the gravest form of robber-farming." P. J. S. Cramer, the former director of coffee research at Buitenzorg (Bogor), later described it more moderately as economically "defensible" but still likely to lead to forest destruction and groundwater supply problems (Cramer 1957, 38).

Emigration southward from the Semendo lands continued apace during the 1920s and 1930s. According to maps produced by O. Sevin, the "pioneer front" almost reached as far as Lampung's southwestern coast, though the highest concentrations remained nearer the South Sumatran border in and just south of the Sumberjaya area. Sevin (1989, 93) emphasized the "aggressive" and "very extensive slash and burn" farming techniques of the Semendo, which he argued must have been used to enable such rapid movement. Kusworo (2004, 75) described the process more carefully, saying that the first aim of the new settlers was to find "fertile and relatively flat land where water could be channeled for wet rice fields." Once those fields were created and houses established (often along a riverbank), upland rice would be planted and coffee gardens introduced. Small groups would go back and forth from an existing settlement to set up the new village, generally assisted by Javanese sharecroppers.

World War II and the disturbed period of Indonesia's independence played havoc with the coffee industry as food production took precedence, though smallholders recovered faster than the estates. While one hundred thousand tons of coffee had been produced in Indonesia in 1925, in 1961 this had dropped to nineteen thousand tons (Mougeot and Levang 1990).

The 1960s and 1970s saw much spontaneous migration of Javanese into the Pasemah coffee lands of Dempo and Pagar Alam, seeking work as sharecroppers. After an international price peak in 1977, following the failure of the Brazilian coffee crop, many were able to purchase their own gardens. Semendo people, on the other hand, continued their movement to Lampung, partly depopulating their homeland. They were followed into the hills of Sumberjaya by Sundanese transmigrants and spontaneous Sundanese and Javanese settlers. In parts of the subdistrict, Javanese now form the majority ethnic group. When opening new areas of forest using pioneering techniques, the Javanese still try to put the blame on Semendo, perpetuating their stereotype as "forest destroyers" (Suyanto et al. 2005).

Sumberjaya Coffee Smallholders versus the Indonesian Department of Forestry, 1985–97

During the 1980s the Suharto government, through its forest classifications, became landlord over huge areas of the national territory, allocating most of the production forest to large corporations as logging concessions, while enclosing other land as protected forest, nature reserves, and national parks.

By 1978, Lampung had outstripped South Sumatra as Indonesia's most important coffee province (McStocker 1987).[12] In the late 1980s growth slowed as the military moved to clear coffee growers from protected forests and national parks and to engage in large-scale reforestation (Kusworo 2000). Evicted transmigrants were forced to move to the lowlands, but other settlers remained in nearby villages, prolonging conflicts. The protected forests and national park in Sumberjaya were greatly expanded by the Department of Forestry from the original Dutch reserve. Semendo villages, established from Dutch times outside the reserve, had strong claims over the lands from which they were newly excluded (Verbist and Gamal Pasya 2004).

The Sumberjaya subdistrict was particularly targeted by the Department of Forestry as it was the watershed for the Way Besai river, feeding lowland water supply and irrigation schemes. Early reforestation efforts used slow-growing, valuable timber species, such as mahogany and *sonokeling* (*Dalbergia latifolia*), but many trees died or were uprooted by coffee garden owners. The latter surreptitiously managed to maintain their cultivation, playing a game of "cat and mouse" (*kucing-kucingan*) in which the foresters would eventually receive a share of the harvest (Kusworo 2004, 157). Following construction of a hydropower project on the Way Besai in 1994, officials became more serious, attempting to reforest the entire catchment with the fast-growing shrub *Calliandra calothyrsus*. In 1995–97 even elephants were introduced by the military for the rapid demolition of gardens and houses. Villagers still spoke bitterly of their hatred for *Calliandra* (fieldwork, July 2001). People were not opposed to forests: they simply needed land on which to farm. One Semendo village was awarded the national environmental award, Kalpataru, for maintaining its village forest against outside pressure, while others kept their closed forests (*hutan tutupan*), especially to conserve springs (Kusworo 2000).

Some villagers earned money by planting timber trees for the Department of Forestry, but then they subsequently destroyed them before they became serious coffee competitors. Trees of "useful" species supplied by the government, such as durian or sugar palms, were allowed to remain. Then came the fall of Suharto in 1998, and, with it, great volatility. Villagers saw the old regime swept away and they no longer feared retribution from the police or the army. The weak rupiah during 1998, coinciding with a temporary rise in international prices, resulted in a bonanza for export crops such as coffee, with prices as high as Rp. 15,000 per kilogram. Almost immediately, the reforested lands were cleared of their *Calliandra*, coffee reappeared, and the villages were rebuilt. Natural forest clearing reached a new peak from 1998 through 2000, but paradoxically there are now more trees in the coffee gardens than on the state-forest land (Verbist, Putra, and Budidarsono 2004). "Wild nature" is being replaced by a planted, but selective, forest.

The activities of the Department of Forestry against the villagers are reminiscent of the struggles against the colonial department of the 1920s. Villagers were especially incensed that their coffee trees were regarded as mere "bushes," yet the shrub *Calliandra* was substituted as a reforestation species. Although the growers had earlier used both bribes and trickery to maintain their cultivation, political events including the decline in the power of the Department of Forestry after decentralization led to victory for the growers, at least in their possession of the land. Unfortunately, the ensuing slump in coffee prices has made this a hollow triumph.

Neoliberalism, the Commodity Chain, and Prices Received by Farmers

Deregulation of the coffee commodity chain after the dismantling of the International Coffee Agreement (ICA) in 1989 moved the institutional framework from one where producers had a voice to an informal and buyer-dominated system.[13] "In the process, a substantial proportion of total income generated in the coffee chain has been transferred from farmers to consuming country operators" (Ponte 2002, 1116). Talbot (2002a, 220) has labeled this situation "the new international inequality," as four transnational corporations control the flow, processing, and distribution of coffee into the core markets and absorb most of the profits. The result has been a collapse in prices to growers that has been described as "the worst coffee crisis ever seen" (Osorio 2004 quoted in Muradian and Pelupessy 2005, 2029). The entry of Vietnam into the low end of the coffee market put further pressure on prices, as Vietnamese coffee is directly competitive with Indonesian robusta. After the brief boom of 1997–98, prices in the coffee lands of southern Sumatra slid quickly to levels below the cost of production, with serious consequences for farmers. The promoting of organic and "bird-friendly" coffee has been suggested as a possible solution, with a price subsidy to farmers (Muradian and Pelupessy 2005), but its applicability to the study area is questionable, as growers do not adhere to strict organic guidelines.

The Coffee Crisis in the Homeland: Semendo Villages in South Sumatra

In the Semendo homeland in South Sumatra, the low coffee prices of 2001–02 saw people forced to adopt a number of survival strategies. A kilogram of coffee sold locally for Rp. 2,000–2,500 per kilogram (below production cost) while a kilogram of rice cost Rp. 2,500–3,500 (author's fieldwork, January 2002). Where they had access to wet rice fields, people relied heavily on this crop for subsistence. They preferred to spend time on their rice fields and neglect their coffee until prices improved. They also turned to the collection of forest products such as rattan and young men stripped the bark from *medang* trees (*Lauraceae* spp.)

for mosquito coils. Use of forest products, a traditional form of forest "rent," remained a buffer against the low coffee prices.

Extensive old family orchards of durian and other fruit trees grew along the lower river valleys, where the produce was marketed as fresh fruit. Agroforests of coffee, rubber, and fruit trees were still found in these valleys. The higher Semendo country was characterized by open spaces with regrowth bracken and *alang-alang*. Although new coffee gardens were still being opened in the forests, most were strictly illegal, as they lay inside the official (1980s) forest boundary. Many gardens were actually located on ancestral fallows or old rubber lands, which the people call *rimba* (old forest). The coffee system was not intensive, with farmers unable to afford much fertiliser and not using shade trees[14] so the leaves often appeared yellow and lacking in nitrogen. Pruning was practiced to prolong the life of the bushes for up to ten or fifteen years, after which they were felled and the coffee replanted in a new forest or bushland area. In more elevated parts of the plateau, some arabica was still being produced. Although arabica prices were supposed to be higher, most traders refused to separate the varieties, just mixing them all together.

The village of Penindaian with its neighbours, Bandar Alam and Tanjung Raksa, had 122 households. A large exodus to Lampung had taken place from 1963 to 1965, after a disastrous fire in 1963, when almost all houses in Penindaian had burned. Much land in the village was owned by *tunggu tubang* who [*hereditary*] had moved away, but still retained ownership rights. *Tunggu tubang* land is usually not sold without extensive negotiation among family members, so it just lies vacant or is occasionally rented out. The large amount of temporarily unused rice land and simply vacant land in Semendo villages was striking.

Rice varieties included tall traditional types in addition to the newer IR64 (*padi pendek*), which was being trialed for the first time using seed stock from a fellow villager, a Javanese migrant. Those seeds were cheaper than those purchased commercially and people were keen to try them, knowing that they could obtain two crops per year and double their rice output. They were unsure, however, about the fertiliser needs of the new crop and had received no assistance from government officers, none of whom had visited the village.[15]

Penindaian and Tanjung Raksa shared access to a twenty-five hectare traditional community forest, similar to the old closed forests, *rimboe larangan*. People were not allowed to farm there, but with permission from village leaders could utilize the forest resources (which still included large trees). Other folk ranged far into the mountains, seeking rattan to make baskets for sale in the district capital.

The coffee lands of Semendo present a picture of a population adopting a range of alternative activities to cope with the low prices.[16] Farmers were innovative, seeking additional crop materials and other income sources, though Javanese migrants and returned Semendo with Lampung experience were acting as catalysts for many of the innovations. Those who had access still depended on the "nature" represented by the forest, or restored the rice fields on which their subsistence depended. They received little government assistance, and many were information poor, but they were forced to manage on their own.[17]

Applying Science to Coffee Systems in Sumberjaya

The World Agroforestry Centre (ICRAF) has been studying the Sumberjaya watershed since 1998, originally to counter government plans to once again remove the settlers.[18] ICRAF scientists are trying to prove that permanent coffee gardens protect the watershed at least as well as the shrub *Calliandra callothyrsus* (Noordwijk et al. 2004). They have encouraged farmers to use shade trees and diversify holdings (Noordwijk 2001; author's fieldwork, July 2001). A study by S. Budidarsono, S. A. Koncoro, and T. P. Tomich (2000) identified a typology of coffee systems, based on vegetation structure complexity, management intensity, and tenurial security. Vegetation structure varied from a simple monocrop to a multistrata, complex agroforestry system. Management ranged from "traditional pioneer" (originally typical of Semendo farmers) through semi-intensive (with shade) to intensive farming with high fertilizer use. Under the category of tenure security, Budidarsono, Koncoro, and Tomich distinguished between privately owned land and state forest land. An economic analysis showed that the complex multistrata coffee system with secure tenure and medium management intensity brought the highest returns, yielding various fruits as well as coffee, whereas the pioneer system offered the lowest return to land and labor.

The question of shade trees is an important one for the region's coffee farmers. In Latin America a rapid conversion occurred during the 1970s and 1980s, following the development of new sun-tolerant, high-yielding coffee varieties (Perfecto et al. 1996). These modern plantations are grown as monocultures without shade but with large amounts of chemical inputs. Although yields are higher than for traditional coffees, there is increased soil erosion, loss of diversity, and high input costs. With lower world coffee prices and more interest by consumers in organically grown produce, shade-grown "bird-friendly" coffees now attract a premium.

A number of studies of the multistrata system recognized by ICRAF in Sumberjaya have aimed to show that it is as sustainable as some of the organic coffees grown in South America (Noordwijk 2001). Although not equal to "natural" forest in characteristics such as carbon stock assessment (Noordwijk et al. 2002), biodiversity (Gillison et al. 2004) or bird assemblages (O'Connor 2006), the multistrata agroforest scores better than either simple shaded coffee systems or unshaded "pioneer" types. Unfortunately, there is as yet no economic recognition of this system's environmental superiority. Robusta coffee brings low prices on world markets, its eventual destination being instant coffee. There have been no incentives for growers to improve the quality of their product, as traders mix all coffees together.[19] A certification system, if introduced, would have to pay careful attention to quality control and evolve different marketing strategies. One possible solution would be to encourage multistrata coffee over larger units, which would then make certification worthwhile, but tenurial and tax incentives would be needed before such a goal could be realized (Noordwijk et al. 2002).

The World Agroforestry Centre has put considerable resources into its "laboratory" of Sumberjaya and several scientific studies have emerged. It has provided advice to growers and also argued the case of growers against the Department of Forestry through its scientific studies. The resources have been mainly in the form of research to prove that the coffee growers have not been degrading the environment, but in fact have been improving it. Some local people (mainly Javanese) have also secured jobs as research assistants. Verbist, Putra, and Budidarsono (2004) noted that only about 7 percent of gardens were of the multistrata type until 2000, but they then increased dramatically since then, mainly as a result of more varied production as coffee prices dropped and the government began encouraging community forestry, for which various trees were supplied. Most farmers with secure land tenure, including most Semendo, now have multistrata coffee, and have planted a variety of local

Figure 10.2. Young women sorting coffee, South Sumatra. Photo credit: L. Potter.

timber trees as well as the government supplied fruit trees. Javanese occupying protection forest land have similarly invested in intensification, believing that they are now immune from eviction (Suyanto et al. 2005; A. Kusworo, personal communication).

The requirements for certification of boutique, "bird-friendly" coffee are more difficult to apply in Sumberjaya than in Latin America. Under current certification schemes, gardens must be guaranteed chemical free for three years, but Lampung farmers still use chemical fertilizers and herbicides if they can afford them. Unlike the position of arabica growers in other parts of Indonesia (such as Bali or Tanah Toraja, Sulawesi) where boutique coffees do exist, a certification system is not guaranteed to bring financial rewards to robusta coffee farmers and is not favored by growers.

However, through the efforts of ICRAF and a local NGO, WATALA (Friends of Nature and Environment), the government has granted some Javanese and Sundanese growers leases for five-year community forestry leases (Hutan Kemasyarakatan, HKm) on their coffee lands (with a possible extension to twenty-five years). The benefits of a community forestry lease are simply that legal tenure over the land is recognized. In an area where there had been so many evictions in the past, such tenure is perceived as valuable. Although groups in four Semendo villages have applied for such leases, to my knowledge none has so far been granted (Kerr, Pender, and Suyanto 2006). In explanation of this anomaly, the researchers stated: "The Sumendo people are known locally for being less inclined to collective action and potentially difficult to work with" (ibid., 12).

I wondered why Semendo people continued to be stereotyped in this way, so I asked two local observers for their thoughts. The first emphasized that Semendo did undertake collective action in protecting forests and constructing irrigation channels, but had stronger communities than the Javanese and Sundanese, so they did not rely on official recognition. He suggested that there were some struggles over land between Javanese and Semendo, with Javanese seeking government assistance for their cause (Observer 1, personal communication). The second observer suggested that many Semendo mistrusted governments of any persuasion, having lost much land to the Department of Forestry in recent times. He also suggested that there was friction between groups, and noted that ICRAF has just started to employ Semendo, which has led to an improvement in perceptions among the largely Javanese researchers (Observer 2, personal communication). Obviously the situation is complex, and these are anecdotal observations only, but the dominance of Javanese among government officials and researchers seems to be perpetuating the myth that Semendo people cannot be trusted with community forestry leases. J. Kerr, J. Pender, and Suyanto also indicated that "bridging social capital" was useful, such as direct links to the Department of Forestry through forestry employees who lived in one successful village. "Bonding social capital," on the other hand, appears to have always been strong among the Semendo, which should encourage their joint application for community forest leases and their ability to manage them.

Although ICRAF views the development of HKm in an entirely positive light, its working out at the local level has also been suggested as a strategy whereby forestry officers "gain greater control not only over the resource, but also over people" (Kusworo 2004, 163–64). There are restrictions imposed on people's behavior in a community forest, especially if they want to remove trees. Prices for some additional products, such as fruit, are low: many farmers are growing small chili under their coffee, a strategy they perceive as essential for survival. If they wish to plant larger and more profitable chili or other vegetables, they will have to cut down some of their trees. Studies of agroforestry elsewhere have noted that, though generally a positive option for poor communities, agroforests may be the site of "contentious political struggle" (Schroeder and Suryanata 1996, 189).

Traditional indigenous knowledge may now be harder to find in modern Sumberjaya. The producers' knowledge of the crop and the techniques employed, together with their effects on and concepts of "nature," have varied over time and by location and culture. A recent study of the indigenous knowledge of Semendo, Sundanese, and Javanese households in Sumberjaya, which encompassed soil erosion, water quality, and land suitability, revealed that they have moved toward "a complex of hybrid origin, rather than a purely indigenous system" (Schalenbourg 2004). The convergence of scientific and indigenous knowledge, aspired to by political ecologists such as Raymond Bryant (1998), seems to have been achieved in Sumberjaya under the impress of many scientific studies (see also Agrawal 1995). The position in the more isolated Semendo homeland remains rather different.

The Semendo, Smallholder Coffee, and the Future

In this chapter I have presented a history of smallholder coffee in parts of southern Sumatra over the past 140 years, with special emphasis on the migratory Semendo group. Case studies drawn from the colonial period presented early favorable assessments of Semendo rice farming and social cohesion. Despite the emphasis on coffee as a commodity throughout the subsequent analysis, it is clear that to the Semendo coffee was only a contingent part of a broader livelihood system, which was centered on wet rice fields and included protected forests. The formal forestry establishment, both in southern Sumatra in the 1920s and in Sumberjaya during the Suharto era, basically misunderstood the dynamics of such systems, characterizing Semendo smallholders as mere "forest destroyers" and physically expelling both them and their Sundanese and Javanese neighbors from the Sumberjaya uplands.

Low international coffee prices have recently encouraged diversity within and beyond the coffee systems, with growers attempting to position themselves as best they can to ensure survival. The position in the South Sumatran homeland, where the concentration of effort remains with rice and forest activities, provides a kind of baseline for the changes that have occurred in the coffee systems of Sumberjaya, as ICRAF and local NGOs in the name of biodiversity and agroforestry have encouraged more tree-based techniques. As they have adapted their coffee systems to fit better with ICRAF's vision for their area, some farmer groups have been able to negotiate with the government and have secured land tenure for up to twenty-five years, provided that they plant trees on their coffee farms and protect remaining forest. The exclusion of Semendo from this development, even though they have transformed their coffee systems from the swiddening "pioneer" type to "multistrata agroforests," indicates a continuation of negative stereotyping of this group. It is obviously important for ICRAF, their NGO helpers, and government agencies to counter such prejudices and enable all groups to enjoy whatever benefits might become available, especially possible new initiatives in payment for environmental services (PES). Although the harsh-flavored robusta coffee will never rival the more delicate arabica to command a price premium in international markets, the development of a mixed coffee agroforest, as an "intermediate" system, has scope for the provision of services that equally may be able to reward growers (Wiersum 2004). The stability of the forest frontier will largely depend on the perception of favorable outcomes being available to all.

The Message Is the Market

Selling Biotechnology and Nation in Malaysia

SANDRA SMELTZER

As one of the world's megadiversity countries, Malaysia has an abundance of unique flora and fauna. In an attempt to capitalize on this rich biodiversity, in 2005 the Malaysian government established BioNexus, a nationwide network of research and development institutions that welcomes relationships with foreign biotechnology companies. The government also introduced the National Biotechnology Policy to provide the necessary regulatory and financial support for this nascent sector of the economy. Prime Minister Abdullah Badawi has promised his citizens that, together, BioNexus and the Biotechnology Policy will help launch Malaysia into the status of a developed nation by the year 2020. Although this strategy may produce some positive agricultural, scientific, and economic results, the government is cultivating the industry within a purely economic framework. As development economist Amartya Sen has argued, this kind of strategy places economic imperatives before politics, the environment, and civic freedoms. These latter concerns are "temporarily" left to the side so the country can focus on achieving its foremost priority—economic growth (Sen 1999). For Sen, a more appropriate human-centered form of economic development concentrates on the removal of "unfreedoms"—for example, poverty, lack of labor opportunities, repression of expression, and neglect of public amenities and services (Sen 1999). In other words, development programs should create environments that provide citizens with opportunities to freely exercise their human agency. In Malaysia, however, the government has placed tight restrictions on its press, favored short-term economic gains over effective environmental protection, and is negotiating a free trade agreement with the United States that will open up domestic natural resources to more extensive patenting, subjecting both nature and people to the twin processes of enclosure and commodification.

In addition to offering a critical overview of Malaysia's new biotechnology strategy and associated policies and laws, in this chapter I also examine how the

government has used the "politics of developmentalism" (Loh 2003, 261) to garner domestic support for its plans and policies. Specific attention is paid to how
the government has used the communitarian rhetoric of "Asian values"—loyalty,
hard work, and political stability—to create "buy-in" for its national projects.
Citizens are told that if they work hard, stay united, and support the government,
they will reap the benefits of development projects, including those associated
with biotechnology. The government has also rhetorically portrayed Malaysia's
natural resources as "precious," guaranteeing their protection in order to assuage
any concerns Malaysian citizens might have about the potential negative consequences of biotechnology activities.

I will then discuss the role played by the Malaysian media in helping to naturalize the government's biotechnology strategy. A political economy analysis of
the domestic mainstream media landscape reveals that there is little room for
citizens to learn about, debate, critique, or participate in the development of
the new biotechnology strategy. Instead, mainstream media tend to uncritically
relay approved messages concerning the benefits of biotechnology. In so doing,
they act as agents in the commodification of Malaysia's environment and its
peoples.

Developing Malaysia's Biotechnology Industry

In the mid-1990s Malaysia began construction of a massive international
high-tech hub. Named the Multimedia Super Corridor (MSC), this Malaysian
imitation of Silicon Valley was expected to launch the country into a position of
power and independence in the new global information economy. Prime Minister Mahathir Mohamad envisioned the MSC as a key element in a larger government strategy called Vision 2020, designed to steer Malaysia toward the status
of "developed nation" by the year 2020. In essence, the strategy was conceived as
a sociopolitical manifesto encouraging Malaysians to work hard, remain united,
and embrace information and communication technologies (ICTs). In return,
citizens were promised that ICTs, the MSC, and Vision 2020 would beget socioeconomic progress for all Malaysians.

In physical terms, the MSC is a nine-mile-wide by thirty-mile-long corridor that stretches from Kuala Lumpur City Centre at one end to the newly
constructed cities of Putrajaya (Malaysia's administrative capital) and Cyberjaya
(the business and residential headquarters of the MSC) at its other end. To obtain official "MSC status," corporations are required to locate at least part of
their operations inside this corridor.[1] In so doing, they are able to take advantage
of the project's Bill of Guarantees, which offers, among other things, exemp-
tion from local ownership requirements, unrestricted employment of local and
foreign workers, generous tax breaks, and the elimination of import duties on
high-tech equipment.

In 2003, Mahathir announced that a biotechnology hub named BioValley would become the newest addition to the MSC. BioValley was designed to capitalize on Malaysia's abundant natural resources and turn the country into an international center for biotechnology industry. The final completion date for the project was set for 2006, at which point the government expected BioValley to house between 200 and 250 biotechnology corporations operating in close quarters with research and development institutes. The entire project was slated to be built on land originally set aside for Malaysia's Entertainment Village (or E-Village), a project the government had hoped would eventually be able to compete with Bollywood and the Hong Kong film industry. When E-Village proved unsuccessful, its land and nascent infrastructure were made available for the development of the BioValley project.

The government's decision to build this biotechnology hub can, in part, be attributed to its recognition that the MSC had not produced the kinds of results it had originally anticipated. A new stream of revenue and greater economic diversification was deemed necessary to keep the country moving toward its Vision 2020 goals in an increasingly competitive global economy. The government also voiced concerns about the potential financial repercussions of delaying the development of a domestic biotechnology industry. As Mahathir's successor, Prime Minister Abdullah Badawi, has stated, "Malaysia possesses the richest biodiversity on the planet. It is a gift, *a competitive advantage* that is God-given and we must find ways to harvest it to the best of our abilities" (Badawi 2003a, emphasis added). Badawi has also warned that Malaysia "must take steps now, failing which we will end up losing to others who will exploit our rich bio-diversity for their own good only" (Badawi 2003b). These statements demonstrate a well-founded concern that with the increasing encroachment of the World Trade Organization's (WTO) Agreement on Trade-Related Aspects of Intellectual Property Rights (TRIPS), there is a real possibility Malaysia may lose control over some of its own natural resources. The government also recognizes that although the Convention on Biological Diversity (CBD) provides a framework designed to protect the biodiversity interests of the developing world, the economic imperatives underpinning the WTO and TRIPS are more interested in the commodification of biodiversity for the benefit of interests located primarily in the developed world.[2] It is not very surprising then, that in an attempt to diversify its economy (especially in the aftermath of the dot-com bust), the government would aim to capitalize on Malaysia's natural "wealth" before others get in the door.

Of course, Malaysia is not alone in its drive to use biotechnology as a means of wealth creation, particularly in the vacuum left behind by attempts around the world to re-create Silicon Valley as the "Holy Grail of economic development" (Sturgeon 2000, 15). In particular, Malaysia's decision to build its biotechnology industry must be understood within the context of the long-standing competitive relationship the country shares with its neighbor to the south, Singapore. In the early 1990s, the Singaporean government launched its Singapore ONE project, a high-tech hub with a technology corridor of ICT science parks, research institutes, and the National University of Singapore. When Malaysia introduced the MSC in 1996, competition for multinational companies and international investment flared between the two governments and their respective projects. In 2000, Singapore unveiled its Biopolis initiative as "a centre for biomedical sciences in Asia and the world" (Biopolis 2006). Soon thereafter, Malaysia pursued its megadiversity advantage and developed BioValley to tap specifically into agrobiotechnology.

For all of the reasons described above, the Malaysian government dedicated a significant amount of time, energy, and money to establishing BioValley; however, it afforded the project only a relatively minor role in political rhetoric between 2003 and 2005. In comparison with the dramatic launch of the MSC, BioValley almost completely slipped under the public radar. The handful of government speeches that focused on BioValley lacked the sensationalism one might expect to accompany this kind of new initiative. Additionally, official websites offered little in the way of background information about the project or explanations of how it would fulfill its mandate of becoming a new engine of economic growth for the country. As one international journalist remarked, "Even after its launch, it was hard to obtain concrete details about the BioValley"; it "was shrouded in mystery" (Cyranoski 2005, 620). The project's understated launch has been interpreted by local pundits as signaling the government's desire to announce its commitment to joining the international biotechnology bandwagon, while lacking strong policy direction or concrete plans to build the industry.

On April 28, 2005, however, Prime Minister Badawi took a significant step toward raising the profile of biotechnology in Malaysia (and, in the process, distanced himself from his predecessor's plans for the industry). Badawi announced the establishment of three new mechanisms designed to invigorate this sector of the economy and address concerns regarding its lack of policy direction: the National Biotechnology Policy, the Malaysian Biotechnology Corporation, and BioNexus. Together, this tripartite strategy signaled that the government was ready to move biotechnology from out of the shadows and into the public eye.

With the mandate of making biotechnology "one of the key drivers of the country's development" (Badawi 2005b), the overarching National Biotechnology Policy promises domestic and international companies significant tax incentives, an accommodating regulatory framework, access to public and private venture capital, and a robust workforce. The government also established the Malaysian Biotechnology Corporation (MBC), a one-stop private agency to facilitate the entry of companies and investors into the Malaysian biotechnology industry, expand research and development, encourage the commercialization of biotechnology, and oversee the implementation of government policies and initiatives.[3] Together, the National Biotechnology Policy and the MBC have been tasked with steering Malaysia's biotechnology industry toward contributing 5 percent of the country's GDP by the year 2020 and creating two hundred thousand new jobs in the areas of agriculture, health care, industrial biotechnology, and bioinformatics (Bernama 2005; Malaysia 2006, 157–69). To help achieve these objectives, the government took the original infrastructure-heavy BioValley project—which failed to produce anticipated results—and subsumed it under "a network or nexus of centres of excellence from existing institutions around the country, to be known as BioNexus Malaysia" (Badawi 2005b). BioNexus will initially be composed of three centers of excellence: agro-biotechnology at the Malaysian Agricultural Research and Development Institute, genomics and molecular biology at the Universiti Kebangsaan Malaysia, and pharmaceuticals and nutraceuticals at the Universiti Putra Malaysia (with a laboratory to be constructed on the original BioValley site) (Malaysia 2006, 158). This three-part strategy of the National Biotechnology Policy, the MBC, and BioNexus will be overseen by the Biotechnology Implementation Council. Chaired by the prime minister, the council will be advised by an International Advisory Panel composed of industry representatives, academics, venture capitalists, and members of myriad think tanks.

The Politics of Developmentalism

As incomes, the middle class, and consumerism began to grow in Malaysia during the 1990s, the government began to shift its focus away from political discourse that overtly featured policies preferential to Malays.[4] In its place, the government introduced rhetoric that concentrated on the "politics of developmentalism," which linked economic growth and development with national pride and collectivity (Loh 2003, 261). The rallying cry "Malaysia Boleh!" (Malaysia Can!) was adopted by Mahathir to encourage Malaysians to work together and embrace "Asian values" of nationalism, loyalty, and unity so the country as a whole could develop. These ideals were contrasted with "Western liberal democracy," which was characterized as an individualistic political system that, if implemented in Malaysia, would only serve to hinder the country's economic development (Teik 2002, 51).

The utilitarian nature of this shift in ethnic discourse should be understood as part of the government's broader strategy "to negotiate and capitalise upon transnational phenomena" in the new knowledge-based economy of the information age (Bunnell 2002, 106). By showcasing the country's cultural diversity, the government hopes to attract tourism and foreign investment, encourage domestic entrepreneurship, and garner support for its projects. By portraying Malaysia as an ethnically harmonious country—one that accepts and even celebrates its cultural diversity—the government promotes an image of political stability and a safe choice for investment. This is particularly important for the biotechnology sector, which tends to require heavy up-front financial commitment with a significant time lag in remuneration. The government also has used Malaysia's diversity to demonstrate that the country shares close ties with other Asian cultures and business communities.

The government also recognizes that non-Malay expertise is required for the success of Malaysia's high-tech and biotechnology sectors. Serious concerns have been raised that Malaysia does not possess the labor force necessary to propel these industries beyond a middle man role and into cutting-edge research and development. At the same time, the country continues to lose top-quality "knowledge workers" to foreign markets. The government has, therefore, promoted Malaysia as a multicultural, inclusive country in which all citizens are treated equally and fairly as a means of signaling to economically advantageous workers—specifically non-Malay Malaysians—that the government wants them to either stay or to come back home to Malaysia (Bunnell 2002, 115–16). This kind of developmentalist rhetoric of cultural inclusivity has also started to play out in the government's campaign to connect the benefits expected to accrue from biotechnology with the needs of the country's agriculturally based population. In addition to promising improvements to the physical infrastructure of underdeveloped regions, Badawi has also stated that the country's agricultural sector, "together with advances in biotechnology, can turn Malaysia's abundant natural resources into a vibrant and lucrative sector of our economy. For the rural population, it can provide sources of new income and new wealth. Ultimately, it will develop the rural areas, strengthen domestic demand and create equitable growth in the country" (Badawi 2004).

Under the Mahathir administration, "the word 'agriculture' and 'farmers' became a dirty word [sic]" (Kuppusamy 2004). Today, it is clear that, rather than viewing agricultural activities as markers of a *developing* country, they have been rhetorically recovered as critical components in Malaysia's march toward *developed* nation status. Therefore, in many respects, "old" commodities associated with agricultural activities are being literally and figuratively reconfigured and repackaged as "new" commodities for a lucrative biotechnology sector. Moreover, the poverty cycle of many agriculturally based Malays (as well as Malay fisherfolk, factory workers, squatters, and so forth) has been used as a political platform by the Parti Islam Se-Malaysia (PAS), which means developmentalist rhetoric linking biotechnology benefits with agricultural activities is politically strategic for Badawi's ruling party, the United Malays National Organisation.

Malaysia's indigenous peoples have also become increasingly valuable to state and federal governments. These citizens often live on biologically diverse—and thus potentially lucrative—land, and many possess valuable knowledge of local flora and fauna. As part of its commitment to the CBD and the Cartagena Protocol on Biosafety (CPB), the federal government is expected to play a central role in "ensuring that the objectives of the CBD are met, and especially to ensure that the equitable sharing of benefits obtained from genetic resources and related traditional knowledge becomes a reality" (Aguilar 2003, 182). Badawi has pledged his support for these objectives, stating that "it should be accepted as a matter of principle that commercial benefits should be fairly and equitably shared with the providers and users of the biological resources" (Badawi 2005a). Therefore, indigenous peoples could, if they chose, benefit financially from the country's burgeoning biotechnology industry; however, as discussed in greater detail below, the government's historical relationship with these citizens points to a very different future.

Another element in the government's campaign to garner support for its biotechnology strategy has been the promotion of Malaysia's natural resources as "precious" and of intrinsic value to Malaysian culture. Badawi has guaranteed state protection of these resources and marketed biotechnology as a safe and benign natural step along the country's path toward modernity. As he stated in 2005, "Malaysia treasures its natural resources. Our primary forests, our pristine beaches, our precious rivers and tributaries—all of these must be conserved and protected" (Badawi 2005a). Consequently, Badawi argues, a balance needs to be struck between, on the one hand, protecting and sustaining the natural environment and, on the other hand, financially benefiting from it. This kind of politically strategic attentiveness to environmental protection and sustainability is used to alleviate potential fears citizens may have about biotechnology, helping to render associated activities benign.

Rhetoric versus Reality

The Malaysian state plays a key role in producing rhetoric to minimize public concern over the relationship between state-facilitated development and environmental sustainability. In so doing, the state has helped to mask the destructive implications of the development path it has championed. As the environmental NGO Sahabat Alam Malaysia (SAM) laments, "The attempt to transform the physical environment into raw material for Malaysia Inc.'s corporate mercantilism is straining natural potentials to [the] breaking point in order to chase dreams of economic grandeur" (SAM 2005, 11).

The extent of this strain is evident in the country's history of deforestation: between 1990 and 2000 Malaysia lost 13.4 percent of its natural forest (FAO 2001). In addition to extensive logging activities in the 1980s and 1990s,[5] the construction of modern infrastructure (e.g., roads, dams, the MSC, golf courses) and commercial agriculture (especially palm oil) have also contributed significantly to a rapid decline in Malaysia's forests (Article 19 and CIJ 2007; McMorrow and Talip 2001; SAM 2005; Vincent and Rozali 2005). The delayed construction of the massive Bakun Dam and its inequitable resettlement program has already devastated land and livelihoods, drawing significant criticism from domestic and international environmentalists and human rights organizations (Choy 2005). The development of the fifteen-hundred-ton Broga incinerator, located in the Sungai Lalang forest reserve on a river basin, has drawn similar ire. A lack of public consultation and transparency in the development of these projects has only served to fuel the fire of discontent. Despite such environmentally destructive activities, the government has actively marketed Malaysia's "green image" at home and abroad to demonstrate its commitment to the environment and protection of the country's natural resources. It has pledged, for example, that Malaysia will maintain a minimum 50 percent "tree cover"; however, this 50 percent marker is misleading for it includes plantation forests and tree-crop cover, which are not considered natural forests (SAM 2005). Nor does the figure address the quality of forests or the "importance of contiguous forest corridors, essential for wildlife to traverse their habitats safely" (SAM 2005, 35).[6]

Moreover, federal and state-level governments are often either unaware of, or unwilling to stop, illegal, environmentally destructive activities taking place within their borders. As a case in point, ramin (an endangered hardwood) has been smuggled into Malaysia from Indonesia and subsequently sold on international markets. This activity directly contravenes the Convention on International Trade in Endangered Species of Wild Fauna and Flora to which Malaysia is a signatory (EIA 2003).

As Malaysia drives toward greater industrialization and rapid growth, air pollution has become another serious environmental and human health hazard for the country (Afroz, Hassan, and Ibrahim 2003; Awang et al. 2000; Sastry 2002). In September and October 1997, Malaysians experienced the deleterious effects of massive air pollution when a large-scale haze infiltrated the country from biomass burning in the Indonesian states of Kalimantan and Sumatra (Afroz, Hassan, and Ibrahim 2003). The education minister, Najib Tun Razak (now deputy prime minister of Malaysia), placed Malaysian academics under a gag order forbidding them from talking to the press about the haze situation and its potential health implications in large part because "such 'speculative findings' were damaging the country's image abroad and harming tourism" (Masood 1997, 107; Netto 1999). The government maintained its position even when particulate matter in the state of Sarawak far exceeded "extremely hazardous" levels (SAM 2005, 146–49).

In addition to withholding health-related information from the public and facilitating environmentally detrimental practices, the Malaysian government has increasingly allowed environmental management to be influenced by private interests. As a particularly problematic case in point, civil society agents (the Coalition Against Water Privatisation) are heavily criticizing the government's continued corporatization and likely privatization of Malaysia's water management, arguing that, as a human right, water should not be commodified.

The government also has a long history of marginalizing the country's in-digenous peoples, viewing them as obstacles along Malaysia's path of progress. This perspective has been used to justify encroachment onto their land, making it available for export-oriented palm oil plantations, dams, and urban sprawl (including the MSC) (Article 19 and CIJ 2007; Bunnell and Nah 2004, 2453; Nicholas 2000, 2003). This history is particularly problematic as indigenous peoples "occupy the last remaining resource frontiers in a nation-state domi-nated by a profiteering system searching for natural resources" (Nicholas 2003, 2). The Malaysian state increasingly regards this population as valuable inasmuch as it possesses useful knowledge for the expansion of Malaysia's biotechnology industry. As the Ninth Malaysia Plan states: "Malaysia will focus on its areas of competitive advantage, including in optimising its rich biodiversity, *leveraging on its multi-ethnic traditional and complementary medicine*" (Malaysia 2006, 27, emphasis added). There are, of course, examples of indigenous peoples resisting attempts by the government and private entities to commodify them and their land (e.g., the Sarawak Peoples Campaign). The CBD also stipulates that bio-prospectors must gain prior informed consent from the country of origin, as well as ensure the "fair and equitable sharing of the benefits arising out of the utiliza-tion of genetic resources" (CBD 1992). Yet, Malaysia does not have a national law to protect indigenous knowledge, and a uniform and legal standard for access and benefit-sharing continues to be negotiated at the international level with no near-term resolution expected. In March 2006, the government announced it was "in the process of formulating and enacting" legislation for such sharing; however, it has not provided a timeline for this process (Malaysia 2006, 165). Potential for abuse is made clear by a promotional brochure for investPenang, a not-for-profit Penang government entity mandated to attract companies to the state: "Penang is...eminently suitable as a one-stop centre for clinical trials as Malaysia's population is ethnically heterogeneous.... This coupled with the fact that Malaysians are still *drug naïve* makes Penang your ideal gateway to Asia" (investPenang 2005, emphasis added).

When combined with plans to expand Malaysia's biotechnology industry and make it one of the country's key economic-growth engines, the lack of national and international protection places the knowledge, natural resources, and liveli-hoods of indigenous peoples in a precarious position.

A Disjuncture between Rhetoric and Reality

As a signatory to the CBD and the CPB, Malaysia must establish a national law to protect the transboundary movement of living modified organisms (LMOs). In 1997, the government began drafting such a law, a Biosafety Bill to protect "human, plant and animal health, the environment and biological diversity, in accordance with the principle of sustainable development, and ethical and cultural norms" (Nagulendran 2006). After eight years and significant pressure from the Ministry of Natural Resources and Environment and domestic NGOs, the bill was finally approved by the cabinet in November 2005 and was passed in the parliament in 2007.

Environmental and human rights organizations contend the delay in establishing a biosafety law and an access and benefit-sharing law can in large part be attributed to governmental concerns that safety regulations will deter international companies from investing in Malaysia. In lieu of a biosafety law, only voluntary guidelines exist for monitoring genetically modified organisms (GMOs)[7] in Malaysia; however, with no legal enforcement or consequences for failing to abide by these guidelines, they remain ineffective. Even though the Biosafety Bill has become an enforceable act, it remains to be seen whether the government will be able to control transboundary movements of GMOs, especially in light of previous examples of the illegal trafficking of other materials.

Of importance, this domestic response to biosafety directly contradicts Malaysia's position at an international level. Within the international community, Malaysia has taken a prominent leadership role, defending the safety and patent rights of the developing world, the need for greater environmental protection, and the importance of traditional knowledge. In fact, the Malaysian government has taken a proactive role in a wide range of multilateral environmental negotiations, including the Basel Convention, the Framework Convention on Climate Change, and especially the Biosafety Protocol. Prime Ministers Badawi and Mahathir have also argued that the WTO and TRIPS do not operate in the best interest of the developing world, and have actively supported the CBD.

This incongruity between domestic and international approaches is also indicative of a struggle taking place between federal ministerial interests. As is the case in most countries, some governmental ministries are more interested in the economic potential of biodiversity, while others are more concerned with its protection. In 2004, the Ministry of Science, Technology and Environment (MOSTE) split into the Ministry of Science, Technology and Innovation (MOSTI) with the Environment section transferred to the Ministry of Natural Resources and Environment (NRE). The creation of the umbrella Ministry of Natural Resources and the Environment was seen by many as a positive step toward addressing "environmental and resource management issues in an integrated and holistic manner" (SAM 2005, 160). Such a holistic approach is especially needed in Malaysia as environmental issues are managed at local, state, and federal levels of government. Yet, there are concerns that MOSTI tends to be heavily probusiness, is nurturing strong relations with American foreign policymakers and corporations, and is headed by a relatively strong minister with a direct line to the prime minister. Moreover, under MOSTI falls not only everything to do with the MSC but also everything to do with domestic biotechnology programs and policies. Yet, the ministry responsible for negotiating multilateral biotechnology and environmental agreements at an international level is NRE.

To be clear, both MOSTI and NRE recognize the need for, and support a balance between, economic growth and the protection of the environment, biodiversity, and human, plant, and animal health. As exemplified by the lack of substantial information in the Ninth Malaysia Plan about biosafety issues, however, it is unclear how the government intends to balance economic growth with safety concerns. In reaction to this absence of clarity, Parliamentary Opposition Leader Lim Kit Siang posed the question: "Foreign investors are being wooed to develop the biotechnology sector[,] so how are we ensuring that we properly regulate access to our biological resources and traditional knowledge, and avoid 'biopiracy'[?]" (2006). Additionally, the Ninth Malaysia Plan makes it very clear that an economically oriented MOSTI is to play the central role in developing the country's biotechnology industry. The plan states that "in collaboration with the relevant ministries," MOSTI "will formulate strategies and implement programmes to harness biotechnology as a source of growth and wealth creation" (Malaysia 2006, 168).

Concerns over Malaysia's probusiness approach to biotechnology have been articulated particularly well by domestic environmental NGOs Third World Network (TWN), Consumers' Association of Penang (CAP), and Sahabat Alam Malaysia (SAM). These organizations are especially worried about what will happen as Malaysia strengthens its economic ties with the United States. Currently, the United States is Malaysia's number-one trading partner and largest foreign direct investor, which places Malaysia in a highly dependent position. Unfortunately, U.S. foreign policy on environmental issues is particularly problematic—it has not ratified the CBD (and is therefore not a member of the CPB) and has discouraged its trading partners from placing any barriers to the transboundary movement of GMOs (Falkner 2005). In March 2006, Malaysia and the United States announced they would begin negotiating a bilateral free trade agreement (FTA) but failed to make President Bush's July 1, 2007, fast-track trade promotion authority deadline (to facilitate an easy passage through the United States Congress). The two countries will likely continue talks well into 2008. In conjunction with other NGOs, activists, and academics, TWN, CAP, and SAM maintain that the agreement will have deleterious consequences for the environment and people of Malaysia and is being negotiated without transparency.[8] One of the more serious concerns expressed about the agreement is the potentiality that U.S. intellectual property rights (IPRs) will be enforceable in Malaysia. These rights extend beyond WTO obligations and would require "longer periods for patent and copyright protection, restrictions on the grounds for compulsory licenses, and exclusive rights over data" (Khor 2006). This would clearly place economics before health concerns and allow natural resources to be "owned" by private, primarily external interests. (This is particularly problematic as "owning" life-forms is antithetical to most indigenous peoples.) The FTA will also deepen the relationship that Malaysia already shares with the United States on a wide range of biotechnology matters. As two examples, the government hired the American-based life sciences firm Burrill & Company to conduct research and analysis for drafting the National Biotechnology Policy and the Massachusetts Institute of Technology has been intimately intertwined with Malaysian policy and program development, including helping to develop the original BioValley strategy through the Malaysia-MIT Biotechnology Partnership Program.

This discussion demonstrates how Malaysia's biotechnology sector has been developed according to the central pillars of neoliberalism. First, key policy elements of the strategy have been heavily influenced by private interests. Second, biosafety and access and benefit sharing have yet to be regulated or enforced within Malaysia. Third, the FTA being negotiated with the United States will make it increasingly difficult for domestic companies to survive, while intellectual property rights are skewed in favor of external private interests. The privatization, deregulation, and liberalization of an industry as important as biotechnology could have serious consequences for Malaysian citizens and their environment. Combined, they open the door for greater commodification of both nature and people, particularly of citizens with little political capital to defend either themselves or their environment.

Media as Agent: Producing Nature and People as Commodities

Domestic NGOs have raised concerns that the government's biotechnology policies and initiatives are being developed without sufficient public consultation or opportunities for citizen feedback. The situation is exacerbated by a lack of critical media coverage about the issues as promises of financial remuneration and the benign benefits of biotechnology are almost always uncritically relayed in the local news. For instance, a 2005 story in the prominent English newspaper the *New Straits Times* reads, "Biotechnology is set to be the driver for a leap-frogging of agricultural innovation in the country.... Biotechnology provides a panacea to productivity" (Arshad 2005). When Prime Minister Badawi attended the 2004 Biotechnology Industry Organization's annual international convention in San Francisco, Malaysian media coverage of the event was overwhelmingly supportive of the government's plans and of the biotechnology industry in general. In its *Malaysia Media Monitors' Diary*, the human rights organization Aliran specifically criticized reports of the event published in the *New Straits Times* and *The Star*, admonishing the papers for jumping on the "biotech bandwagon" and "acting like PR arms of biotech industry" (Aliran 2004). Aliran also rebuked the papers for neglecting to mention "that many groups and individuals in the U.S. had demonstrated and protested against" the convention (Aliran 2004).

When the mainstream media *have* offered some critical assessment of biotechnology issues, the reporting has tended to be more pragmatic in nature. Attention is focused on what Malaysia needs to do to make the government's biotechnology strategy work (e.g., the workforce or venture capital necessary to make it an economic success), rather than on investigating issues related to environmental protection, traditional knowledge, or the morality of certain biotechnology endeavors.

Although the government sees Malaysia's cultural diversity as potentially advantageous for economic growth and development, this diversity must be kept in check to ensure that Malaysians work together toward common economic goals—as defined by the government—and remain supportive of the country's leadership. This means any civil unrest or challenge to the government—or its programs and policies—is treated as dangerous to Malaysia's economic stability and progress. As Amartya Sen has argued, this economic rationale is used by elites throughout the developing world to justify the repression of a free press "for the good of the whole" (1999, 148–59). To ensure that public discourse is adequately managed and the status quo remains intact, the vast majority of Malaysian media are concentrated in the hands of the government and the politically supportive economic elite. The media are also subjected to strict regulations and are under constant threat of losing their licenses or being sued if they publish or broadcast something deemed to be critical of the government or against the "national interest" of the country (Anuar 2005; McDaniel 2002; Siong 2004). Moreover, the private media are careful not to alienate their primary source of financial support—advertisers. As Dallas Smythe famously made obvious, the audience *is* the commodity for mass communication (1977). When a significant portion of a media outlet's revenue comes from advertising—69 percent for Malaysian newspapers in 2004 (Press Guide 2005, A-29)—editors and owners tend to self-censor to ensure that coverage of stories remains within "appropriate" boundaries.

Nevertheless, the political and economic control of Malaysia's media is not absolute. First, there are a number of alternative media outlets, especially online critical newspapers and journalistic blogs, operating in the country. Despite run-ins with the police and threats of reprisals, these media continue to challenge the government's news monopoly. Second, mainstream media personnel are not a homogeneous, passive group toeing the party line. As John Hilley explains, "Media production in Malaysia is of a more subtle nature....This is not to negate the particular institutional controls within the Malaysian media, but to acknowledge the hegemonic interactions and conflicts" operating with the system (2001, 168). For example, there are a handful of savvy and critical mainstream journalists knowledgeable about biotechnology issues who try to gently push the envelope in their reporting. In addition, over the past few years there has been an increase in the number of mainstream newspaper stories and television programs dedicated to environmental issues. However, the vast majority of coverage tends toward piecemeal, safe stories about specific issues such as water privatization or air quality indices. Although these issues must obviously be discussed, they are done so in a fragmented manner, offering little in-depth contextual information or connections to broader environmental and human rights issues. The only newspaper to specifically address biotechnology (at least at the time of writing) is *The Edge Weekly* and its online daily edition, *The Edge Daily*. Focusing specifically on business and investment issues, this paper offers rather critical business-oriented coverage, which the government has most likely allowed because the paper's target audience is relatively small.[9] What this means, however, is that the only newspaper providing some critical coverage of biotechnology issues is specifically dedicated to business concerns, which frames biotechnology as an economic and investment issue, rather than one of environmental and social concern.

With the government's promise not to censor the Internet,[10] a wide range of online "politically contentious" journalism has sprung up over the last few years (George 2006).[11] The foremost goal of these media is to challenge "the consensus that powerful interests try to shape and sustain through the mainstream media" (George 2006, 3). Although the audience share of these media remains relatively limited, they have opened up space in Malaysia for the exchange of critical ideas, opinions, and perspectives; however, these alternative media have also offered little in the way of critical discussions regarding Malaysia's biotechnology future. As a result, they have helped to naturalize biotechnology activities by remaining surprisingly silent about the issue.

Mapping the Future of Biotechnology in Malaysia

While commercially driven biotechnology endeavors are not necessarily problematic in and of themselves, the industry's development in Malaysia is unfolding in such a way that both the physical environment and people with little sociopolitical and economic clout—particularly the country's indigenous population—may be under threat. Despite the expected influx of domestic and foreign biotechnology companies, the potential for new jobs, higher GDP, and scientific discoveries, the sector is expanding rapidly with practically no parameters in place to protect citizens and the environment. The Malaysian state has made rhetorical overtures about the importance of protecting the country's natural resources and of sharing equitably biotechnology remunerations, and Prime Minister Badawi has stated that "all of us—the public sector, private sector, civil society and members of the public—should be engaged in the biodiversity governance dialogue" (2005a). Yet, the government has limited debate about biotechnology—a fact exemplified by the dearth of critical reporting in the mainstream news. The government has also developed the sector by prioritizing economic objectives over social and environmental concerns. Specifically, the government has delayed the implementation of biosafety regulations and of access and benefit-sharing policies.

This has allowed state-level governments within Malaysia to independently negotiate projects with foreign companies and research institutes. Without enforceable federal laws, some state authorities have made deals that may not be in the best interest of their citizens and local environments. This is even more problematic considering that only nonbinding guidelines regulate clinical trials in Malaysia. This lax regulatory environment positions the country as an attractive locale for trials, as human subjects are not adequately protected (Netto 2007). There is thus a need to map these myriad state-level biotechnology initiatives and agreements, and to analyze the potential negative implications as people and nature become commodities.

Also in need of careful scrutiny is the free trade agreement with the United States, which threatens to open the door even wider for external private interests to own and control Malaysia's natural resources. A wide range of civil society agents are trying to raise awareness about the potential ramifications of the agreement, helping citizens understand its terms and encouraging public debate on its merits. Whether and how these agents use mainstream and especially alternative forms of communication will be something to watch for in the future.

Even if an appropriate, countrywide regulatory framework were to be introduced, the biotechnology industry in Malaysia is already expanding beyond the federal government's control, especially as individual states engage in their own negotiations with domestic and international businesses and organizations. This makes the work of the country's civil society actors all the more crucial.

New Concepts, New Natures?

Revisiting Commodity Production in Southern Thailand

PETER VANDERGEEST

In this chapter I make a set of observations on two kinds of histories. The first outlines the shifting modes of integration into commodity networks over the past twenty years in the district of Satingpra, Thailand, and the associated landscape changes. Commodity production has long been a feature of livelihood practice in Satingpra, and rural people have shaped landscapes as they engage in commodity production and exchange. Over the past twenty years, however, there have been dramatic shifts in how this site has been integrated into commodity networks. Shrimp farming and wage labor in nearby towns have displaced the production of palm sugar as villagers' major sources of cash income, and in doing so they have brought a series of influential new actors into being. Shrimp farming in particular has dramatically remade both the landscape and the actors who have a significant presence in the area. These actors are both local (e.g., shrimp farmers, feed suppliers, and protesting villagers) and translocal (e.g., multinational corporations, academics, and NGOs located throughout the world). Although not all these actors are physically present, they are all involved in the remaking of livelihoods; the creation, appropriation, and movement of new economic values; and the refashioning of socionatures in Satingpra.

A second set of observations concerns the ways that our understandings of changing agrarian economies and politics are partly an artifact of new approaches to understanding agrarian transitions. In writing this chapter, I found it difficult

The ideas and information on which this paper is based have benefited from my participation in the Major Collaborative Research Initiative on Agrarian Transitions in Southeast Asia, funded by the Social Sciences and Humanities Research Council of Canada (SSHRCC). It is also draws on research funded by two SSHRCC standard grants led by Mark Flaherty, and was facilitated by research assistance provided by Keith Barney and Jaroon Kanjanapan.

to separate out shifting understandings of agrarian change from shifts in our research methods and concepts. On the one hand, my methods and concepts have changed over the past two decades: terms such as socionatures were absent in 1985, and commodity chain analysis and related network approaches were not yet part of our toolkit of methods and concepts. In more recent research, new concepts have pushed aside the terminology and methods derived from agrarian political economy that I employed during the 1980s. On the other hand, there have been significant changes in how villagers participate in commodity relations, independent of changes in analytical concepts and research methods. Inevitably, then, our comparisons of what a place such as Satingpra looked like over two historical periods will be shaped by both the concepts through which we look at these sites and by changes in the sites themselves.

Concepts

My research has shifted from an agrarian studies approach to one organized in good part by network concepts. Agrarian studies refers to an approach to understanding agrarian change that was organized through the lens of primarily Marxist-derived conceptual tools.[1] Research in agrarian studies typically highlighted class-based collective action, property relations, and commoditization (Bernstein and Byres 2001; Hart et al. 1989). This approach to studying agrarian change has been displaced gradually by a series of other approaches, including community studies and commodity chain analyses. The latter is now strongly influenced by network theories.

Network approaches have ensnared many scholars in part because they promised a solution to theoretical problems that preoccupied academics throughout the 1990s. In particular, network metaphors helped dissolve some of the dualisms and essentialisms that bothered many agrarian scholars, including those between nature/society and state/private. Network metaphors also seemed to provide a convincing way of understanding global processes and connections. Actor-network theory (ANT) has been particularly attractive for many agro-food scholars because it provided a theoretically legitimate way to say academically what seemed like common sense—that biophysical processes matter, and that social processes are always natural processes as well. Elements of ANT could be easily absorbed into the commodity chain approach by adding nonhuman actants. More broadly, the term "socionatures" has become a shorthand way of indicating allegiance to the idea that concepts such as social and nature need to be displaced by terms that do not make these distinctions.

At the same time, many writers have drawn on network theories with much ambivalence, and some reject them outright, for good reasons. Although conceptual dualisms can always be subjected to deconstruction, eliminating them entirely also means losing the distinctions that give our categories "traction."

When every social or socionatural phenomenon becomes a network, then the concept loses its analytical purchase (Holton, 2005, 210). Network approaches tend to lose sight of concepts and collective actors that cannot be easily reduced to network effects—such as class, ethnicity, and gender. For example, the incursion of ANT into commodity chain analysis has directed more attention to the biological characteristics of agro-commodities (e.g., Friedberg 2001, 353; FitzSimmons and Goodman 1998), but studies using this approach have typically paid less attention to the broader socioecological contexts of agricultural production. Accounts of the production of socionatural landscapes have emerged in a separate environmental studies literature, for example, in the critiques of protected areas as a way of protecting nature (e.g., Neumann 1998; see also introduction to this book).

Dissatisfaction with the limits of these new approaches has provoked moves to bring back some of the concerns of the agrarian studies approach. This is not a simple return, however, as scholars are not abandoning their interest in social processes and forms of collective action that had been passed over in the previous phase of agrarian studies. Many of these actors will appear in the stories below, but it is worth highlighting one in particular. Both development agencies and activist groups have latched onto the idea of "local community" as a ubiquitous rural collective actor. Community emerged as a shorthand way of referring to relatively small groups of people whose capacity to act collectively was assumed to be based on dense forms of interaction and shared interests created through long histories of living near each other. Agrarian studies scholars are wont to dismiss the idea of local community as a form of agrarian populism,[2] and to deconstruct the term for how it obfuscates property, class, and gender relations (e.g., Li 2001, 2002a; Agrawal and Gibson 2001). Despite the skeptical commentaries, however, the idea of local community has proven resilient. It seems unavoidable, because it has uses that cannot be captured by other terms. It allows activists and scholars to discuss forms of place-based collective action that cannot easily be identified with class, ethnicity, and so on. It is also useful for writers who are oriented toward larger scale processes such as globalization, and who need a shorthand way of referring to local actors.

In the remainder of this chapter I will outline my engagements with these different approaches to understanding agrarian change. I will present material from research I did during my MA and PhD research in the Songkla Lake area during 1985 and 1987–88. Over the past twenty years I have continued to do research in this area, at first on land and tree tenure (1990s) and then more specifically on shrimp farming as part of a commodity-based research project. My accounts of the changes I have observed are followed by reflections on the ways that my shifting methods and concepts have shaped how I collected data, identified actors, and told stories.

Class and Socionatures in Palm Sugar Production

My research during the 1980s was carried out in two phases: the first for a master's thesis, the second for a dissertation. In 1985, I conducted a household-based survey and interviewed older villagers to obtain a locally based history of the region. My aim was to understand rural differentiation in a manner that was consistent with the methods and problematics of agrarian studies. In particular, I was interested in producing an account of the impact of commodification on class and stratification.

During 1987–88, in the second phase of my research, I eschewed household surveys, and instead focused my work on uncovering hidden narratives of resistance (Scott 1985) and outlining how the increasing presence of a developmentalist state was reorganizing rural politics. My methods included extensive key informant interviewing and an analysis of the changing expressions of politics in shadow-play performances that local villagers had taped over a period of three decades. I also continued to rely on the 1985 surveys. As students of agrarian change often did, I classified the sixty-nine households that I surveyed into three "strata," based on ownership of land and other productive resources. My analysis (see Vandergeest 1989) was organized by the assumption that these strata could be understood as actors whose actions were shaped by class interests, though not necessarily in a self-conscious or organized way.

The three most important commodities produced in the district during this period were palm sugar, rice, and fish. Forty-five of the sixty-nine households in the survey derived most of their cash income from tapping the palmyra palm for sugar. A typical household would tap some twenty-five palm trees by climbing them twice a day to change bamboo collectors over a four-to-eight-month tapping season. Most poor and middle-level households relied almost entirely on sugar production for cash income, while many of the nontapping households in my survey derived most of their income from the further processing or trading of palm sugar. Villagers used the cash income to purchase fish, vegetables, eggs, and other food, to pay for schooling, transportation, and health care, or to buy other productive resources such as nets, ducks, boats, and livestock.

Most households grew rice, primarily for their own consumption. Poorer households in my survey rented much of the land they used for rice production; wealthier households rented out land, retaining only enough to produce rice for their own consumption; and "middle" strata households mostly grew rice on their own land. Fishing for everyday consumption was important everywhere and a few households in my survey were small-scale commercial fishers. Since I was interested in palm sugar production, the survey did not include villages known to specialize in fishing in the lagoon, where most people were often Muslim. It was in these specialized fishing villages that the strongest opposition to shrimp farming later emerged, out of concern about how shrimp farming might affect fishing resources.

Many people in palm sugar–producing villages participated in local labor markets on a part-time basis. Men, for example, often worked several months a year as manual labor driving and loading trucks, in construction, or on the trawlers that operated out of Songkla. Women along the main highway deshelled wild-caught shrimp that were delivered to them daily from fish processing factories in the Songkla–Hat Yai corridor to the south. But the sale of labor was the major source of income for only four surveyed households, and was the second most important source of income for an additional nineteen households. These low figures could be attributed in part to the way that people who took up full-time wage labor in the nearby cities would normally take up residence in these cities, as the roads, buses, and ferries involved in taking the trip to Songkla made daily commuting difficult.

It was palm sugar production that really attracted my interest in relation to class differentiation. I drew on my interviews to construct a historical narrative that outlined how the expansion of palm sugar production advantaged the poorer households, an argument that was out of step with agrarian studies scholarship that emphasized how commodification marginalized poorer villagers. Although villagers had long produced palm sugar as a local specialization, and exchanged it for products produced elsewhere in the region (tree resins, rice), it had not always occupied such a central place in the Satingpra economy. Before World War II, rice was the more important commodity for shaping class relations. Local stratification was based largely on ownership of rice land and on labor debts that had evolved out of local forms of personal slavery that were prevalent in the area until World War II. During and after World War II, shortages of refined sugar led to high local prices, later institutionalized by government policies that stabilized sugar prices above international levels as a way of supporting the influential Thai sugar-processing industry. Wartime sugar shortages expanded the regional market for Satingpra sugar in southern Thailand and northern Malaysia. That expansion continued after the war due to stable prices, the growing road system, and a preference for palm sugar in sweets, curries, and other local foods.

Although the expansion of palm sugar production may have been facilitated by war and national-level politics, my argument was that the actual increase in production occurred through the collective actions of poorer and middle peasants, as a way of extracting themselves from dependency relations on the local landowning elites. Production was facilitated by the relatively open access to the resources needed for tapping trees and boiling sap. Although the palm trees were planted on the bunds between privately owned rice fields, access to palm trees for tapping was effectively open. The high value attached to the palm trees for sugar and many other uses (lumber, thatching, fruits, burning for fertilizer, fuelwood) had contributed to a culture of planting continuous rows of trees between rice fields. The number of trees was thus far in excess of the number tapped, even with the high population densities (four hundred people per square kilometer in the district). Only recently had landowners began charging rents, and these rents were very small. Palm fronds could also be collected as fuel for boiling down the sap without any cost, although most fuel was rubber wood made available by the rubber replanting program further inland.

At the same time, the peak period for sugar production coincided with the rice harvest. Poorer villagers were able to generate enough cash income from palm sugar to monetize and pay off what were labor debts to landowners, and thus they were able to stop working for these landowners during the rice harvest. Former landowners, unable to find labor to harvest rice, abandoned rice farming except for a few fields for their own consumption. They instead rented out or sold their land to poorer households, who then combined rice cultivation with palm sugar production as their major livelihood activities. Thus the expansion of palm sugar indirectly also increased their access to land for farming rice. The result was a transformation in class relations that increased poor farmers' control of land, labor, and income.

My research also provided a detailed account of state development activities, although at the time I did not frame this as regulation, certainly not the regulation of production. In retrospect, however, I can write that the major government involvement in regulating production (other than unsuccessful attempts to introduce high-yield rice varieties) were laws prohibiting the home production of liquor from sugar. These laws had little effect, as the distilleries on the other side of the lake continued as a major market for palm syrup, and as villagers in Satingpra continued to enjoy their homemade spirits.

At the same time, the district government was a strong presence. When I began my research, researchers had to obtain formal permission in the district center, and most "development" was channeled through district governments. *Kamnan* (chief of the *tambon,* comprised of about ten administrative villages) were still the dominant figures at the *tambon* level. These power structures had evolved from the previous century, when local *chao muang* ruled small and large *muang* relatively autonomously. Although administrative reforms had displaced the *chao,* the provincial governors, district officers, and *kamnan* retained much of the overarching power of the old *chao* through their control of most state activity in their respective domains. Agricultural, fisheries, and other officials reported not only to their departmental superiors in Bangkok but also to the civil authorities. I point this out because of how decentralization and new commodity networks later began to displace this kind of authority.

How does this production regime produce socionatures, in today's terminology? I paid close attention to the question of how ecological processes shaped class relations—my research was influenced not only by agrarian studies but also by cultural ecology, during a time when what is now called political ecology was just emerging. More than that, however, the fieldwork results seemed to demand that I work ecology into my explanations of social change. It was clear that the lush, cultivated landscape of trees and rice fields was produced through the way that villagers participated in commodity networks in interaction with the activity of palm trees and rice: the seasonality of sugar production and the rice harvest, the prolific growth of palm fronds that could be used for fuel, and the ecological niches in which farmers planted trees were as important to the commodity network as were the actions of rural classes, merchants, and consumers. My analysis recognized this by emphasizing ecological activities, though at the time I would have resisted any notion that trees and rice plants might be actors.

Communities, Networks, and Shrimp Socionatures

Bulletin from Public Citizen

FOR IMMEDIATE RELEASE

Record-Breaking Numbers Reveal Consumers' Insatiable Appetite for Popular Seafood

WASHINGTON, D.C.—A record-setting billion pounds of shrimp was imported for seafood lovers in the United States in 2003, but most consumers don't realize where the popular food comes from, said Public Citizen today.... The group again urged consumers to be cautious when buying and eating shrimp.

Shrimp aquaculture uses a factory-farming model that douses shrimp with pesticides, antibiotics and other chemicals; most shrimp farms are in Southeast Asia, where labor and environmental standards are considerably weaker than in the United States. Recent news reports have tied some of the devastating effects of last month's tsunami to the destruction of mangroves....Mangroves are often destroyed to make room for shrimp farms. When they're cut down, a natural barrier to the ocean is eliminated, making it easier for tidal waves to reach the shore....

...Public Citizen has been urging consumers to pay attention to whether the shrimp is farm-raised or wild-caught....
Public Citizen urges consumers to buy only wild-caught shrimp.

In the years following my degree research, I periodically returned to Satingpra District to visit friends, follow local events, and follow up on research questions around land and tree tenure. Starting in the mid-1990s I reengaged with the area through a research project focused on shrimp farming. My methods were in part organized by the fact that I was not able to visit more than a few weeks at a time, once or twice a year. This meant more long-distance reliance on my local research assistant, also my host when I stayed in the area. He reported to me on key events, clipped the local newspapers, and toward the end of the research conducted interviews with shrimp farmers. In part to compensate for this inability to do detailed local research, and in part because I began using some of the techniques of commodity chain analysis, I also directed my attention to the global controversies surrounding shrimp farming.

The first major shrimp farms along this part of the east coast were large contract-farming schemes built by agribusiness corporations in the 1980s about one hundred kilometers north of where I was doing PhD research. Several of these corporations purchased large tracts of smallholder rice land and converted them into shrimp farms. The farmers from whom they had purchased land were among the farmers that were contracted to grow shrimp, following the instructions of the company's university-trained experts. After a few years these schemes collapsed in mutual accusations of cheating, stealing, and technical incompetence, but in the meantime nearby villagers had started to build their own shrimp farms. The allure of lucrative incomes, an order of magnitude greater than what was possible through existing livelihood options, induced a rush into shrimp farming. Key facilitating factors included the government's accelerated land titling program, which helped make land available as collateral for bank credit, and the availability of a surface water infrastructure previously used for rice farming. A second wave of rapid growth followed in 1998 after the financial crisis of 1997 drove down the value of the baht. The price obtained by shrimp farmers doubled, while many local land speculators who found that they were unable to sell land sought to recoup their investments through the construction of shrimp farms.

According to data collected in 2004 and 2005 in fisheries offices in districts bordering the lagoon, there were 1,164 farms with an average total farm area of 1.07 hectares that used water from the Songkla Lake lagoon, an area that included parts of the Satingpra District. These data are incomplete as not all offices collected data on all farms, but they give an idea of the extent and structure of shrimp farming in the lagoon watershed. Most shrimp farms were built by farmers who dug out shrimp farming ponds in their rice land, although some were built in the mangroves and other wet forests that lined the southern part of the lake. The larger farms were often owned by residents in the local towns, many of whom purchased rural land during the period of land speculation.

Shrimp farming has become central to the regional economy in many parts of the Songkla Lake area, but the impact has been spatially uneven and accompanied by other major changes in livelihood strategies. A growing number of people now commute on a daily basis to work in the Hat Yai–Songkla corridor. This is facilitated by continued expansion of paved roads, the building of a bridge across the mouth of the lagoon at Songkla city, and the booming economy in the Songkla–Hat Yai area. Seafood processing for export is especially important, an activity tied to the construction of a deep-sea port in Songkla. In Satingpra, the old economy has not disappeared, but it has declined. Only a minority of households now produce palm sugar, although palm tree stands remain dense away from the coastal shrimp farming zone. In many districts rice farming is considered something only older people do, although there are significant areas to the north and south ends of the lagoon where commercial rice farming and fruit production remain important. In the lower, more saline parts of the lagoon, many villagers obtain supplementary income from raising sea bass in cages.

The influx of money that has accompanied shrimp farming and wage labor has dramatically transformed both the socionatural landscape and people's access to material goods. Near the Gulf of Thailand, and the lagoon, large strips of land have been turned into ponds for raising shrimp. Some of the global reaction against shrimp farming is provoked by the unappealing landscape aesthetics.

Figure 12.1. Sugar palm and rice, Satingpra District, Thailand, October 1981.
Credit: P. Vandergeest.

Farms are typically surrounded by the jumbled infrastructure of shrimp farming: ditches, piping, pumps, aerators, huts, lighting, and so on. Salinization through seepage often kills nearby vegetation, sometimes leaving dead sugar palm trees standing out against the horizon. The main local environmental and social controversies in Songkla Province include the salinization of rice fields, pollution of surface and groundwater, and water pollution due to poor sediment disposal. Between crops, farmers need to remove the sediments that accumulate at the bottom of the ponds; these sediments are nutrient rich and reduce dissolved oxygen if they end up in water bodies.

Unpredictable ecological characteristics makes shrimp farming an easy illustration for arguments that nonhuman actants such as viruses, bacteria, and the physiological processes of shrimp have the capability of both shaping, and undermining, industrial agro-food production systems. Farmed shrimp are susceptible to a series of viruses that can wipe out entire crop areas, and the spatial movements of the industry globally have been driven in part by periodic disease episodes that temporarily increase prices until new production zones emerge or old ones expand and intensify. These epidemics have sometimes left large areas of

Figure 12.2. Shrimp farming, Satingpra District, Thailand, June 1994. Credit: P. Vandergeest.

shrimp farms idle or abandoned, provoking critics to describe shrimp farming as a slash-and-burn industry that illustrates why export-oriented food production in ecologically sensitive areas to satisfy the appetites of the global wealthy is unjust and destructive (e.g., Shiva 2000).

I have, however, found it difficult to sustain this view in the face of the rapid changes I have encountered around Songkla Lake. In particular, it is hard to ignore the degree to which the livelihoods of many people have become dependent on shrimp farming. Even the main alternative, wage labor, is partly based on this industry. Shrimp farming has brought a huge influx of money into the Songkla Lake area, and not all of it has been appropriated by corporations or large farmers. It is common now to see villagers who were formerly fishers, palm sugar tappers, or rice farmers driving pickup trucks with cellular phones in hand. Moreover, the image of abandoned wastelands belies the way that many shrimp farmers in this area have been adept at recuperating their ponds after disease episodes and other problems, in part through collective self-regulation around water and sediment disposal. Because the majority of farmers own and operate small farms on their family land, they have limited alternatives for making a livelihood other than finding ways of maintaining shrimp production. At the same time, the boom-and-bust cycles of shrimp farming have led not only to new wealth but also to unimaginable debt, debt that some villagers will never repay. The district abounds with stories of new wealth, despair, and violence, much of it associated with shrimp farming.

The environmental and social impacts of shrimp farming have provoked significant opposition to shrimp farming around Songkla Lake. Rice farmers have circulated petitions and staged large demonstrations to register their complaints about salinization. Fishers have pressed local governments to act against shrimp farmers whose sediment disposal has degraded water quality. There have been countless individual encounters around shrimp farm siting and pollution. In some cases, the goal was to stop shrimp farming from entering a zone that villagers considered ecologically vulnerable, but in other cases the focus was on changing management practices, including water and sediment disposal techniques, and stopping the underground seepage of saline water.

In an effort to document the effectiveness of this kind of local "regulation," we interviewed about twenty shrimp farmers during 2001 and 2002, as well as members of local governments in ten *tambon* (subdistricts and some non–shrimp farming villagers. My conclusion (Vandergeest 2007) was that effective regulation (at the time) was almost entirely the result of the collective actions of local villagers or shrimp farmers who shared water infrastructure, as well as regulation by local government bodies. In other words, shrimp farmers who were using better disposal methods for sediments, and who were being stopped from siting shrimp farms in certain areas, were being forced to do so largely because of pressure from other villagers and shrimp farmers. Sanctions used by villagers who sought to actively regulate shrimp farming took many forms, ranging from indirect social pressure to theft and violence. The Department of Fisheries, who has the mandate to regulate shrimp-farming effluents and management practices, had no significant presence, although this is now changing rapidly in response to buyer pressure for traceability and certification. The processing companies who purchased shrimp limited their regulation of shrimp farming practices to those that affect shrimp quality, understood primarily in terms of size, freshness, and antibiotic residue. They did not involve themselves in the environmental and social impacts. Local NGOs had some influence in facilitating collective action to regulate shrimp farming in some areas, though the dangers associated with conflicts with some shrimp farmers meant that their activities were generally not visible.

Among government agencies, it was the civil authorities, not the Department of Fisheries, that were most active in regulating shrimp farming. Their mandate includes the resolution of civil conflicts, and they were the target of demonstrations, petitions, and other villager actions. A key moment occurred in 1998 when the prime minister responded to the controversy over the inland spread of shrimp farming by ordering the governors of coastal provinces to have their provinces zoned into fresh and brackish water areas, with shrimp farming banned in fresh water zones. Governors in coastal provinces found that the ambiguity of what was fresh or brackish forced them away from using purely technical criteria in making zoning decisions. The governor of Songkla Province resolved the problem by asking the tambon administrative organizations (TAO) to zone their *tambon*. TAOs are made up of an elected council plus administrative officers; as the locus of decentralization in Thailand, they have displaced much of the former power of the *tambon kamnan*. The province also made shrimp-farm operations subject to the laws and to the conditions set out by the TAO. This approach made it possible in some areas for village-level opponents of shrimp farming to combine with district and provincial civil authorities to use the zoning process as a vehicle for containing the spread of shrimp farms, as well as making permission to engage in shrimp farming conditional on specified management practices. Although these provisions were often not enforced, in about half of the eleven *tambon* where I obtained information on this, the spatial limits on shrimp farming had held, and the management provisions often provided leverage to local villagers seeking to regulate specific practices.

Shrimp farming is contested not only among villagers but also by transnational activist networks. The activities of organizations based in consumer countries are particularly visible to consumers of electronic media. Anyone with access to the Internet can learn about shrimp farming controversies by checking the websites of Public Citizen, the Environmental Justice Foundation, Sierra Club Canada, the Monterey Bay Aquarium, Chef's Collaborative, the Mangrove Action Project, the World Wide Fund for Nature (WWF), and more. From the point of view of many food activists, the solution to the controversies surrounding farmed shrimp might seem simple. Here is a global commodity that exemplifies all the problems of global markets (Shiva 2000). We should all simply stop eating farmed shrimp. Governments in shrimp-exporting countries should ban or at the very least severely curtail shrimp-farming operations. Greater community food self-reliance should be promoted in both southern and northern countries. Organizations such as Public Citizen might be understood as adopting this position in their support of import duties and recommendations that U.S. consumers eat wild-caught American shrimp. In 2004–05, the Southern Shrimpers Alliance, composed of participants in the wild-caught shrimp industry, was able to convince the U.S. government to impose antidumping duties on shrimp exports from six major producing countries, including Thailand. The duties were in effect a U.S. tax on producers, with proceeds redistributed to supporters of the antidumping petitions in the U.S. shrimp industry, in accordance with the provisions of the so-called Byrd Amendment, which mandates the distribution of anti-dumping duties to companies that petition the U.S. government for trade protection.

But many environmental NGOs are now refraining from supporting boycotts of farmed shrimp. Instead, they often suggest that consumers should seek out farmed shrimp that has been certified as having been produced through sustainable management practices, such as organic shrimp. Although there are significant differences of opinion among environmental groups (MAP 2006), many are now following broader trends in the environmental movement, to promote working with industry to certify shrimp for production practices that address the concerns of the different groups—whether this means not locating in mangroves, not using antibiotics and other chemicals, or respecting the livelihoods of local communities. Participants in these NGO–industrial collaborations (Gereffi, Garcia-Johnson, and Sasser 2001) include the Food and Agriculture Organization, the World Bank, retailers and retailing organizations, restaurant chains, environmental groups such as the WWF and Conservation International, and industry organizations such as the Aquaculture Certification Council (ACC).[3]

In Thailand, the Department of Fisheries has been particularly aggressive in pursuing certification, in part as a way of positioning the Thai industry as a producer of high-quality shrimp. The department has put together a program to enroll shrimp farmers in an environmentally oriented certification scheme, the Thai Code of Conduct, as well as the less demanding Good Aquaculture Practices (GAP) program. Provisions in the Code of Conduct draw on templates for "best management practices" (Bene 2005) in shrimp farming that circulate internationally.

As of February 2006, according to interviews and district-level data, most shrimp farmers around Songkla Lake were being enrolled in the GAP program, as it was being required by the processing firms who buy shrimp from farmers. Enrollment in the Code of Conduct was slower, with only a few larger farms certified in Songkla Province, and 140 farms listed as certified on the Department of Fisheries website. However, this could change with announcements by major buyers in the United States and Europe (including Wal-Mart and Darden) of plans to buy only shrimp certified by the ACC, and EurepGAP's progress in creating its own complex standards in part through consultation with NGOs. Either the Thai Code of Conduct will need to be recognized by northern-based certification institutions like the ACC and EurepGAP or farmers will have to be directly certified by these private schemes. Barriers to certification for smaller farmers, such as elaborate procedures and high costs, could eliminate the many small farms in my research site.

What has been noticeable to me about these new regulatory collaborations is that the people who are most directly affected, the shrimp farmers themselves, are seldom enrolled in any meaningful way into these networks. Nor do the certification templates that circulate through these networks provide for any meaningful participation by affected people in setting, monitoring, and enforcing standards. These exclusions characterize not only industry-led certification schemes but also those promoted by organic certifiers and by environmental groups such as the WWF. This lack of attention to local communities has been contested by NGOs whose work combines conservation with community development or social justice (e.g., Redmanglar Internacional 2003, MAP 2006), but these contestations have so far not had much impact on these regimes. In Thailand, GAP and Code of Conduct certification processes are similarly implemented entirely by Department of Fisheries officials who make periodic visits to farms, without any consultation even with the TAOs. The exclusion of affected people from certification processes seems all the more glaring when contrasted to my field research, which found that local people, or local "communities," were the most effective regulators of shrimp farming, and that some TAOs had also been pushed into taking effective regulatory actions. The effect is to insert the views and actions of distant retailers, restaurant chains, NGOs, and perhaps consumers (depending on views about relative autonomy in consumer choice) into the creation of standards that farmers may need to meet and document if they are to continue selling their shrimp. Certification programs are making consumers of shrimp, the WWF, Conservation International, Public Citizen, the Monterey Bay Aquarium, and innumerable other organizations a significant presence in assessing and shaping ecologies in the Songkla Lake area. The question will be, on whose terms, and with what involvement for people whose lives are being reorganized by these commodity networks?

Comparative Methodological Reflections

My research in Satingpra during the 1980s was located in the concepts and methods of agrarian studies: I assumed the process of commoditization was driven by class-based actions, and I focused on the often antagonistic relations between "peasants" and a developmentalist state. This was true in both the first phase, when my research was focused on political economy and commoditization, and the second phase, when my interests turned to cultural interpretation and resistance.

As I remember this research from the perspective of the present, I can claim that I also paid careful attention to what we now call socionatures, outlining how ecological activities were entangled with agrarian transformations in ways that also produced a specific kind of productive landscape. In effect, I was bringing ideas from "cultural ecology" to bear on agrarian studies. However, I did not explicitly locate Satingpra in transnational commodity or activist networks, although I did follow the sugar commodity network to Bangkok to learn about the politics of sugar pricing. I also did not use the idea of community as a collective actor.

It is difficult to know what the results might have been had I paid more attention to transnational networks or community-based collective action during the 1980s. There were arguably no equivalents to the current activities of transnational NGOs and corporations in transforming livelihoods and landscapes in

Satingpra. This is not to imply that Satingpra was isolated. My research during the 1980s was also about the way that Satingpra was incorporated into larger-scale processes. But what drew my interest were questions about the way Satingpra villagers were incorporated into national administrative practices and a national economy, which were in turn organized through development discourses. This was partly because these were the questions that animated me and other researchers at the time, but perhaps also partly because corporations, transnational commodity networks, and NGOs were not glaringly present in the way that they are today. Both my analytic tools, and the modes of insertion of Satingpra into larger economic and political relationships, have changed.

Similarly in relation to community action: if there was a parallel during the 1980s, it might have concerned the lack of participation by villagers in formulating rural development policies. I explored this idea, but organized my findings in the language of peasant-state relations and class relations. Far from invoking the idea of community as a collective actor seeking to participate in making development, I wrote instead about how the idea of the community was produced through different kinds of development and nation-building practices, and I expressed skepticism about the idea of community as an autonomous, harmonious collective actor (Vandergeest 1996; 1991).

Comparing my current research on shrimp farming to my earlier research on palm sugar points to my virtual abandonment of traditional agrarian studies concepts in favor of approaches framed by the agro-food studies literature, commodity chain analysis, network analysis, and community-based natural resource management (CBNRM). Rather than do an analysis of changing class relations with regard to shrimp production, my research has focused on the many collective actors and activities that surround the production, processing, trade, marketing, consumption, and contestation of shrimp. This shift can be partly explained by the availability of new research methods and concepts. As a global commodity, and as the object of intense struggles, farmed shrimp became an enticing subject for academic work. Is it a healthy food, a substitute for depleted ocean fisheries, and a way of bringing wealth to previously marginalized coastal zones? Or is it the paradigm case of destructive, slash-and-burn development, leaving degraded coastal landscapes, undermined livelihoods, and violence in its wake?

Network approaches have proven particularly useful to me for tracing these circulating commodities and contested meanings, and thus it is network approaches that have organized how I have collected and analyzed data on the industry. I have been involved with interviewing not only shrimp farmers and traders in Satingpra but also processors, marketers, and fisheries officials in Bangkok; supermarkets and restaurant chains in Bangkok; and seafood consumers at upscale health-oriented markets in Minneapolis (Skladany and Vandergeest 2004). The growing market for shrimp, and the way that environmental groups have turned to campaigns aimed at changing consumer behavior, have led us to collect information from websites on shrimp consumption, marketing, and NGO campaigns. What should we think about Conservation International's decision to work with the ACC, Wal-Mart, and Dardon (Red Lobster) around certification? Is it possible for certification schemes to include local "communities" in setting, monitoring, and enforcing standards? What if new, buyer-driven regulation undermines shrimp farming in places such as Satingpra, where farmed shrimp is now the mainstay of the local economy?

My analysis is now populated by diverse collective actors who played no role in my earlier work, and who would not easily find a location in the agrarian studies framework of several decades ago. These include not only transnational actors but also actors in the Songkla Lake area. Most obviously, and in contrast to my previous skepticism, I have found myself writing about "local communities" as actors. I have tried to do so in ways that address the criticisms of the concept of local community as an autonomous and homogeneous actor. I thus make it clear that I understand communities as comprised of shifting local networks that express local power relations and that can include both local NGOs and state institutions such as the TAO. At the same time, I have arguably adopted this concept because it was useful in describing forms of collective action that would have been difficult to imagine a mere two decades earlier, and that are not easily resolved into class-based actors.

My writing on shrimp farming also shows certain continuities with my earlier work. I have mentioned the attention to ecological processes. Another has been my interest in finding critical perspectives on shrimp farming among villagers in Satingpra, a contemporary version of the "hidden narratives" of peasant resistance. But now I am reluctant to frame these actions as simple resistance, although that characterization is accurate in some cases. Where there is resistance, moreover, it is no longer resistance to the government's development agenda. Instead, it takes diverse forms, ranging from shrimp farmers seeking better deals from corporations to local fishers and farmers seeking to ban shrimp farms or to contain the more destructive practices of shrimp farmers.

As mentioned in the introduction to this book, the comparison with my earlier research on commodities illustrates how the ways that we understand commodities and commoditization derives in part from our particular positioning at different points in time and changing academic concepts and methods. Yet my changing approach to research has also followed changes in the ways that Satingpra as a site has been integrated into "translocal" networks, and the changing forms of collective action in Satingpra. My visits to the district confronted me with the ways that the lucrative but highly unstable shrimp farming industry was transforming people's lives. It seemed impossible to properly understand these changes without understanding how farmed shrimp is very much a contested, transnational commodity. It also was not possible for me to ignore the many ways that people in Satingpra acted to make the area a production site, and also to constrain, oppose, or regulate shrimp farming.

These shifts in my research approach, however, have left me uneasy both with what I see as weaknesses in network approaches more generally and, more specifically, with the way I have not located the local politics of shrimp into a better understanding of agrarian change and local differences. Network approaches have helped me trace how diverse actors can come together in collaborative action, but they have been less helpful for thinking about what gives these actors distinct identities and capabilities. For example, what makes a class a class, and not a community? What gives different state agencies specific kinds of identities (civil administrations, Department of Fisheries) that orient how they act in relation to shrimp farming?

More specifically in relation to agrarian change: network approaches by themselves have not enabled me to locate the ways that the people living in the Songkla Lake basin participate in shrimp farming, or act collectively to regulate or oppose shrimp farming. Who is involved, in terms of ethnicity, occupation, class, gender, local government links, and why? Clumping this complexity together into the term "community," although useful in relation to arguments addressing transnational actors in the commodity network, has the effect of hiding local differences that are fundamental to understanding how people in Satingpra experience shrimp farming. Answering these sorts of questions implies a return to some of the research frameworks that I drew on in my earlier work: How has shrimp farming and the more general economic change differentially affected the livelihoods of people of different economic status? How might economic status, gender, religion, or other differences shape participation in collective action? There is no necessary contradiction in merging the two approaches to better understand how transnational networks and flows are transforming the lives of people in Satingpra, other than the time and resources necessary to accomplish both kinds of studies.

Final Reflections on Concepts and Methods

Although the Satingpra of the 1980s presented itself to me as an incredibly dynamic and complex place, by the year 2000 it had become too easy to remember that world as relatively simple and isolated. Yet it is difficult to argue that the economy was more or less commodified during these two periods, or even less dynamic. The key differences lie in the reach, complexity, and relative stability of the commodity networks that palm sugar and farmed shrimp brought to the region. New academic concepts and methods that focus attention on transnational commodity networks have helped me understand these changes.

I have highlighted how palm sugar and shrimp production produced distinct landscapes—one, a lush landscape of rice fields and palm trees; the other, large ponds surrounded by machinery and dying vegetation. The concept of socio-natures, however, involves more than the idea that "natures" are produced socially. It should also draw attention to the ways that ecological processes shape the production of commodities and, thus, social relations. In the case of palm sugar, socionatural activities helped create a situation in which relatively poor rural people were able to improve their economic situations relative to the past. Sugar production from palm trees was also relatively predictable, and with a predictable local market, allowed for a relatively stable income. Instability was based mostly on whether there was enough healthy male labor available for climbing trees. In contrast, the socionatures of shrimp are highly unstable, with crops easily wiped out by shrimp diseases. One effect has been to induce vulnerable shrimp farmers to act collectively to regulate water effluent quality and sediment disposal.

Palm sugar and shrimp are also associated with very different kinds of politics. In the case of palm sugar, my analysis described a class politics, in which palm sugar production allowed poorer producers to extract themselves from debt de-pendency and gain better access to land and productive resources. Although it may not have been readily apparent, my analysis was able to show how this was in part an ecological politics—a politics that was shaped by ecological processes. In the case of shrimp, the ecological politics are front and center. In Satingpra, collective mobilization emerged because of the perceived threats to livelihood and quality of life posed by the ecology of shrimp farming, although this mobi-lization was also enabled by broader political changes in Thailand over the past two decades. The ecological politics of shrimp farming is dramatically different from that of sugar production in other ways as well: most obviously, in the spa-tiality of political action. The struggles around shrimp farming link Satingpra to actors situated in sites located on the other side of the world. Finally, there is a much greater diversity of actors involved in these struggles—from NGOs in the United States to the FAO to academics to multinational corporations to local governments and local NGOs.

In this chapter I have posed the question of the degree to which the differences outlined here are also a product of my changing research methods and conceptual frameworks. Twenty years ago I wrote about the politics of palm sugar as a class politics—but class politics was what I was looking for when I framed my research primarily through the lens of agrarian studies. More recently I have written about the politics of shrimp as a network politics, but that is what I was looking for when I framed my research through the lens of commodity chain analysis and network-influenced approaches to CBNRM. In the end, these shifts in analysis cannot be understood as primarily the result of either changing concepts and methods, or of socionatural changes in Satingpra, but as the outcome of both. At the same time, examining my current work through the lens of agrarian studies highlights how it would be useful to work some of the questions and concepts of agrarian studies into contemporary network approaches. Doing so would give the network analyses more "traction" through a richer account of how collective actors and their capacities are constituted, and it would make for a more nuanced analysis of how people's lives and livelihoods have been differentially remade through the socionatures of shrimp farming.

If I changed my methods in part because it made sense for me to do so in the face of what was presented to me in my field site as urgent questions, then my final question concerns the uniqueness or generality of this site. Did new conceptual frameworks emphasizing global networks and local politics emerge in part because many other sites were going through similar transformations? Is this case study representative of regional trends toward the increasing importance of transnational, high-value, high-impact agro-food commodities? These questions suggest that case studies like that presented here could be usefully complemented with a regional analysis of changes in commodity production and the regulatory practices associated with these changes.

Concluding Comparisons

Products and Processes of Commodification in Southeast Asia

JOSEPH NEVINS and NANCY LEE PELUSO

Coffee growers in Sumatra; wild mushroom pickers in the U.S. Pacific Northwest; female garment workers in southern Vietnam; shrimp farmers in Thailand; and steel workers in Indonesia: What do they all have in common?

In addition to being involved in the production and circulation of commodities, all of them are actors in the sense that they are not mere cogs in an economic machine, but individuals and parts of collectivities that shape the conditions under which commodities are made, traded, and consumed. As such, these actors are producers of histories, geographies, social relations, and "Nature"—just as they are shaped by forces of time, space, and society as well as by the physical environment. In these regards, they are both the makers of Southeast Asia and its literal embodiment.

This book has tried to put human faces on commodity processes and to enable its readers to imagine concretely the histories and geographies of socionatural change due to recent forms of commodity production in Southeast Asia. In doing so, it has examined a wide variety of commodities that are new to recent spatial and temporal contexts within the region, and others that have long helped define the people and places of Southeast Asia.

The book has also helped to illuminate the connections between seemingly disparate people and places that make production of specific commodities possible. At the same time, it has also demonstrated how such links—given their complexity, depth, and reach—and the actors behind them help to obscure commodification processes and their origins and effects, their benefits and detriments, and how they both make and destroy, give life or livelihoods and take them away. Commodification always engenders disturbance as it inevitably involves upheavals—what Joseph Schumpeter (1975) referred to as "creative destruction"—that reshape social, cultural, political, and geographic relations as much as economic ones. And given that power relations are always at play, the resulting disturbances produce and remake hierarchical social arrangements along various axes of difference (e.g., race, class, gender, rural/urban, nation).

Hence, to comprehend the relationship between Southeast Asia and commodity production in the twenty-first century is also to grasp three critical theoretical assertions that the chapters in this book ground in diverse Southeast Asian settings. First, commodification is intrinsically spatial in that the production, trade, and consumption of commodities occur in, involve, link, and produce particular spaces. These spaces—from a global scale to that of the human body, from the coffee-trading boards of London and New York to individual coffee growers within Southeast Asia—both reflect and actively reproduce socioeconomic disparities.

Second, commodification is an embodied social and cultural process. It is one that must be read through people's lives and deaths, relationships, and institutions. This means not only those directly involved in the production, trade, and consumption of a particular commodity, but those embedded within the larger social and spatial fabrics out of which the commodity emerges and that ties them together, while reshaping them in complex ways.

Third, commodification is a multifaceted process that unfolds in varied ways across space, time, and society; it is, in other words, highly and inherently contingent, in addition to being uneven in how its benefits and detriments travel across and embed themselves in sociogeographic spaces. In the case of declining prices and increased volatility in the global coffee market (see Potter, chapter 10), for example, it is not only how different subjects respond to these phenomena that influences outcomes along the commodity chain but also the material conditions that shape and reflect people, places, and institutions that informs their ability to respond in particular ways.

Just as commodification is contingent and uneven, so, too, is neoliberalism. As readily as we could talk about violent dispossession and the production of poverty related to a particular commodity, we could tell a different tale about the wealth-related manifestations of neoliberalized development in Southeast Asia, focusing on the skyscrapers of Kuala Lumpur, the nouveau riche in Saigon, the region's foreign investors in Japan, South Korea, and China, or those in the United States, Europe, and Australia.

To say this is not to deny the similarities that commodification produces in an age of globalization and neoliberalism. Like modernity and globalization more broadly, commodification in a neoliberalized age is a double-edged sword: it leads to vastly improved opportunities for some and profound insecurity for others (see Giddens 1990). And like other processes of accumulation that create hierarchical sociogeographic arrangements, commodification in a capitalist-dominated world produces and reflects a landscape of the good life for some and dispossession for all too many. We have tried to show that commodification today embodies ways of seeing and acting that favor particular ways of being while rendering others difficult or impossible.

In addition to illuminating shifts in the region's commodification processes, the chapters in this book have attempted to bridge the gaps between materialist and constructionist approaches by combining the strengths of political economy with cultural studies of commodity production (Bridge and Smith 2003). Our contributions have been of two sorts. Contributors pushed the boundaries of established theoretical framings in commodity studies. Second, many contributors introduced or extended our understandings of new terms, frames, and concepts in commodity studies, in part because of their focus on Southeast Asian productions of people, places, and nature.

Several new themes have thus emerged from and animated this collection. The contributions by Barney, Biggs, and Gellert, for instance, demonstrate some of the concrete effects of Chinese capital and markets on new and existing land and water use practices, particularly the ways Chinese capital and markets may be leading global or transnational patterns of enclosure. Moreover, they show that forest and agrarian enclosures are taking place in different ways than classic private (e.g., Thompson 1975; Williams 1973; Watts 1983) or state modes have done in Europe, the United States, and other parts of Southeast Asia (Hirsch 1990; Peluso 1992; James McCarthy 2004). New forms of public-private alliances between global or international capital and state actors in economies transitioning from socialist or other authoritarian modes of rule drive and shape enclosure, where varied state interests in establishing territorial control articulates, sometimes in unexpected ways, with the motives and anticipated effects of these big projects. China-as-consumer/market also looms large in Barney's story of pulp plantations in Laos; Gellert's timber-producing, though decentralized, Indonesian forest managers; and Vandergeest and Fougères's chapters on shrimp and fish production.

Several other chapters demonstrate that it is not simply the biggest country that makes a difference, but rather the richest and most resourceful investors. Intricate webs of social relations often define the high ends of the commodity chain, as shown by Tsing's unpacking of management-capital relationships between foreign (Korean and Asian-Canadian) managers and Japanese "odorless" capital investment, with suggestive glimpses of political maneuvering. Taiwanese provide the capital driving factory production in Tran's story of Vietnamese garment workers, with other East Asians as managers. Their actions create tensions between long-important ideologies of state power—the worker state—and the profit goals of these companies, which then play out in the relations between the workers and the managers, in addition to between citizens and the state. Buyers in Hong Kong are at the beginnings and ends of Fougères's transformative live fish commodity chains encircling Sulawesi. And, though markets for Myanmar's gems may be driving some of the enclosures and changes in access for small-scale miners in the countryside, MacLean has shown us that the ways these are taking place and their outcomes are neither "neoliberal" in form nor consistent with the neoliberal exceptions identified by Ong (2006).

Most authors here have discussed transformations in landscapes or socionatures, some of which are massive, others exposed through their spatialized micropolitics. The conversion of ways of seeing, being in, and controlling "nature" is, in some of these chapters, a revolutionary effect of the post-2000 present. Radical, new, or especially vast transformations characterize the agrarian environments of Laos (Barney), Myanmar (MacLean), Thailand (Vandergeest), and Vietnam (Biggs). At the same time, ongoing transformations, occasionally shifting erratically to new forms, are no less revolutionary in the lives of those forced to accept them or contesting the push to change, as we have seen particularly in forest-based cases in Indonesia and Malaysia (Tsing, Gellert, Li, Smeltzer). Still others seem to be mobilized not by capital or state imperatives alone, but by smaller-scale actors—Southeast Asian mushroom collectors in the United States (Tsing), Sulawesi fishers (Fougères), coffee farmers (Potter)—on their own or in concert with local capital and governments. In all of these, it is the historically layered social relationships of place that shape the specificities of these circumstances.

Taken together, the chapters illustrate how the various ways in which dialogue, discursive strategies, and competing representations depict and reproduce power relations, here seen in foresters' and conservationists' representations of coffee or cocoa growers (Potter, Li), factory managers' efforts to produce efficient and obedient laboring subjects (Rudnyckyj, Tran), or news media reporting that defends, demeans, or reshapes nations' citizen-subjects (Smeltzer, Tran). The physical effects of laboring on otherwise objectified bodies and "resources" is also critically important (Tsing, Tran, Rudnyckyj, MacLean, Potter, Smeltzer). The papers by Gellert, MacLean, Fougères, Potter, and Vandergeest demonstrate the production of both space and territories through the movement of people and capital intended to produce "resources" in "nature." All are telling stories about what Gellert calls "scalar dialectics"—the ways changes in governance and access create changes in the modes and sites of resource production and trade, and the ways in which different spatial levels of organization and practice continuously produce and alter one another.

The chapters also avoid the economistic tendencies of some commodity chain analyses to treat commodities in linear fashion, thus missing the dynamic, non-linear interrelationships between moments of production, circulation, and consumption. Initially growing out of world-systems theory, that approach recognized that commodities are produced in multiple sites, involving numerous and complex sets of relations. However, commodity chain analyses typically retained fixed notions of commodities through each stage or "link," and missed how commodities could be "indigenized," "hybridized," or otherwise appropriated in concept, representation, and form during their commodity lives, thus remaking them in terms of their meanings, values, and effects on users (Castree 2001; Miller 1995; Stone, Haugerud, and Little 2000). As several contributors note, ethnographic approaches to understanding commodity chains enable closer and more critical examinations of the moments, sites, and agents associated with the production and trade of a product and related transactions (Barney, Fougères, Gellert, Potter, Tsing, Vandergeest). The resulting analyses are richer for their focus on both so-cial and socionatural relationships, as well as on concepts of circuits and networks rather than "chains" (see Hughes and Reimer 2004). As exemplars of political ecology, these chapters also provide a practical entry through which to explore interconnections between, and the production of, temporal, spatial, and politi-cal scales (Blaikie 1985; Peet and Watts 1996; Gellert this volume). They clarify not only the benefits and costs of making and selling commodities but also the shifting social relations produced through and productive of those commodities (Bestor 2001). They show why, when marketization and commodification are destructive of nature and people, effective challenges to them will have to take place across scales (Peck and Tickell 2002).

Like globalization, neoliberalization is not an end state, but a process. A focus on neoliberalism as a thing rather than as a process runs the risk of missing the dynamic, contingent, contradictory, and unpredictable nature of this process. The chapters in this book have powerfully demonstrated this point. Perhaps most important is that neoliberal changes in local, national, regional, or global markets are always mediated by place-based histories (Hart 2006; Ong 2006; Massey 1993). For example, one striking effect of reading these chapters together is the recognition of the critical differences between the former or present so-cialist states (Laos, Vietnam, Myanmar) and those where authoritarianism has combined with state and private capitalism at present or in the past (Indonesia, Malaysia, Thailand). Commodities and commodification provide useful lenses for relational comparisons of that sort, and demonstrate perhaps that what has been more important to the shaping of commodity production and trade in the twenty-first century is not the colonial past, but the forms that these nation-states took after discarding the yokes of colonialism.

Double movements, which we spent some time on in the introduction to this book, also appear in many of the contributions. Their appearances are anything but automatic or predictable, thus pushing Polanyi's classic analysis of what he called "the Great Transformation." The smallholders, some shifting cultivators, who appear in the stories by Barney, Li, Potter, and MacLean, act and react to changing conditions of capital accumulation in a variety of ways. For the three socialist or socialist-transition political economies included as cases here (Vietnam, Laos, Myanmar), neoliberalization of global political economies pro-vides opportunistic moments for military, party, or other governing elites. These opportunities differ due to the varied histories and geographies with which they articulate, and they are in constant motion.

The authors in this book have made additional important contributions by suggesting new or more refined ways of conceptualizing commoditization processes, enclosure, territorialization, and ongoing primitive accumulation, coining terms that extend well-worn ideas: "leading edges" (Tsing), "scalar dialectics" (Gellert), "guerrilla mining" (MacLean), "aquarian questions" (Fougères), "metacommodification" (Biggs), "worshipping work" (Rudnyckyj). The creation of new frontiers animates this—indeed each of the terms just mentioned gets at some dimension of frontier politics. The details of the chapters, however, bring these abstract notions to life. MacLean, for example, comes in at a moment that might be considered part of a Biggsian point of "reconnaissance"—where violent and enclosing actors seek out the spoils of war at the same time that they wage small and larger scale wars. Reading both MacLean and Tsing, we get a feeling of a Wild West frontierlike context, created by decades of violent upheaval. At the other extreme, Tran's workers are trying to discipline capital and to make capital treat them as human beings, while the new sources of capital and its managers try to discipline the workers. Finally, the frontiers of privatization—where state capitalism of various forms is transitioning to new modes of accumulation—are shown by our contributors to be frontiers of subject production as well, of which Rudnyckyj's enterprising Islamic subjects demonstrate many nuanced dimensions.

The production of nature and people as commodities has a deep history in Southeast Asia. Even in their most recent globalized iterations, however, contingency, history, and spatiality are still primary factors affecting their production and their journeys to market. As new commodity frontiers are "discovered," invented, announced, and produced, what remains constant is the knowledge that these processes are at once contingent, connected, and procreative—not just reactive. Our common goal in this book has been to peel back the obscuring layers of superficial economic "facts" to reveal the inherently sociospatial processes just below the surface, out of which commodities old and new are made.

Notes

Introduction

1. There are exceptions, of course, many of which abound in the political ecology literature. See, e.g., Watts 1983; Peluso 1992; Prudham 2005; Heynan and Robbins 2005.

2. See, e.g., Appadurai 1986a; Kopyotoff 1986; Taussig 1986.

3. For other books exploring commoditization elsewhere in the world, see, e.g., Appadurai 1986a; Smith 1984; Haugerud, Stone, and Little 2000.

4. Rigg 1997; Chia and Perry 2003.

5. Many scholars of Southeast Asia identify these "factors" as key to the area's "regional identity." See, e.g., Chia and Perry 2003. Note, however, that Chia and Perry do not use analytics of enclosure, state violence, or primitive accumulation, but emphasize the common cold war experience, the Asian values rhetoric of national regimes, and the resource-rich geographies of the region.

6. Key milestones were the U.S.-orchestrated overthrow of the democratic socialist government of Salvador Allende in Chile in 1973 and its replacement with a free-market fundamentalist state and Washington's proxy war against the Sandinista government of Nicaragua during the 1980s.

7. Adam Smith recognized this problem in *The Wealth of Nations*, first published in 1776. In it, he celebrated the "discovery" of what he called America and Europeans' figuring out the route to India via the sea around the Cape of Good Hope. He also rejoiced the linking of distant parts of the world through ties of commerce and investment, and the accumulation of great amounts of wealth as a result. But Smith also decried the detrimental impacts of these developments, and worried about the indigenous populations—those on the receiving end of European expansion: "What benefits, or what misfortunes to mankind may hereafter result from these great events, no human wisdom can foresee....Their general tendency would seem to be beneficial. To the natives however...all the commercial benefits which can have resulted from those events have been sunk and lost in the dreadful misfortunes which they have occasioned" (quoted in Alexander 1996, 15) (see also Perelman 2000).

8. For the forestry sector and the way this took place, see Peluso and Vandergeest 2001 and Vandergeest and Peluso 2006a, 2006b.

9. In medieval England, the term "commodity" signified anything that had utility or use value, something that satisfied a human desire. Hence, cows, fields, rivers, and ports were all commodities. Gradually, the term "commodity" came to mean anything that could be bought or sold. Thus, the notion of exchange value replaced that of use value in terms of defining a commodity (Rowling 1987).

10. In terms of nation-states, successful developmental states—ones that play an important role in economic growth—are necessarily autonomous and embedded. They are embedded in social relations that tie the state to society so as to allow institutional means for negotiating goals and policies. This "embedded autonomy" provides the foundation for successful state intervention in economic activity. See Evans 1995.

11. Rowling (1987) argues that money is unique among commodities because it cannot be consumed.

12. On the classics, see, e.g., Williams 1973; Thompson 1975; Marx 1992. On state enclosures, see Vandergeest and Peluso 2006a, 2006b; Sivaramakrishnan 1999; James McCarthy 2004; Watts 1983.

13. For recent articles on new enclosures, see, e.g., www.thecommoner.com and www.midnightnotes.com.

1. Contingent Commodities

1. My approach to commodities combines insights from cultural studies (e.g., Taussig 2004) and world systems theory (e.g., Gereffi and Korzeniewicz 1994), stretching each.

2. *Webster's New International Dictionary of the English Language,* 2nd ed. (Springfield, Mass.: G. C. Merriam, 1961).

3. See Brown 1999. Kodeco also works in oil, plywood, cement, and more. See Kirksey (2001) and Aditjondro (2000).

4. See, however, Shin (n.d.).

5. Despite the inconsistency, I offer Korean names in the preferred usage of the individual. Thus *Choi* Gye Wol and *Kwon* Ta Ha contrast with Yongjin *Kim* in surname order.

6. After World War II, Japan turned to Korea as a staging ground for industrial development. Because of Korean resentment of direct Japanese investment, Japan developed a "putting-out" approach in which Korean firms could flourish with Japanese money, equipment, and trade advantages. Japan, in turn, could bypass U.S. quotas on Japanese products and move less-profitable industries to Korea, clearing the decks for new initiatives (Castley 1997).

7. The fate of West Papua, a Dutch colony both before and after World War II, was much debated in the 1950s and 1960s. In 1969, a delegation of 1,025 Papuans approved the transfer of the territory to the Republic of Indonesia, in what was supposed to be a UN-certified "Act of Free Choice." Many Papuans would have preferred independence, and struggles over this issue continue into the present. Choi seems to have entertained some segment of those being groomed to join Indonesia.

8. *Bahasa* is Indonesian for language; thus, "Indonesian" is *Bahasa Indonesia.* Kwon's naming of the pidgin as Bahasa Kodeco suggests the importance to him of the Indonesian-ness of this pidgin. It reaches out to Indonesian workers, accommodating their difference.

9. "Natives" here refers to Indonesian nationals.

10. Yongjin Kim explains: "Chungcheong dialect is so close to standard Korean that it is easy to pass as a standard Korean speaker. . . . When someone keeps this dialect, he or she is considered to be unrefined, unfashionable, clumsy, humble, or else proud of his local origins."

11. In Korean, as in English, the term "PX" is associated with the military. Kwon seems to be drawing a military parallel.

12. Don Brenneis (personal communication) brought out this point for me. He notes that the status of Korean as itself quite recently a subordinated language makes the book's claim to the easy legibility of a Korean vocabulary-based pidgin a political assertion.

13. By the 1990s, Kodeco was also firmly entrenched in the complementary interplay of legal and illegal logging. The combination increased the pace of deforestation, driving local residents to look for livelihood opportunities in both the legal and illegal sectors of resource extraction. For more details, see Tsing 2004.

14. In December 1998, for example, villagers occupied Kodeco's golf course, claiming that compensation for their land had not been paid (*Banjarmasin Post*, December 22, 1998). In March and April of 1999, another group occupied Kodeco's main offices, demanding compensation for one of Kodeco's coconut plantations (*Banjarmasin Post*, March 11, 1999, and April 15, 1999). From 2000 to 2002, Meratus Dayaks mobilized against Kodeco (Tsing 2004, 208–12; Wulan et al. 2004, 19–26).

15. Dayaks filed a number of NGO-supported lawsuits concerning orchard destruction; I know about these only through fieldwork conversations. None, to my knowledge, were successful.

16. Rebecca McClain (personal communication) pointed out this event to me. See her insightful dissertation (2000) on wild mushroom politics in Oregon.

17. Japanese matsutake have been in sharp decline since the 1970s because of the destruction of red pines—matsutakes' hosts—by nematodes as well as the changing nature of Japanese forests, which has also discouraged red pines. The high prices in Oregon in 1993 have never been equaled before or after. Japanese importers set the price in relation to global supply: as more mushrooms arrive in Japan from China, North and South Korea, northern Europe, and other areas, North American matsutake continue to decline in value. Meanwhile, due to trading strategies, in a single location and season, the price may shift radically, for example, in central Oregon in 2006, from $5 to $50 per pound.

18. Companies supplying Japan with seafood, North American vegetables, and log homes have been important. Statistical and summary information is difficult to present because of the secrecy of this high-stakes trade.

19. Pickers and buyers in Oregon commonly believe that Japanese value matsutake as an aphrodisiac. My preliminary interviews with Japanese buyers and consumers do not confirm this idea. Matsutake, however, is considered a phallus symbol, and polite speech may sometimes avoid direct reference to the mushroom. Premodern aristocrats used euphemisms such as "autumn aroma."

20. Christine Chin (1998) provocatively makes this argument in her study of the making of the middle class in Malaysia.

2. What's New with the Old?

1. The logics of commodification and territorialization and the relationship between them are underlying themes of this chapter but are also sufficiently complex as to deserve fuller theoretical treatment beyond the scope of this chapter.

2. Reformers in the environmentalist movement had hoped the new law would recognize local and indigenous (*adat*) rights to forests and forest land. The new law was limited in its progressive elements, however, not surprisingly given the nontransparent, "shadow" process in the Department of Forestry that produced it (Colchester et al. 2006, 24).

3. Peraturan Pemerintah tentang Tata Hutan dan Penyusunan Rencana Pengelolaan Hutan, Pemanfaatan Hutan dan Punggunaan Kawasan Hutan (Government Regulation on Forest Arrangements and Planning of Forest Management, Forest Use, and Forest Estate Use).

4. "The Logging of West Papua," *Down to Earth* 55 (November 2002). Available at http://dte.gn.apc.org/55WP.htm, accessed September 26, 2007.

5. The joint ministerial decree was signed December 12, 2002. The by-laws (AD/ART) of BRIK were established on January 16, 2003. The licensing process known as ETPIK was based on a decree from the Minister of Industry and Trade (SK No. 32) signed on January 22, 2003; after endorsement by BRIK, it went into effect on March 15, 2003. (Diagram of BRIK system provided to author, August 2005.)

6. Interviews with members of APKINDO, September 2004, and ASMINDO, July 2005.

7. Registered Forest Industry Products Exporters (Eksportir Terdaftar Produk Industri Kehutanan, or ETPIK).

8. Surat Keterangan Sahnya Hasil Hutan, or SKSHH.

9. "BRIK—A Flawed Approach," *Down to Earth* 60 (February 2004). Available at http://dte.gn.apc.org/60FOR.HTM, accessed September 26, 2007.

10. Data provided by BRIK, August 2005. This "realization" in 2005 is only 65 percent of the volume "requested," as opposed to 80–85 percent in the previous two years. The relationship between the two is not clear, however.

11. Indonesian Forum for Environment (WALHI—Friends of the Earth Indonesia).

12. Field interviews during 2004–5 with a variety of private executives and government officials in Jakarta and Tokyo revealed nostalgia for the "glory days" of Hasan and APKINDO.

13. "NGO Opposes Higher Logging Quota Policy," *Jakarta Post,* November 29, 2005.

14. The newly elected governor of Aceh declared a complete logging moratorium on June 6, 2007, but it is too early to examine the effects of this policy.

3. Contesting "Flexibility"

1. See (1996) for how Vietnamese textile and garment industries underwent three major transformations linking them with different types of capital since national reunification in 1975.

2. I agree with Amoore's argument that resistances can be contradictory, with fragmented identities and interests (Amoore 2005, 13), and concur with Mittelman and Chin (2005) that the conduct and meaning of resistance often are culturally embedded.

3. A large literature exists on flexible global production system, patriarchal relations in factories, and their negative effects on workers in Asia and Latin America since the early 1980s: Nash and Fernandez-Kelly 1983; Beneria and Roldan 1987; Ong 1987 and 1997; Harvey 1990; Bonacich et al. 1994; Trân 2001.

4. General Statistics Office, http://www.gso.gov.vn/default.aspx?tabid=387&idmid=3&ItemID=614, accessed October 1, 2007.

5. One should not overgeneralize these comments to all workers. More research is needed to look into cultural differences among migrant and local workers.

6. Under the planned economy, labor unions and the state worked hand in hand in the corporatist system. The VGCL had control over the production process, division of labor, wages, and income distribution to all stakeholders (Norlund 1996).

7. See Trân (2005) for other types of state media such as the labor union television programs.

4. Worshipping Work

1. *Pengajian* are Islamic study sessions in which chapters from the Qur'an are read and discussed.

2. Zainuddin MZ was an Islamic preacher who appeared on television before becoming involved in party politics. He held presidential aspirations in the 2004 elections, but he was unable to run because his party did not reach the necessary threshold of support in parliamentary elections required to run a presidential candidate.

3. An exclamation of derision.

4. This project is similar to Max Weber's argument that Protestant ethics share a certain affinity with modern, Western capitalism. However, there are important differences. For Weber an ethical orientation that emerged from the revisions made by Protestant theologians was conducive to an austerely rationalized, capitalist way of life (Weber 1990). The relationship for Weber was contingent and unintentional. It was sheer coincidence that the maxims of Protestantism gave rise to this methodical way of life. For spiritual reformers in contemporary Indonesia and elsewhere who link corporate success to religious piety, there is an explicit program aimed at simultaneous moral, political, and economic reform. In this configuration, religion is explicitly invoked in order to transform a set of economic practices. For a fuller discussion of this relationship, see Rudnyckyj 2006.

5. KERJA KERAS MERUPAKAN SEBAGIAN AMAL IBADAH KITA.

6. Menjadi "AGENT OF CHANGING" yang independen dan disegani dalam proses transformasi nilai nilai spiritual melalui pengembangan manusia bersumber daya berbasis spiritual (www.esq.co.id).

7. See Watson 2005 for an overview of this organization and its founder.

8. Djohan actually used the acronym "KKN" here, which stands for *korupsi, kolusi, dan nepotisme* (corruption, collusion, and nepotism). This acronym is commonly used to refer to a bribe.

9. The New Order refers to the period that coincides with Suharto's tenure as national leader. Suharto coined the term to contrast the period of his rule with the "Old Order" under Sukarno.

10. ESQ offers a variety of different kind of trainings. The most elaborate (and most expensive) is the four-day "executive" training, usually held in the main conference center in Jakarta. There are also two-day "regular" trainings, which are commonly done on the road in other parts of Indonesia, as well as a two-day training for teens and a one-day training for kids. At Krakatau Steel most trainings were three-day "professional" trainings.

11. Clifford Geertz provides an account of delivering the *talqin* in eastern Java (Geertz 1960, 71) and Bowen describes a similar ceremony in Gayo (Bowen 1984, 24–25).

5. China and the Production of Forestlands in Lao PDR

1. Commercial FGYH plantations in Southeast Asia usually involve hybrid strains of eucalyptus and acacia.

2. The village names and all personal names in this chapter have been changed. The subhead for this section is a statement from the *headman* of Sivilay village, Khammouane.

3. The government of Laos has a 15 percent share in LPFL.

4. Rice shortages at ban Sivilay are historical, but the very serious rice shortages typical of the last decade are widely linked to increased wet season flooding due to the operations of the Theun-Hinboun Power Company (THPC). The THPC project is an inter-basin diversion project which transfers a significant volume of water from the Theun River into the Hinboun River. Upstream erosion effects associated with this project have likely altered the natural flooding regime along the middle to lower Hinboun River. With the exception of five households that have small areas of unaffected paddy, villagers in ban Sivilay have not planted a wet rice paddy crop

since 2002. Although the company has launched a compensation and mitigation program, the poorer households in Sivilay village by and large have not been enrolled. The primary response to this loss of paddy has been a shift further into upland farming and a greater reliance on swidden agriculture.

5. Oji Seishi. Presentation by Seiro Tokunaga, Vientiane.

6. I thank Michael Dwyer for clarifying this point. See also Vandergeest and Peluso (1995).

7. Foppes and Ketphanh (2004) write: "NTFPs [non-timber forest products] are estimated to contribute 40–50 percent of cash income of Lao rural households. A similar amount of 50 percent of average household cash income is used to buy rice (more for the poorer families). NTFPs are therefore the most important safety net or coping strategy for the rural poor in Lao PDR."

8. For example, see Vientiane Times. 2007. "Villagers Preserve Local Forests." February 1, 2007.

9. Lao PDR ranked in the bottom cluster in the World Bank's 2006 Country Policy And Institutional Assessment (World Bank 2006).

6. Water Power

1. The first telegraph lines in Cochinchina were laid by the navy in 1863 with over three hundred kilometers of low-grade wire running from Saigon to provincial posts as well as to Phnom Penh in 1864. See Comité Agricole et Industriel de la Cochinchine (1878) and Boüinais (1884).

2. In Greek mythology, Penelope was the wife of Ulysses. During his absence in the Trojan Wars, she fended off suitors by promising to choose one when she finished weaving a robe. To avoid this day coming, she undid her weaving each night. The "work of Penelope" is used to describe a project perpetually under construction with no foreseeable end.

3. Ông Diều, taped interview with David Biggs, April 19, 2002.

4. U.S. agricultural development programs in Vietnam actually preceded the 1954 Geneva Accords and were focused around Hanoi beginning with the Đồng Quân settlement in 1953.

5. For a survey of Hoover Dam's construction, see Wm. [William] Joe Simonds, "The Boulder Canyon Project: Hoover Dam," http://www.usbr.gov/history/hoover.htm.

6. Ông Rỡ, taped interview with David Biggs, April 12, 2002.

7. Contested Commodifications

1. For a review of contestations around the commodification of nature in different approaches to conservation, see McAfee 1999.

2. My translation from a taped interview, 2003.

3. See McAfee (1999, 139) and Fairhead and Leach (1996).

4. See Henley (2005, 84, 352–59, 546–60) and Weber, Faust, and Kreisel (2003, 414).

5. See Elson (1997, 100–102).

6. I describe this conjuncture in more detail in Li (2007).

7. See also Ellen (1986).

8. I cite the draft plan with permission of TNC's Palu office. According to TNC staff, the plan finally signed by the Minister of Forestry in 2004 was scaled down and "more pragmatic."

9. On the replacement of swidden with cacao in Moa, see Belsky and Siebert (2003).

10. The report was an appendix to TNC (2002a).

11. The governmental project of engaging people in new practices as a way to create environmental subjects is closely examined in Agrawal (2005).

12. The figure of 26 percent included two legal agricultural enclaves inside the main park boundary, but significantly exceeded them (TNC 2002b, 1:67, 76).

13. See Tsing (1999) for a vivid account of the ascription of nature loving to Kalimantan villagers. On the role of scarcity, see Ellen (1986).

14. Forest demarcation in the colonial and contemporary period and the treatment of customary rights is described in Peluso and Vandergeest (2001).

15. Forest Trends (2003). See http://www.rightsandresources.org/ (accessed January 30, 2007) for an updated statement of their platform.

8. Sovereignty in Burma after the Entrepreneurial Turn

1. In 1989, the military regime changed the country's name to Myanmar. Many Burmese, regardless of their ethnicity, object to the change either because it was done by military fiat or because they perceive it to privilege ethnic Burmans, who constitute approximately 60 percent of the country's population (Houtman 1999, 15–120). For these reasons, I will refer to the country as Burma and use the pre-1989 place names throughout.

2. The term "regime" collectively refers to both the state's bureaucracy and the state's armed forces.

9. Old Markets, New Commodities

1. The Basic Fisheries Law (Articles 3, 1985, and 8, 2004) outlaws the use of dissolved cyanide to capture fish, the predominant practice in Pulau Rantau. I therefore use pseudonyms for the islands to avoid incriminating people interviewed.

2. On the "consensus," see Williamson (1990). "Fracturing" refers to the intensification of debates around the appropriateness of neoliberal policies in the late 1990s (see Stiglitz 2002, 16, 20). Stiglitz is a former chief economist and senior vice president at the World Bank.

10. Production of People and Nature, Rice, and Coffee

1. The coffee uplands include parts of the modern provinces of South Sumatra, Bengkulu, and Lampung (fig. 10.1).

2. The district boundaries shown on the map refer to the period before decentralization in 2001.

3. The localities are here named after the dominant ethnic group, which follows local practice. The "Pasemah" lands include the district of Lahat and the town of Pagar Alam, while the "Semendo" lands include three subdistricts in the district of Muara Enim.

4. The *marga* was a traditional grouping of villages in southern Sumatra, originally administered by a specific clan. Dutch changes to land ownership in the 1850s restricted the extent of marga lands, allowing space for migrant clans to establish new groupings (Kingston 1987).

5. Debate was especially heated in 1894 and 1895, when difficulties in marketing the coffee and obtaining labor were emphasized. Labor was imported from Java, as local farmers refused to work for Europeans (Hagenaar 1894–95).

6. Translations from Dutch texts by the author and Annieke van Woerkom.

7. The 1896 Brazilian coffee crisis, in which growers flooded the market, resulted in low prices for years, "initiating a boom and bust coffee cycle which continues to this day" (Pendergrast 1999, 78).

8. Robusta coffee typically grows taller than arabica and can reach a height of twelve meters.

9. A *ladang* is a swidden field.

10. "The elected head of the *marga*, the *pesirah*, with his council, gave permission to clear land, respecting existing customary rights and conservation areas. Slopes, riverbanks and areas around springs were not usually allowed to be cleared" (Charras and Pain 1993, 67). The *marga* groupings were abolished in 1982, following the Suharto government's Village Regulation of 1979, which allowed each village to receive government grants.

11. The coffee area around Lake Ranau used laborers from Bantam, and even Chinese were employed in some locations.

12. In 1978, Lampung led South Sumatra in both area and production. Since 2002, however, low coffee prices have brought reductions in coffee area in both provinces. South Sumatra has now regained supremacy, though overall yields remain below those of Lampung.

13. From 1962 the ICA used a quota system to restrict production and keep prices stable. However, since the entry of Vietnam into the market, the supply of coffee has been greatly above demand and the ICA has not worked, though it has been renegotiated.

14. Some return migrants from Lampung have begun introducing shade trees.

15. Villagers were angry that a farm training program run by the district in October 2000, supposedly lasting two days and including four hours on rice intensification, finished after an hour and a half. More recent information shows some increase in government attention to the area, with the provision of IR64 rice seed as part of a program to improve yields (*Berita Muara Enim*, April 12, 2006).

16. Prices subsequently rose to an average of Rp. 8,000 per kilogram in June 2005, but not before many farmers in Lampung had switched to other crops. In South Sumatra, farmers complained that they needed a price of Rp. 10,000 before they could make much profit, as costs had also increased ("Harga kopi membaik," *Kompas*, March 30, 2005; "Kopi petik merah di Lampung," *Tempointeraktif*, September 6, 2005; "Petani tak nikmati membaiknya harga kopi," *Kompas*, August 18, 2005).

17. One farmer asked the author to explain why prices were so low, and was amazed when competition from Vietnam was mentioned. What Appadurai (1986b, 42) has described as a "paradigm of merchant bridges across large gaps in knowledge between producer and consumer" was widespread in Semendo.

18. The World Agroforestry Centre, formerly known as the International Center for Research on Forestry, and still using the old name for its current acronym, ICRAF, was founded in 1978. It conducts research to promote more sustainable forestry practices, focused on four global themes: land and people, environmental services, strengthening institutions and trees and markets. Its headquarters is in Nairobi. See http://www.worldagroforestrycentre.org.

19. The quality of West Lampung coffee is still below world standard, meaning that they receive only Rp. 7,5008,000 per kilogram, instead of the international price of Rp. 10,000 for robusta ("Petani kopi tidak menikmati harga bagus," *Kompas*, April 11, 2006).

11. The Message Is the Market

1. In 2005, the government added Kedah's Kulim High Tech Park and Penang Cybercity to its list of MSC designated "zones."

2. Malaysia is a member of the WTO, a party to TRIPS, and a signatory to the CBD.

3. See description for the Malaysian Biotechnology Corporation (BiotechCorp), http://www.biotechcorp.com.my/aboutus/malaysiabiotechcorp.htm.

4. This shift in Malaysia's ethnic discourse does not, however, mean that preferential policies have been abandoned. Although not as publicly advocated or discussed as in the past, they remain at the forefront of government policy.

5. In 2005, the Malaysian government announced mandatory prison terms for anyone found guilty of illegal logging (Forest Conservation Portal 2005). It remains to be seen whether the government can, and will, follow through on this new method of control.

6. Additionally, it is difficult to properly assess the extent of Malaysia's biodiversity, much less the destruction of it, as the available data tends to be incomplete and inconsistent across various government ministries and agencies (SAM 2005).

7. The term GMO encompasses a wider range of organisms than does LMO, which refers only to genetically modified organisms that are still alive.

8. For additional information on the NGOs' concerns, refer to their website on the issue: www.ftamalaysia.org.

9. In 2005, the circulation of *The Edge Weekly* in peninsular Malaysia was 23,216 (Press Guide 2005, A-12).

10. This pledge should be viewed solely as an economic strategy to attract international business to the country's fledgling high-tech sector, especially the MSC.

11. Of note, there currently exists no politically contentious journalism on television.

12. New Concepts, New Natures?

1. I include here the turn to a more cultural approach since the mid-1980s, influenced by writers such as Stuart Hall, Raymond Williams, and E. P. Thompson, all of whom identify with Gramscian approaches. See, for example, Scott (1985). In recent years poststructuralist critiques of essentialism and Foucaultian concepts of discipline and governmentality have also been influential among agrarian studies scholars. Here, however, I define agrarian studies in relation to its roots in Marxist political economy and Marxist cultural studies, in order to obtain conceptual traction from making a distinction between the Marxist-influenced approaches and those more influenced by poststructuralism or network theories, or both.

2. For example, the introduction by Bernstein and Byres (2001) to the *Journal of Agrarian Change* does not mention community in its review of rural politics, except indirectly in discussions of agrarian populism, a term that has long been used to dismiss social movements that are not based on class mobilization.

3. The Aquaculture Certification Council was incorporated in 2003 and is based in Washington State. See www.aquaculturecertification.org.

References

Abdullah, Taufik. 1986. "The Pesantren in Historical Perspective." In *Islam and Society in Southeast Asia*, edited by T. Abdullah and S. Siddique, 80–107. Singapore: Institute of Southeast Asian Studies.

Adas, M. 1989. *Machines as the Measure of Men: Science, Technology, and Ideologies of Western Dominance.* Ithaca: Cornell University Press.

———. 2006. *Dominance by Design: Technological Imperatives and America's Civilizing Mission.* Cambridge: Harvard University Press.

Aditjondro, George. 2000. "Chopping the Global Tentacles of the Suharto Oligarchy." http://www.unhas.ac.id/~rhiza/gja1.html.

Afroz, Rafia, Mohd Nasir Hassan, and Noor Akma Ibrahim. 2003. "Review of Air Pollution and Health Impacts in Malaysia." *Environmental Research* 92: 71–77.

Agrawal, A. 1995. "Indigenous and Scientific Knowledge: Some Critical Comments." *Indigenous Knowledge and Development Monitor* 3.

———. 2001. "State Formation in Community Spaces? Decentralization of Control over Forests in the Kumaon Himalaya, India." *Journal of Asian Studies* 60, no. 1: 9–40.

———. 2005. *Environmentality: Technologies of Government and the Making of Subjects.* Durham: Duke University Press.

Agrawal, Arun, and Clark Gibson, eds. 2001. *Communities and the Environment.* New Brunswick, N.J.: Rutgers University Press.

Aguilar, Grethel. 2003. "Access to Genetic Resources and Protection of Traditional Knowledge in Indigenous Territories." In *Trading in Knowledge: Development Perspectives on TRIPS, Trade and Sustainability*, edited by Christophe Bellmann, Graham Dutfield, and Ricardo Meléndez-Ortiz, 175–83. London: Earthscan.

Albion, Robert Greenhalgh. 1926. *Forests and Sea Power: The Timber Problem of the Royal Navy, 1652–1862.* Cambridge: Harvard University Press.

Alexander, Titus. 1996. *Unravelling Global Apartheid: An Overview of World Politics.* Cambridge, Mass.: Blackwell.

Aliran. 2004. "Media Acting Like PR Arms of Biotech Industry." *Malaysian Media Monitors' Diary.* http://www.aliran.com/charter/monitors/2004/06/media-acting-like-pr-arms-of-biotech.html.

Alternative ASEAN Network on Burma (ALTSEAN). 2005. "Call for FATF to Maintain Burma's NCCT Status." http://www.altsean.org/FATF%20briefer%20may%202005.pdf.

Amoore, Louise. 2005. "Introduction: Global Resistance—Global Politics." In *The Global Resistance Reader,* edited by Louise Amoore, 1–13. New York: Routledge.

Anderson, Benedict. 1991. *Imagined Communities: Reflections on the Origin and Spread of Nationalism.* London: Verso.

Anuar, Mustafa K. 2005. "Politics and the Media in Malaysia." *Kasarinlan: Philippine Journal of Third World Studies* 20, no. 1: 25–47.

Appadurai, Arjun. 1986a. "Introduction: Commodities and the Politics of Value." In *The Social Life of Things,* edited by A. Appadurai, 3–63. Cambridge: Cambridge University Press.

———. 1986b. *The Social Life of Things: Commodities in Cultural Perspective.* Cambridge: Cambridge University Press.

Appelbaum, Richard. 2005. "Fighting Sweatshops: Problems of Enforcing Global Labor Standards." In *Critical Globalization Studies,* edited by W. Robinson and R. Appelbaum, 369–78. New York: Routledge.

Arnold, David. 1996. *The Problem of Nature: Environment, Culture, and European Expansion.* Cambridge: Blackwell Press.

Arshad, Fatimah Mohd. 2005. "COMMENT: Biotech Thrust for Agriculture." *New Straits Times: New Sunday Times Online,* October 8. http://ikdpm.upm.edu.my/en/NST.pdf.

Article 19 and Centre for Independent Journalism. 2007. "A Haze of Secrecy: Access to Environmental Information in Malaysia," January. http://www.article19.org/pdfs/publications/malaysia-a-haze-of-secrecy.pdf.

Asad, Talal. 1993. *Genealogies of Religion: Discipline and Reasons of Power in Christianity and Islam.* Baltimore: Johns Hopkins University Press.

Asian Development Bank. 1993. *Report and Recommendation of the President to the Board of Directors on a Proposed Loan and Technical Assistance Grants to the Lao PDT for the Industrial Tree Plantation Project.* Manila: ADB.

———. 2002. *Mid-term Evaluation of CSIADCP Performance in Qualitative and Substantive Terms, Volume 2—Annexes.* Palu, Indonesia: CSIADCP (Provincial Coordination Unit, BAPPEDA).

———. 2003. *PPTA Tree Plantation for Livelihood Improvement Project: Final Report.* Bangkok: MIDAS Agronomics Co.

———. 2005a. Forest Plantations Development Project. *Report and Recommendation of the President to the Board of Directors.* Manila: ADB.

———. 2005b. *Key Indicators of Developing Asian and Pacific Countries.* Manila: ADB.

———. 2005c. *Operations Manual of the Lao Plantation Authority.* Supplementary appendix C. Manila: ADB.

ASMINDO. 2004. "Reposisi Peran dan Fungsi BRIK" [Repositioning the Role and Function of BRIK]. *Asmindo Image* 3: 14–15.

Atz, J. 1971. *Aquarium Fishes: Their Beauty, History, and Care.* New York: Viking Press.

Awang, Muhamad Bin, Abu Bakar Jaafar, Ahmad Makmom Abdullah, Marzuki Bin Ismail, Mohd Nasir Hassan, Ramdzani Abdullah, Shamsuddin Johan, and Hamdan Noor. 2000.

"Air Quality in Malaysia: Impacts, Management Issues and Future Challenges." *Respirology* 5, no. 2: 183–96.

Badawi, Abdullah Ahmad. 2003a. "The Inauguration of Incredible India 2003." http://www.pmo.gov.my/WebNotesApp/PMMain.nsf/0/b992c6411770d4c948256df2000e1b18?OpenDocument.

———. 2003b. "Malaysia: Patenting to Protect Our Flora, Fauna." http://forests.org/articles/reader.asp?linkid=21505.

——— 2004. "Dinner Hosted by the U.S.-ASEAN Business Council." http://www.pmo.gov.my/WebNotesApp/PMMain.nsf/0/4f26340191d5a46848256ed8001c8cc7?OpenDocument.

———. 2005a. "Biodiversity for the Benefit of Present and Future Generations." http://www.pmo.gov.my/WebNotesApp/PMMain.nsf/0/9da932611750fc1848256f96000402b6?OpenDocument.

———. 2005b. "BIOMALAYSIA 2005." http://www.pmo.gov.my/WebNotesApp/PMMain.nsf/0/1822c85b82aa7d8948256ff1001034f4?OpenDocument.

Bailey, C. 1988. "The Political Economy of Marine Fisheries Development in Indonesia." *Indonesia* 46: 25–38.

Baird, I., and B. Shoemaker. 2005. *Aiding or Abetting? Internal Resettlement and International Aid Agencies in the Lao PDR.* Toronto: Probe International.

Barber, C., and V. Pratt. 1997. *Sullied Seas: Strategies for Combating Cyanide Fishing in Southeast Asia and Beyond.* Washington, D.C.: World Resources Institute; Manila: International Marinelife Alliance.

Barham, Bradford, Stephen G. Bunker, and Denis O'Hearn. 1994. "Raw Material Industries in Resource-Rich Regions." In *States, Firms, and Raw Materials,* edited by B. Barham, S. G. Bunker, and D. O'Hearn, 3–38. Madison: University of Wisconsin Press.

Barr, Christopher M. 1998. "Bob Hasan, the Rise of Apkindo, and the Shifting Dynamics of Control in Indonesia's Timber Sector." *Indonesia* 65: 1–36.

———. 2002. "HPH Timber Concession Reform: Questioning the 'Sustainable Logging' Paradigm." In *Which Way Forward? People, Forests, and Policymaking in Indonesia,* edited by C. J. P. Colfer and I. A. P. Resosudarmo, 191–220. Washington, D.C.: Resources for the Future.

Barry, Andrew. 2001. *Political Machines: Governing a Technological Society.* London: Athlone Press.

Barry, Andrew, Thomas Osborne, and Nikolas Rose, eds. 1996. *Foucault and Political Reason: Liberalism, Neo-liberalism, and Rationalities of Government.* Chicago: University of Chicago Press.

Baviskar, Amita. 1995. *In the Belly of the River: Tribal Conflicts over Development in the Narmada Valley.* New York: Oxford University Press.

Beard, Victoria. 2003. "Learning Radical Planning: The Power of Collective Action." *Planning Theory* 2: 13–35.

Bello, Walden. 1998. "East Asia: On the Eve of the Great Transformation?" *Review of International Political Economy* 5, no. 3: 424–44.

Belsky, J. M., and S. F. Siebert. 2003. "Cultivating Cacao: Implications of Sun-Grown Cacao on Local Food Security and Environmental Sustainability." *Agriculture and Human Values* 20: 277–85.

Bene, Christophe. 2005. "The Good, the Bad and the Ugly: Discourse, Policy Controversies and the Role of Science in the Politics of Shrimp Farming Development." *Development Policy Review* 23, no. 5: 585–614.

Beneria, Lourdes, and Martha Roldan. 1987. *The Crossroads of Class and Gender: Industrial Homework, Subcontracting, and Household Dynamics in Mexico City.* Chicago: University of Chicago Press.

Berger, John. 1973. *Ways of Seeing.* New York: Viking Press.

Bernama (Malaysian National News Agency). 2005. "Abdullah Unveils Ambitious National Biotechnology Policy." http://www.bernama.com/bernama/v3/news_business.php?id=131532.

Bernstein, H., and T. J. Byres. 2001. "From Peasant Studies to Agrarian Change." *Journal of Agrarian Change* 1, no. 1: 1–56.

Bestor, Theodore. 2001. "Supply-Side Sushi: Commodity, Market, and the Global City." *American Anthropologist* 103, no. 1: 76–95.

Biggs, David. 2006. "Reclamation Nations: The U.S. Bureau of Reclamation's Role in Water Management and Nation Building in the Mekong Valley, 1945–1975." *Comparative Technology Transfer and Society* 4, no. 3: 225–46.

Biopolis. 2006. "Introduction to Biopolis: About Us." http://www.one-north.com/pages/lifeXchange/bio_intro.asp.

Black, E. R. 1969. *Alternative in Southeast Asia.* New York: Praeger.

Blackburn, Robin. 1997. *The Making of New World Slavery: From the Baroque to the Modern 1492–1800.* New York: Verso.

Blaikie, Piers. 1985. *The Political Economy of Soil Erosion in Developing Countries.* London: Longmann.

Block, Fred. 2001. Introduction to *The Great Transformation: The Political and Economic Origins of Our Time,* by Karl Polyanyi, xviii–xxxviii. Reprint ed. Boston: Beacon Press.

Blomley, Nicholas. 2003. "Law, Property, and the Geography of Violence: The Frontier, the Survey, and the Grid." *Annals of the Association of American Geographers* 93, no. 1: 121–41.

Blum, William. 2003. *Killing Hope: U.S. Military and CIA Interventions since World War II.* Monroe, Maine: Common Courage Press.

Blussé, Leonard. 1991. "In Praise of Commodities: An Essay on the Cross-cultural Trade in Edible Bird's-Nests." In *Emporia, Commodities, and Entrepreneurs in Asian Maritime Trade, c. 1400–1750,* edited by R. Ptak and D. Rothermund, 317–35. Stuttgart: Franz Steiner Verlag.

Bonacich, Edna. 2005. "Labor and the Global Logistics Revolution." In *Critical Globalization Studies,* edited by W. Robinson and R. Appelbaum, 359–68. New York: Routledge.

Bonacich, Edna, Lucie Cheng, Norma Chinchilla, Nora Hamilton, and Paul Ong, eds. 1994. *Global Production: The Apparel Industry in the Pacific Rim.* Philadelphia: Temple University Press.

Boomgaard, Peter. 1997. "Introducing Environmental Histories of Indonesia." In *Landscapes: Explorations in the Environmental History of Indonesia,* edited by P. Boomgaard, F. Colombijn, and D. Henley. Leiden: KITLV Press.

Borsuk, Richard. 2003. "Suharto Crony Stays Busy Behind Bars: 'Bob' Hasan Starts Business, Pulls Strings at Olympics." *Asian Wall Street Journal,* August 13. http://www.mongabay.com/external/bob_hasan_indonesia.htm, accessed November 21, 2005.

Boüinais, A., and A. Paulus. 1884. *La cochinchine contemporaine*. Paris: Challamel Aîné.

Bowen, John R. 1984. "Death and the History of Islam in Highland Aceh." *Indonesia* 38: 21–38.

Boxer, C. R. 1969. *The Portuguese Seaborne Empire, 1415–1825*. London: Hutchinson and Company.

Boyd, William, W. Scott Prudham, and R. A. Schurman. 2001. "Industrial Dynamics and the Problem of Nature." *Society and Natural Resources* 14: 555–70.

Brady, M. 2004. "China's Forest Products Industrial Policy and Its International Implications." Presentation at CIFOR–Forest Trends "Workshop on China Forest Products Trade," Beijing, China, June 2–5.

Breman, Jan, and Gunawan Wiradi. 2002. *Good Times and Bad Times in Rural Java: Case Study of Socioeconomic Dynamics in Two Villages towards the End of the Twentieth Century*. Leiden: KITLV Press.

Brenner, Neil. 2001. "The Limits to Scale? Methodological Reflections on Scalar Structuration." *Progress in Human Geography* 25, no. 4: 591–614.

Bridge, Gavin. 2002. "Grounding Globalization: The Prospects and Perils of Linking Economic Processes of Globalization to Environmental Outcomes." *Economic Geography* 78, no. 3: 361–86.

Bridge, Gavin, and Adrian Smith. 2003. "Intimate Encounters: Culture-Economy-Commodity." *Environment and Planning D: Society and Space* 21, no. 3: 257–68.

Brossard de Corbigny, J. M. 1878. "Notice sur les travaux de canalisation de la Cochinchine Française." *Revue Maritime et Coloniale* 59.

Brown, David. W. 1999. *Addicted to Rent: Corporate and Spatial Distribution of Forest Resources in Indonesia; Implications for Forest Sustainability and Government Policy*. http://www.geocities.com/davidbrown_id/Atr_main.html.

Brown, J. Christopher, and Mark Purcell. 2005. "There's Nothing Inherent about Scale: Political Ecology, the Local Trap, and the Politics of Development in the Brazilian Amazon." *Geoforum* 36, no. 5: 607–24.

Brush, Stephen. 1999. "Bioprospecting the Public Domain." *Cultural Anthropology* 14, no. 4: 535–55.

Bryant, Raymond. 1994. "Shifting the Cultivator: The Politics of Teak Regeneration in Colonial Burma." *Modern Asian Studies* 28, no. 2: 225–50.

———. 1996. "Asserting Sovereignty through Natural Resource Use: Karen Forest Management on the Thai-Burmese Border." In *Resources, Nations, and Indigenous Peoples*, edited by R. Howitt, J. Connell, and P. Hirsch, 32–41. Melbourne: Oxford University Press.

———. 1997. *The Political Ecology of Forestry in Burma, 1824–1994*. Honolulu: University of Hawaii Press.

———. 1998. "Power, Knowledge, and Political Ecology in the Third World: A Review." *Progress in Physical Geography* 22, no. 1: 79–94.

Budidarsono, S., S. A. Koncoro, and T. P. Tomich. 2000. *A Profitability Assessment of Robusta Coffee Systems in Sumberjaya Watershed, Lampung, Sumatra, Indonesia*. Southeast Asia Policy Research Working Paper No. 16. Bogor, Indonesia: ICRAF SEA.

Bunker, Stephen G. 1985. *Underdeveloping the Amazon*. Chicago: University of Chicago Press.

Bunnell, Tim. 2002. "(Re)positioning Malaysia: High-Tech Networks and the Multicultural Rescripting of National Identity." *Political Geography* 21, no. 1: 105–24.

Bunnell, Tim, and Alice M. Nah. 2004. "Counter-Global Cases for Places: Contesting Displacement in the Globalizing Kuala Lumpur Metropolitan Area." *Urban Studies* 41, no. 1: 2447–67.

Burkhard, Gunter. 2002a. *Natural Resource Management in Central Sulawesi: Past Experience and Future Prospects.* Palu, Indonesia: STORMA.

———. 2002b. *Stability or Sustainability: Dimensions of Socio-economic Security in a Rain Forest Margin.* Palu, Indonesia: STORMA.

Burma Border Consortium. 2003. *Reclaiming the Right to Rice: Food Security and Internal Displacement in Eastern Burma.* Bangkok: BBC.

Butcher, J. 2004. *The Closing of the Frontier: A History of the Marine Fisheries of Southeast Asia, c. 1850–2000.* Singapore: Institute of Southeast Asian Studies.

Caraway, Teri L. 2007. *Assembling Women: The Feminization of Global Manufacturing.* Ithaca: Cornell University Press.

CARE. 2002. *Report on the Interim Evaluation of CARE International Indonesia Project: Protection of Tropical Forests through Environmental Conservation of Marginal Lands (PTF-ECML) Phase II.* Report prepared by Oyvind Sandbukt and Rudy Syaf. Palu, Indonesia: CARE.

———. 2003. *Protection of Tropical Forests through Environmental Conservation of Marginal Lands (PTF-ECML) Phase II, 2001–2005, Second Annual Report.* Jakarta: CARE International Indonesia.

Casson, Anne, and Krystof Obidzinski. 2002. "From New Order to Regional Autonomy: Shifting Dynamics of 'Illegal' Logging in Kalimantan, Indonesia." *World Development* 30, no. 12: 2133–51.

Castley, Robert. 1997. *Korea's Economic Miracle: The Crucial Role of Japan.* New York: St. Martin's.

Castree, Noel. 1995. "The Nature of Produced Nature: Materiality and Knowledge Construction in Marxism." *Antipode* 27, no. 1: 12–48.

———. 2001. "Commodity Fetishism, Geographical Imaginations, and Imaginative Geographies (Commentary)." *Environment and Planning A* 33, no. 9: 1519–25.

———. 2003. "Commodifying What Nature?" *Progress in Human Geography* 27, no. 3: 273–97.

CBD (Convention on Biological Diversity). 1992. "Access to Genetic Resources and Benefit-Sharing." http://www.biodiv.org/programmes/socio-eco/benefit/default.aspx.

Chalfin, Brenda. 2004. *Shea Butter Republic: State Power, Global Markets, and the Making of an Indigenous Commodity.* New York: Routledge.

Chapin, Mac. 2005. "A Challenge to Conservationists." *World Watch*, November.

Charras, M., and M. Pain. 1993. "First Book: Major Changes in Southern Sumatra." In *Spontaneous Settlements in Indonesia*, edited by M. Charras and M. Pain, 37–98. Jakarta: CNRS-ORSTOM, Departemen Transmigrasi.

Chia Lin Sien, and Martin Perry. 2003. Introduction to *Southeast Asia Transformed: A Geography of Change*, edited by Chia Lin Sien, 1–47. Singapore: Institute of Southeast Asian Studies.

Chin, Christine. 1998. *In Service and Servitude: Foreign Female Domestic Workers and the Malaysian "Modernity" Project.* New York: Columbia University Press.

Chomsky, Noam. 1993. *Year 501: The Conquest Continues.* Boston: South End Press.

Choy, Yee Keong. 2005. "Sustainable Development—An Institutional Enclave (with Special Reference to the Bakun Dam-Induced Develoment Strategy in Malaysia)." *Journal of Economic Issues* 39, no. 4: 951–71.

Clarence-Smith, William Gervase. 1992. "Planters and Smallholders in Portuguese Timor in the Nineteenth and Twentieth Centuries." *Indonesia Circle* 57: 15–30.

Clarence-Smith, W. G., and S. Topik. 2003. *The Global Coffee Economy in Africa, Asia and Latin America, 1500–1989*. Cambridge: Cambridge University Press.

Colchester, Marcus, with Marco Boscolo, Arnoldo Contreras-Hermosilla, Filippo Del Gatto, Jessica Dempsey, Guillaume Lescuyer, Krystof Obidzinski, Denis Pommier, Michael Richards, Sulaiman N. Sembiring, Luca Tacconi, Maria Teresa Vargas Rios and Adrian Wells. 2006. *Justice in the Forest: Rural Livelihoods and Forest Law Enforcement*. Bogor, Indonesia: Center for International Forestry Research (CIFOR).

Comaroff, Jean, and John Comaroff. 2000a. *Millennial Capitalism and the Culture of Neoliberalism*. Durham: University of North Carolina Press.

——. 2000b. "Millennial Capitalism: First Thoughts on a Second Coming." *Public Culture* 12, no. 2: 291–343.

Comité Agricole et Industriel de la Cochinchine. 1878. *La cochinchine française en 1878*. Paris: Challamel Ainé.

Cooke, N., and T. Li, eds. 2004. *Water Frontier: Commerce and the Chinese in the Lower Mekong Region, 1750–1880*. Lanham, Md.: Rowman and Littlefield.

Coronil, Fernando. 1997. *The Magical State: Nature, Money, and Modernity in Venezuela*. Chicago: University of Chicago Press.

Correia, David. 2005. "From Agropastoralism to Sustained Yield Forestry: Industrial Restructuring, Rural Change, and the Land-Grant Commons in Northern New Mexico." *Capitalism Nature Socialism* 16, no. 1: 25–44.

Cossalter, C. 2004a. "Does China Have a Comparative Advantage for Growing Pulpwood?" Paper presented to the "International Forum on Investment and Finance in China's Forestry Sector," Beijing, June 2–5.

——. 2004b. "Pulp Industry Expansion and New Wood Fiber Demand in Southern China." Paper presented to the "Future of Forests in East Asia and China" conference, Kuala Lumpur, October 7–8.

Cramer, P. J. S. 1957. *A Review of Literature of Coffee Research in Indonesia*. Edited by F. L. Wellman. Turialba, Costa Rica: Inter-American Institute of Agricultural Sciences.

Cronon, William. 1996. "The Trouble with Wilderness; Or, Getting Back to the Wrong Nature." In *Uncommon Ground*, edited by W. Cronon. New York: W. W. Norton.

Curran, L. M., S. N. Trigg, A. K. McDonald, D. Astiani, Y. M. Hardiono, P. Siregar, I. Caniago, and E. Kasischke. 2004. "Lowland Forest Loss in Protected Areas of Indonesian Borneo." *Science* 303: 1000–1003.

Cyranoski, David. 2005. "Malaysian Biotechnology: The Valley of Ghosts." *Nature* 436, no. 7051: 620–21.

Dauvergne, Peter. 1997. *Shadows in the Forest: Japan and the Politics of Timber in Southeast Asia*. Cambridge: MIT Press.

De Angelis, Massimo. 1999. "Marx's Theory of Primitive Accumulation: A Suggested Reinterpretation." http:///homepages.uel.ac.uk/M.DeAngelis/PRIMACCA.htm.

De Angelis, Massimo. 2004. "Separating the Doing and the Deed: Capital and the Continuous Character of Enclosures." *Historical Materialism* 12, no. 2: 57–87.

De Bruyn Kops, G. F. 1919. *Overzicht van Zuid-Sumatra*. Amsterdam: de Bussy.

Demeritt, David. 1998. "Science, Social Constructivism and Nature." In *Remaking Reality: Nature at the Millennium*, edited by Bruce Braun and Noel Castree, 173–93. London: Routledge.

Departemen Kehutanan. 2004. *Data strategis kehutanan*. Jakarta: Forestry Statistics Division, Department of Forestry, Republic of Indonesia.

Dienst van het Boschwezen. 1921–22. *Verslag van den Dienst van het Boschwezen in Nederlandsch-Indie over de jaren 1921 en 1922*. Weltevreden, Batavia: Landsdrukkerij.

Dove, Michael. 1988. *The Real and Imagined Role of Culture in Development: Case Studies from Indonesia*. Honolulu: University of Hawaii Press.

———. 1996. "So Far from Power, So Near to the Forest: A Structural Analysis of Gain and Blame in Tropical Forest Development." In *Borneo in Transition: People, Forests, Conservation, and Development*, edited by C. Padoch and N. L. Peluso. Kuala Lumpur: Oxford University Press.

Drayton, Richard. 2000. *Nature's Government: Science, Imperial Britain, and the "Improvement" of the World*. New Haven: Yale University Press.

Dreyfuss, Robert. 2000. "Apocalypse Still." *Mother Jones*, February, 42–51.

Ducourtieux, Olivier, Jean-Richard Laffort, and Silinthone Sacklokham. 2005. "Land Policy and Farming Practices in Laos." *Development and Change* 36, no. 3: 499–526.

EarthRights International. 2007. *Turning Treasure into Tears: Mining, Dams, and Deforestation in Shwegyin Township, Pegu Division, Burma*. Washington, D.C.: ERI.

EarthRights International and Karen Environmental and Social Network. 2003. *Capitalizing on Conflict*. Washington, D.C.: ERI.

EIA (Environmental Investigation Agency). 2003. "Environmental Investigators Expose Laundering of Illegal Indonesian Timber by Malaysia and Singapore." http://www.eia-international.org/cgi/news/news.cgi?t=template&a=133&source=.

EIA/Telapak. 2005. *The Last Frontier: Illegal Logging in Papua and China's Massive Timber Theft*. Washington D.C.: Environmental Investigation Agency; Bogor, Indonesia: Telapak.

Ekbladh, D. 2002. "'Mr. TVA': Grass-roots Development, David Lilienthal, and the Rise and Fall of the Tennessee Valley Authority as a Symbol for U.S. Overseas Development, 1933–1973." *Diplomatic History* 26, no. 3: 335–74.

Ellen, Roy F. 1986. "What Black Elk Left Unsaid: On the Illusory Images of Green Primitivism." *Anthropology Today* 2, no. 6: 8–12.

Elson. R. E. 1997. *The End of the Peasantry in Southeast Asia: A Social and Economic History of Peasant Livelihood*. London: Macmillan.

Evans, Peter. 1995. *Embedded Autonomy: States and Industrial Transformation*. Princeton: Princeton University Press.

Evrard, O., and Y. Goudineau. 2004. "Planned Resettlement, Unexpected Migration and Cultural Trauma in Laos." *Development and Change* 35, no. 5: 937–62.

Fairhead, James, and Melissa Leach. 1996. *Misreading the African Landscape: Society and Ecology in a Forest-Savanna Mosaic*. Cambridge: Cambridge University Press.

Falkner, Robert. 2005. "American Hegemony and the Global Environment." *International Studies Review* 7: 585–99.

FAO (Food and Agriculture Organisation, United Nations). 2001. *Global Forest Resources Assessment 2000: Main Report.* FAO Forestry Paper No. 140. Rome: FAO.

Farid, Hilmar. 2005. "Indonesia's Original Sin: Mass Killings and Capitalist Expansion, 1965–66." *Inter-Asia Cultural Studies* 6, no. 1: 3–16.

Fasseur, Cornelis. 1992. *The Politics of Colonial Exploitation: Java, the Dutch, and the Cultivation System.* Translated by R. E. Elson and Ary Kraal, edited by R. E. Elson. Ithaca: Cornell University, Southeast Asia Program.

Fauzi, Noer, ed. 2005. *Memahami gerakan-gerakan rakyat Dunia Ketiga.* Yogyakarta, Indonesia: Insist Press.

Ferguson, J. 1990. *The Anti-Politics Machine: Development, Depoliticization, and Bureaucratic Power in Lesotho.* Cambridge: Cambridge University Press.

———. 2005. "Seeing Like an Oil Company: Space, Security, and Global Capital in Neoliberal Africa." *American Anthropologist* 107, no. 3: 377–82.

Ferguson, James, and Akhil Gupta. 2002. "Spatializing States: Toward an Ethnography of Neoliberal Governmentality." *American Ethnologist* 29, no. 4: 981–1002.

Fernandes, Leela. 1997. *Producing Workers: The Politics of Gender, Class, and Culture in the Calcutta Jute Mills.* Philadelphia: University of Pennsylvania Press.

Fernando, M. R. 2003. "Coffee Cultivation in Java, 1830–1917." In *The Global Coffee Economy in Africa, Asia, and Latin America, 1500–1989,* edited by William Gervase Clarence-Smith and Steven Topik, 157–72. Cambridge: Cambridge University Press.

FitzSimmons, M., and D. Goodman. 1998. "Incorporating Nature: Environmental Narratives and the Reproduction of Food." In *Remaking Reality: Nature at the Millennium,* edited by B. Braun and N. Castree, 194–220. London: Routledge.

Foppes, J., and S. Ketphanh. 2004. "NWFP Use and Household Food Security in Lao PDR." In *Proceedings of the Symposium on Biodiversity and Food Security,* October 14. Vientiane: Ministry of Agriculture and Forestry, Food and Agriculture Organization. http://www.fao.org/world/laos/Publications/SymposiumBiodiversityFoodSecurity.pdf, accessed October 2, 2007.

Forbes, H. O. 1885. *A Naturalist's Wanderings in the Eastern Archipelago: A Narrative of Travel and Exploration from 1878 to 1883.* New York: Harper and Brothers.

Forest Conservation Portal. 2005. "Malaysia to Introduce Prison Sentences for Illegal Logging." http://forests.org/articles/reader.asp?linkid=45624.

Forest Trends. 2003. "The Katoomba Group: Who We Are." http://www.katoombagroup.org/Katoomba/whoweare/htm, accessed April 26, 2005.

Foucault, Michel. 1970. *The Order of Things: An Archaeology of the Human Sciences.* London: Tavistock.

Fougères, D. 2005. "Aquarian Capitalism and Transition in Indonesia." PhD diss., University of California, Berkeley.

Fox, James J., Dedi Supriadi Adhuri, and Ida Aju Pradnja Resosudarmo. 2005. "Unfinished Edifice or Pandora's Box? Decentralization and Resource Management in Indonesia." In *The Politics and Economics of Indonesia's Natural Resources, Indonesia Update Series,* edited by B. P. Resosudarmo, 92–108. Singapore: Institute of Southeast Asian Studies, in collaboration with the Australian National University.

Freeman, Carla. 2000. *High Tech and High Heels in the Global Economy: Women, Work, and Pink-Collar Identities in the Caribbean.* Durham: Duke University Press.

Friedberg, Susanne. 2001. "On the Trail of the Global Green Bean: Methodological Considerations in Multi-Site Ethnography." *Global Networks* 1, no. 4: 353–68.

Furnivall, J. S. 1956. *Colonial Policy and Practice: A Comparative Study of Burma and Netherlands India.* New York: New York University Press.

Galudra, Gamma, and Martua Sirait. 2006. "The Unfinished Debate: Socio-legal and Science Discourses on Forest Land Use and Tenure Policy in 20th Century Indonesia." Paper presented at international meeting of the International Association for the Study of Common Property, Bali, Indonesia, June 19–24.

Geertz, Clifford. 1960. *The Religion of Java.* Glencoe, Ill.: Free Press.

Gellert, Paul K. 2003. "Renegotiating a Timber Commodity Chain: Lessons from Indonesia on the Political Construction of Global Commodity Chains." *Sociological Forum* 18: 53–84.

———. 2005a. "The Shifting Natures of 'Development': Growth, Crisis and Recovery in Indonesia's Forests." *World Development* 33: 1345–64.

———. 2005b. "For a Sociology of 'Socionature': Ontology and the Commodity-Based Approach." In *Nature, Raw Materials, and Political Economy: Research in Rural Sociology and Development,* edited by P. S. Ciccantell, G. Seidman, and D. A. Smith, 65–91. Amsterdam: Elsevier JAI.

George, Cherian. 2006. *Contentious Journalism and the Internet: Towards Democratic Discourse in Malaysia and Singapore.* Singapore: Singapore University Press.

Gerard, F., and F. Ruf, eds. 2001. *Agriculture in Crisis: People, Commodities, and Natural Resources in Indonesia, 1996–2000.* Montpellier, France: Cirad.

Gereffi, G., R. Garcia-Johnson, and E. Sasser. 2001. "The NGO-Industrial Complex." *Foreign Affairs* 125: 56–65.

Gereffi, Gary, and Miguel Korzeniewicz, eds. 1994. *Commodity Chains and Global Capitalism.* Westport, Conn.: Praeger.

Giddens, Anthony. 1990. *The Consequences of Modernity.* Stanford: Stanford University Press.

Gillison, Andrew N., Nining Liswanti, Suseno Budidarsono, Meine van Noordwijk, and T. P. Tomich. 2004. "Impact of Cropping Methods on Biodiversity in Coffee Agroecosystems in Sumatra, Indonesia." *Ecology and Society* 9, no. 2: 7.

Glassman, Jim. 2006. "Primitive Accumulation, Accumulation by Dispossession, Accumulation by 'Extra-Economic' Means." *Progress in Human Geography* 30, no. 5: 608–25.

Goldman, M. 2001. "Constructing an Environmental State: Eco-Governmentality and Other Transnational Practices of a 'Green' World Bank." *Social Problems* 48, no. 4: 499–523.

———. 2005. *Imperial Nature: The World Bank and Struggles for Justice in the Age of Globalization.* New Haven: Yale University Press.

Gordon, H. 1954. "The Economic Theory of a Common-Property Resource: The Fishery." *Journal of Political Economy* 62: 124–42.

Gorkom, K. W. van. 1884. *De Oost-Indische cultures tot handel en nijverheid.* Amsterdam: de Bussy.

Gouvernement Général de l'Indochine. 1911. *Voies d'eau de la Cochinchine.* Saigon: Imprimerie Nouvelle.

———. 1930. *Dragages du Cochinchine: Canal Rachgia-Hatien.* Saigon: n.p.

Gramberg, J. S. G. 1866. "Schets der Kesam, Semendo, Makakauw en Blalauw." *Tijdschrift voor Taal, Land en Volkenkunde* deel 15 vijfde serie deel 1: 446–74.

Griffiths, Philip Jones. 2003. *Agent Orange: "Collateral Damage" in Vietnam*. London: Trolley.

Grove, Richard. 1995. *Green Imperialism: Colonial Expansion, Tropical Island Edens and the Origins of Environmentalism, 1600–1860*. Cambridge: Cambridge University Press.

Guin, Jerry. 1997. *Matsutake Mushroom: "White" Goldrush of the 1990s*. Happy Camp, Calif.: Naturegraph Publishers.

Gungwu, Wang. 1958. "The Nanhai Trade: A Study of the Early History of Chinese Trade in the South China Sea." *Journal of the Malayan Branch of the Royal Asiatic Society* 31, no. 2: 1–138.

Hà Linh Quân. 2004. "Workers' Lives in Industrial Zones and Export Processing Zones." *Labor*, September 14. http://www1.laodong.com.vn/pls/bld/display$.htnoid ung (36,112120).

Hagenaar, R. Jr. 1894–95. "Over Koffie in Palembang." *Tijdschrift voor het Binnenlandsch Bestuur* deel 4, 650–55; 793–96; deel 10, 278–79; deel 11 20–37; 38–42.

Hall, D. G. E. 1981 [1955]. *A History of Southeast Asia*. 4th ed. New York: St. Martin's.

Hall, Stuart. 1996. "The Problem of Ideology: Marxism without Guarantees." In *Stuart Hall: Critical Dialogues in Cultural Studies*, edited by David Morley and Kuan-Hsing Chen, 25–46. New York: Routledge.

Hansen, Thomas B., and Finn Stepputat. 2006. "Sovereignty Revisited." *Annual Review of Anthropology* 35: 295–315.

Haraway, Donna. 1989. *Primate Visions: Gender, Race, and Nature in the World of Modern Science*. New York: Routledge.

Hardin, Rebecca. 2002. *Concessionary Politics in the Western Congo Basin: History and Culture in Forest Use*. Environmental Governance in Africa Working Paper No. 6. Washington, D.C.: World Resources Institute. http://pdf.wri.org/eaa_wp6.pdf.

Hart, Gillian. 2002. *Disabling Globalization: Places of Power in Post-Apartheid South Africa*. Berkeley: University of California Press.

———. 2004. "Geography and Development: Critical Ethnographies." *Progress in Human Geography* 28, no. 1: 91–100.

———. 2006. "Denaturalizing Dispossession: Critical Ethnography in the Age of Resurgent Imperialism." *Antipode* 38, no. 5: 977–1004.

Hart, Gillian, Andrew Turton, Benjamin White, Brian Fegan, and Lim Teck Ghee. 1989. *Agrarian Transformations: Local Processes and the State in Southeast Asia*. Berkeley: University of California Press.

Harvey, David. 1990. *The Condition of Postmodernity: An Enquiry into the Origins of Cultural Change*. Cambridge, Mass.: Blackwell.

———. 1996. *Justice, Nature and the Geography of Difference*. Malden, Mass.: Blackwell.

———. 2003. *The New Imperialism*. Oxford: Oxford University Press.

———. 2005. *A Brief History of Neoliberalism*. Oxford: Oxford University Press.

Hatch, Walter, and Kozo Yamamura. 1996. *Asia in Japan's Embrace: Building a Regional Production Alliance*. Cambridge: Cambridge University Press.

Haugerud, Angelique, M. Priscilla Stone, and Peter D. Little. 2000. *Commodities and Globalization: Anthropological Perspectives*. Lanham, Md.: Rowman and Littlefield.

Hayden, Cori. 2003. *When Nature Goes Public: The Making and Unmaking of Bioprospecting in Mexico.* Princeton: Princeton University Press.

Heertz, Noreena. 2004. *The Debt Threat: How Debt Is Destroying the Developing World.* New York: HarperBusiness.

Henley, David. 2005. *Fertility, Food, and Fever: Population, Economy and Environment in North and Central Sulawesi, 1600–1930.* Leiden: KITLV Press.

Heppner, Kevin. 2005. "Sovereignty, Survival, and Resistance: Contending Perspectives on Karen Internal Displacement in Burma." Karen Human Rights Group. http://www.khrg.org/papers/wp2005w1.htm.

Heynan, Nik, and Harold A. Perkins. 2005. "Scalar Dialectics in Green: Urban Private Property and the Contradictions of the Neoliberalization of Nature." *Capitalism Nature Socialism* 16, no. 1: 99–113.

Heynan, Nik, and Paul Robbins. 2005. "The Neoliberalization of Nature: Governance, Privatization, Enclosure, and Valuation—Editors' Introduction." *Capitalism Nature Socialism* 16, no. 1: 5–8.

Hilley, John. 2001. *Malaysia: Mahathirism, Hegemony and the New Opposition.* London: Zed.

Hirsch, Philip. 1990. *Development Dilemmas in Rural Thailand.* New York: Oxford University Press.

———. 1993. *The Village in Perspective: Community and Locality in Rural Thailand.* Chiang Mai, Thailand: Social Research Institute.

Ho Chi Minh City Labor Federation. 2004. *Agenda for Women Workers.*

Hoàng Dũng. 2005. "Resolving All Workers' Demands." *The Laborer,* May 12. http://www.nld.com.vn/tintuc/chinh-tri-xa-hoi/118071.asp.

Hoedt, Th. G. E. 1929. *Mededeeling over het Boeboekvraagstuk in Zuid-Sumatra.* Batavia: Rygrok and Co.

Holton, R. J. 2005. "Network Discourses: Proliferation, Critique and Synthesis." *Global Networks* 5, no. 2: 209–15.

Hong Van. 2005. "Issuing the strike decree is equivalent to 'giving birth to the son before the father.'" *The Laborer,* August 8. http://www.nld.com.vn/tintuc/cong-doan/quyen nghia-vu/124151.asp.

Horkheimer, Max, and Theodor W. Adorno. 1972. *Dialectic of Enlightenment.* New York: Seabury Press.

Houtman, Gustaaf. 1999. *Mental Culture in Burmese Crisis Politics.* Tokyo: University of Foreign Studies.

Huddle, F. P. 1972. *The Mekong Project: Opportunities and Problems of Regionalism.* Washington, D.C.: U.S. Government Printing Office.

Hughes, Alex, and Suzanne Reimer. 2004. Introduction to *Geographies of Commodity Chains,* edited by Alex Hughes and Suzanne Reimer, 1–16. London: Routledge.

Huitema, W. K. 1935. *Gevolkingskoffie: Met een inleiding tot hare geschiedenis op Java en Sumatra.* Wageningen: Veenman and Zonen.

Ingersoll, J. 1969. *The Social Feasibility of Pa Mong Irrigation: Requirement and Reality.* Washington, D.C.: Bureau of Reclamation, Department of the Interior.

International Water Power and Dam Construction. 1997. "China's Challenge" (November): 36–37.

International Water Power and Dam Construction. 2005. "News: Mekong Hydro Plants Revived." http://www.waterpowermagazine.com/story.asp?sectioncode=130&storyCode=2 031732, accessed June 26, 2006.

investPenang. 2005. *Biotechnology Gateway.* Penang, Malaysia: investPenang.

Iwabuchi, Koichi. 2002. *Recentering Globalization: Popular Culture and Japanese Transnationalism.* Durham: Duke University Press.

Jackson, Peter. 1999. "Commodity Cultures: The Traffic in Things." *Transactions of the Institute of British Geographers* 24, no. 1: 95–108.

Johannes, R., and M. Riepen. 1995. *Environmental, Economic, and Social Implications of the Live Reef Fish Trade in Asia and the Western Pacific.* Washington, D.C.: Nature Conservancy.

Jomo, K., C. Chung, B. Folk, I. ul-Haque, P. Phongpaichit, B. Simatupang, and M. Tateishi. 1997. *Southeast Asia's Misunderstood Miracle: Industrial Policy and Economic Development in Thailand, Malaysia, and Indonesia.* Boulder, Colo.: Westview Press.

Jonas, Andrew E. G. 2006. "Pro Scale: Further Reflections on the 'Scale Debate' in Human Geography." *Transactions of the Institute of British Geographers* 31: 399–406.

Kamerling, Z. 1905–06. "De Toekomst van Sumatra." *Tijdschrift voor Nijverheid en Landbouw in Nederlandsch Indie* 71, 359–522, 623–721; 72, 139–92; 73, 75–114.

Kamm, Henry. 1995. "Decades-Old U.S. Bombs Still Killing Laotians." *New York Times,* August 10.

Karen Environmental and Social Action Network (KESAN). 2003. *Thulie Kawwei.* Chiang Mai, Thailand: KESAN.

Katsigris, E., G. Bull, and A. White. 2004. "The China Forest Products Trade: Overview of Asia-Pacific Supplying Countries, Impacts and Implications." *International Forestry Review* 6, nos. 3–4: 237–53.

Katz, Cindi. 1998. "Whose Nature, Whose Culture? Private Production of Space and the Preservation of Nature." In *Remaking Reality: Nature at the Millennium,* edited by Bruce Braun and Noel Castree, 46–63. London: Routledge.

Kerr, J., J. Pender, and Suyanto. 2006. "Property Rights and Environmental Services in Lampung Province, Indonesia." Paper presented to the 11th conference of the International Association for the Study of Common Property, Bali, Indonesia, June 19–23. http://dlc. dlib.indiana.edu/archive/00001935, accessed July 15, 2006.

Khor, Martin. 2006. "Challenges on Road to US-Malaysia FTA." http://www.twnside.org. sg/title2/gtrends95.htm.

Kingston, J. B. 1987. "The Manipulation of Tradition in Java's Shadow: Transmigration, Decentralization, and the Ethical Policy in Colonial Lampung." PhD diss., Columbia University.

Kirksey, Eben. 2001. "Washed Away." *Guardian,* August 1. http://society.guardian.co.uk/ societyguardian/story/0,7843,530165,00.html.

Kligman, Gail. 1998. *The Politics of Duplicity: Controlling Reproduction in Ceaucescu's Romania.* Berkeley: University of California Press.

Knapen, Han. 2001. *Forests of Fortune? The Environmental History of Southeast Borneo, 1600–1880.* Leiden: KITLV Press.

Kolko, Gabriel. 1988. *Confronting the Third World: United States Foreign Policy, 1945–1980.* New York: Pantheon.

Koning, Juliette. 2000. *Women and Households in Indonesia: Cultural Notions and Social Practices.* Richmond, England: Curzon.

Kopytoff, Igor. 1986. "The Cultural Biography of Things: Commoditization as Process." In *The Social Life of Things*, edited by A. Appadurai, 64–91. Cambridge: Cambridge University Press.

Kraft van Ermel, W. K. L. 1892. "De Koffiecultuur in een gedeelte der residentie Palembang." *Tijdschrift voor het Binnenlandsch Bestuur* 7: 1–42.

Kuppusamy, Baradan. 2004. "Malaysian PM Vows Pro-Farmers Agenda." http://www.checkbiotech.org/root/index.cfm?fuseaction=news&doc_id=8530&start=1&control=216&page_start=1&page_nr=101&pg=1.

Kusworo, A. 2000. *Perambah hutan atau kambing hitam? Potret sengketa kawasan hutan di Lampung.* Bogor, Indonesia: Pustaka Latin.

———. 2004. "Pursuing Livelihoods, Imagining Development: Smallholders in Highland Lampung, Indonesia." PhD diss., Australian National University.

Kwon, Tae Ha. 1994. *They Call Me the King of Kalimantan.* Seoul: JoongAng Daily Press.

Labor Law Counsel Forum. 2005. "Advancing Social Security Benefits for Workers." *The Laborer*, May 17. http://www.nld.com.vn/tintuc/cong-doan/tu-van/118326.asp.

Ladejinsky, W. 1955. "South Vietnam Revisited." In *Agrarian Reform as Unfinished Business: The Selected Papers of Wolf Ladejinsky*, edited by Louis J. Walinsky, 243–67. New York: Oxford University Press.

Lambrecht, Curtis. 2004. "Oxymoronic Development: The Military as Benefactor in the Border Regions of Burma." In *Civilizing the Margins: Southeast Asian Government Policies for the Development of Minorities*, edited by C. Duncan, 150–81. Ithaca: Cornell University Press.

Latham, M. E. 2000. *Modernization as Ideology: American Social Science and "Nation Building" in the Kennedy Era.* Chapel Hill: University of North Carolina Press.

Latour, Bruno. 1993. *We Have Never Been Modern.* Translated by Catherine Porter. Cambridge: Harvard University Press.

———. 2005. *Reassembling the Social: An Introduction to Actor-Network Theory.* New York: Oxford University Press.

Law, J. 1992. "Notes on the Theory of the Actor-Network: Ordering, Strategy, and Heterogeneity." *Systemic Practice and Action Research* 5, no. 4: 379–93.

Lê Thùy. 2004. "Increasing Strikes in Ho Chi Minh City and Complex Development." *The Laborer*, December 30. http://www.nld.com.vn/tintuc/chinh-tri-xa-hoi/108261.asp.

Lee, Ching Kwan. 1998. *Gender and the South China Miracle: Two Worlds of Factory Women.* Berkeley: University of California Press.

Leftwich, Adrian. 1994. "Governance, the State and the Politics of Development." *Development and Change* 25: 363–86.

Lens, Sidney. 2003. *The Forging of the American Empire: From the Revolution to Vietnam, a History of U.S. Imperialism.* London: Pluto Press, in conjunction with Haymarket Books, Chicago.

Leslie, D., and S. Reimer. 1999. "Spatializing Commodity Chains." *Progress in Human Geography* 23: 401–20.

Letterkerker, C. 1916. *Land en Volk van Sumatra.* Leiden: Brill.

Li, Tania Murray. 2001. "Boundary Work: Community, Market, and State Reconsidered." In *Communities and the Environment*, edited by A. Agrawal and C. C. Gibson, 157–79. New Brunswick, N.J.: Rutgers University Press.

——. 2002a. "Engaging Simplifications: Community-Based Resource Management, Market Processes, and State Agendas in Upland Southeast Asia." *World Development* 30, no. 2: 265–83.

——. 2002b. "Local Histories, Global Markets: Cocoa and Class in Upland Sulawesi." *Development and Change* 33, 3: 415–37.

——. 2007. *The Will to Improve: Governmentality, Development, and the Practice of Politics.* Durham: Duke University Press.

——, ed. 1999. *Transforming the Indonesian Uplands: Marginality, Power, and Production.* Amsterdam: Harwood Academic.

Lie, John. 1998. *Han Unbound: The Political Economy of South Korea.* Stanford: Stanford University Press.

Lilienthal, D. E. 1976. *The Journals of David E. Lilienthal.* Vol. 6. New York: Harper and Row.

Lim, Kit Siang. 2006. "Biotechnology—6 Points." http://blog.limkitsiang.com/?p=432.

Livingston, J. Sterling. 1988. "Pygmalion in Management." *Harvard Business Review* 65, no. 5: 121–30.

Loh Kok Wah, Francis. 2003. "Towards a New Politics of Fragmentation and Contestation." In *New Politics in Malaysia*, edited by Francis Loh Kok Wah and Johan Saravanamuttu, 253–82. Singapore: Institute of Southeast Asian Studies.

Lohman, Larry. 1993. "Green Orientalism." *Ecologist* 23, no. 6: 202–4.

Lowe, C. 2000. "Global Markets, Local Injustice in Southeast Asian Seas: The Live Fish Trade and Local Fishers in the Togean Islands of Sulawesi." In *People, Plants, and Justice: The Politics of Nature Conservation*, edited by C. Zerner, 234–58. New York: Columbia University Press.

Lucas, Anton, and Carol Warren. 2003. "The State, the People and Their Mediators: The Struggle over Agrarian Law Reform in Post–New Order Indonesia." *Indonesia* 76: 87–126.

Lugo, Alejandro. 1990. "Cultural Production and Reproduction in Ciudad Juarez, Mexico: Tropes at Play among Maquiladora Workers." *Cultural Anthropology* 5, no. 2: 173–96.

Lynch, Caitrin. 2007. *Juki Girls, Good Girls: Gender and Cultural Politics in Sri Lanka's Global Garment Industry.* Ithaca: Cornell University Press.

Macknight, C. 1976. *The Voyage to Marege: Macassan Trepangers in Northern Australia.* Carlton, Australia: Melbourne University Press.

MacLean, Ken. 2007. "Spaces of Extraction: Actually Existing Governance along the Riverine Networks of Nyaunglebin District." In *Myanmar: The State, Society and the Environment*, edited by Monique Skidmore and Trevor Wilson, 246–67. Canberra: Asia-Pacific Press, Australian National University.

MacPherson, C. B. 1978. *Property: Mainstream and Critical Perspectives.* Toronto: University of Toronto Press.

Malaysia. Economic Planning Unit, Prime Minister's Department. 2006. "Ninth Malaysia Plan." http://www.epu.jpm.my/rm9/html/english.htm.

Mann, S. 1990. *Agrarian Capitalism in Theory and Practice*. Chapel Hill: University of North Carolina Press.

Mansfield, Becky. 2005. "Beyond Rescaling: Reintegrating the 'National' as a Dimension of Scalar Relations." *Progress in Human Geography* 29: 458–73.

MAP (Mangrove Action Project). 2006. "Wal-Mart and Darden Restaurants Announce Future Sourcing of 'Certified' Farm-Raised Shrimp: Will Consumers Be Served "Green" Shrimp, or a Green-wash?" http://www.earthisland.org/map/walmart.htm.

Marchand, Marianne, and Anne Sisson Runyan. 2000. *Gender and Global Restructuring: Sightings, Sites and Resistances*. New York: Routledge.

Marshall, Jonathan. 1995. *To Have and Have Not: Southeast Asian Raw Materials and the Origins of the Pacific War*. Berkeley: University of California Press.

Marston, Sallie A., John Paul Jones III, and Keith Woodward. 2005. "Human Geography without Scale." *Transactions of the Institute of British Geographers* 30: 416–32.

Marx, Karl. 1972 [1867]. *Capital*. Vol. 1. New York: New World.

———. 1992 [1867]. *Capital*. Vol. 1. Reprint ed. New York: International Publishers.

Masood, Ehsan. 1997. "Malaysia Backs 'Gag' on Haze Scientists." *Nature* 390, no. 6656: 107.

Massey, Doreen. 1993. "Power-Geometry and a Progressive Sense of Place." In *Mapping the Futures: Local Cultures, Global Change*, edited by J. Bird et al., 59–69. London: Routledge.

Maung Maung Gyi. 1983. *Burmese Political Values: The Socio-political Roots of Authoritarianism*. New York: Praeger.

Maung U Saw. 1999. "Recent Developments in the Mineral Sector of Myanmar." In *Sustainable Development of Land and Mineral Resources in Asia and the Pacific*, vol. 5, 113–38. Bangkok: United Nations.

McAfee, Kathleen. 1999. "Selling Nature to Save It? Biodiversity and Green Developmentalism." *Environment and Planning D: Society and Space* 17, no. 2: 133–54.

McCarthy, James. 2004. "Privatizing Conditions of Production: Trade Agreements as Neoliberal Environmental Governance." *Geoforum* 35, no. 3: 327–41.

McCarthy, James, and W. Scott Prudham. 2004. "Neo-liberal Nature and the Nature of Neo-liberalism." *Geoforum* 35: 275–83.

McCarthy, John. 2004. "Changing to Gray: Decentralization and the Emergence of Volatile Socio-legal Configurations in Central Kalimantan, Indonesia." *World Development* 32, no. 7: 1199–1223.

McDaniel, Drew. 2002. *Electronic Tigers of Southeast Asia: The Politics of Media, Technology, and National Development*. Ames: Iowa State University Press.

McDole, Catherine. 1969. *A Report on Socio-cultural Conditions in the Pa Mong Study Area of Northeast Thailand*. AID Contract 493–461. Bangkok: U.S. Operations Mission Thailand.

McGilvray, F., and T. Chan. 2001. *The Trade in Live Reef Food Fish: A Hong Kong Perspective*. Hong Kong: International Marinelife Alliance—Hong Kong.

McKay, Steven C. 2006. *Satanic Mills or Silicon Islands? The Politics of High-Tech Production in the Philippines*. Ithaca: Cornell University Press.

McLain, Rebecca. 2000. "Controlling the Forest Understory: Wild Mushroom Politics in Central Oregon." PhD diss., University of Washington.

McMichael, P. 1997. "Rethinking Globalization: The Agrarian Question Revisited." *Review of International Political Economy* 4, no. 4: 630–62.

McMorrow, Julia, and Mustapa Abdul Talip. 2001. "Decline of Forest Area in Sabah, Malaysia: Relationship to State Policies, Land Code and Land Capability." *Global Environmental Change* 11: 217–30.

McStocker, R. 1987. "The Indonesian Coffee Industry." *Bulletin of Indonesian Economic Studies* 25, no. 1:40–69.

Merchant, Carolyn. 1980. *The Death of Nature: Women, Ecology, and the Scientific Revolution: A Feminist Reappraisal of the Scientific Revolution.* San Francisco: Harper and Row.

Midnight Notes Collective. 1990. "The New Enclosures." Midnight Notes No. 10. http://www.midnightnotes.org/newenclos.html.

Miller, Daniel. 1995. "Consumption and Commodities." *Annual Review of Anthropology* 24: 141–61.

Miller, Peter, and Nikolas Rose. 1990. "Governing Economic Life." *Economy and Society* 19, no. 1: 1–31.

Ministry of Agriculture and Forestry. 2005. *Forestry Strategy to the Year 2020.* Vientaine: Lao PDR, Ministry of Agriculture and Forestry.

Ministry of Planning and Investment, Vietnam. 2006. *Report on Foreign Investment in Vietnam.*

Mitchell, Timothy. 1991. "The Limits of the State: Beyond Statist Approaches and Their Critics." *American Political Science Review* 85, no. 1: 77–96.

———. 2002. *Rule of Experts: Egypt, Techno-politics, Modernity.* Berkeley: University of California Press.

Mittelman, James, and Christine B. N. Chin. 2005. "Conceptualizing Resistance to Globalization." In *The Global Resistance Reader,* edited by Louise Amoore, 17–27. New York: Routledge.

MOLISA (Ministry of Labor), Ministry of Planning and Investment, VGCL, Taiwanese Trade Association. 2004. *About Labor Relations in Dong Nai and Binh Duong Provinces,* September. Hanoi.

Moody, Roger. 2000. *Gravediggers: A Report on Mining in Burma.* Vancouver: Canada Asia Pacific Resource Network.

Moore, Donald S. 2005. *Suffering for Territory: Race, Place, and Power in Zimbabwe.* Durham: Duke University Press.

Moore, Donald S., Jake Kosek, and Anand Pandian. 2003. *Race, Nation, and the Politics of Difference.* Durham: Duke University Press.

Morton, Giles. 2000. *Nathaniel's Nutmeg, or the True and Incredible Adventures of the Spice Trader Who Changed the Course of History.* New York: Penguin.

Mougeot, E., and P. Levang. 1990. *Marketing of Rice, Cassava and Coffee in Lampung, Indonesia.* Jakarta: ORSTOM and Departemen Transmigrasi, Biro Perencanaan, Republik Indonesia [Transmigration Department, Planning Bureau, Republic of Indonesia].

Multatuli. 1987 [1860]. *Max Havelaar: or the Coffee Auctions of the Dutch Trading Company.* Translated, with notes, by Roy Edwards. London: Penguin.

Muradian, R., and W. Pelupessy. 2005. "Governing the Coffee Chain: The Role of Voluntary Regulatory Systems." *World Development* 33, no. 12: 2029–44.

Murdoch, J. 1998. "The Spaces of Actor-Network Theory." *Geoforum* 29, no. 4: 357–74.

Nagulendran, K. 2006. "Biosafety." Presentation at "Current Issues in Biosafety, Bioethics and Bio-communication" conference, University of Malaya, Malaysia, February 21.

Nakahara, M. 1984. "Muslim Merchants in Nan-Hai." In *Islam in Asia: Southeast and East Asia*, edited by R. Israeli and A. H. Johns. Jerusalem: Magnes Press, Hebrew University.

Nash, June, and Maria Patricia Fernandez-Kelly. 1983. *Women, Men, and the International Division of Labor*. Albany: State University of New York Press.

National Archives and Records Administration—Denver [NARA-D]. 1950a. "Project for Reconnaissance Survey of Hydroelectric and Irrigation Projects in Underdeveloped Countries Which Might Justify Assistance under the Point IV Program." RG115, box 4.

———. 1950b. "International Affairs, 1943–49." RG 115, box 5.

The Nature Conservancy. 2001. "Laporan kegiatan pemetaan bersama masyarakat di 10 (sepuluh) desa sekitar TNLL." Palu, Indonesia: The Nature Conservancy.

———. 2002a. *Building Conservation Capacity and Partnerships at Lore Lindu National Park, Sixth and Final Report to National Resources Management II Program, USAID*. Palu, Indonesia: The Nature Conservancy.

———. 2002b. *Draft Management Plan, Lore Lindu National Park*. Palu, Indonesia: Taman Nasional Lore Lindu / The Nature Conservancy.

Netherlands Delta Development Team. 1974. *Recommendations concerning Agricultural Development with Improved Water Control in the Mekong Delta: Main Report*. Bangkok: Mekong Committee.

Netto, Anil. 1999. "Academics Speak Out at Their Own Risk." *Asia Times Online*, June 16. http://www.atimes.com/se-asia/AF16Ae01.html.

———. 2007. "HEALTH-ASIA: Rat Race on for Clinical Trials Bonanza." Inter Press Service news agency. http://www.ipsnews.net/news.asp?idnews=36411.

Neumann, R. P. 1998. *Imposing Wilderness: Struggles over Livelihood and Nature Preservation in Africa*. Berkeley: University of California Press.

Nevins, Joseph. 2003. "Restitution over Coffee: Truth, Reconciliation, and Environmental Violence in East Timor." *Political Geography* 22, no. 6: 677–701.

———. 2005. *A Not-So-Distant Horror: Mass Violence in East Timor*. Ithaca: Cornell University Press.

Nguyen Thi Dieu. 1999. *The Mekong River and the Struggle for Indochina: Water, War, and Peace*. Westport, Conn.: Praeger.

Nicholas, Colin. 2000. *The Orang Asli and the Contest for Resources: Orang Asli Politics, Development and Identity in Peninsular Malaysia*. Copenhagen: International Work Group for Indigenous Affairs.

———. 2003. "Orang Asli Resource Politics: Manipulating Property Regimes through Representivity." Presentation at RCSD conference on "Politics of the Commons: Articulating Development and Strengthening Local Practices," Chiangmai, Thailand, July 11–14. *Digital Library of the Commons*. http://dlc.dlib.indiana.edu/archive/00001090/.

Noordwijk, M. van. 2001. "Forest Conversion and Watershed Functions in the Humid Tropics." Background for Sumberjaya 2001 research planning meeting, January 28–29, 33–41.

Noordwijk, M. van, Subekti Rahayu, Kurniatun Hairiah, Y. C. Wulan, A. Farida, and B. Verbist. 2002. "Carbon Stock Assessment for a Forest-to-Coffee Conversion Landscape in Sumber-Jaya (Lampung, Indonesia): From Allometric Equations to Land Use Change Analysis." *Science in China* (Series C) 45, Supp. 75–86.

Nordstrom, Carolyn. 2000. "Shadows and Sovereigns." *Theory, Culture, and Society* 17, no. 4: 35–54.

Norlund, Irene. 1996. "Democracy and Trade Unions in Vietnam: Riding a Honda in Low Gear." *Copenhagen Journal of Asian Studies* 4: 73–99.

Obidzinski, Krystof. 2005. "Illegal Logging in Indonesia: Myth and Reality." In *The Politics and Economics of Indonesia's Natural Resources*, edited by B. P. Resosudarmo, 193–205. Singapore: Institute of Southeast Asian Studies, in collaboration with the Australian National University.

Obidzinski, Krystof, and C. Barr. 2003. *The Effects of Decentralisation on Forests and Forest Industries in Berau District, East Kalimantan.* Case Study 9 on Decentralisation. Bogor, Indonesia: CIFOR.

O'Connor, James R. 1973. *The Fiscal Crisis of the State.* New York: St. Martin's Press.

——. 1988. "Capitalism, Nature, Socialism: A Theoretical Introduction." *Capitalism Nature Socialism* 1, no. 1: 11–38.

——. 1996. "The Second Contradiction of Capitalism." In *The Greening of Marxism*, edited by Ted Benton. New York: Guilford Press.

O'Connor, T. 2006. "Birds in Coffee Agroforestry Systems in Lampung, Sumatra." PhD diss., University of Adelaide.

Ohmae, Kenichi. 1995. *The End of the Nation-State: The Rise of Regional Economies.* London: Harper Collins.

Ong, Aihwa. 1987. *Spirits of Resistance and Capitalist Discipline: Factory Women in Malaysia.* Albany: State University of New York Press.

——. 1997. "The Gender and Labor Politics of Postmodernity." In *The Politics of Culture in the Shadow of Capital*, edited by Lisa Lowe and David Lloyd, 61–97. Durham: Duke University Press.

——. 2000. "Graduated Sovereignty in South-East Asia." *Theory, Culture, and Society* 17, no. 4: 55–75.

——. 2006. *Neoliberalism as Exception: Mutations in Citizenship and Sovereignty.* Durham: Duke University Press.

Osorio, N. 2004. "Lessons from the World Coffee Crisis: A Serious Problem for Sustainable Development." Submission to UNCTAD XI Sao Paulo, Brazil, June 2004, International Coffee Organization (ICO), London.

Owen, Norman G., ed. 2004. *The Emergence of Modern Southeast Asia: A New History.* Honolulu: University of Hawaii Press.

Pa Mong Resettlement Research Project. 1982. *Pa Mong Resettlement Research Project: Final Report.* Ann Arbor: Department of Geography and Center for South and Southeast Asian Studies, University of Michigan.

Patlis, Jason. 2005. "New Legal Initiatives for Natural Resource Management in a Changing Indonesia: The Promise, the Fear, and the Unknown." In *The Politics and Economics of Indonesia's Natural Resources*, edited by B. P. Resosudarmo, 231–47. Singapore: Institute of Southeast Asian Studies, in collaboration with the Australian National University.

Pauw ten Kate, H. 1869. "Rapport van de Marga Semindo Darat, Afdeeling Kommering Ogan-Oeloe en Enim Residentie Palembang." *Tijdschrift voor Indische Taal Land en Volkenkunde*, deel 17, vifde serie deel 3: 525–47.

Peck, Jamie, and Adam Tickell. 2002. "Neoliberalizing Space." *Antipode* 34, no. 3: 380–404.

Peet, Richard, and Michael Watts, eds. 1996. *Liberation Ecologies: Environment, Development, Social Movements.* New York: Routledge, 1996.

Peluso, Nancy Lee. 1992. *Rich Forests, Poor People: Resource Control and Resistance in Java.* Berkeley: University of California Press.

———. 1993. "Coercing Conservation? The Politics of State Resource Control." *Global Environmental Change* 3, no. 2: 199–218.

Peluso, Nancy Lee, and Peter Vandergeest. n.d. "The Forests are Surrounding the Cities! Emergencies, Insurgencies, and the Construction of Political Forests in Southeast Asia." In *Knowing Nature, Transforming Ecologies: Science, Power, and Practice,* edited by Matthew Turner, Mara Goldman, and Paul Nadasdy. Forthcoming from University of Chicago Press.

——— 2001. "Genealogies of Forest Law and Customary Rights in Indonesia, Malaysia, and Thailand." *Journal of Asian Studies* 60, no. 3: 761–812.

Peluso, Nancy Lee, and Michael Watts, eds. 2001a. *Violent Environments.* Ithaca: Cornell University Press.

———. 2001b. "Violent Environments." In *Violent Environments,* edited by N. L. Peluso and M. Watts, 1–38. Ithaca: Cornell University Press.

Pendergrast, M. 1999. *Uncommon Grounds: The History of Coffee and How It Transformed Our World.* New York: Basic Books.

Perelman, Michael. 2000. *The Invention of Capitalism: Classical Political Economy and the Secret History of Primitive Accumulation.* Durham: Duke University Press.

Perfecto, I., R. A. Rice, R. Greenberg, M. E. van der Voort. 1996. "Shade Coffee: A Disappearing Refuge for Biodiversity." *BioScience* 46, no. 8: 598–608.

Perkins, J. 2004. *Confessions of an Economic Hit Man.* San Francisco: Berrett-Koehler.

Perry, Elizabeth. 1993, *Shanghai on Strike: The Politics of Chinese Labor.* Stanford: Stanford University Press.

Pham, Ho. 2004. "Successful Arbitration of 57 Cases of Labor Disputes." *The Laborer,* November 17. http://www.nld.com.vn/tintuc/cong-doan/quyen-nghia-vu/104861.asp.

Polanyi, Karl. 2001 [1944]. *The Great Transformation: The Political and Economic Origins of Our Time.* Boston: Beacon Press.

———. 2005 [1957]. "The Self-Regulating Market and the Fictitious Commodities: Labor, Land and Money." In *The Global Resistance Reader,* edited by Louise Amoore, 48–53. New York: Routledge.

Ponte, S. 2002. "The 'Latte Revolution'? Regulation, Markets and Consumption in the Global Coffee Chain." *World Development* 30, no. 7: 1099–1122.

Porter, T. M. 1995. *Trust in Numbers: The Pursuit of Objectivity in Science and Public Life.* Princeton: Princeton University Press.

Press Guide 2005. 2006. Kuala Lumpur: Perception Media.

PriceWaterhouseCoopers. 2006. "Global Forest, Paper, and Packaging Industry Survey: 2006 Edition." http://www.pwc.com/fpp/.

Prins, J. 1935. "Eenige gegevens betreffende Semendo en Semendo'sch volksrecht." *Tijdschrift voor Indische Taal, Land en Volkenkunde,* deel 75 aflevering 1, 237–66.

Prudham, S. 2005. *Knock on Wood: Nature as Commodity in Douglas-Fir Country.* London: Routledge.

Public Citizen. 2005. "Shrimp Stockpile: Importing America's Favorite Seafood." http:// www.citizen.org/publications/.

Rabinow, Paul. 1986. "Representations Are Social Facts: Modernity and Post-modernity in Anthropology." In *Writing Culture: The Poetics and Politics of Ethnography*, edited by J. Clifford and G. E. Marcus, 234–261. Berkeley: University of California Press.

Redmanglar Internacional. 2003. "Statement on Certification." http://www.library.enaca. org/certification/publications.

Reid, Anthony. 1993. "Islamization and Christianization in Southeast Asia: The Critical Phase, 1550–1650." In *Southeast Asia in the Early Modern Era: Trade, Power, and Belief*, edited by A. Reid, 151–79. Ithaca: Cornell University Press.

———. 2000. *Charting the Shape of Early Modern Southeast Asia*. Singapore: Institute of Southeast Asian Studies.

Reid, Anthony, ed., with Jennifer Brewster. 1983. *Slavery, Bondage, and Dependency in Southeast Asia*. New York: St. Martins Press.

Rénaud, J. 1879. "Étude sur l'approfondissement du canal de Vinh-té et l'amélioration du port d'Hatien." *Excursions et Reconnaissances* no. 1.

Resosudarmo, Ida Aju Pradnja. 2004. "Closer to People and Trees: Will Decentralisation Work for the People and the Forests of Indonesia?" *European Journal of Development Research* 16 (March): 110–32.

Ribot, Jesse C. 1998. "Theorizing Access: Forest Profits along Senegal's Charcoal Commodity Chain." *Development and Change* 29, no. 2: 307–41.

———. 2002. *Democratic Decentralization of Natural Resources: Institutionalizing Popular Participation*. Washington, D.C.: World Resources Institute.

Ribot, Jesse C., and Nancy L. Peluso. 2003. "A Theory of Access." *Rural Sociology* 68: 153–81.

Ridder, J. 1988. *Maritime Trade Networks in Transition: The Buginese of South Sulawesi*. Wageningen, Netherlands: Wageningen Agricultural University.

Rigg, Jonathan. 2003. *Southeast Asia: The Human Landscape of Modernization and Development*. London: Routledge.

Robinson, Geoffrey. 1995. *The Dark Side of Paradise: Political Violence in Bali*. Ithaca: Cornell University Press.

Rock, Michael. 2003. "The Politics of Development Policy and Development Policy Reform in New Order Indonesia." Working Papers of the William Davidson Institute, Paper no. 632. Ann Arbor: University of Michigan Business School.

Roitman, Janet. 2001. "New Sovereigns? Regulatory Authority in the Chad Basin." In *Intervention and Transnationalism in Africa: Global-Local Networks of Power*, edited by T. Callaghy, R. Kassimir, and R. Latham, 240–63. Cambridge: Cambridge University Press.

———. 2005. "The Garrison-Entrepôt: A Mode of Governing in the Chad Basin." In *Global Assemblages: Technology, Politics, and Ethics as Anthropological Problems*, edited by Aihwa Ong and Stephen Collier, 417–36. Berkeley: University of California Press.

Roosa, John. 2006. *Pretext for Mass Murder: The September 30th Movement and Suharto's Coup d'Etat in Indonesia*. Madison: University of Wisconsin Press.

Rose, Nikolas S. 1999. *Powers of Freedom: Reframing Political Thought*. Cambridge: Cambridge University Press.

Rowling, Nick. 1987. *Commodities: How the World Was Taken to Market.* London: Free Association.

Royen, J. W. van. 1927. *De Palembangsche marga en haar grond- en waterrechten.* Proefschrift ter verkrijging van den graad van Doctor in de Rechtsgeleerdheid aan de Rijksuniversiteit te Leiden. Leiden: Adriani.

Rudnyckyj, Daromir. 2004. "Technologies of Servitude: Governmentality and Indonesian Transnational Labor Migration." *Anthropological Quarterly* 77, no. 3: 407–34.

———. 2006. "Islamic Reform and Spiritual Economy in Contemporary Indonesia." PhD diss., University of California, Berkeley.

Sahlins, Peter. 1994. *Forest Rites: The War of the Demoiselles in Nineteenth-Century France.* Cambridge: Harvard University Press.

Said, Edward W. 1978. *Orientalism.* New York: Pantheon.

SAM (Sahabat Alam Malaysia). 2005. *Malaysian Environment in Crisis.* Penang, Malaysia: Consumers' Association of Penang.

Samsu, I. Suramenggala, H. Komarudin, and Y. Ngau. 2005. *The Impacts of Forestry Decentralization on District Finances, Local Community and Spatial Planning: A Case Study in Bulungan District, East Kalimantan.* Decentralization Case Study 12. Bogor, Indonesia: CIFOR.

Sastry, Narayan. 2002. "Forest Fires, Air Pollution, and Mortality in Southeast Asia." *Demography* 39, no. 1: 1–23.

Sawyer, Suzana. 2001. "Fictions of Sovereignty: Of Prosthetic Petro-Capitalism, Neoliberal States, and Phantom-like Citizens in Ecuador." *Journal of Latin American Anthropology* 6, no. 1: 156–97.

———. 2004. *Crude Chronicles: Indigenous Politics, Multinational Oil, and Neoliberalism in Ecuador.* Durham: Duke University Press.

Schaaf, C. H., and R. H. Fifield. 1963. *The Lower Mekong: Challenge to Cooperation in Southeast Asia.* Princeton, N.J.: D. van Nostrand.

Schalenbourg, W. 2004. "Farmers' Local Ecological Knowledge of Soil and Watershed Functions in Sumberjaya, Sumatra, Indonesia." PhD diss., Katholieke Universiteit Leuven, Netherlands. http://www.ethesis.net/sumberjaya/sumberjaya_inhoud.htm, accessed September 13, 2005.

Scheper-Hughes, Nancy. 1992. *Death without Weeping: The Violence of Everyday Life in Brazil.* Berkeley: University of California Press.

———. 2002. "The Global Traffic in Human Organs." In *The Anthropology of Globalization*, edited by Jonathan Xavier Inda and Renato Rosaldo, 270–308. Malden, Mass.: Blackwell.

Schroeder, R. A., and K. Suryanata. 1996. "Gender and Class Power in Agroforestry Systems." In *Liberation Ecologies: Environment, Development, Social Movements*, edited by R. Peet and M. Watts, 188–204. London: Routledge.

Schumpeter, Joseph A. 1975 [1942]. *Capitalism, Socialism, and Democracy.* 3rd ed. New York: Harper and Row.

Schwarz, Adam. 1994. *A Nation in Waiting: Indonesia in the 1990s.* Boulder, Colo.: Westview Press.

Scott, James. 1976. *The Moral Economy of the Peasant.* New Haven: Yale University Press.

———. 1985. *Weapons of the Weak: Everyday Forms of Peasant Resistance*. New Haven: Yale University Press.

———. 1998a. "Freedom and Freehold: Space, People, and State Simplification in Southeast Asia." In *Asian Freedoms: The Idea of Freedom in East and Southeast Asia*, edited by D. Kelly and A. Reid, 37–64. Cambridge: Cambridge University Press.

———. 1998b. *Seeing Like a State*. New Haven: Yale University Press.

Selth, Andrew. 1996. *Transforming the Tatmadaw: The Burmese Armed Forces since 1988*. Canberra: Australia National University.

Sen, Amartya. 1999. *Development as Freedom*. New York: Anchor.

Setten, D. J. G. van. 1922. "Iets over het ladangen in het algemeen en in de Residentie Palembang in het bijzonder, een en ander in verband met de door sommige boschbouwkundigen voorgestane bosch politiek." *Teysmannia* 33: 104–20.

Sevin, O. 1989. "History and Settlement." In *Transmigration and Spontaneous Migrations in Indonesia: Lampung Province*. Jakarta: ORSTOM, Departemen Transmigrasi [Department of Transmigration].

Shin, Yoon Hwan. N.d. "The Korean *Community* in Southeast Asia: A Case Study of Koreans in Jakarta in the Mid-1990s."

Shiva, V. 2000. *Stolen Harvest: The Hijacking of the Global Food Supply*. Cambridge, Mass.: South End Press.

Sikor, T., and T. Pham. 2005. "The Dynamics of Commoditization in a Vietnamese Uplands Village, 1980–2000." *Journal of Agrarian Change* 5, no. 3: 405–28.

Simbolon, Johannes. 2003. "Choi, South Korea's Pioneer in RI." *Jakarta Post*, Business News, December 15, reprinted in *Irian News*, December 15, 2003. http://www.kabar-irian.com/pipermail/kabar-irian/2003-December/0.

Siong, Tong Yee. 2004. "*Malaysiakini*: Treading a Tightrope of Political Pressure and Market Forces." In *Asian Cyberactivism: Freedom of Expression and Media Censorship*, edited by Steven Gan, James Gomez, and Uwe Johannen, 276–315. Singapore: Friedrich Naumann Stifung.

Sivaramakrishnan, K. 1999. *Modern Forests*. Stanford: Stanford University Press.

Skladany, Mike, and Peter Vandergeest. 2004. "Catch of the Day." *Alternatives* 30, no. 2: 22–24.

Smith, Martin. 1999. "Ethnic Conflict and the Challenge of Civil Society in Burma." In *Strengthening Civil Society in Burma*, edited by Burma Center Netherlands, 15–53. Chiang Mai, Thailand: Silkworm.

Smith, Neil. 1984. *Uneven Development: Nature, Capital and the Production of Space*. New York: Basil Blackwell.

———. 1996. "Spaces of Vulnerability: The Space of Flows and the Politics of Scale." *Critique of Anthropology* 16: 63–77.

Smythe, Dallas. 1977. "Communications: Blind Spot of Western Marxism." *Canadian Journal of Political and Social Theory* 1, no. 3: 1–27.

Social Sciences Library—Hanoi. 1881. "Rapports présentés à S.E. Ministre de la Marine et des Colonies sur les grands travaux projetés en Cochinchine." Folio 4°/904(3).

Société Géographique de l'Indochine. 1925. "Plan topographie de la Province de Cantho: 1/100.000." Hanoi: Société Géographique de l'Indochine.

Soper, Kate. 1995. *What Is Nature?* Oxford: Basil Blackwell.

Southeast Asia Technology Company. 1978. *Study of Environmental Impact of the Nam Pong Project.* Bangkok: National Energy Administration.

State Planning Committee (SPC). 2000. *Poverty in the Lao PDR: Participatory Poverty Assessment.* Vientiane.

Steinberg, David. 2005. "Burma/Myanmar: The Role of the Military in the Economy." *Burma Economic Watch* 1: 51–78.

Stellman, Jeanne Mager, Steven D. Stellman, Richard Christian, Tracy Weber, and Carrie Tomasello. 2003. "The Extent and Patterns of Usage of Agent Orange and Other Herbicides in Vietnam." *Nature* 422: 681–87.

Stiglitz, J. 2002. *Globalization and Its Discontents.* New York: W. W. Norton.

Stoler, Ann Laura. 1985. *Capitalism and Confrontation in Sumatra's Plantation Belt, 1870–1979.* New Haven: Yale University Press.

Stone, M. Priscilla, Angelique Haugerud, and Peter D. Little. 2000. "Commodities and Globalization: Anthropological Perspectives." In *Commodities and Globalization: Anthropological Perspectives,* edited by Angelique Haugerud, M. Priscilla Stone, and Peter D. Little, 1–29. New York: Rowman and Littlefield.

Stone, R. D., and Claudia D'Andrea. 2001. *Tropical Forests and the Human Spirit: Journeys to the Brink of Hope.* Berkeley: University of California Press.

Stuart-Fox, M. 2004. "The Political Culture of Corruption in the Lao People's Democratic Republic." Political Economy of Development Working Paper 1. Williamsburg: College of William and Mary.

Sturgeon, Timothy J. 2000. "How Silicon Valley Came to Be." In *Understanding Silicon Valley: The Anatomy of an Entrepreneurial Region,* edited by Martin Kenney, 15–47. Stanford: Stanford University Press.

Suarga, Riza, Popi Komalasari, and Hidayat. 2004. *Revitalisasi kehutanan Indonesia: Mempertahankan eksistensi dan memperkokoh peran ke depan.* Jakarta: Masyarakat Perhutanan Indonesia.

Sun, X., E. Katsigris, and A. White. 2004. *Meeting China's Demand for Forest Products.* Washington, D.C.: Forest Trends.

Sutherland, H. 2000. "Trepang and Wangkang: The China Trade of Eighteenth-Century Makassar, c. 1720s–1840s." In *Authority and Enterprise among the Peoples of South Sulawesi,* edited by R. Tol, K. van Dijk, and G. Acciaioli, 73–94. Leiden: KITLV Press.

Suyanto, S., Rizki Pandu Permana, Noviana Khususiyah, and Laxman Joshi. 2005. "Land Tenure, Agroforestry Adoption, and Reduction of Fire Hazard in a Forest Zone: A Case Study from Lampung, Sumatra, Indonesia." *Agroforestry Systems* 65: 1–11.

Swyngedouw, Erik. 1997. "Neither Global nor Local: 'Glocalization' and the Politics of Scale." In *Spaces of Globalization: Reasserting the Power of the Local,* edited by K. Cox, 37–166. New York: Guilford Press.

———. 1999. "Modernity and Hybridity: Nature, *Regeneracionismo,* and the Production of the Spanish Waterscape, 1890–1930." *Annals of the Association of American Geographers* 89: 443–65.

———. 2004. "Scaled Geographies: Nature, Place, and the Politics of Scale." In *Scale and Geographic Inquiry: Nature, Society, and Method,* edited by E. Sheppard and R. B. McMaster, 129–53. Malden, Mass.: Blackwell.

Talbot, John M. 2002a. "Information, Finance and the New International Inequality: The Case of Coffee." *Journal of World Systems Research* 8, no. 2: 214–50.

——. 2002b. "Tropical Commodity Chains, Forward Integration Strategies, and International Inequality: Coffee, Cocoa, and Tea." *Review of International Political Economy* 9, no. 4: 701–34.

Tarling, Nicholas. 2001. *Imperialism in Southeast Asia: "A fleeting, passing phase."* London: Routledge.

Taussig, Michael. 1986. *Shamanism, Colonialism, and the Wild Man: A Study in Terror and Healing.* Chicago: University of Chicago Press.

——. 2004. *My Cocaine Museum.* Chicago: University of Chicago Press.

Taylor, Robert. 2002. "Freedom in Burma and Thailand: Inside Or Outside the State?" In *The Idea of Freedom in Asia and Africa,* edited by Robert Taylor, 143–181. Stanford: Stanford University Press.

Teik, Khoo Boo. 2002. "Nationalism, Capitalism and 'Asian Values.'" In *Democracy in Malaysia: Discourses and Practices,* edited by Francis Loh Kok Wah and Khoo Boo Teik, 51–73. Richmond, England: Curzon.

Tergast, G. C. W. 1930. *Monographie over de Bevolkingskoffiecultuur in Nederlandsch Indie: Mededeeling van de Afdeeling Landbouw,* No. 15.

Thai Burma Border Consortium. 2005. *Internal Displacement and Protection in Eastern Burma.* Bangkok: TBBC.

——. 2006. *Internal Displacement in Eastern Burma: 2006 Survey.* Bangkok: TBBC.

Thee, Kian Wie. 2002. "The Soeharto Era and After: Stability, Development, and Crisis, 1966–2000." In *The Emergence of a National Economy: An Economic History of Indonesia, 1800–2000,* edited by H. W. Dick, V. Houben, T. Lindblad, and K. W. Thee, 194–243. Honolulu: University of Hawaii Press.

Thompson, E. P. 1971. "The Moral Economy of the English Crowd in the Eighteenth Century." *Past and Present* 50, no. 1: 76–136.

——. 1975. *Whigs and Hunters: The Origins of the Black Act.* New York: Pantheon.

Thongchai, Winichakul. 1994. *Siam Mapped: The History of the Geo-Body of a Nation.* Honolulu: University of Hawai'i Press.

Thorenaar, A. 1922. "Land—en Boschbouw in Palembang." *Tectona* 15: 763–81.

Thùy Anh. 1924. "Land—en Boschbouw in Palembang." *Tectona* 17: 759–91.

Thùy Anh. 2005. "The Best Way to Minimize Strikes." *The Laborer,* August 30. http://www.nld.com.vn/tintuc/cong-doan/quyen-nghia-vu/125688.asp.

Topik, Steven and William Gervaise Clarence-Smith. 2003. "Introduction: Coffee and Global Development." In *The Global Coffee Economy in Africa, Asia and Latin America, 1500–1989,* edited by William Gervaise Clarence Smith and Steven Topik. Cambridge: Cambridge University Press.

Trần, Angie Ngọc. 1996. "Through the Eye of the Needle: Vietnamese Textile and Garment Industries Rejoining the Global Economy." *Crossroads: An Interdisciplinary Journal of Southeast Asian Studies* 10, no. 2: 83–126.

——. 2001. "Global Subcontracting and Women Workers in Comparative Perspective." In *Globalization and Third World Socialism: Cuba and Vietnam,* edited by Claes Brundenius and John Weeks, 217–36. Hampshire, England: Palgrave.

———. 2005. "Sewing for the Global Economy: Thread of Resistance in Vietnamese Textile and Garment Industries." In *Critical Globalization Studies*, edited by W. Robinson and R. Appelbaum, 379–92. New York: Routledge.

———. 2007a. "The Third Sleeve: Emerging Labor Newspapers and the Response of the Labor Unions and the State to Workers' Resistance in Vietnam." *Labor Studies Journal* 32, no. 3 (September): 257–79.

———. 2007b. "Alternatives to the 'Race to the Bottom': Minimum Wage Strikes in Vietnam and Their Aftermath." *Labor Studies Journal* 32, no. 4 (December): 430–51.

Trần Đức. 2004. "Dong Nai Province: Forty-four Strikes in 2004." *The Laborer*, December 28. http://www.nld.com.vn/tintuc/cong-doan/108100.asp.

Trần Hiệp. 2005. "The Second Night Singing with Workers." *The Laborer*, August 24. http://www.nld.com.vn/tintuc/van-hoa/125298.asp.

Trouillot, Michel-Rolph. 2001. "Anthropology of the State in the Age of Globalization: Close Encounters of the Deceptive Kind." *Current Anthropology* 42, no. 1: 125–38.

Tsing, Anna. 1999. "Becoming a Tribal Elder, and Other Green Development Fantasies." In *Transforming the Indonesian Uplands: Marginality, Power and Production*, edited by Tania Murray Li. London: Routledge.

———. 2000. "Inside the Economy of Appearances." *Public Culture* 12, no. 1: 115–44.

———. 2004. *Friction: An Ethnography of Global Connection*. Princeton: Princeton University Press.

Turrell, R. 1988. "Conquest and Concession: The Case of the Burma Ruby Mines." *Modern Asian Studies* 22, no. 1: 141–63.

U.S. Government Printing Office. 1966. *Public Papers of the Presidents of the United States: Lyndon B. Johnson, 1965*. Vol. I. Washington, D.C.: U.S. GPO.

Vandergeest, Peter. 1989. "Peasant Strategies in a World Context." *Human Organization* 48, no. 2: 117–25.

———. 1991. "Gifts and Rights." *Development and Change* 22: 421–43.

———. 1996. "Real Villages." In *Constructing the Countryside*, edited by E. Melanie Dupuis and Peter Vandergeest, 279–302. Philadelphia: Temple University Press.

———. 2003. "Land to Some Tillers: Development-Induced Displacement in Laos." *International Social Science Journal* 55, no. 1: 47–56.

———. 2007. "Certification and Communities: Alternatives for Regulating the Environmental and Social Impacts of Shrimp Farming." *World Development* 35, no. 7: 1152–71.

Vandergeest, Peter, and Nancy L. Peluso. 1995. "Territorialization and State Power in Thailand." *Theory and Society* 24: 385–426.

———. 2006a. "Empires of Forestry: Professional Forestry and State Power in Southeast Asia, Part 1." *Environment and History* 12, no. 1: 31–64.

———. 2006b. "Empires of Forestry: Professional Forestry and State Power in Southeast Asia, Part 2." *Environment and History* 12, no. 4: 359–93.

Verbist, B., and Gamal Pasya. 2004. "Perspektif sejarah status kawasan hutan, konflik dan negosiasi di Sumberjaya, Lampung Barat, Propinsi Lampung." *Agrivita* 26, no. 1: 20–28.

Verbist, B., Andree Ekadinata Putra, and Suseno Budidarsono. 2004. "Penyebab guna lahan dan akibatnya terhadap fungsi dearah aliran sungai (DAS) pada lansekap agroforestri berbasis kopi di Sumatera." *Agrivita* 26, no. 1: 29–38.

Verdery, Katherine. 1994. "Beyond the Nation in Eastern Europe." *Social Text* 4: 1–19.

Vietnam National Archives Center #2 [VNA2]. 1893. Fonds Goucoch. Folio IA 19/174. Ajudication de travaux de dragages a effectuer en Cochinchine pour l'amelioration du réseau des voies de navigation intérieure.

Vietnam National Archives Center #2 [VNA2]. 1900. Fonds Goucoch. Folio IA 13/232 (1). Au sujet du percement d'un canal demandé par MM Duval et Guéry.

———. 1902. Fonds Goucoch. Folio IA 13/232(1). Decision 3378 of Governor-General.

———. 1904. Fonds Goucoch. Folio IA13/308(12). Nombre de stères de bois a bruler vérifies.

———. 1936. Tòa Đại Biêu Chính Phủ Nam Viêt [TDBCPNV]. Folio E.02/71. Monographie de Rach-Gia.

———. 1944. General Delegate of South Vietnam Record Group. Folio H.6/20. Riziculture et hydraulique agricole, August 29.

———. 1966. Publication NL 504. Dredging Program Report.

Vĩnh Tùng. 2003. "Conference on Solutions to Resolve Labor Conflicts in Go Vap District." *The Laborer*, June 30. http://www.nld.com.vn/tintuc/cong-doan/45844.asp.

Vincent, Jeffrey R. and Rozali Mohamed Ali. 2005. *Managing Natural Wealth: Environment and Development in Malaysia.* Washington, D.C.: Resources for the Future.

Vlekke, Bernard. 1959. *Nusantara: A History of Indonesia.* Chicago: Quadrangle Books; The Hague: W. van Hoeve.

Vonk, H. 1937. "Systematisch beheer van het ladangareaal in Palembang." *Landbouw* 8, no. 9: 357–73.

Walker, Andrew. 2004. "Seeing Farmers for the Trees: Community Forestry and the Arborealisation of Agriculture in Northern Thailand." *Asia Pacific Viewpoint* 45, no. 3: 311–24.

Wallerstein, Immanuel M. 1974. *The Modern World-System.* New York: Academic Press.

———. 2004. *World-Systems Analysis: An Introduction.* Durham: Duke University Press.

Watson, C. W. 2005. "A Popular Indonesian Preacher: The Significance of Aa Gymnastiar." *Journal of the Royal Anthropological Institute* 11, no. 4: 773–92.

Watts, Michael. 1983. *Silent Violence: Food, Famine, and Peasantry in Northern Nigeria.* Berkeley: University of California Press.

———. 1999. "Commodities." In *Introducing Human Geographies*, edited by P. Cloke, P. Crang, and M. Goodwin, 305–15. New York: Arnold.

Watts, M., and D. Goodman. 1997. "Agrarian Questions: Global Appetite, Local Metabolism; Nature, Culture, and Industry in Fin-de-Siècle Agro-Food Systems." In *Globalising Food: Agrarian Questions and Global Restructuring*, edited by D. Goodman and M. Watts, 1–32. London: Routledge.

Weber, Max. 1990 [1905]. *The Protestant Ethic and the Spirit of Capitalism.* London: Unwin Hyman.

Weber, Robert, Heiko Faust, and Werner Kreisel. 2003. "Colonial Interventions on the Cultural Landscape of Central Sulawesi by the 'Ethical Policy': Impacts of the Dutch Rule in Palu and Kulawi, 1905–1942." *Asian Journal of Social Science* 31, no. 2: 398–434.

White, A., X. Sun, and K. Canby. 2006. *China and the Global Market for Forest Products.* Washington, D.C.: Forest Trends.

White, Gilbert F., E. de Vries, H. B. Dunkerley, and J. V. Krutilla. 1962. *Economic and Social Aspects of Lower Mekong Development: A Report to the Committee for Coordination of Investigations of the Lower Mekong Basin.* Bangkok: ECAFE.

White, P. W., and W. E. Garrett. 1968. "The Mekong: River of Terror and Hope." *National Geographic* 134, no. 6: 737–89.

Wiersum, K. F. 2004. "Forest Gardens as an 'Intermediate' Land-Use System in the Nature-Culture Continuum: Characteristics and Future Potential." *Agroforestry Systems* 61: 123–34.

Williams, Raymond. 1973. *The Country and the City.* New York: Oxford University Press.

Williamson, J. 1990. "What Washington Means by Policy Reform: Introduction." In *Latin American Adjustment: How Much Has Happened?*, edited by J. Williamson, 1–20. Washington, D.C.: Institute for International Economics.

Willis, Paul. 1977. *Learning to Labor: How Working Class Kids Get Working Class Jobs.* New York: Columbia University Press.

Wolf, Eric. 1982. *Europe and the People without History.* Berkeley: University of California Press.

Wolters, Oliver W. 1967. *Early Indonesian Commerce: A Study of the Origins of Srivijaya.* Ithaca: Cornell University Press.

World Bank. 2006. *Millennium Development Goals Global Monitoring Report, Part II,* July 25. http://web.worldbank.org.

Wulan, Yuliana Cahya, Yurdi Yasmi, Christiana Purba, and Eva Wollenberg. 2004. *Analisa konflik: Sektor kehutanan di Indonesia.* Bogor, Indonesia: Center for International Forestry Research.

Yayasan Tanah Merdeka (YTM). 2003. *Notulensi dialog masyarakat mataue dan Balai Taman Nasional Lore Lindu, Balai Desa Mataure, 14 Agustus 2003.* Palu, Indonesia: Yayasan Tanah Merdeka.

Zachman, N. 1973. "Indonesian Fisheries Development and Management." *Journal of the Fisheries Research Board of Canada* 30, no. 1: 2335–40.

Zimmer, Oliver. 1998. "In Search of Natural Identity: Alpine Landscape and the Reconstruction of the Swiss Nation." *Comparative Studies in Society and History* 40, no. 4: 637–65.

Contributors

KEITH BARNEY is a PhD candidate in the Department of Geography at York University (Canada). He conducted field research in Laos from 2004 to 2006 and has consulted on forestry management issues in Asia for the Centre for International Forestry Research (CIFOR), Rights and Resources Initiative, and Forest Trends.

DAVID BIGGS is Assistant Professor of History at the University of California at Riverside. He received his PhD in History from the University of Washington in 2004. He has published widely on Vietnam's environmental history and is finishing a book on the environmental history of the Mekong Delta. His continuing research delves into environmental aspects of the Vietnam War and American intervention in Southeast Asia.

DORIAN FOUGÈRES is a Special Assistant for Strategic Planning at the CALFED Bay-Delta Science Program, and an Assistant Facilitator at the Center for Collaborative Policy, both in Sacramento, where he works on integrating scientific information and practices with public policy. He received his PhD in Environmental Science, Policy, and Management from UC Berkeley in 2005. His doctoral research was on the political ecology of fisheries and aquaculture in Sulawesi, Indonesia.

PAUL K. GELLERT is Assistant Professor of Sociology at the University of Tennessee. His work focuses on the political economy of natural resources and development in Indonesia and the Asian region. He has written widely on timber production in Indonesia and regional timber markets, including a recent piece in the *ANNALS of the American Academy of Political and Social Science.*

TANIA MURRAY LI is Professor in the Department of Anthropology at University of Toronto. She holds a senior Canada Research Chair in the Political Economy and Culture of the Asia-Pacific region. Since 1990, her research has focused on questions of culture, economy, environment, and development in Indonesia's upland regions. She is editor of *Transforming the Indonesian Uplands: Marginality,*

Power and Production (Routledge, 1999), and author of *The Will to Improve: Governmentality, Development, and the Practice of Politics* (Duke, 2007).

KEN MACLEAN is Assistant Professor in the Department of International Development, Community, and Environment (IDCE) at Clark University. He holds a PhD in Anthropology and a MSc in Environmental Justice from the University of Michigan. MacLean has authored numerous research monographs, academic articles, and policy briefs on contemporary Burma, and has served as the Associate Director of EarthRights International's Burma Project. Other research interests include aspects of contemporary Vietnam.

JOSEPH NEVINS is Associate Professor in the Department of Earth Science and Geography at Vassar College. He has written extensively on violence, justice, and spatiality. His most recent books are *A Not-So-Distant Horror: Mass Violence in East Timor* (Cornell, 2005) and *Operation Gatekeeper: The Rise of the "Illegal Alien" and the Making of the U.S.-Mexico Boundary* (Routledge, 2002).

NANCY LEE PELUSO is Professor of Society and Environment in the Department of Environmental Science, Policy, and Management at University of California at Berkeley, and codirector of the Berkeley Workshop in Environmental Politics. She has been conducting research and publishing on forest and agrarian politics in Indonesia for more than twenty years. Her books include *Rich Forests, Poor People: Resource Control and Resistance in Java* (UC Press, 1992) and *Violent Environments* (Cornell, 2001), coedited with Michael Watts.

LESLEY POTTER is Visiting Fellow in the Department of Human Geography at the Research School of Pacific and Asian Studies at the Australian National University. She retired as Associate Professor of Geographical and Environmental Studies at the University of Adelaide in 2003. Her research and publication work over the past twenty-five years has focused on the histories of important natural resource commodities and cash crops in different parts of Indonesia. She is coauthor, with Harold Brookfield and Yvonne Byron, of *In Place of the Forest* (United Nations University, 1995).

DAROMIR RUDNYCKYJ is Assistant Professor of Pacific and Asian Studies at the University of Victoria, Canada. His research examines Islam and globalization in Indonesia, Malaysia, Singapore, and Brunei. Previous research projects analyzed the networks and institutions that enable labor migration from Indonesia throughout the Indian and Pacific Ocean regions.

SANDRA SMELTZER is Assistant Professor in the Faculty of Information and Media Studies at the University of Western Ontario. She has a PhD in Communication from Carleton University. Her recent research has focused on the cultural implications of information and communication technologies, including the rise of political blogging and environmental journalism in Malaysia.

ANGIE NGỌC Trầ n is Professor of Political Economy at California State University, Monterey Bay. She has written extensively on gendered division of labor, migrant workers, garment and electronics workers in Vietnam and California, strikes,

Vietnamese socialist state and market economy, labor unions and newspapers, with recent articles in *Labor Studies Journal* and *Amerasia Journal*. She is coeditor, with Melanie Beresford, of *Reaching for the Dream: Challenges of Sustainable Development in Vietnam* (NIAS Press, 2004).

ANNA TSING is Professor of Anthropology at the University of California at Santa Cruz. She is the author of *Friction: An Ethnography of Global Connection* (Princeton, 2005) and *In the Realm of the Diamond Queen: Marginality in an Out-of-the-Way Place* (Princeton, 1993). She is coeditor, with Paul Greenough, of *Nature in the Global South: Environmental Projects in South and Southeast Asia* (Duke, 2003).

PETER VANDERGEEST is Director of the York Centre for Asian Research and Associate Professor of Sociology at York University. He has written widely on the cultural politics of the environment and development in Southeast Asia, including the social aspects of forestry, with publications in the *Journal of Asian Studies*, *Theory and Society*, *Environment and History*, and *World Development*. His current research is on contemporary agrarian transitions in Southeast Asia and the privatization of environmental governance for aquaculture salmon and shrimp.

Index

Page numbers in italics indicate figures.

actor-network theory, 122, 207
Adas, Michael, 119
Aditya-Birla Group (India), 105
Agrarian Law of 1870 (Java), 178
agrarian studies approach, 207
Aliran (human rights organization), 202
"alternative civilizing projects," 12
APKINDO, 44, 46, 52
Appadurai, Arjun, 238n17
Aquaculture Certification Council, 218, 239n3
aquarium trade, 164
Asad, Talal, 76
Asian Development Bank, 91, 100, 101, 125, 126
Asian financial crisis, 10–11, 14
  Indonesia, 14, 78, 80, 171–72
  Thailand, 11, 14, 213
"Asian values," 10, 192
authoritarianism, 2–3, 10–11
Au village (Indonesia), 133, 134

Badan Revitalisasi Industri Kehutanan, 52–53
Badawi, Abdullah, 197, 200, 204
  biotechnology strategy, advocacy of, 191, 193, 194, 196, 202
Bahasa Kodeco, 33–34, 36, 232n8
Bakun Dam (Malaysia), 197–98
Ban Sivilay (Laos), 24, 235–36n4

Land and Forest Allocation map, 99
LFPL plantation project and, 93–96
Barney, Keith, 20, 227
Barr, Christopher M., 104
Basic Fisheries Law (Indonesia), 237n1
Bernstein, H., 239n2
BGA-Oji Plantation Concession, *94*
Biggs, D., *112*, 227
BioNexus Malaysia, 191, 195
Biosafety Bill (Malaysia, 2007), 199–200
Biotechnology Implementation Council (Malaysia), 195
BioValley project (Malaysia), 193, 194, 195
Blaikie, Piers, 16
Body Shop (retail firm), 23
Borsuk, Richard, 52
Brazilian coffee crisis (1896), 237n7
Brenneis, Don, 233n12
Broga incinerator (Malaysia), 198
Brown, J. Christopher, 50
Budidarsono, S., 186, 187
Burkard, Gunter, 137
Burma, 140–57
  colonial administrative rule, 152
  entrepreneurial turn, 142–44, 145–46
  forced displacement of populations, 150, 152–53, 154–55
  guerilla mining, 148, 149

CPSIA information can be obtained
at www.ICGtesting.com
Printed in the USA
LVOW13s0546231217
560542LV00007B/144/P